*Women and Christianity*

**Recent Titles in
Women and Religion in the World**

Women and Judaism
*Rabbi Malka Drucker*

# Women and Christianity

CHERYL A. KIRK-DUGGAN AND
KAREN JO TORJESEN, EDITORS

Women and Religion in the World
Cheryl A. Kirk-Duggan, Lillian Ashcraft-Eason
and Karen Jo Torjesen, Series Editors

**PRAEGER**
*An Imprint of ABC-CLIO, LLC*

A B C 🠻 C L I O

Santa Barbara, California • Denver, Colorado • Oxford, England

**Library of Congress Cataloging-in-Publication Data**

Women and Christianity / Cheryl A. Kirk-Duggan and Karen Jo Torjesen, editors.
   p. cm. — (Women and religion in the world)
   Includes bibliographical references (p.     ) and index.
   ISBN 978-0-275-99155-5 (alk. paper) — ISBN 978-0-313-08271-9 (ebook)
   1. Women in Christianity.   2. Christian women—Social conditions.   3. Feminism—Religious
aspects—Christianity.   I. Kirk-Duggan, Cheryl A.   II. Torjesen, Karen Jo, 1945–
   BV639.W7W592   2010
   270.082—dc22       2009030412

14   13   12   11   10       1   2   3   4   5

This book is also available on the World Wide Web as an eBook.
Visit www.abc-clio.com for details.

ABC-CLIO, LLC
130 Cremona Drive, P.O. Box 1911
Santa Barbara, California 93116-1911

This book is printed on acid-free paper ∞

Manufactured in the United States of America

*In honor of women of faith ~*
*grandmothers, mothers, other mothers,*
*daughters, sisters, and sister friends*
*who daily make a transformative difference,*
*even when no one is watching*

# Contents

# Acknowledgments

This project has been one of communal collaboration, networking, and antiphonal poetry, as we called and invited a wonderful group of global scholars to participate in this magnificent project. Our appreciation to Suzanne Staszak-Silva for the invitation to launch the Women and Religion in the World series and for Lindsay Claire guiding us to bring closure with excellence.

In deepest appreciation to all of the educational and religious institutions and women's groups, in the academy and in churches across the globe, who have invited women to teach, do consulting, preach, pastor, and engage their constituencies regarding women's religious experience, the impact of faith on their lives, and the interconnections between the oppression women encounter and how they move to experience transformation in the midst of patriarchal sexism, misogyny, and other venues of oppression, including class, race, heterosexism, and ability. We stand amidst the legacies of the former Center for Women and Religion, Graduate Theological Union, Berkeley, California, and the Claremont Graduate University Women's Studies in Religion program, Claremont, California.

In deepest thanks for all of the scholars and activists who have written about, and advocated on behalf of the health, well-being, and transformation of all women, men, children, and their communities.

In heartfelt gratitude for the legacies of such giants as Sojourner Truth, Harriet Tubman, The Grimké Sisters, Ida Wells Barnett, Eleanor Roosevelt, Gloria Steinem, bell hooks, Marian Wright Edelman, Alice Walker, Toni Morrison, Sonja Sanchez, Nikki Giovanni, Elizabeth Schüssler Fiorenza, Rosemary Radford Ruether, Ada Maria Isasi Diaz, Emilie Townes, Katie G. Cannon, Cheryl Townsend Gilkes, Jacqueline Grant, Kwok Pui Lan, Mary Ellen Gaylord, and Margo L. Goldsmith.

A special thanks to women in our most intimate communities who helped love us into being the scholars and leaders we have become; to our grandmothers, mothers, sisters, sister-friends, colleagues, staff, and students who support our daily journey: for all of their support and love, for their tireless work to make a difference.

Karen especially thanks Margo L. Goldsmith, patron of the Women's Studies in Religion program; and, Cheryl thanks Mike, her best buddy, friend, and confidante who supports our research, writing, her life; to Dedurie Vanessa, my beloved sister, who bolsters me daily. To the Shaw University community and my church home, Young Missionary Temple C.M.E. Church, Raleigh, North Carolina—to all we give thanks.

# Introduction

*Cheryl A. Kirk-Duggan and Karen Jo Torjesen*

Women have been active in Christianity since its inception. When going against Eastern customs and ethos, Jesus taught women, related to them, and engaged them with respect. He never condemned them, acted as if they were inferior, or as if they were property. While the received biblical texts do not indicate women were disciples, Mary Magdalene, in all four gospels, is present during the passion, death, crucifixion, and resurrection of Jesus the Christ, the Messiah for Christians. Paul, a missionary and founder of the Christian church, writes letters to groups of people and churches throughout the Greco-Roman world. Many of the Pauline texts speak of liberation, salvation, and religious life. Yet, many of them written under Paul's name, but not by Paul, speak of women's subordination, submission, and oppression in the name of faith. Some of these texts were written as Christianity became more public and the writers adapted and edited divinely inspired stories to match the cultural norms of that day, where the equality, inclusion, and liberative stances for women incorporated by Jesus were diminished. In the early house churches, the rule was more egalitarian, and women were often in charge as long as Christian communities aligned themselves with social structures of the private arena.

When Constantine made Christianity the state religion in the Greco-Roman world, Christian practice became even more exclusive. The Greco-Roman world created a dichotomy of public versus private, where house (*oikos*) indicated private (the realm of female, indoor, stationary, natural, inferior), while public (*polis*) pertained to male, outdoor, mobile, civilized, and superior. There is a distinction between public and private space; who occupies it, and how it is experienced, often is based upon gender: male (honor, the exercise of authority), female (shame, her chastity). Even early philosophers, the source of thought for many theologians, viewed women as inferior. For Aristotle, women's emotions, loves, fears, anger, and speech were undisciplined. This concept allowed society to exclude women, children, and slaves from political power. Thus, philosophical conceptions of the rational self bore political and social consequences in the ancient world. Greco-Roman gender systems have shaped Western attitudes toward women and sexuality for 2,000 years.

Ancient writers often used sex to intimidate and shame, and made female leaders out to be disreputable and promiscuous. Many Christian leaders embraced this public/private dichotomy. Christians adopted the Greco-Roman virtue system. Men equaled justice, courage, and self-mastery; women equaled chastity, obedience, and silence. Men's virtue had social and personal functions at the intersection of public life and honor. Women gained honor with sexual purity. Chastity equaled sexual fidelity. Understanding these ideologies is critical to seeing the process of how women became marginalized and were scapegoated in Christianity. The quest for equality and liberation from early Christianity through today, then, involves the societal reality that male honor pertains to leadership, valor, strength, and women's honor pertains to her sexuality and chastity, a reality normative for Western thought in general, and Christianity in particular.

This volume understands the historical and religious patriarchal framing of Christianity, as it explores numerous experiences of women and their Christian faith, under five rubrics: women, family, and environment; socio-economics, politics, and authority; body, mind, and spirit; sex, power, and vulnerability; women, worldview, and religious practice. The volume particularly explores issues of oppression and liberation and how women have worked for transformation, noting the earliest modern organized quests for women's liberation. The chapters include global voices, passionate stories, and profound lived experiences of injustice and justice in a 21st-century world of Christianities.

The first women's movement in Christianity, in the United States, emerged out of the struggle to liberate the slaves in the American south during the 19th century. Christian women calling for the emancipation of slaves encountered opposition, sometimes violent. These women speaking and preaching against slavery first in homes and then in rented halls were attacked for their intrusion into the male world of politics and public speaking. The radical leaders of the abolitionist movement called for equal rights for women as they defended the human rights of the enslaved. After the success of the abolitionist movement they began another campaign for the emancipation of women, demanding the right to vote. Their suffrage movement was considered a radical movement: women marched and demonstrated; they were imprisoned, beaten and came back to march again. Society labeled these women radicals because they transgressed the Victorian ideals of womanhood, the doctrine of separate spheres, domestic and public, that confined women's activities to family life and the moral education of children. This ideal of womanhood was held up by Christian preachers and supported with biblical authority.

Elizabeth Cady Stanton, one of the movement's leaders, insisted that women could not secure their full rights until they tackled the role of Christianity in excluding women from public life. Although none of her sisters in the movement supported her, Stanton taught herself Hebrew and Greek, studied the stories and the biblical passages used to exclude women, challenged them, and provided alternate readings. She then made her own translations of the Bible with a commentary that she had published as *The Women's Bible*.

The campaign for the equal rights for women did not gain a following until the 20th century. Here again, the struggle for equal rights for women followed the long and painful struggle for the civil rights of diasporic Africans in the 1960s, who, though liberated from slavery, still lived as an oppressed minority. Although poor women of all races had frequently worked outside the home, by the mid-20th century, Euro-American women were integrated into the public sphere as wage earners in the fields of business, education, and government, particularly middle-class women. Now they began to seek the same protections from discrimination and equal access for which African Americans and their supporters were campaigning throughout the 1960s.

In this period, the earlier ideological critique of the role of Christianity in supporting the separate spheres ideology was taken up again. Women were seeking leadership roles in churches and separate spheres, where doctrines denied them roles as pastors, preachers, and priests. Within the churches, these women challenged the interpretations of Christianity that insisted on women's subordination and segregation from the public sphere and called for a revolution in the way the Christian religion was understood.

In the 1970s, for the first time, women were admitted into theological seminaries, were trained in biblical languages and the interpretation of scripture, studied the theological tradition, and participated in discussions of ethics. They brought to their studies a new perspective, that of women; they had different questions, raised different issues. Above all, they were struck by the absence of women and women's voices in the heritage of Christianity. As newly minted scholars, they created a new field of study, publishing books on feminist theology that integrated women's experience of Christianity into the "God talk" of theologians, new commentaries on the Bible that reexamined the contributions of women, and feminist works on ethics, history, sociology, counseling, liturgy, preaching, ministerial leadership, and spirituality. Many of the women contributing to this volume have contributed to this body of scholarship. All of them are inheritors of this growing legacy of feminist writings.

Under the impetus of the women's movement, U.S. society began to pay attention to issues that were buried under codes of secrecy and shame. In the consciousness raising groups of the 1960s and 1970s, women told each other their stories for the first time. Here they discovered that their isolated experiences of domestic violence and sexual violence were in fact far more common than they could have imagined—that the problem was systemic. Their analysis of the scope of the problems probed the roots of domestic violence in patriarchal attitudes toward women and sexuality. Their activism produced the first battered women's shelters and the first march, "Take Back the Night," calling attention to the fact that rape was widespread. Campaigns for reforms in the legal and judicial systems followed, training programs for police, and counseling for victims.

Feminist scholars studying Christianity took up these issues raised by activists. Their analysis included an examination of the ways in which the Bible, Christian theology, and Christian gender and social ethics were appropriated to give religious legitimation to the subordination of women, the devaluation of the body, and the denigration of female sexuality. Christian teachings on marriage had given a religious meaning to male authority in the household, assigning a sacramental character to the subordination of a wife to a husband as a symbol of the relationship between Christ and the church.

The lower evaluation of the female body derives in part from patriarchal cultures that are home to Christianity and in part from the theological meaning given to the incarnation. For the Greek philosophical traditions that have shaped Western culture, both body and femaleness are distanced from the transcendent, conceptualized as immaterial and pure rationality. For the theological tradition that adopted this worldview, body and femaleness represent the lower orders of being that still originate with God. Both women and nature are subordinated within this theological tradition, creating a linkage that feminists concerned about ecological issues must engage. The notion of a God incarnate in a male body dignifies maleness, so for example, in the Catholic Church only men can become priests because the work of representing Christ can only be done in a male body.

Christian attitudes toward sexuality were shaped under the profound influence of ascetic and monastic movements, beginning in the fourth centuries CE. Those who renounced the world also renounced sexual relations, seeing sexuality as incommensurate with spirituality. As celibacy was imposed on an all male priesthood, female sexuality appeared especially threatening, leading to sermons and tracts decrying the dangers of association with females. The double standard of sexual morality of patriarchal cultures arises from the necessity of controlling female reproductive sexuality; wives are viewed as the sexual property of their husbands, remnants of Hebrew or Old Testament scriptures, where females were property of their fathers and then their husbands, after marriage.

A feminist critique of Christian scholars encapsulated above is always accompanied by creative work. Critique grows out of the fundamental impulse toward change and transformation and drives the continuing evolution of Christianity as it responds to its contemporary context. The chapters gathered in this book reflect that fundamental impulse. The authors here critique the use of certain passages of the Bible to support the gender values of patriarchal cultures. At the same time, Christian scripture is mined for all the ways that it empowers women, encourages female agency, affirms women's experience, and speaks of the divine with female metaphors. Women scholars are imagining new Christian models of family, motherhood, and husband/wife relationships that break loose from the patriarchal moorings Christian teachings on the family have inherited within the Christian theological tradition.

Another central task is redeeming female sexuality, disentangling it from the idea of dangerous or sinful or seductive sexuality. This creative theological and cultural work flows into the political activism of confronting sexual violence. Sexual violence has been rendered invisible by the ideas that husbands have sexual rights over women and that women are complicit in rape, unless they exemplify the ideals of chastity. By redefining the meanings of women's sexuality, women create an alternative view of themselves from which to resist the imposition of masculinist values on their sexual behavior.

Experience has been an important category in the development of women's scholarship; women explored the impact of a theology or biblical interpretation on women's experience. Women's experience was the vantage point for the critique of aspects of the Christian tradition. Women's experience also counted as an important resource for knowledge. Christianity needed to be understood from a perspective of women's experience, and women needed to recast Christian liturgies, theologies, and interpretations also in the language of their own experience. Further, experience is valued as a way of both capturing and communicating particular dimensions of Christianity. To this end, feminist scholarship welcomes the voice of women and includes writing that is done in the first person. An astute analysis of one's own experience that marks the interaction between societal notions of gender, sexuality, and family is able to assess the effect of Christian teachings and values and becomes the foundation for working creatively toward a reform of those values.

Christianity has become a global religion, through its assimilation by the Roman and Byzantine empires, through its medieval missions to Europe, then through the colonization of the Americas and Africa. When Christianity interacts with other global and local religions, a confluence of patriarchal heritages—African religions and Christianity, Christianity and Confucianism—impacts women. This volume shows how women living across multiple traditions critique and transform those traditions within their own cultural contexts. Some women discover in these other traditions resources for engaging their own; for example, the wisdom of indigenous religions has much to offer ecofeminism. Activism on behalf of women has also become transnational with networks on women's reproductive health, the welfare of women workers criss-crossing national boundaries.

The ethical thinking of these scholars is embedded in the social, economic, and political realities of women's daily lives. The experience of African American women, Hispanic women, and Asian American women is critical for their analysis and their ethical imperatives. The global and local contexts are so intertwined, that ethical thinking around transforming women's lived realities includes assessing the impact of globalization and structural adjustment on women in India and Sri Lanka as well as migrant Asian workers in the United States. Black feminist, Womanist, Latina, and Asian American female scholars along with feminist scholars worldwide have been engaged since the 1980s in research and activism around women's liberation.

Religions are dynamic, continuously evolving, responding to new cultures, to new technologies, new ideas, and changing social relations. Christianity of the 19th century was shaped by evangelization; Christianity of the 20th and 21st centuries is shaped by immigration. The transition from agricultural societies to industrial societies shifted the patterns of social relations from the multigenerational family to the nuclear family, and beyond. This volume seeks to present Christianity as a lived religion in all its complexity as it responds to the challenges—social, political, and economic—of its age.

The articles here present Christianity as a work in progress; they show how Christianity shapes women's lives in every dimension, not just the spiritual. These articles also show how women are contributing to the ongoing evolution of Christianity through their lives, through their understandings of Christianity and through their activism as they seek to realize their vision of Christianity within society. This volume is designed to give an accurate portrayal of the diversity and complexity of Christianity as a lived religion by focusing on the points where Christian women are engaging contemporary issues, as mentioned earlier, regarding the categories of women, family, and environment; socioeconomics, politics and authority; body, mind, and spirit; sexuality, power, and vulnerability; and women, worldview, and religious practice. These scholars write with passion, academic excellence, interest, and a commitment to the transformation of all of society.

In the section titled *Women, Family, Environment,* Kathlyn A. Breazeale, feminist process theologian and dancer, follows the historical development of the concept of the ideal Christian wife in Western culture, which remains prevalent today. She explores religious, economic, and political factors used to construct this archetype or model and historically traces six models of the ideal Christian wife archetype through scripture, miracle and mystery plays, street puppet theater, woodcuts and capitalism, and in two contemporary films: all of which have been used to teach children, youth, and adults about desired behavior to fulfill the ideal and to warn about potential lethal consequences of disobedience to this ideal.

Tuere Bowles, a historian and ethnographer, investigates how faith and spirituality undergird daily lives and practices of black women activists in the environmental justice movement. Their faith and spirituality anchors their decision-making, sustains activism, and frames environmental justice efforts. She provides information regarding historical social movements; relates, compares, and contrasts experiences of exemplary black women activists, regarding their motivations for engaging in social action, how they sustain their efforts, how they value wisdom and knowledge in their practice; and the impact that their activism has had on their own lives and those of their communities.

Karen Baker-Fletcher, constructive theologian, creates a poetic engagement of scripture, theology, and nature to make sense of alternative understandings of God in ways that voting people of faith might support. After examining biblical texts regarding creation, including notions of dominion, the essay continues with views of God; a poetic response to natural disaster; biblical theological reflections on creation and suffering; and a creative dance of the Spirit of God.

The section *Socioeconomics, Politics, Authority* begins with an essay by Judith Johnson, a feminist/Catholic theologian at the internet university called Global Ministries University, who also works as an activist for women's ordination. The essay explores the movement of Roman Catholic women fighting for ordination following the rubric of *aggiornamento,* a new wind blowing, following Vatican II. After reviewing the historic beginnings of this movement and the first women's Catholic ordination conferences, she explores the cultural and intellectual context of women's priestly ordination, the inception of the Women's Conference on Ordination (WCO), and the women's theological revolution related to ordination. Her essay also examines gender wars and the papal response, 21st-century milestones related to women's ordination, and the historic Danube Seven's ordination and excommunication.

Social ethicist Pamela K. Brubaker investigates women's political activism in relation to United States' Christian and interfaith organizations: the Roman Catholic Church, the World Council of Churches, and transnational feminist networks. She explores daily life issues regarding equality as a political issue and questions moral agency, or the capacity for a person to determine for themselves their value systems, and how they behave related to those value systems, which is a complicated matrix regarding the meaning of, access to, and use of authority.

Joan M. Martin, a social ethicist, discusses women's moral agency amidst their work experience as they sustain sources of revenue for themselves, their families, and their communities. She engages a Christian womanist/feminist ethic as her methodological framework to focus on women's lived experience of work and labor. Engaging a Christian womanist/feminist ethic as a justice-seeking ethic, she also sets out notions and principles of a moral framework in solidarity with women's lived experience toward justice and dignity in work, where work and labor are synonyms regarding women's livelihood or occupational engagement within the family, church, and society. She uses the concept of "toil" to frame the description and quality of paid or unpaid work, when it is imperceptible, unacknowledged, disrespected, exploitative, and deprives women of their full human equality and dignity in relation to the work of men.

The section on *Body, Mind, Spirit* begins with the chapter by Jean T. Corey, a scholar of English and Literature, who explores the connections and relationships between mothering and a woman's body, mind, and spirit for women of faith. She studies health, faith, and motherhood to challenge and extend one's understanding of body, mind, and spirit. She analyzes motherhood in public and private spaces, studies new ways of connecting the role of mothers and their body, mind, and spirit framed by history, public, and private experiences; wrestles with the spirituality of resistance and growth against disempowerment and dehumanizing situations; investigates how religion and culture understand motherhood; reflects on the spirituality of mothering; and, concludes by envisioning a new world of mothers, othermothers, and their children as she suggests a way of knowing which allows women to engage in the kind of mother work toward envisioning a new world.

Soyoung Baik-Chey, researcher, theologian, and Christian social ethicist, analyzes how historical construction as opposed to natural instinct leads Korean Christian women to struggle with incongruence between their ontological capabilities and their cultural presuppositions. She reflects on how Korean Christian women internalized cultural-religious teachings of Christianity and Confucianism, requiring them to practice a self-sacrificing, self-denying devotion to benefit others. She analyzes Confucian and Christian cultural-religious heritages, questions their androcentric Christian and

Confucian interpretations on women and love, and suggests a theological rethinking of body, mind, and spirit in a harmonious and integrated way of being and loving.

Linda E. Thomas, professor of theology and anthropology, examines HIV/AIDS, African women, and the Bible in conversation with related realities in the United States, using statistics and realities as a preface to analyzing HIV/AIDS in South Africa for two reasons. Her essay shows the global nature of this story, this pandemic crisis, and honors the holistic ministries of St. John's Apostolic Faith Mission in South Africa, noting how much work needs to be done regarding sexuality in an effectively public way.

The studies in *Sex, Power, Vulnerability* begin with a chapter by Marie M. Fortune, pastor and activist, theologian and author committed to ending sexual and domestic violence, who questions sexual violence and the dynamics of an appropriate Christian sexual ethics. After reflecting on the violence and violations of sexual violence, the essay examines the witness of Hebrew scripture and the issue of sexual violence as property crimes, explores child abuse and incest, analyzes sexual harassment and exploitation of vulnerability, and investigates contemporary Christian traditions regarding sexual violence.

Marie Cartier, an artist, scholar, activist, poet, and playwright, makes connections between butch femme lesbian reality, queer theory, and spirituality, via Christianity. Connecting theology and lived religious reality with butch femme realities is central to this work. Her essay explores how pre-Stonewall lesbians viewed the body to define themselves and the sense of community they developed in the lesbian bars of the period. Such community building functioned through a sense of common faith in each other and was the grounding for a theology of community that made sacred seeing and befriending each other, in a world where there was no other space that allowed for a communal religious experience. Methodologically, each section begins with a question to establish clarification around definitions, identities, norms for particular behaviors, matters of history and heritage to help unpack the complexities of butch femme realities.

Shari Julian, author, forensic psychologist, and consultant, examines the dichotomies of messages surrounding women's power, faith, social roles, and cultural norms, particularly that of the widow, while analyzing women's lived experiences. Mining how faith and social norms conscribe women in ways that distort their experience of power and identity and render them vulnerable within a sexist, male-biased culture, she explores the myth and reality of female power interface with church teachings, hierarchy, faith, law, ethics, norms, gender, sexuality, and a dualist social ethic. This chapter analyzes how women are responsible for the values and behaviors of women and men but how men basically determine criteria for measuring the success of those values and norms.

In the final category, *Women, Worldview, Religious Practice,* Althea Spencer Miller, a biblical scholar with a concern for the role of the biblical interpretation in its sociopolitical usage, investigates portions of Caribbean women's history through the lens of gender and sexuality to understand the processes that constructed this irony. She examines colonial sexual behavior and slave sexual behavior as resistance, and traces ways Christianity perpetuated the regnant gender ideology, amidst the churches' complicit misogyny; and how the church/state doctrines and philosophies micromanaged personal morality—especially that of women.

Amy Hoyt, a feminist ethnographer, investigates women within the Church of Jesus Christ of Latter-day Saints (LDS) to view how maternal practices, specifically childbirth and raising children, shape traditional religious women and contribute to their religious devotion. Drawing upon an ethnographic study, she explores how maternal practices are religious practices that act to alter the interior of women, particularly women from a U.S. LDS community she worked with. After introducing LDS history and ethnographic demographics, the essay explores its methodology, examines pedagogies of maternity as religious praxis and its theoretical implications, analyzes notions of agency and subjectivity, and reflects on pedagogies and transformative gifts of parenthood.

These chapters invite you to expand your horizons about the way in which you envision the impact Christianity has on the lives of women who engage their Christian faith in their lived experiences. Their faith is not a matter of window dressing on Sundays, but a part of the essential fabric of their lives. Practicing their faith by no means secures them a perfect, easy life. Like all humanity, their lives are fraught with difficulty, challenges, disappointments, and grave pain; yet Christianity is not about glorifying pain or suffering. Their Christian faith allows them a view of life that brings hope and possibility, helps them experience life in community as covenant, and allows them to experience the gifts of salvation, the lessons, and the love of Christ which he modeled and taught: God is love; God created us out of love for us to live in love with God, ourselves, our neighbors; our sins can be forgiven; there is life after death; God loves us just as we are and wants the very best for us. Ergo, the totality of the life of Jesus the Christ is his message of love, redemption, and eternal life. For women, this faith, following these principles, provides an opportunity for liberation.

# PART I

# Women, Family, Environment

# CHAPTER 1

# There Goes the Bride: A Snapshot of the Ideal Christian Wife

*Kathlyn A. Breazeale*

The archetype of the wife in Western culture had an ominous beginning. Two wives, Pandora and Eve, were held responsible for the miseries, death, and sin of humankind. The story of Eve's creation by Yahweh and her partnership with Adam is recorded in Genesis 1–3, and Pandora is considered to be the "first Greek bride" who is "given in marriage by Zeus" in Greek mythology. Sixteenth-century artist Jean Cousin merges Eve and Pandora into one figure in a painting of a reclining nude woman holding an apple branch in her right hand as her right arm rests on a human skull. A serpent coils around her left arm as her left hand rests on a vase.[1] Created in response to sacred stories and images of wives as the source of human suffering, the idealized Christian wife has been constructed as the opposite of Pandora and Eve. Whereas a wife was responsible for all the human family's sorrows, the ideal wife must provide the good for her own family including her husband, children, and community.

Male writers recording the creative power of a male God wrote and elaborated on the sacred stories of Pandora and Eve.[2] Fear of female power is one subtext of these stories; thus, the idealized wife model is an attempt to subordinate and control female power so that the wife uses all her power to benefit her husband. Furthermore, the stories of Pandora and Eve function as cautionary tales for husbands: evil occurs when husbands do not control their wives. These stories have been used to provide religious justification for

3

the political and economic domination of wives by their husbands, as well as cultural norms that reinforce this domination.

Yet sacred stories are not the only sources that reveal a society's ideal of the wife. One must examine popular portrayals in the arts directed to the common people, as well as learned treatises written by scholars for other scholars. Thus, I chose the diversity of literatures analyzed in this chapter to access popular culture in each historical period. This chapter traces the historical development of the concept of the ideal Christian wife in Western culture, which remains prevalent today, by examining religious, economic, and political factors used to construct this archetype.[3] I demonstrate how the texts for defining "wife" shift from biblical scripture to the miracle and mystery plays of the medieval church, and then to the street drama and woodcut illustrations of the Renaissance and Reformation period. I examine the influence of capitalism and the resulting needs of the new middle class on religious beliefs about the role of the Christian wife. Following the historical overview, I discuss how Christian archetypes of two wives—Eve and Mary—continue to influence the portrayal of wives as good or bad in contemporary films. Because the purpose of this chapter is to analyze idealized images or models of the wife, I have selected popular images of the wife used to educate and prescribe behavior, rather than descriptive accounts of actual historical women.[4]

## PROVERBS 31: AN ECONOMIC IDEAL WIFE

The model of the ideal wife, the Queen Mother whose son is king, found in Proverbs 31:10–31, portrays a wife who uses all her power to benefit her husband.[5] The focus is entirely on the work this ideal wife does on behalf of the entire household; there is no mention of intimacy or concern for her well-being.

The verses in this chapter are an acrostic poem where each verse begins with the succeeding letter of the Hebrew alphabet. The book of Proverbs is a collection of wisdom teachings edited during the early postexilic period (the later part of the sixth century BCE) by elite men who "were the bureaucrats or 'sages' of society, working in court circles as counselors and educators" (Fontaine 1992, 145). The purpose of the Book of Proverbs was to give religious and moral instruction to young Jewish men. One can only speculate as to if and how young Jewish women were instructed with the ideal wife images in 31:10–31. Although Proverbs is predominantly literature of the upper class, Carole R. Fontaine suggests that these images were "held up as a goal to which *all wives* [emphasis mine], regardless of their social status, ought to aspire" (1992, 152).

Although women were considered property in biblical times, authors and editors of Proverbs clearly recognized the power of women as Phyllis Bird argues: "in Proverbs . . . [women are not] simply sexual objects; they are persons of intelligence and will, who, from the male's point of view expressed here, either make or break a man. The man must learn to recognize the two types and abstain from harmful relationships" (Bird 1974, 60). In Proverbs, Wisdom symbolizes the good woman and Folly symbolizes the bad and dangerous woman.[6] Women are divided into two categories based on their usefulness to men.

The upper-class wife of Proverbs 31:10–31 is useful to her husband because she "does him good and not harm all the days of her life" (verse 12).[7] She "does good" by providing domestic and business management services. Her labor enables her husband and children to live well as her husband performs public service (verse 23). Rising before dawn, she willingly makes beautiful and warm clothing for all her household, she travels to get food, and she supervises her female servants (verses 13–15, 19, 21–22). As an astute businesswoman with strong arms who works long into the night, she buys a field, plants a vineyard, and makes linen garments and sashes that she sells to the merchant (verses 16–18, 24). She has strength, dignity, a sense of humor, wisdom, kindness, and is generous to the poor and needy (verses 20, 25–26). She is never idle (verse 27). Her children and her husband believe that she is happy (verse 28). Her husband trusts her, profits from her, and praises her (verses 11, 29). In conclusion, the author/editor of this text denigrates female charm and beauty while praising a woman who "fears the Lord" (verse 30); such a woman should receive a share of the profits and public praise (verse 31). Ultimately, the virtuous woman does not exist because the Hebrew words, particularly the military and praise language toward the end of the text used to describe the "virtuous woman," are terms used to describe a god or a man.[8] Therefore, the woman described in these verses does not ultimately exist; in reality, "she" is a man or god.

In summary, this is an economic model of the ideal wife. Her value is compared to material wealth: she is "far more precious than jewels" (verse 10). In this model, there is no mention of the ideal wife's spiritual practices/religious responsibilities or physical/sexual attributes. As Phyllis Bird notes, the texts describes and characterizes the ideal wife nonsexually, as provider for husband and home; apparently, they are the entire focus of her time, talent, and energies. Her personhood gets lost; in this way she "does her husband good" (1974, 58). The ideal wife portrayed in Proverbs 31 is indeed the opposite of Pandora and Eve. The Proverbs wife provides only benefits for her husband and family, whereas Pandora and Eve are held responsible for the suffering and death of humankind.

## THE HOUSEHOLD CODES: A POLITICAL IDEAL WIFE

Depictions of women as wives are rare in the Christian Testament as the drama of the early Christian communities features virgins, prostitutes, mothers, and widows. While Jesus does mention wives in his prohibitions against divorce, wives are absent from his parables. And of all the women named as Christian apostles, prophets, missionaries and leaders of house churches, only Prisca is explicitly referred to as a wife (Acts 18:2).[9] Yet Elisabeth Schüssler Fiorenza notes that Prisca is not defined as a wife; rather, she is characterized by her "commitment to partnership in the work of the gospel" (1983, 173).

Perhaps one reason for this scarcity of images of women as wives is the anti-marriage sentiment evident in the teachings of Jesus and Paul. For example, Luke 14:26 records Jesus as declaring that those who do not "hate" their relatives, including wives, cannot be his disciples. And while Paul gives prescriptions for wives in I Corinthians 7:2–5, 10–11, 13–16 and 39, these verses are found in the same chapter in which Paul elaborates his preference for celibacy in verses 7–8, 25–38 and 40.[10]

Recent biblical scholars have interpreted the antifamily and pro-celibacy texts as evidence for the anti-patriarchal focus of the Jesus Movement. The power and authority of the *paterfamilias,* the father of the patriarchal household, was undercut by these admonitions to either reject one's family or to remain unmarried (Fiorenza 1983, 225).[11] Following Paul's teaching in 1 Corinthians 7:11 and 15, a wife who converted to Christianity had the option of leaving her unbelieving husband if he wanted a divorce, and she could choose to remain unmarried. Furthermore as a Christian convert, she had the opportunity to gain power and authority as a Christian leader that was not possible for her in the traditional role of wife.

This anti-marriage stance led to conflict both with the Roman social world outside the Christian communities and with those inside the communities, who became uncomfortable with women having authority over men, when Christianity became more mainstream and adapted to Greco-Roman culture. Prior to the third and fourth centuries CE, women were leaders in churches.[12] Evidence of this conflict regarding women's authority is found in the household codes that prescribe subordinate behavior for wives in Colossians 3:18, Ephesians 5:22–24, 33, 1 Peter 3:1–6 and Titus 2:4–5.[13] Derived from Aristotle's philosophical politics (fourth century BCE), the household codes were a set of rules specifying proper behavior in the patriarchal household between three pairs: husband and wife, father and children, master and slaves. By the first century CE, these codes had been adopted as the guide for ethical conduct throughout the Hellenistic world, including Hellenistic Judaism (Swidler 1979, 332).[14] These codes were adapted by Christian writers to give theological justification for the subordination of wives to husbands from a Christian perspective.

For example, Mary Rose D'Angelo argues that in Colossians, the declaration of the universal lordship of Christ is used to affirm "the patriarchal rule of the masters of this world" (1994, 322). In this text that appears to be the earliest use of the household code in a canonical book, Colossians 3:18 commands: "Wives, be subject to your husbands, as is fitting in the Lord." Here the word *kyrios*, usually translated "Lord," may refer both to Christ and to a husband as *kyrios*, the "usual title for any male superior, . . . the master of a slave, the husband or guardian (*tutor*) of a woman, or the head of a family . . ." (D'Angelo 1994, 321–22).[15]

The theological basis for the ideal submissive Christian wife found in Colossians is elaborated in Ephesians 5:21–33. In verses 22–24, this submission is strengthened by explicitly associating the husband with the Lord or Christ and the wife with the church.[16] Verse 24 leaves no doubt that this subjection is comprehensive: "Just as the church is subject to Christ, so also wives ought to be, in everything, to their husbands." As Fiorenza observes, "Ephesians christologically cements the inferior position of the wife in the marriage relationship" (1983, 270). Elizabeth Johnson suggests yet another ramification of using this Christ-church relationship as an image of human marriage: the author of Ephesians 5:31 quotes Genesis 2:24, where husband and wife become one flesh, to locate marriage within creation, not in social order. Ephesians sets up parallels: the church mirroring creation and the household mirroring the church (1992, 341). The ideal wife is to be submissive to her husband in the church as well as in the home.

While the verses in Ephesians are addressed to Christian wives married to Christian husbands, 1 Peter 3:1–6 is addressed to wives under the control of non-Christian husbands. In contrast to the option for Christian wives to separate from their non-Christian husbands stated in 1 Corinthians 7 (verses 11, 15), 1 Peter 3:1–2 commands wives "to accept the authority of your husbands, so that, even if some of them do not obey the word, they may be won over without a word by their wives' conduct when they see the purity and reverence of your lives." This text silences the wife's voice as a missionary and teacher.

Admonished to follow the example of Sarah who "obeyed Abraham and called him lord," the Christian wife is to accept the authority of her husband even if she is afraid: "You have become her daughters as long as you do what is good and never let fears alarm you" (verse 6). The source of these fears may have been personal, fear of an abusive husband,[17] or communal as the Christians addressed by Peter were encouraged to imitate Christ by enduring the suffering they were experiencing due to being persecuted for their beliefs (verses 2:12, 4:12–16, 5:8–9). Christian wives were one focus of the persecution because according to Roman law, a wife was required to practice the same religion as her husband. Wives who converted to Christianity threatened the stability of the household and the state because in Greco-Roman society, the state was conceived as constituted by patriarchal households (Schüssler Fiorenza 1983, 263–66). Thus, "the burden of alleviating tension between the Christian community and the Greco-Roman household and the state falls squarely on Christian wives and slaves" (Corley 1994, 353). Like wives, slaves were also required by Greco-Roman law to practice the religion of their master. In her analysis of this relationship between wives, slaves, and masters, Clarice J. Martin demonstrates how the household codes, rules of domestic behavior, "reflect an attempt to restrict the enthusiasm of women and slaves" so that the patriarchal household is restored and validated as a Christian household (1991, 213).

Wives literally portrayed their vital role in reducing the tension between Christian communities and Greco-Roman society when they complied (or not) with the command for a modest appearance to be consistent with their silent and submissive behavior: "Do not adorn yourselves outwardly by braiding your hair, and by wearing gold ornaments or fine clothing; rather, let your adornment be the inner self with the lasting beauty of a gentle and quiet spirit, which is very precious in God's sight (1 Peter 3:3–4)." In Greco-Roman society, women who exhibited liberated behavior, that is, who practiced speaking in public, wearing bright colors, and elaborately arranging their hair, were suspected of also behaving as courtesans or prostitutes. Thus, Corley suggests the author of 1 Peter is reflecting "the stereotypical Hellenistic slander that was being leveled against Christian women in Asia Minor . . . [which] indicates that the Christian women may have occasioned such slander by their apparently 'liberated' behavior" (1994, 352).

Evidence of Christian wives' liberated behavior is also found in Titus 2. This text is unique as compared to the other household codes in that instructions for the proper behavior of husbands are not included with the instructions for wives. Linda M. Maloney asserts this omission demonstrates that "the particular 'hot spot,' in the author's view, was defiance of social convention on the part of . . . married or marriageable women . . ." (1994, 367). The author of Titus admonishes wives "to love their husbands, to love their children, to be self-controlled, chaste, good managers of the household, kind, being submissive to their husbands, so that the word of God may not be discredited" (2:4–5). There is no public role for the ideal Christian wife, and one purpose of this text was "to limit the role of women in the church . . ." (Dewey 1992, 353).

Household codes reflect an older, conservative view of women that conflicted with both "the great range of activities and leadership roles undertaken by Jewish women in the first centuries" and "the more emancipatory ideas" circulating among pagans in the Roman Empire (Tanzer 1994, 330–331). In reading between the lines of the household codes and 1 Timothy 2:9–15 (which admonishes all women to dress modestly and "learn in silence with full submission"), Luise Schottroff finds evidence of a history of women's resistance to oppression during the first and second centuries CE (1995, 69–78). Schottroff declares that Christian women shook up established order and exposed women's oppression. These liberators refused to stay in their assigned places of domestic baby makers or the role of ascetic widow, the *univira*; they took a verbal stand in public (1995, 73).

To summarize, the household codes of Colossians, Ephesians, 1 Peter, and Titus all portray the most important characteristic of the ideal Christian wife as her subjection to her husband. This subjection is defined as silent acceptance of the husband's authority, modest attire, and confining her activity to her home. Thus, in contrast to the economic model of Proverbs 31, the household codes construct a political model of the ideal wife. In the midst of controversy and persecution, society demands her submissive behavior to reduce political conflict in the household, the church, and the larger non-Christian community. The ideal wife's value is her subordination allegedly as explicitly ordained by God. The codes provide a spirituality for wives that are missing in Proverbs 31. Now the portrait of the biblical ideal wife is more complete.

## MEDIEVAL MIRACLE AND MYSTERY PLAYS: A RELATIONAL IDEAL WIFE

The text for conveying Christian ideals changed in the medieval period from written to dramatic. The informal gatherings of Christian communities for worship and instruction in the people's own language had developed into the formal setting of the mass spoken in Latin. After the fall of the Roman Empire and the subsequent development of regional languages (for example, French, Spanish, German, and English), Latin survived only among the educated classes in the West and in the liturgies and documents of the Catholic Church. Since the great majority of the population was not educated and therefore did not understand Latin, the priests began to dramatize portions of the life of Jesus Christ as a means of instruction. These biblical plays were first developed as part of the daily liturgy in the monasteries founded by St. Benedict in the 5th century. By the late 10th century, the story of the visit of the women to the empty tomb was enacted by priests at the altar on Easter Day (Muir 1995, 13–15). Beginning in the 13th century, these dramas expanded from the altar to the street and developed into a cycle of plays performed in the vernacular by members of local craft guilds. However, the church continued to influence the content of the scripts as most of the plays were written and revised by clerics (Happe 1975, 21–22). The plays were also known as the Corpus Christi plays because they were originally performed during the feast of Corpus Christi established in 1311 by the Council of Vienne (Happe 1975, 19).

The cycle of miracle and mystery plays portrayed the biblical story of God's plan for salvation from creation to the final Day of Judgment, and "the celebration of the Passion of Christ [was] the chief object of these plays" (Happe 1975, 24). Produced at regular intervals for approximately 200 years, these plays were intended to instruct all social classes and involved the effort of the entire community.[18] Surviving manuscripts in Italian, French, German, Spanish, and English attest that the plays were produced throughout Western Europe.[19] Two of the most popular plays portrayed the image of the wife: *Adam and Eve* and *Noah*.

In Chester, England, the Adam and Eve play was initially produced by the Tanners who provided white leather costumes for Eve and Adam to simulate the appearance of nakedness (Happe 1975, 62). Yet in a French production, the pair wore "fine garments (*sollempnes vestes*) symbolic of their glorious state" (Muir 1995, 69). The script for this play closely followed the text of Genesis 2 and 3 with additions that reinforced the responsibility of Eve and all women/wives for sin and evil.

For example, in the Chester version of the play, the Devil proclaims woman's proclivity to wrong doing in a speech given prior to the temptation translated as "Woman will do what she is forbidden to do for any trivial excuse" (Happe 1975, 69, 653–54). And after eating the apple, Adam declares to Eve he knew when she was created and named "Eve" that she would be the cause of misery for man (Happe 1975, 72). The implication in the reference to Eve's name, which means "life," is that Eve is "the mother of all who live and sin" (Happe 1975, 654). In *The Play of Adam*, the earliest surviving play in French, Adam resists the temptation of the Devil on two occasions before Eve succumbs (Odenkirchen 1976, 55–69). And after eating the apple, Adam laments: "*Jo ai guerpi mun criator, Par le conseil de mal uxor*," translated as "I have rejected my creator because of the counsel given me by an evil wife" (Odenkirchen 1976, 84–85).

In contrast to Eve the evil wife, the majority of the Noah plays portray Mrs. Noah as good and obedient to her husband and God. However, some of the Noah plays, mainly the English versions, draw on an Eastern legend that makes Mrs. Noah succumb "to a temptation of the devil . . . and seek to prevent Noah's salvation" (Muir 1995, 73). In one version, the devil entices Mrs. Noah to get Noah drunk so he will tell her everything. In fourth century Gnostic writings, early medieval folk-tales, and many church murals, Mrs. Noah, with Satan or alone, tries to destroy the Ark and therefore delay or disrupt the plan of salvation.[20] Although the scene with the Devil is missing, Mrs. Noah appears as willful and disobedient in the English cycle plays of York, Towneley, and Chester. In the Towneley version, Mrs. Noah disobeys her husband's command to enter the Ark three times, using her desire to spin as her excuse. The conflict between the couple escalates as Noah strikes Mrs. Noah and she strikes back (Happe 1975, 105, 112). Finally, Mrs. Noah acquiesces. After entering the Ark, she becomes a good wife. She obediently steers the Ark with the tiller following Noah's request, and she offers help and advice in navigating and sending forth birds to determine if dry land can be found (Happe 1975, 113–15).

In contrast to the Towneley version, the Chester play portrays Mrs. Noah as refusing to board the ark without her women friends, her "gossips," because they have loved her and she wants to save them from drowning. She tells Noah he will have to get a new wife if these women are not allowed on the ark (Hopper and Lahey 1962, 101). After consultation with Noah, the three sons drag their mother onto the ark. When Noah welcomes her on board, Mrs. Noah strikes Noah on the ear (Happe 1975, 127) and she does not speak again in the play.

The popularity of the English version of Mrs. Noah is evident in the iconography of English churches. Images of her appear on one of the bosses in the nave of Norwich Cathedral and in the stained glass windows of both York Minster and Malvern Priory (Anderson 1963, 107).[21] She also appears in the literature of the period as Chaucer mentions her in *The Miller's Tale*.[22]

In summary, the medieval plays follow Proverbs 31 and the household codes in categorizing a wife as either good or bad depending on her relationship to her husband. A wife's relationship with her women friends is not valued. Furthermore, the additions to Genesis 2 and 3 reinforce the belief that wives are by nature inferior to husbands. Before the fall (which is really not a fall, but an expulsion as God puts them out), the Devil denounces woman's nature with no parallel reference to man's nature, and Adam successfully resists the Devil's temptation whereas Eve does not. The wife is also spiritually inferior as both Eve and Mrs. Noah encourage their husband to disobey God. Eve and Mrs. Noah are portrayed as bad wives because they think and act for themselves. Their power is not subordinated to their husbands or God.[23]

## SECULAR STREET DRAMA: PUNCH AND JUDY—THE BATTERED WIFE

The miracle and mystery plays added characters, emotions, commentaries, and debates to the biblical texts. Such freedom of interpretation could not

survive the religious upheaval of the 16th-century reformation and coun-
terreformation movements (Muir 1995, 9). The French plays, the *Mystères,*
were suppressed by an enactment of the Parlement de Paris in 1548, and
the last recorded performance of a complete cycle in England appears to
have been at Coventry in 1580 (Happe 1975, 24). Yet the religious image of
the wife continued to be dramatically portrayed in the puppet theater of the
streets and fairs as "the Biblical themes that had quite disappeared from the
human stage were still preserved by the puppets" (Speaight 1955, 64).

Throughout Elizabethan England, the puppets presented Eve as the evil
wife in *The Creation of the World* (Speaight 1955, 64, 78). The medieval
characterization of Mrs. Noah as the abrasive wife continued in the secular
character of Judy, originally named Joan, the wife of Punch.[24] By 1705, *The
Creation of the World* included a scene "showing Punch and his wife dancing in Noah's Ark . . ." (Speaight 1955, 92). A script from 1730 echoes the
verbal and physical conflict of the medieval Noah and Mrs. Noah. Punch
declares: "Joan you are the plague of my life, A rope would be welcomer [*sic*]
than such a wife." Punch continues by lamenting Joan's "thundering tongue"
and proclaims that the unmarried man is "happy" because he does not have a
wife to scold him. Joan replies by pointing out Punch's "hunch" and his "great
strutting belly." She asserts he is declaring war against her, and she threatens
to "beat [his] fat guts to a jelly" (Speaight 1955, 169–70).

By 1825, Punch was hailed on the streets of London as "the most popular performer in the world" (Speaight 1955, 182). In 1828 when the Punch
and Judy script was first published, the fighting between Punch and Judy
ended by Punch killing Judy as he declares: "To lose a wife is to get a fortune"
(Speaight 1955, 189, 191). As this drama continued to be performed into the
20th century, Judy's death became standardized in the plot. Her task is to
dance and quarrel with Punch, bring Punch the Baby, become enraged when
the Baby disappears, and then become a domestic-abuse victim from blows
Punch lands on her (Speaight 1955, 192, 195). In the majority of the plays
performed in the 19th and 20th centuries, Punch is not punished for his
behavior as he defeats the Devil in the final scene of the play.

Sanctioning the death of Judy at the hands of her husband is the ultimate
outcome of the contempt for wives portrayed in the medieval plays about Eve
and Mrs. Noah. Perhaps Judy's death as a wife was deemed justified because
Eve, the first wife, was held responsible for the death of humankind. Judy's story
functions as a cautionary tale to wives who do not conform to the image of the
wife advocated by Proverbs 31 and the household codes. When Punch declares
he will "get a fortune" by losing his bad wife, his words image the reverse of the
good wife in Proverbs 31 who is "far more precious than jewels" (verse 10b). Just
as Proverbs was used for the instruction of youth, unfortunately the Punch and
Judy play came to be regarded as a play for children (Speaight 1955, 214–17).

## RENAISSANCE AND REFORMATION: WOODCUTS AND CAPITALISM—A SILENT, MORAL IDEAL WIFE

The invention of the printing press in the 15th century provided a new means for portraying the image of the ideal Christian wife. Similar to the miracle and mystery plays, the press provided a method for communicating with the majority of the population who did not know Latin. Two examples illustrate popular images of both the bad wife and the good wife.

The bad wife is shown in a woodcut (Gotha, circa 1533) titled "A Husband Who Does Not Rule" or "The Prize of the Devout Woman" (Ozment 1983, 52–53 and Roper 1989, 258–59). The husband is shown on his hands and knees harnessed to a cart loaded with a large wooden tub filled with laundry. As he pulls the cart, his wife stands over him with a whip in one hand, his sword in her other hand, and his purse and codpiece slung over her arm. In the verses accompanying this woodcut (Ozment 1983, 52–53), the husband laments that he "took" a wife, referring to her as a "shrewish scold." The wife replies that he deserves to "be beaten" because he has been "carousing about" and not providing clothing and food for her and the children. This wife is bad because she is asserting power over her husband; she is carrying the symbols of male authority: sword, purse, and codpiece. Yet the author of these verses evidences sympathy for the wife through the words of the "wise man," one of the four persons walking behind the cart. This man has the last word, and he admonishes men to stay with their wives "in love and suffering, And always be patient." Furthermore, if the husband has "much worry and care," he is to consider this "as God's will."[25]

In contrast to the wife with a whip, the good wife stands still and silent in "A Wise Woman" (Vienna, circa 1525; Ozment 1983, 66–67). Prefaced by the declaration that "any woman who does as she [the wise woman] instructs protects her honor well," the verses in boxes on either side of the woman explain each part of her appearance. Her eyes are wide open—she sees "keenly as the hawk" to "discern the honest from the false" and "guard" herself against one "who against my honor plots." A large key is next to her left ear—she opens her ears to "hear God's word, Which keeps the pious on their guard." In her right hand, she holds a mirror displaying a crucifix—she will "despise pride" and "behold herself in the mirror of Christ." Her lips are bound together with a padlock—she wears this "golden lock" so she will "say no harmful words Or wound another's honor." A turtle dove is sitting on her chest—she has a "steadfast heart" that is "faithful" to her husband so that "No fault of his will break my loyalty." Two serpents are wrapped around her waist—she is "girded with serpents" to protect herself "from the poison of scandal, From evil love, and shameful play." A small pillow is under her left arm and she holds a large pitcher in her left hand—she will "serve the aged freely And thereby gain eternal life." Her feet are horses' hoofs—she will be "steadfast in honor. And not fall into sin. . . . This image of the good wife protecting her honor illustrates the silent submission demanded by the household codes. This image also evidences the influence of capitalism on the good wife ideal: through her honor, a woman must demonstrate she is good enough to earn a husband.

The concept that a woman could make herself good enough to win a husband and earn his love was as new as the notion that men could make money rather than inherit it. Capitalism provided men who were not born to the nobility the economic means to propose marriage, yet there were not enough noble women for them to marry. Thus, the criteria for determining who was a good woman for marriage changed from the woman's social class to her individual morals (Heyn 1997, 59–60). This change is still evident in the definition of "lady." Contemporary usage of "lady" denotes morality whereas the original definition indicated a woman of the upper class. As the feudal system collapsed during this period of fundamental economic upheaval, the new middle-class good wife ideal was a critical factor for establishing capitalism.

Although capitalism created a new class for husbands, the wife's subordinate status remained the same. Following Proverbs 31, the new Protestant theology reaffirmed that a wife's economic power was to be controlled by her husband. Lyndal Roper demonstrates how Protestant theology developed to support the rise of middle-class husbands through the growing economic importance of the guilds: ". . . the politics of the Reformation gave voice to the interests and perceptions of the married craftsmen who ruled over their wives and organized the household's subordinate labour force of men and women" (Roper 1989, 3).

In summary, Protestant theology reinforced the subordination of wives to husbands to ensure the stability of the new economic and moral social order. This theological strategy of wife subordination is familiar: the same strategy was advocated by the early Christians in the household codes to reduce their conflict with Roman society. And in the decades following the rise of capitalism, the street theater portrayal of Judy's death at the hands of Punch reminded viewers of all ages that insubordinate wives could suffer lethal consequences.

## FROM SACRED SCRIPTURE TO THE SILVER SCREEN: THE IMPOSSIBLE IDEAL WIFE

[F]ilms . . . provide a key means for millions of Americans to grapple with religious issues, mythic archetypes, and fundamental ideological concerns.
(Martin and Ostwalt 1995, viii)

As described in the previous sections, the form of the popular text for defining the Christian wife has developed from written to dramatic to illustrated. On January 31, 1898, another change occurred with the screening of the first photographic film, *The Passion Play of Oberammergau*. This film was "directly patterned after medieval Passion plays" (Miles 1996, 6).[26] Whereas the bad wife may be portrayed on the screen as emulating Eve, the good wife confronts the impossible challenge of emulating the goodness of the Virgin Mary, Mother of Jesus.

The construction of Mary as the opposite of Eve has been well documented and discussed by recent scholars. Eve is the supreme example of woman's inherent inferior and evil nature, while Mary is the model of goodness that all women should emulate. However, as Virgin and Mother, the Mary model is impossible for human women to achieve.[27] In light of this scholarship, my point here is to demonstrate how wives in particular are denigrated by the dichotomy between the two archetypes of Mary and Eve.

In the Catholic Church that celebrated virginity and celibacy, wives occupied the lowest rung on the moral ladder. By definition, wives are not virgins; wives are sexually active. Thus, as Anne Baring and Jules Cashford observe: "If they [women] could not emulate Mary's virginity, they were condemned to align themselves with Eve" (1993, 539). This condemnation of women was especially applied to wives as Rosemary Radford Ruether notes: "The married woman was the epitome of the carnal Eve. Her subordination and need for punishment were fully stressed" (1989, 34).[28] In Protestant theology, the wife's subordination within marriage was her punishment for Eve's sin according to Martin Luther, who argued that Eve had to be under her husband's power because of her complicity with original sin; thus God commands that husbands must rule, wives must obey (Luther 1958, 202–3 [1535–45]). Thus, the Protestant Reformation did not include a reformation of the association of wives with Eve and sin. In both Catholic and Protestant marriages, the wife as Eve "must be subdued, guarded, and maintained in such a way that she can do no further harm" (Phillips 1984, 118).

To redeem Eve's sin, "Mary had to be perpetually virgin, untainted by sexual relationship with another human being" because the doctrine of original sin proclaimed that sin was transmitted through sexual intercourse (Baring and Cashford 1993, 572). Thus, although Mary is technically a wife, she was originally almost never portrayed as a wife. In early iconography and apocryphal stories of Mary and Joseph, "Joseph is generally depicted as an older man, who, symbolically, is thereby transformed from her nuptial husband into her father" (Baring and Cashford 1993, 563).[29] Mary, the wife of Joseph, was not compatible with Mary, the virgin, who gave birth to the Son of God.

However, beginning in the end of the 14th century with the influence of the emerging middle-class ideal and a rise in the importance of Joseph, the image of Mary was changed to portray the ideal wife of the household codes (Warner 1976, 189–91). She was imaged as "obedient, respectful, humble, quiet, and modest. . . . Even her silence in the Gospels is turned to good account, becoming an example to all women to hold their tongues" (Warner 1976, 190). Thus, Mary became the ultimate model for the good wife ideal that is impossible for real wives to fulfill.

The impossibility of real women to fulfill the good wife ideal is portrayed to the extreme in the original version of *The Stepford Wives* (1975). In this film about suburban, white, upper-middle-class wives and husbands, each wife is systematically murdered by a robot who, with cooperation from the husband, has been created as an idealized version of the human wife. Each robot wife has a Barbie-doll figure and is programmed to totally please her husband, including offering excessive praise for his sexual abilities. Although the human Joanna, the central character, is portrayed as sexually desirable to her husband, one of the robot wives reveals that "our sex life is better."

This film chastises wives who have desires of their own. Joanna's husband complains that her interest in becoming a professional photographer interferes with her responsibility to be a good mother, and he reminds her that they moved from New York City to Stepford for the benefit of their children. Charmaine, another Stepford wife, is an avid tennis player. Yet after she is replaced by a robot, "Charmaine" has her tennis court destroyed so her husband can have the heated swimming pool he always wanted. The robot wife Charmaine declares: "I want to please him now. . . . All I ever thought about before was just me."

The robot wives also please their husbands by staying home. When Joanna and her best friend try to start a consciousness-raising group, they discover that previously there had been such a group in Stepford, and this group was the "first women's club to ask any of those liberation ladies to come lecture." But now the robot wives are too busy ironing, cooking, and cleaning their houses. They declare they are happier now as they support their husbands who work so many hours each day.

*The Stepford Wives* (1975) release date followed the Supreme Court's legalization of abortion in 1973 and Congressional approval of the Equal Rights Amendment in 1971–72 (although ultimately this amendment did not become law because it was not ratified by the required number of states). This film can be read as a male fantasy of retribution against women who dare to become "liberated."[30] Near the end of the film, Joanna is unsuccessful in her desperate attempt to find her children and flee Stepford. In one of the most chilling scenes just before she is to be murdered, Joanna asks the man in change, "Why?" He replies:

> *Because we can.* We've found a way of doing it [having someone service us, no matter what] that's just perfect. . . . Wouldn't you like *some perfect stud* waiting on you around the house, praising you, servicing you, whispering how your sagging flesh was beautiful no matter how you looked? [emphasis added]

"Because we can." This is the voice of patriarchy warning women that reject-ing the good wife ideal can have fatal consequences. The human wives who, like the archetype Eve, have their own desires and do not fully submit to their husbands, are replaced by obedient robot wives. Furthermore, the robot wife is programmed to kill the human wife so that the men do not have to commit this act. This programming exemplifies Mary Daly's analysis that patriarchy perpetuates itself through the actions of women against women.[31] While there are no references to religion in this film, the religious belief that God commands husbands to rule over wives (Genesis 3:16) and wives to be obedient (Ephesians 5:22, without regard for Ephesians 5:21) is graphically portrayed.

In contrast, religious beliefs about the good wife ideal are explicit in *Breaking the Waves* (1996). This film tells the story of Bess, who lives in a village on a windswept coast of Scotland and is a member of a small, conser-vative Christian church. The women are not allowed to speak during church services or to be present at the grave for burials. Throughout the film Bess is shown praying aloud to God. With her eyes open, Bess speaks to God in a high-pitched, child-like voice. Then Bess closes her eyes, and God talks back to her in words spoken by Bess with a stern, harsh voice.

Bess is portrayed as a warm-hearted and generous young woman who is a virgin when she marries Jan, an "outsider" who works on an oil rig off the coast. In marriage, Bess discovers her sexual passion and ecstasy. She is supremely happy. In prayer, she promises God: "I'll be good, I'll be really, really good" because she hears God reminding her that "God giveth and God taketh away." When Jan returns to the oil rig for his work shift, Bess is dev-astated. She weeps and wails and even delays the departure of the plane carrying the oil rig workers so that Jan must comfort her. In prayer, God upholds the good wife ideal as God accuses Bess of being selfish, of putting her own feelings first, of not considering how her behavior affected Jan. In response, Bess once again promises to be "a good girl." Unable to bear her grief over Jan's absence, Bess begs God to bring Jan home. Jan does come home sooner than expected because he has an accident on the rig that leaves him paralyzed from the neck down. Bess believes Jan's condition is her fault due to her prayer for his return.

After the accident, Jan asks Bess to "get a lover for my sake." He tells her: "It will be you and me. Do it for me." At first Bess refuses. Then in prayer, she hears God telling her: "Prove to me you love him and then I'll let him live." As Jan's condition worsens, Bess begins to live the life of a prostitute. She asks God, "Am I going to hell?" And God responds, "Whom do you want to save? Yourself or Jan?" Jan survives a series of critical operations, and Bess becomes convinced that her promiscuous behavior is responsible. In conversations with her sister-in-law and then with her doctor, Bess proclaims: "He is my husband and God has said I must honor him. . . . I don't make love with them. I make love with Jan and I save him from dying. . . . God gives everyone something to be good at. . . . I'm good at this."

Eventually, Bess becomes convinced she must die in order for Jan to live, so she chooses to go to men on a boat who are known for their cruelty to prostitutes. Bess prays as she goes to the boat, and she believes God is with her. Bess dies from her ordeal, and Jan recovers so that he is able to walk with crutches. After Bess's doctor testifies at the inquiry regarding her death, the judge asks, "Do you want the records of the court to state that the deceased was suffering from being good? Perhaps this was the psychological defect that led to her death?" Because of her sexual behavior, Bess is condemned to hell by the elders of her church. In response, Jan and his friends steal her body from the morgue and bury her at sea. The next morning, the men hear bells ringing in the clouds above the boat.

Advertised as "a love story with no limits," this disturbing film raises provocative questions about a wife caught in the dichotomy between the bad Eve and good Mary archetypes. Bess is portrayed as obsessed with being "a good girl" and with proving her love for her husband. Bess is judged as mentally ill by others. Is the film suggesting that the good wife ideal is a form of mental illness? Bess believes her love for her husband will save him. The church elders believe Bess is a sinner going to hell. What are we to believe about Bess? Is she a saint, a sinner, or a candidate for a psychiatric ward? With the "bells of heaven" ringing after Bess's burial, is this film a glorification of the ultimate self-sacrificial love of a good wife? Or is the film a critique of religious beliefs about the good wife ideal?

*The Stepford Wives* and *Breaking the Waves* demonstrate that the wives are powerless to create a healthy marriage relationship when confronted with forces beyond their control. Symbolically, these forces are represented by male-created robotics technology and a voice of God that sounds like the voices of the male church elders. These forces reinforce the husband's power. Joanna's husband chooses to replace her with a robot wife, and Bess's God values her husband's life more than her life. Both Joanna and Bess die to fulfill their husband's desires.

In conclusion, although the archetypes of Eve and Mary are still portrayed in contemporary films, neither archetype is helpful for contemporary women and men seeking to create a mutual power-sharing marriage partnership.[32] Both archetypes separate a wife from knowledge of her own power and desire. Eve, the wife who has this knowledge is bad, while the good wife Mary is not permitted to acquire such knowledge. The current divorce rate of 65 percent in the United States (Heyn 1997, 18) is evidence that these models of the wife based on traditional religious beliefs are not functioning for the majority of couples. The fact that wives initiate 60 to 75 percent of these divorces suggests that new images of the wife must be created. How could the role of wife be changed? As religious and cultural beliefs about marriage are being questioned, contemporary films become contemporary texts to struggle with what it means to be a wife.

## Conclusion: A Call to Change the Ideal

This analysis of historical and contemporary ideal wife archetypes has come full circle. The opening and closing scenes are the same: the ideal Christian wife is the subordinate wife. Her subordination is political, economic, and ordained by God. She silently and obediently accepts her inferior nature and status. Her morality and honor are judged according to her submission of her power to her husband. Many churches in the 21st century embrace this theology implicitly; others state such doctrines explicitly, as has the Southern Baptist Convention.[33]

Six models have been examined to trace the historical development of the ideal Christian wife archetype: the Economic Ideal Wife of Proverbs 31; the Political Ideal Wife of the New Testament household codes; the Relational Ideal Wife of the Medieval miracle and mystery plays; the Battered Wife of the Punch and Judy street puppet theater; the Silent, Moral Ideal Wife of the Renaissance and Reformation woodcuts and capitalism; and the Impossible Ideal Wife as portrayed in two contemporary films. I have analyzed how these diverse texts and art forms have been used as educational tools for children, youth, and adults: both to prescribe behavior to fulfill the ideal and to warn about the sometimes fatal consequences of noncompliance with this ideal.

How dangerous is it to be a wife or girlfriend in the United States today? On average, every day more than three women are murdered by their husbands or boyfriends.[34] Every nine seconds a woman in this country is beaten by her husband or boyfriend,[35] and nearly one-third of women (31%) report being physically or sexually abused by a husband or boyfriend at some point in their lives.[36] These statistics are staggering and indicate that intimate partner violence violates *one in four women* in the United States, women in all population groups across the differences of race, class, and religion.[37]

There is no difference in these statistics for women who are Christian. These statistics are a piercing call to church congregations to be involved in reducing violence against women and girls.[38]

In addition to reducing violence, Jesus's actions and teachings provide Christians with a mandate to reclaim the radical mutuality demonstrated by Jesus's treatment of women, including women who did not conform to social rules for acceptable female behavior. For example, Jesus did not condemn the woman caught in adultery (John 8:3–11), and he encouraged Mary as a student when Martha wanted her help in the kitchen (Luke 10:38–42). Furthermore, violence against wives is reprehensible for Christians given Jesus's core teachings of "do to others as you would have them do to you" (Matt. 7:12) and "love your neighbor as yourself" (Matt. 19:19). These teachings should certainly apply to one's closest neighbor, one's wife. The subordinate good wife ideal is not compatible with the gospel of love proclaimed by Jesus. Yet why has this ideal endured among some Christians?

One reason is offered by journalist Dalma Heyn who argues that the good wife ideal, like religious ideas, endures *"because of its extraordinary psychological value"* [emphasis Heyn's] (Heyn 1997, 83): "The idea of Wife suggests, as does the idea of a god, that, . . . the cares of the world will be eased, or even erased, by a benevolent and caring heart; and that home will be a place of comfort and nurturance" (Heyn 1997, 86). Yet, given the domestic violence statistics cited above, the home is *not* a place of "comfort and nurturance" for many wives and girlfriends who are psychologically terrorized, beaten, and murdered. Now is the time for Christians to take the lead in challenging the doctrine of subordination that leaves women and girls vulnerable to men and boys who believe they can use violence to enforce this subordination. By changing the traditional good wife ideal, more wives and girlfriends may be safe in their own homes. This safety would be truly ideal.

## NOTES

1. See Claudine Leduc, "Marriage in Ancient Greece," in *A History of Women in the West: I. From Ancient Goddesses to Christian Saints*, ed. Pauline Schmitt Pantel (Cambridge: The Belknap Press of Harvard University Press, 1992), 235. Furthermore, Barbara Smith suggests that the Pandora myth "gives us a kind of recipe of acquisition by which a young girl is transformed from *parthenos* ["maiden"] into *gune* ["woman" and "wife"]. See Smith, "Greece," in *The Feminist Companion to Mythology*, ed. Carolyne Larrington (London: Pandora Press, 1992), 96. Francoise Borin discusses Cousin's painting *Eva Prima Pandora* in "Judging by Images," in *A History of Women in the West: III. Renaissance and Enlightenment Paradoxes*, eds. Natalie Zemon Davis and Arlette Farge (Cambridge: The Belknap Press of Harvard university Press, 1993), 193–95.

2. For synopses of the stories and discussion of Pandora and Eve, see Baring and Cashford 1993, 486–91, 515–18; and Phillips 1984, 16–37.

3. For more comprehensive historical analyses, see Marilyn Yalom, *A History of the Wife* (New York: HarperCollins Publishers, 2001); and Stephanie Coontz, *Marriage, A History: How Love Conquered Marriage* (New York: Penguin Books, 2006).

4. I am grateful to Cheryl Kirk-Duggan and Karen Jo Torjesen for their valuable suggestions and careful reading of this essay, and to my colleagues in the Religion Department at Pacific Lutheran University for their helpful responses to an earlier draft.

5. See Bruce K. Waltke, *The Book of Proverbs: Chapters 15–31* (Grand Rapids, MI: William B. Eerdmans, 2005), 510. For an alternative view of this text, see Kathleen M. O'Connor who argues that this text describes the nature of a life lived with wisdom rather than the ideal marriage partner in *The Wisdom Literature: Message of Biblical Spirituality* (Wilmington: Michael Glazier, 1988), 77.

6. For further feminist analysis of Wisdom and Folly in Proverbs 1–9, see Carol A. Newsom, "Woman and the Discourse of Patriarchal Wisdom: A Study of Proverbs 1–9," in *Gender and Difference in Ancient Israel*, edited by Peggy L. Day (Minneapolis, MN: Fortress Press, 1989), 142–60; Alice Ogden Bellis, *Helpmates, Harlots, and Heroes: Women's Stories in the Hebrew Bible* (Louisville: Westminster/John Knox Press, 1994), 193–97; and Katharine Doob Sakenfeld, *Just Wives?: Stories of Power & Survival in the Old Testament & Today* (Louisville: Westminster/John Knox Press, 2003), 126–33.

7. All biblical quotations and references in this chapter are from the *New Revised Standard Version*.

8. Randall C Bailey, "Doing the Wrong Thing: Male-Female Relationships in the Hebrew Canon," in *We Belong Together: The Churches in Solidarity with Women*, ed. Sarah Cunningham (New York: Friendship Press, 1992), 32–34.

9. For discussions of women's leadership in the early Christian communities, see Fiorenza, 1983, 160–204; and Karen Jo Torjesen, *When Women Were Priests: Women's Leadership in the Early Church & the Scandal of their Subordination in the Rise of Christianity* (New York: HarperSanFrancisco, 1993).

10. For a discussion of how these anti-marriage teachings were understood by the first Christian theologians, see Elizabeth A. Clark and Herbert Richardson, *Women and Religion: The Original Sourcebook of Women in Christian Thought* (New York: HarperSanFrancisco, 1996), 19–66. For a critique of how these teachings have been interpreted by Christians throughout the centuries including the contemporary Christian Right, see Rosemary Radford Ruether, *Christianity and the Making of the Modern Family* (Boston: Beacon, 2000).

11. See also S. Scott Barchy, "Undermining Ancient Patriarchy: The Apostle Paul's Vision of a Society of Siblings," *Biblical Theology Bulletin* 29, n. 2 (Summer 1999): 68–78; and "Who Should Be Called Father?: Paul of Tarsus between the Jesus Tradition and *Patria Potestas*," *Biblical Theology Bulletin* 33, no. 4 (Winter 2003): 135–47.

12. Two examples of detailed analyses of women's leadership in this early period are Torjesen, *When Women Were Priests*; and Carolyn Osiek, Margaret Y. MacDonald, and Janet H. Tulloch, *A Woman's Place: House Churches in Earliest Christianity* (Minneapolis, MN: Fortress Press, 2005). I am grateful to Annal Frenz for bringing *A Woman's Place* to my attention.

13. I am focusing on these texts, rather than the prescriptions of Paul in I Corinthians 7, because the ideal wife as defined by the household codes was intended to be "viewed" by both the Christian communities and the social world beyond the church. I wish to thank Sarah S. Forth for calling my attention to the image of wives in the household codes and for suggesting sources to initiate my research of these codes and Proverbs 31.

14. For further discussions of the political and religious context of the household codes, see Corley 1994, 351; and Fiorenza, 1983, 254–59.

15. D'Angelo also argues that "Colossians raises the question of the ways that slavery and the subjugation of women collaborate in sustaining the patriarchal order" (1994, 315, 321–22). For a discussion that argues this point with examples from other Household Codes texts, see Martin, 1991.

16. However, Catherine Clark Kroeger begins her analysis of this text with verse 21 to argue that these verses promote mutual submission. See Kroeger, "Let's Look again at the Biblical Concept of Submission," in *Violence against Women and Children: A Christian Theological Sourcebook*, ed. Carol J. Adams and Marie M. Fortune (New York: Continuum, 1995), 135–40.

17. Corley finds the implication that wives should submit to sexual abuse in the reference to Sarah obeying Abraham because Sarah was given to Pharaoh "on account of her beauty." Corley discusses how these verses have been used by contemporary pastors to counsel women to stay in abusive marriages. See Corley, 1994, pages 353–57.

18. The Passion Play still being performed in Oberammergau, Germany, is evidence of the ongoing attraction of these plays.

19. For more detailed discussions of the history, development, and production of the miracle and mystery plays, see Muir 1995, 1–61; Happe 1975, 9–35; and Hopper & Lahey 1962, 1–29.

20. In some stories, Mrs. Noah successfully delays the building of the ark for 100 years. See Hopper and Lahey 1962, 36.

21. The Norwich Cathedral boss portrays "a young man apparently pleading with a very rigid looking female"; the window at York "shows the Ark afloat, with Noah praying in the bows and one of the sons apparently still reasoning with his mother"; in the Malvern window, the couple is shown in front of the ark as "Noah fingers his beard with rueful embarrassment and his wife's stiffly raised hand is poised like a chopper, ready to cut off any further argument" (Anderson 1963, 107–8).

22. Chaucer's reference is in lines 353–4: "sorrow of Noah and all his fellowship That he had ere he got his wife to ship . . ." (Anderson 1963, 107).

23. For further analysis of how women were portrayed in the miracle and mystery plays, including Mrs. Noah, see Katie Normington, *Gender and Medieval Drama* (Woodbridge, Suffolk: D. S. Brewer, 2004).

24. Punch can be traced from the character Pulcinella in the Commedia dell'Arte of Italy (begun in the early 1500s) and from Polichinelle, a traditional figure in French farce (Speaight 1955, 15–18, 40–43). In England, the puppet's name was shortened to Punch.

25. For a less sympathetic interpretation, see Roper 1989, 258–59.

26. This film "featured thirteen tableaux of about a minute each from the trial and death of Jesus." An Episcopal priest, Hannibal Goodwin, was the inventor of photographic film. See Miles 1996, 6.

27. See for example, Mary Daly, *Beyond God the Father: Toward a Philosophy of Women's Liberation* (Boston: Beacon Press, 1973); Warner 1976; Phillips 1984; and Baring and Cashford 1993.

28. See also Ruether, "Virginal Feminism in the Fathers of the Church," in *Religion and Sexism: Images of Woman in the Jewish and Christian Traditions*, ed. Rosemary Radford Ruether (New York: Simon and Schuster, 1974), 150–83.

29. For examples of this iconography that portray Joseph as an elderly man, see Warner 1976, Plates I, II, and III, Figure 4. For the exception, see Warner 1976, Figure 25.

30. For further analysis of films as retribution against women, see Susan Faludi, "Fatal and Fetal Visions: The Backlash in the Movies," in *Backlash: The Undeclared War Against American Women* (New York: Doubleday, 1991), 112–39; and Molly Haskell, *From Reverence to Rape: The Treatment of Women in the Movies*, 2nd ed. (Chicago: University of Chicago Press, 1987).

31. See Mary Daly, *Gynecology: The Metaethics of Radical Feminism* (Boston: Beacon Press, 1978), 8.

32. See Kathlyn A. Breazeale, *Mutual Empowerment: A Theology of Marriage, Intimacy, and Redemption* (Minneapolis, MN: Fortress Press, 2008).

33. In 1998, the Southern Baptist Convention passed a resolution that: "A wife is to submit herself graciously to the servant leadership of her husband even as the church willingly submits to the headship of Christ." See Kenneth L. Woodward, "Using the Bully Pulpit?" *Newsweek*, June 22, 1998, 69.

34. See "Bureau of Justice Statistics Crime Data Brief," *Intimate Partner Violence, 1993–2001* (February 2003), cited in "Domestic Violence Is a Serious, Widespread Social Problem in America: The Facts," 2005, http://endabuse.org/resources/facts/.

35. See "Battering Statistics" compiled in October 1996 by the Los Angeles Commission on Assaults Against Women, 605 West Olympic Boulevard, Suite 400, Los Angeles, CA, 90015.

36. See *Health Concerns across a Woman's Lifespan: 1998 Survey of Women's Health* (The Commonwealth Fund, May 1999), cited in "Domestic Violence Is a Serious, Widespread Social Problem in America: The Facts," http://endabuse.org/resources/facts/.

37. See L. Heise and C. Garcia-Moreno, "Violence by Intimate Partners," *World Report on Violence and Health* (Geneva: World Health Organization, 2002), cited in "Intimate Partner Violence: Fact Sheet," National Center for Injury Prevention and Control, http://www.cdc.gov/ncipc/factsheets/ipvfacts.htm.

38. Four excellent resources that address how the church should respond to violence against women are Monica A. Coleman, *The Dinah Project: A Handbook for Congregational Response to Sexual Violence* (Cleveland, OH: Pilgrim Press, 2004), Nancy Nason-Clark, *The Battered Wife: How Christians Confront Family Violence* (Louisville, KY: Westminster John Knox Press, 1997), Pamela Cooper-White, *The Cry of Tamar: Violence against Women and the Church's Response* (Minneapolis, MN: Fortress Press, 1995), and Carol J. Adams, *Woman-Battering* (Minneapolis, MN: Fortress Press, 1994).

## References

Anderson, M. D. 1963. *Drama and Imagery in English Medieval Churches.* London: Cambridge University Press.

Baring, Anne and Jules Cashford. 1993. *The Myth of the Goddess: Evolution of an Image.* London: Arkana Penguin Books.

Bird, Phyllis. 1974. "Images of Women in the Old Testament." In *Religion and Sexism: Images of Woman in the Jewish and Christian Tradition,* ed. Rosemary Radford Ruether, 41–88. New York: Simon and Schuster.

*Breaking the Waves.* [1996] 2000. DVD. Directed by Lars von Trier. Santa Monica, CA: Artisan Entertainment.

Corley, Kathleen E. 1994. "1 Peter." In *Searching the Scriptures, Vol. Two: A Feminist Commentary,* ed. Elisabeth Schüssler Fiorenza, 349–60. New York: Crossroad.

D'Angelo, Mary Rose. 1994. "Colossians." In *Searching the Scriptures, Vol. Two: Feminist Commentary,* ed. Elisabeth Schüssler Fiorenza, 313–24. New York: Crossroad.

Dewey, Joanna. 1992. "1 Timothy," "2 Timothy," and "Titus." In *The Women's Bible Commentary,* ed. Carol A. Newsom and Sharon H. Ringe, 353–61. London: SPCK and Louisville: Westminster/John Knox Press.

Fontaine, Carole R. 1992. "Proverbs." In *The Women's Bible Commentary,* ed. Carol A. Newsom and Sharon H. Ringe, 145–52. London: SPCK and Louisville: Westminster/John Knox Press.

Happe, Peter, ed. 1975. *English Mystery Plays.* New York: Penguin Books.

Heyn, Dalma. 1997. *Marriage Shock: The Transformation of Women into Wives.* New York: Villard Books.

Hopper, Vincent F. and Gerald B. Lahey, eds. 1962. *Medieval Mysteries, Moralities, and Interludes.* New York: Barron's Educational Series, Inc.

Luther, Martin. 1958. "Lectures on Genesis [1535–45]." In *Luther's Works.* Trans. George V. Schick. Ed. Jaroslav Pelikan. Vol. 1. St Louis: Concordia Publishing House.

Maloney, Linda M. 1994. "The Pastoral Epistles." In *Searching the Scriptures, Vol. Two: A Feminist Commentary,* ed. Elisabeth Schüssler Fiorenza, 361–80. New York: Crossroad.

Martin, Clarice J. 1991. "The *Haustafeln* (Household Codes) in African American Biblical Interpretation: 'Free Slaves' and 'Subordinate Women.'" In *Stony the Road We Trod: African American Biblical Interpretation*, ed. Cain Hope Felder, 206–31. Minneapolis: Fortress Press.

Martin, Joel W. and Conrad E. Ostwalt Jr. 1995. *Screening the Sacred: Religion, Myth, and Ideology in Popular American Film.* Boulder: Westview Press.

Miles, Margaret R. 1996. *Seeing and Believing: Religion and Values in the Movies.* Boston: Beacon Press.

Muir, Lynette R. 1995. *The Biblical Drama of Medieval Europe.* Cambridge: Cambridge University Press.

Odenkirchen, Carl J., Trans. 1976. *The Play of Adam.* Brookline, MA and Leyden: Classical Folia Editions.

Ozment, Steven. 1983. *When Fathers Ruled: Family Life in Reformation Europe.* Cambridge and London: Harvard University Press.

Phillips, John A. 1984. *Eve: The History of an Idea.* San Francisco: Harper & Row.

Roper, Lyndal. 1989. *The Holy Household: Women and Morals in Reformation Augsburg.* Oxford: Clarendon Press.

Ruether, Rosemary Radford. 1989. "The Western Religious Tradition and Violence Against Women in the Home." In *Christianity, Patriarchy, and Abuse: A Feminist Critique*, eds. Joanne Carlson Brown and Carole R. Bohn, 31–41. Cleveland: The Pilgrim Press.

Schottroff, Luise. 1995. *Lydia's Impatient Sisters: A Feminist Social History of Early Christianity.* Translated by Barbara and Martin Rumscheidt. Louisville: Westminster /John Knox Press.

Schüssler Fiorenza, Elisabeth. 1983. *In Memory of Her: A Feminist Theological Reconstruction of Christian Origins.* New York: Crossroad.

Speaight, George. 1955. *The History of the English Puppet Theater.* New York: John de Graff.

*The Stepford Wives.* [1975] 2004. DVD. Directed by Bryan Forbes. Hollywood: Paramount.

Swidler, Leonard. 1979. *Biblical Affirmations of Woman.* Philadelphia: The Westminster Press.

Tanzer, Sarah J. 1994. Ephesians. In *Searching the Scriptures, Vol. Two: A Feminist Commentary*, ed. Elisabeth Schüssler Fiorenza, 325–48. New York: Crossroad.

Warner, Marina. 1976. *Alone of All Her Sex: The Myth and the Cult of the Virgin Mary.* New York: Alfred A. Knopf.

CHAPTER 2

# Righteous Anger and Sustaining Faith: Black Women's Activism in the Environmental Justice Movement

*Tuere Bowles*

Environmental injustices still occur in the United States despite improvements in environmental protection over recent decades. People of color and low-income groups bear a more disproportionate burden of environmental health hazards in their homes, neighborhoods, and places of employment than their white and middle-class counterparts (Bryant & Mohai, 1992; Bullard, 2000; Bullard & Johnson, 2000; Institute of Medicine [IOM], 1999; United Church of Christ—Commission for Racial Justice, 1987). Recognizing these disparities, grassroots activists, local community groups, environmental justice networks, lawyers, and academics have joined together in a social justice struggle known as the environmental justice (EJ) movement. EJ activists believe all people, regardless of race, ethnicity, or income should enjoy access to safe, healthy environments (*Principles of Environmental Justice*, 1991).

For generations, black women have led struggles and fought for socioeconomic and environmental justice. Their activism has sometimes been in the forefront but more often in shadowed spaces of men within social movements (Mullings, 1997; Springer, 1999). Often, men take public roles on national and international levels while black women provide base, local leadership and behind-the-scenes activism upon which social movements are built. The environmental justice movement is no different. Untold numbers of black women dedicate their lives to fighting environmental threats to their families, homes, communities, and workplaces. Given that black women represent significant numbers of the environmental justice movement (Di Chiro, 1998; Taylor, 2000), it provides a superb context for understanding how their faith and spirituality shapes their activism.

This chapter explores how faith and spirituality undergird daily lives and practices of black women activists in the environmental justice movement. For these women activists, their faith and spirituality anchors their decision-making, sustains activism, and frames environmental justice efforts. In the chapter, I explore historical social movements and identify the involvement of exemplary black women. Then, I contrast selected historical exemplars with current environmental justice activists regarding their motivations for engaging in social action, how they sustain their efforts, how they strategically employ their voice in protest, and why they value wisdom in their practice. I conclude by interpreting the narratives and providing implications for practice.

## HISTORICAL SOCIAL MOVEMENTS AND BIOGRAPHICAL COMPOSITES

This section highlights three exemplary black women activists of faith: Frances Ellen Watkins Harper, Nannie Helen Burroughs, and Septima Poinsette Clark, lives positioned within distinctive, larger social movements vital to their social justice struggle. The brief biographies only provide a snapshot of the women and are distilled accounts of their lives from various published sources, such as: *When and Where I Enter: The Impact of Black Women on Race and Sex in America* by Paula Giddings (1984); *Afro-American Women Writers: 1746–1933* by A. A. Shockley (1988); *African American Women and Social Action: The Clubwomen and Volunteerism from Jim Crow to the New Deal, 1896–1936* by F. L. Cash (2001); and *Women in the Civil Rights Movement: Trailblazers and Torchbearers, 1941–1965* edited by V. L. Crawford and B. Woods (1990). Biographical composites were modeled after the article titled "Fannie Coppin, Mary Shadd Cary, and Charlotte Grimke: Three African American Women Who Made a Difference" by E. A. Peterson (2002). The social movements identified are loosely constructed and the time frames serve as signposts in recounting the history. For example, many historians and activists could justifiably argue that the human rights movement in the United States began in 1492 with the colonization of North America and the genocide of Native and indigenous people. Similarly, the civil rights movement really began in 1865 after the end of the Civil War and continues to the present day. So, again, the time periods are loosely constructed. Also, the theoretical work undergirding this section strongly pulls from critical social theory that "encompasses bodies of knowledge and sets of institutional practices that actively grapple with the central questions facing groups of people differentially placed in specific political, social, and historic contexts characterized by injustice" (Collins, 1998, p. 230).

## ANTI-SLAVERY MOVEMENT (1619–1865): EXEMPLAR FRANCES ELLEN WATKINS HARPER

The year 1619 marks the beginning of slavery, the peculiar institution, in the United States for those of African Descent. Thus, from West African shores, to the sardine packed ships of middle passage, to the auction block and on slave plantations, many African women and men resisted enslavement. The African slave trade ended in 1807, yet slavery persisted, primarily in the South, until 1865. Countless Underground Railroad conductors such as Harriet Ross Tubman (1820–1913), planned and led escapes of enslaved persons to freedom in the northern United States and Canada. Many abolitionists, particularly freed blacks of the North, spoke out against slavery's injustices and cruelty. Sojourner Truth (1797–1883), born into slavery and later granted emancipation in 1828, was one such person. She worked on behalf of the Anti-Slavery movement and for women's rights.

Frances Ellen Watkins Harper (1825–1911), an exemplary late 19th-century poet, essayist, novelist, and antislavery activist, was born to free parents in Baltimore, Maryland. Her parents passed during her first few years of life. She was educated in a black school where she studied scripture, composition, and abolition. As an adult in 1850, she taught at Union Seminary, Columbus, Ohio, which later became Wilberforce University. There, she became the school's first black female vocational instructor. In 1853, after hearing about a free black man who was placed into slavery, who tried to escape, but later died from exposure, Harper committed to the abolitionist cause.

In 1854, Harper moved to Philadelphia, lived at an Underground Railroad station, visited other antislavery offices and began her antislavery lecturing and activist career. Hired by the Pennsylvania Anti-Slavery society, she championed emancipation in lecturing two to three times per day. In 1860, she married Fenton Harper and limited her public speaking and teaching. After his death in 1864, she reemerged into the public scene again as a lecturer, author, and reformer. Watkins Harper spoke on a wide variety of topics; she spoke and taught in adult education settings, like women's club meetings, Sunday schools, churches, schools, town meetings, and homes. Hence, Watkins Harper's teaching and activism spanned antebellum, Civil War, and Reconstruction periods.

## RECONSTRUCTION PERIOD (1865–1877), WOMEN'S SUFFRAGE (1848–1920), & BLACK WOMEN'S CLUB MOVEMENTS (1896–1936): EXEMPLAR NANNIE HELEN BURROUGHS

The reconstruction era followed the American Civil War. The 13th Amendment (1865) declared slavery to be illegal in the United States. The 14th Amendment (1868) made blacks born in the United States citizens and the 15th Amendment (1870) enfranchised black men. A violent popular movement emerged in the South known as the Ku Klux Klan out of protest, outrage, and fear of blacks. The 19th Amendment (1920) enfranchised women. Yet, benefits of the previous amendments were not fully exercised for African Americans due to segregation (*Plessy v. Ferguson*, 1896), poll tax, literacy tests, the Grandfather clause, Jim Crow laws, and Black Codes.

Despite the treacherous times, black women, educators, and activists included continued to pursue social justice and racial uplift. For example, in 1896, Mary Church Terrell, Ida B. Wells-Barnett, Margaret Murray Washington, Fanny Jackson Coppin, Frances Ellen Watkins Harper, Charlotte Forten Grimke, and Harriet Tubman met in Washington, D.C., to form the National Association of Colored Women (NACW). An exemplar of this expansive period is Nannie Helen Burroughs.

Nannie Helen Burroughs (1883–1961) was an outstanding writer, educator, and Baptist leader. She also founded the National Trade and Professional School for Women and Girls in Washington, D.C. She held firm religious beliefs and later became President of the Women's Auxiliary of the National Baptist Convention. Unable to become a teacher of domestic science because of being denied by the Board of Education in the District of Columbia, Burroughs later started her own school to give girls options.

In the 1900s, Burroughs began the Women's Industrial Club, which offered short-term lodging to black women and taught them basic domestic skills. She held evening classes for club members majoring in business. Later, she developed and ran a self-help venture, Cooperative Industrial, Inc., which provided free facilities for a medical clinic, a hairdressing salon, and a variety store. In 1909, with help of the National Baptist Convention, she started the National Trade and Professional School for Women and Girls with the motto: "We Specialize in the Wholly Impossible." The curriculum emphasized practical and professional skills for women.

## 1960s CIVIL RIGHTS MOVEMENT (1955–1965): EXEMPLAR: SEPTIMA POINSETTE CLARK

The 1960s civil rights movement is most memorable for many today. Rosa Parks, an activist, member, and secretary of local Alabama NAACP chapter and participant of the Highlander Folk School decided in 1955 not to give up her bus seat to a white patron. Although Parks was not the first to resist public transportation inequities, her action led to the Montgomery Bus Boycott. The national attention, among many other contributing factors, spurred a national civil rights movement. Key events that transpired during this time period included the vicious, heinous hate-crime murder of Emmett Till, student-led sit-ins, the Freedom Rides, and the March on Washington (1963). Also, key legislation passed by Congress included the Civil Rights Act (1964) and the Voting Rights Act (1965).

Septima Poinsette Clark (1898–1987), an exemplar, was born and reared in Charleston, South Carolina. In 1916, upon graduating from Avery Normal Institute, she became the director of education for the Highlander Folk School and the director of training of the Southern Christian Leadership Conference (SCLC). Clark taught at the Promise Land School on John Island, South Carolina, during a time when blacks could not teach in the Charleston public schools. She returned to Charleston in 1919 and taught at the Avery Institute, her alma mater. After an unsuccessful marriage and birth of a child, Clark later settled in Columbia, South Carolina, where she began working with the National Association of Colored People (NAACP) to prepare for a court case that would force the Columbia Public schools to make salaries of black and white teachers equal.

In 1956, South Carolina passed a statute prohibiting city employees from joining civil rights organizations. Refusing to relinquish her NAACP membership, Clark was forced to resign from teaching. This began her tenure at the Highlander Folk School, first as a workshop director and later as director of training. Workshops at Highlander prompted the beginning of the Johns Island, South Carolina, Citizenship Schools. Singularly, Highlander could no longer manage the responsibility of running citizenship schools. The Southern Christian Leadership Conference (SCLC) expressed interest in directing the program in 1961. Consequently, Clark became the director of training for the SCLC. Over her lifetime, Clark's community work included the Federation Women's Group, the Teachers' Association of South Carolina, Alpha Kappa Alpha Sorority, Inc., and the National Council of Negro Women, to name a few. This intertwined nature of activism and faith are certainly prevalent in the biographical sketches of the exemplars.

## THE INTERSECTION OF FAITH AND SOCIAL ACTION FOR EXEMPLARS

As evidenced by Watkins Harper, Burroughs, and Clark, their faith led them to engage for collective freedom and survival toward social change within society. These women had significant turning points and epiphanies that led them to a deeper committed life of social action for social change. Recognizing injustices, their faith and activism took them to many battlefronts.

Moreover, social change requires persons to understand they are agents and have power to act. Power from within involves a personal and group sense of agency—the capacity for people to take action on behalf of themselves or others to transform the world (Tisdell, 2001) as Clark celebrates in her biography, *Ready from Within*. From a moral center and strong faith, these exemplary women had hope for a better future and society for everyone.

## PORTRAITS OF BLACK WOMEN ENVIRONMENTAL JUSTICE ACTIVISTS

The stories of black women environmental justice activists underscore how faith shapes their practices. Narrative stories provide a deeper way of knowing and seeing the world, building on African epistemology and black feminist thought (Collins, 1990, 2000). Since narratives can "educate, empower, and emancipate" (Langellier, 1999, p. 447), excerpts of stories and vignettes from 16 black women activists ranging from ages 36 to 78 inform this study. Self-identified activists ranging from 6 to 22 years, their education levels spanned from grade school to the doctorate. Marital/partner status varied; most had children, and 9 of the 16 activists had previous social movement involvement, from civil rights, women's rights, and peace to the mainstream environmental movement. Table 2.1 depicts the pseudonyms and corresponding demographic information for activists. Each narrative was analyzed separately by fragmenting the data (Charmaz, 2002), analyzing across the data set to identify recurring patterns, themes and concepts.

## MOTIVATING FACTORS

Black women's motivation to engage in environmental justice struggles included a predisposition for social justice issues and causes, passion for homeplace, and defining moment(s). Their choice to engage initiates from both intrinsic and contextual reasons.

### PREDISPOSITION FOR SOCIAL JUSTICE ISSUES AND CAUSES

The first theme is predisposition for social justice issues and causes. Most activist women were wired to do activist work, evident because they felt this work was "innate and embedded" and they "always knew" they would do it, or they traced a family legacy of activism.

**Table 2.1** Black Women EJ Activists' Demographics

| Pseudonym | Age | Marital Status | Children | Education | Prior SM Activism | Years in EJ Movement |
|---|---|---|---|---|---|---|
| Barbara | 56 | Divorced | 2 | PhD | No | 22 |
| Deborah | 51 | Single | 0 | JD | No | 12 |
| Emily | 50 | Divorced | 1 | Bachelor's | Yes | 10 |
| Emma | 78 | Widowed | 7 | GED | Yes | 22 |
| Esther | 53 | Divorced | 3 | Grade School | Yes | 20 |
| Frances | 65 | Divorced | 1 | Master's | Yes | 15 |
| Fredericka | 39 | Single | 0 | Bachelor's | No | 15 |
| Georgianna | 78 | Married | 3 | Bachelor's | No | 8 |
| Janice | 61 | Divorced | 0 | Master's | No | 13 |
| Johnnie | 45 | Single | 1 | HS Diploma | No | 10 |
| LaTanya | 44 | Single | 0 | JD | Yes | 12 |
| Madelyn | 53 | Married | 2 | Bachelor's | No | 8 |
| Mahalia | 63 | Divorced | 2 | Bachelor's | Yes | 10 |
| Malaika | 36 | Single | 0 | JD | Yes | 9 |
| Pamela | 64 | Divorced | 1 | Associate's | Yes | 6 |
| Vashti | 45 | Married | 0 | Master's | Yes | 18 |

Note. SM—Social Movement; EJ—Environmental Justice

Environmental Justice activists shared that they always knew that they would pursue activist's causes. Vashti, a 45-year-old activist and educator, reflects:

> I was one of those kids, . . . who, you know, they knew what they wanted to do. And . . . I knew that I wanted to be a civil rights advocate and I knew that I wanted to be a lawyer. Again, I just had that feeling that that was what I had a gift for; and . . . had a really strong interest in . . . So, I had all these really strong feelings about what I didn't want to do but I had an equally strong, strong feeling about what I did want to do.

Although Vashti did not become a lawyer, she definitely pursued her work in civil rights.

Malaika, a 36-year-old attorney and cofounder of a nonprofit human rights legal firm, similarly knew at an early age, that she wanted to do this type of work. Malaika comments:

> I grew up in a social justice activist family and I always knew I was going to do work for social justice as an adult. And also knew that when I was a child that I wanted to be a lawyer and do this work . . . I should say that . . . I didn't ever, for one moment think it would have anything to do with the environment.

Malaika became a lawyer. Yet, she also reports a family history of activism.

The idea of family activism resonated with two other participants who spoke affectionately about their mothers' or grandmothers' influence. When I probed Malaika for examples about her social justice activist family background, she reflected:

> Well, yeah . . . my grandmother was a strong activist and a very spiritual woman as well. And so, growing up with her, her guidance, her teaching, her love that I wanted to be just like her. And so, . . . I wanted to work . . . for correcting problems that creates a situation for people who are living less than their fullest potential and are surrounded by injustices that kind of deprive them of that ability and that opportunity to live to their fullest potential and enjoy their lives.

When asked what motivated her to do this work, Pamela, a 64-year-old executive director of a community center, pondered and concluded: "I guess it is embedded in me. It's just something that I just have inside . . . of working in the community." Like others with family histories of social activism, Deborah, a 51-year-old environmental lawyer and consultant, exclaimed that the next generation of environmental justice activists will be sons and daughters of current activists. She foretells:

> The first generation in the Environmental Justice field came more out of civil rights and tenants' rights and nuclear rights . . . The young people now, by virtue of the struggle their parents and their predecessors engaged in, have a leg up. A lot of them are going to school for these studies now having watched their parents, having marched the marches, having been in the demonstrations, understanding the community side of the issue, they want to problem solve.

Thus, women in the environmental justice movement report both a historical tradition and a future trend of passing the baton of activist work through the generations.

## Passion for Homeplace

hooks (1990), a black feminist scholar, coined the term "homeplace" to signify a sacred and safe place where one can learn cultural lessons, be affirmed, nurtured, and learn how to resist injustice in a white supremacist society. Most participants talked ardently and forcefully about the homes, neighborhoods, and communities that they are fighting to protect. With tremendous frustration, Janice, a 61-year-old activist and retired schoolteacher, shared how industry invaded her community:

> This community is over 100 years old. In fact, my church I attend is 104 [years old]. So we were *here before industry even thought about coming into our community. THEY INVADED US*, we did not invade them! . . . Industry came here in the fifties and we have not been the same. This was a rural area where people fish, hunt, swim, everything . . . that's our livelihood for some of us. Now, it's been polluted. It's polluted by [an International Refinery], it's polluted from the Superfund site where 11 companies dump their waste materials in an open pit and bury it . . .

Likewise, Mahalia, a 63-year-old-activist and retired school teacher, shared steps she took in initiating an environmental justice campaign on behalf of her community, which sits on a parcel of land given to freed slaves following emancipation:

> You start where you are and use what you got and in the environmental justice movement. I started in my front yard. What do I have? I have a facility in front of me making noise. I'm four generation complaining about the ills, what happened. Guess what? I got information from oral history. . .

She later explained further how for generations her community's property has been encroached upon by different industries.

All 16 women interviewed passionately shared that their homes, neighborhoods, and communities were of value and importance to them. Vashti spoke fondly of the place where she grew up and worked as an activist for almost 40 years:

> I'm originally from [a historic community in the Northeast], born and raised and lived there until the summer of '98 when my husband and I were getting married and I was moving here. So, I lived in [that community] from the time I was born until I was almost forty years when I moved. And it has a lot to do with sort of who I am and why I do what I do because I grew up in [that] community, I went to school there, I went to college and graduate school in [that] community. And I have a deep, deep, deep, deep passion about that place. . . . I'm most passionate about trying to right some of the historical wrongs as well as the contemporary problems that face and challenge [in that] community. . . . I have received some extraordinary gifts from that community. And of course, one wouldn't often think that given the public perception of [my] community which for too very long has been about all kinds of social malaise and poverty and crime, crime and more crime and drugs. . . . But for me it has always been place of enormous, enormous gifts and I've gone on to do some fairly remarkable things and all of it I attribute to having had the wonderful upbringing that I did in that community.

Vashti's passion for her place of birth motivated her activism, and she was among the first to organize and establish an environmental justice organization. Hence, one's passionate commitment to place is a significant factor for prompting environmental justice activism.

## Defining Moment(s)

The final theme under motivating factors is defining moments. All women in this study pinpointed a definitive moment or series of moments when their environmental justice activism began. Two avenues emerged that characterized defining moments—an environmental justice movement insider informs citizens and impacted communities of risks, threats, and harms; or, community residents collaboratively put the pieces of the puzzle together as to who or what is negatively impacting their health and welfare.

An exemplary experience of how participants ignited their environmental justice activism is evident in Frances's story. Frances is a 65-year-old retired college professor and grassroots activist. Because of representatives from a state network coming to her community to share information,

Frances's eyes were opened to local environmental degradation. She recounted the details:

> I have lived [here] for eighteen years and I was aware of the bad smells but I didn't have any physical problems that I knew of. I was aware of bad smells and I had to put together smells with what is causing those smells . . . you know, chemicals and chemicals affect your body. . . . And the people from [the Environmental Network] came out to our community and just wanted to talk with us. And they started sharing some data with us . . . . One of the things that impressed me the most was that [the Company], which is a hazardous waste facility right next to where we live, had groundwater contamination and had this plume that migrated a mile from site. And at first when somebody showed me the chemicals . . . well, my mouth dropped open. "You mean this stuff is our groundwater?" And there was no telling what is coming out in the air that we didn't even know about. And that was like a defining moment for me—. . . That's the moment I got involved.

Upon first learning from other movement insiders about what was going on in their communities, the majority reported being stunned and awestruck. However, some communities did not have the good fortune of folks letting them know in advance; they had to put the pieces of the puzzle together on their own. Esther, a 53-year-old activist, detailed this process:

> I was working with the first African American mayor for [a southern city], and there was a program that came about of affordable homes, targeting African Americans. I had just arrived in [my new southern city] from [another West Coast metropolitan city] with my three children and my husband at the time and we were staying in a small house, nice place; but we were looking for a house to buy. And with me working the mayor's office, [I] knew about the program and thought "this is fantastic. I'll check into it and get the information and perhaps we can get one of these homes." Had no idea that the homes that they were building and the construction that was going to start would be on top of the city's dump, okay? So, that's how I got involved through the mayor's office, realizing after a few years that I was living on top of a dump and people started dying. . . . When you have five and six people in one block that died from unknown cancerous and brain tumors and respiratory problems, then your antenna go up and you start research . . . or I did, along with other neighbors. And we invited the mayor over and the house was packed with people and we demanded answers. What was going on? The rumors were that this was a toxic dump, why didn't anyone tell us? Why was this community just targeted for African Americans and what was going to happen to people here?

Esther's story is heart wrenching. Yet, it was under Esther's leadership that the community later devised a health survey to identify the exact number of neighbors affected and they later launched a lawsuit against the city.

In summary, black women environmental justice activists shared that they had distinctive backgrounds and experiences that prepared and prompted them for activist work, either a predisposition to social justice issues and causes, or a family history of activism. Further, a strong connection to their local place of dwelling was significant for their activism. In all cases, women were concerned about their local neighborhoods' health and vitality. Finally, participants in this study reported factors that typically included contact from another movement insider or residents putting the pieces of the puzzle together based on observations of illnesses in their communities.

## SUSTAINING FACTORS

Like motivating factors, sustaining factors that encouraged women to con-tinue this work included these themes: spirituality, social responsibility, com-munal engagement, and righteous anger. Women reported more than one sustaining factor.

### SPIRITUALITY

The majority of these women reported that they were sustained by their spiritual purpose/calling and a deep and abiding faith in God. Mahalia, in particular, believed that her environmental justice work aligned with her spir-itual calling: that "God teaches me," and she self-identifies as an "Evangelist-Activist." Johnnie, a 45-year-old regional organizer, firmly believes that she is called to be where she is and doing the type of work she does:

> The call, my call to do this work that I do? How else can I explain it? I think it's where I need to be; because I need to be here. . . . This is my time . . . I think God put me here for a reason . . . And, I need to be here. That's my calling.

Thus, Johnnie's commitment to her work and involvement in EJ is sustained through her sense of divine calling.

Yet, Emily, a 50-year-old grassroots activist, somewhat struggling with her spiritual purpose, is encouraged through friends who remind her that she has a purpose:

> Well, spiritually I feel like that all of us have a purpose for being here. And, I think that sometimes God continues to put you in the same place every

time until you learn a lesson that He is trying to teach. And, I think that's where I am. And, I have a friend that tells me, "You need to stop fighting what God has carved out for you."

Interestingly, two women shared spiritual conversions as a result of being involved in the environmental justice movement. Georgianna, a 78-year-old grassroots activist and retired schoolteacher, who helped fight the foreign company that wanted to locate in your community, whose pollution caused sinus problems, chest colds, and arthritis, noted:

> I like to say that I'm an ongoing work of God. So many things happened to me when I joined the EJ movement and being friends with [another neighboring activist] because she's a very spiritual person. . . . She got me to read the Bible and I knew of God. That's what she says, "so many people know God but they don't know Him and have a relationship with Him."

Likewise, in Malaika's conversion experience, she spoke of being transformed through her activism and work in the environmental justice movement:

> Well, I became a Christian just recently and that's because of the work that I'm doing in communities. And just, again, being deeply inspired and I guess transformed by the people that I've worked with . . . [who] have that strength through their belief and love of God. . . . So, philosophically, I mean, if you look at the life that Jesus led, it's not different from the [injustice] issues that are covered in the environmental justice movement.

Moreover, most women repeatedly reported that they were sustained in their activist struggles by their faith in God.

## Social Responsibility

Second, many participants spoke about a strong sense of social responsibility as a sustaining factor in their activist work, particularly regarding making a difference and their quest for truth and justice. Barbara says:

> I have the kind of personality where "my self-esteem is intact." . . . But I don't live for the applause. But I do, in fact, live for making a difference! I really want to feel that at the end of my life I contributed something.

Janice echoes Barbara regarding making a difference:

> Making a difference in order to have justice for all of us. It's not right to infringe on other people and making their life miserable and depreciating

their property and giving them poor health and NOT HIRING YOU as a worker or employee when you have located in their community.

Thus, making a difference was very important to women and that desire sustained them in their work. Making a difference, however, was also coupled with other sustaining factors.

Deborah, when asked what keeps her going in day-to-day struggles, adamantly replied:

> Truth! . . . I feel a compunction to make it TRUE. In other words, the truth is that we are pretty dog gone screwed up as a result of the way things are. And, the only way we are going to make progress out of this morass that we are in is to tell the truth and be true to that. So, I have learned how to temper my truth-telling so that people don't want to stab me on my way out of the room anymore . . . So, in my work with my clients my aim is to get them to understand the truth and act on it accordingly.

Barbara puts into context how an entire community is sustained through their belief in what is right, determination and faith in God:

> The one thing that we have . . . is determination and the feeling that what we're doing is *right!* That it's right! And we believe that we have God's blessings and His support. And because we're right we go into a battle . . . , which actually *stuns* the large entities because they can't believe that this little small group of people would have the gumption, you know, to fight them in the manner in which we do.

Thus, Barbara's reflections provide a wide-angle lens to how one's individual sustaining factors are made manifest in a collective struggle against powerful opponents.

## COMMUNAL ENGAGEMENT

Third, over half of the respondents reported communal engagement and interaction with other activists as a strong sustaining factor, often coupled with dynamics like justice, hearing stories, and so forth. Madelyn's experience in the environmental justice movement is exemplary of what most women reported. When asked what keeps her going, Madelyn concluded:

> Oh, well, shoot, what keeps me going is just . . . you know, I'm the luckiest person in the world because I work with people . . . they are just amazing people; and yeah, some of them are feisty, . . . some of them are just real fun-loving, some can be sort of crotchety, but it is all wonderful. And

knowing that I'm doing something good . . . that is really helpful, something that is steering the direction for justice keeps me up . . . I do it because I get to work with just really incredible people.

Malaika's story also illustrates how a number of things keep her going; for example, interaction with the people, doing something good, justice, and so forth.

LaTanya, a 44-year-old lawyer and environmental justice activist, echoes Malaika's sentiments. Working with interesting people, in part sustains LaTanya's work. She finds the work "so interesting, I meet the best people in the world and people want to talk about it like yourself, got to meet you, you know, and so that's what keeps me going."

Vashti shared that what really allowed her to persist in her work was the sister camaraderie:

Oh, I'd say [my closest friend and Organization Co-founder] kept me going a lot and I kept her going a lot. We always had each other. And there was some vicious, vicious, times that we went through but we always had each other, always. My mother was a tremendous source of inspiration and pride to me. She was very, very proud of the work that we were doing. . . . Whenever we had functions, . . . my mother always cooked so she was like the chef of sort of our political organizing. . . . It was a royal battle for a really, really long time. Some days it is still a battle but not at the same level as it used to be and so I'd say mostly what we had is that we had . . . a community of people, a community of women. And so, . . . whatever our local dynamic was, our national dynamic was that this was a movement [whose] leadership was overwhelmingly female.

Vashti was sustained through her female cofounder of an organization, the help of her mother, political and environmental groups she worked with in her local community, and a national circle of women environmental justice activists. Likewise, LaTanya also expressed her admiration of elder women:

Well, my inspiration has come from the older women and everybody reminds me of my grandmother. And the women are great and they are the backbone of the movement, they are the ones who know what is going on in the communities and the older ones particular, the elders, they didn't get a lot of credit. And the other interesting thing about that is that they do everything. EJ . . . for the design fights, . . . for the housing, . . . voting fights, . . . who was making all the food? It was the women.

In addition to working with people and the sister camaraderie that goes on in environmental justice movements, many women talked about being encouraged by hearing stories of others in the movement. Madelyn maintained:

> Gosh, listening to other success stories, where they have been, where they are going and what they have accomplished. Some of them struggled very, very hard . . . And people didn't think it could be done but . . . if we put God in the center of what it is that we are doing, nothing is impossible . . . My motivation is that nothing is impossible if you put God ahead of . . . other people and their success stories and listening to them talk about putting God before what it is they are doing . . . it makes those impossible situations possible.

Though Fredericka, a 39-year-old organizer and environmental justice activist, didn't hear these stories within the movement, she is sustained in her work by hearing stories of her parents:

> I was born in the middle of the sixties, the middle of the civil rights movement and I think somehow that part of me and the fact that my parents lived in the south and . . . they weren't part of the movement but they were certainly a part of the effects of the civil rights movement and the fact that they still tell me stories . . . I think that oral history . . . has been a driving force for me to want to see change happen.

In sum, communal engagement via interaction with people, sister camaraderie and hearing stories in community also helped to sustain the work of activists in this study.

## RIGHTEOUS ANGER

The fourth sustaining factor was righteous anger. For three women in the study, anger served as the primary sustaining activism force. Yet, five additional women spoke often of being angry because of different issues and failed environmental justice causes; however, it was not reported as what sustained their work. Often, this anger is toward government for failing to enforce current laws and regulations to protect people or industry as a potent foe. Esther noted:

> My passion is fueled by my anger because if I live on [a street] in a white-gated community none of this would have happened. I wouldn't have to have fought for the twenty years. . . . I'm angry that the developers . . . were not forthright in coming together and giving people the information of what was really going on prior to building this subdivision. . . . They knew that this was a dumpsite, why put people on this dumpsite? And if so, why

not excavate it—clean it before you develop it? That angered me. It was like . . . putting good money into a bad project, you know? That was one layer of anger. The other layers have been with the bureaucratic system and there are many layers of anger there. The layers have been fueled over and over again. . . . I'm going to go on and on and on. And eventually they will get tired of hearing me; they will get tired of what's going on in this community and do something about it.

Frances also shared Esther's anger. Frances declared:

I have the strong sense of right and wrong. I have a strong sense of what my government is supposed to do. I mean, I've read the Constitution; I've read the Declaration of Independence; I know the Pledge of Allegiance; I know all that good stuff that is in the history books and it is a crock of crap, okay? And it suddenly hits you "this stuff is nothing, it means nothing" This government is supposed to but it doesn't . . . well, I'm really pissed off. . . . Your heart goes out when you see people who are really suffering and so that is what gives me strength. . . . And it makes me very angry and anger can overcome fear, trust me . . . and that sense of injustice will keep me going.

In sum, the motivating factors included a predisposition to social justice issues and causes, passion for place, and defining moments. The sustaining factors included spirituality, social responsibility, community engagement, and righteous anger.

## PREVAILING STRATEGIES USED IN PRACTICE

Once fully engaged in environmental justice causes, black women activists employed vital strategies to successfully advance local and national causes. Two prevailing strategies that are particularly unique to this group of women include big mouthing and using wisdom.

### BIG MOUTHING

Big mouthing, for the women in this study, means to be forcefully and passionately outspoken about what you know to be true. Emma calls this having a "big mouth." She pointed out other women in the struggle who had a "big mouth" reflecting through her environmental justice archives. Most of these activist women believed their mouth to be their greatest asset and tool.

Esther self-identifies as the "mouth of the south" and attributes that as to why her neighbors selected her to be the spokesperson for many years in her community's fight against local authorities for their homes built on top of a toxic waste dump. She laughed and elaborated,

> I'm not afraid to speak up to the point that it would chill some people to say some of the things that I've said to people that I know are responsible. . . . I am in my fifties, my children are grown, I've lived a good life. I thank God that I have had a few minor aches and pains but if God didn't do anything else, He gave me a voice and I will speak about the atrocities that have happened to the people in this community . . . I don't shout, I'm passionate about what takes place here.

Similar to Esther's observation, Mahalia firmly believes that her mouth is a gift from God. She reflected:

> I have a skill, what is that skill? I can talk! I was criticized a lot as I got older. All I could hear people say, "She talks too much, she talks too much" and if I had listened to that, I would have never used the skill God gave me . . . we need to learn now to change how we plant seeds into people who have skills that is given to them by God.

Many women viewed their mouth and the ability to communicate as an asset and gift of God. Thus, the concept of big mouthing, a means for women to speak with authority and raise attention to critical issues in their communities, is akin to speaking truth to power. On different occasions, Fredericka talked about persons who taught her to speak truth to power and how she teaches communities to speak truth to power:

> Telling those who are in the seat of power or letting them know, first of all, when they do things right. And not being afraid to let them know when they are not doing the right thing. So, it's just plainly telling them the truth!

Deborah also self-identifies as a "truth-teller." Thus, because women activists have knowledge and are not afraid to display it publicly, they are empowered to speak forcefully and powerfully.

## USING WISDOM

In addition to big mouthing, the second common strategy black women employed in practice was using wisdom. By using wisdom, women knew when to speak, when not to speak and/or when to ignore critics and detractors; how to make decisions and solve problems. Moreover, women gained wisdom through spiritual means such as prayer, divine inspiration, and reading Holy texts; common sense; and life experiences.

Emma shared that in her environmental struggles, she could only rely on what God gave her—wisdom! At 78 years of age, she boldly reported,

> I have to let it be known that I only had what God give me, you know? . . . **WISDOM!** God give me **wisdom** because He always put me in the right place at the right time that whatever He give me in this mouth, whatever I have to use this mouth to do and say, I have already seen it, I've already heard it. . . I've been **there** . . . I know what's I'm talking about!

Emma totally depended on her divine wisdom for communicating and experiences. She also used wisdom to figure out when not to speak. Emma illustrated this by sharing a story about her early civil rights involvement and how activists knew that the next strategy was a full bus boycott, but no one said anything until the time was right. Emma explained:

> That thing was being in the works all awhile [we knew what was] going to happen. We didn't know where, how it was going to be done. But we *knew* it was going to be done. But then when Rosa Parks did it, then all of us knew, see? . . . Those people don't run [around talking publicly about the strategy]. . . . But I got sense enough to know that when I see the big people not saying anything . . . the time's not right.

Emma tempers her "loose mouth" with good sense or wisdom to know when to speak and when not to speak about what she knows. Mahalia talks about using wisdom as a strategy from her self-initiated Bible studies, particularly lessons learned from King Solomon in the Bible.

Many women reported using wisdom based on the collective experiences of folks, especially movement elders. Emily shared how her older friends encouraged her to "move forward":

> I enjoy talking with older people about their experiences and things they have done and how they overcame some of their adversities. And, they have helped me to become much more spiritual, . . . introspective, follow my heart, follow my mind. [The elders would say,] "Don't allow people to discourage you just because they don't like what you're doing or what you are saying . . . You know, they've told me that I am very sensitive. Sometimes overly sensitive . . . But you know, you just got to brush yourself off and keep right on going.

Emily's recollections of how elder friends both talked to and encouraged her are exemplary of how she employs the wisdom of the elders in her everyday practice.

Likewise, Frances has learned to rely on what she terms mother wit, which she learned from others in the movement:

> And I've learned a lot from people who have to rely on mother wit and it's important! And I think I've gained more mother wit as a result of working with people like this . . . now I am saying throw the book away and that's what I'm saying to EPA all the time, "Throw your book away. It hasn't got the information we need. It's not working."

Thus, wisdom, mother wit, and good common sense served as a viable strategy that women employed in their activism.

## Conclusion

For Black women environmental justice activists, faith serves as the epicenter of all they do in practice. In the face of deleterious forces with power elites, black women activists survive the paradox of righteous anger regarding unjust issues while maintaining a sustaining faith. Their faith, however, conjoins at both the individual and collective levels.

At the individual level, black women environmental justice activists inevitably engage in informal spiritual formation as a result of simply participating in the movement. Although there is no formal curriculum or established spiritual director, they attend to the dynamics of faith and living out their call to serve in action. In the pursuit of environmental justice, their faith serves as a template for making meaning out of their experiences. They absorb vital information, which is often technical, scientific, and related to policy; learn environmental laws and regulations; engage in planning, decision-making, coalition building, and community organizing. For many of the grassroots activists, they do all of the aforementioned with limited formal training but with a heavy reliance on divine wisdom and a willingness to serve as a mouthpiece. Their personal faith helps them to gain a sense of competence emerging from their confidence in the transcendent that they can do, as Nellie Helen Burroughs says, "the wholly impossible."

In addition to making meaning of their experiences, black women environmental justice activists attain new movement roles beyond the traditional mother, spouse, sister, or friend. Based upon their immersion and sustained environmental justice commitment, activist women draw upon their faith to reconstruct new self-identities in the movement such as *evangelist-activist, educator-activist*, and *griot-activist*. The evangelist-activist role, for example, represents the women who see themselves as truth-tellers. The activists in this study are not licensed or ordained clergypersons, but are deeply in tuned with the Divine and have no problem speaking biblical truth to power. In the environmental justice movement, the evangelist-activist links the biblical story to the gross environmental injustices with the hope of creating change. On the other hand, the educator-activists draws upon their formal education, informal education, or divine wisdom to support the growth and development of movement adherents. Finally, the griot-activist serves as the cultural bearer for the movement by typically leading movement participants in spirituals, hymns, and chants during meetings and protest marches or sharing stories of past prevails. For black women environmental justice activists, their faith extends beyond the individual meaning making and reconstruction of self-identities to the communal.

At the communal level, black women environmental justice activists value an interconnectedness with others, particularly strong sister camaraderie, in enacting their faith for committed social change. The concept of interconnectedness is supported by the empirical research findings in *Common Fire: Lives of Commitment in a Complex World* that sought to understand how those who are committed to the common good are sustained. The authors found that "Knowing that one is among friends and colleagues who share a common purpose can remind the weary of their own commitments and help to create a kind of synergy that both gives and receives new strength and reorders one's perspective" (p. 208). Clearly engaging within a community helps to sustain those committed to the common good.

In sum, black women's faith in the environmental justice movement extends to addressing large social forces and dynamics. Participating in the environmental justice movement is their individual and corporate faith in action, as they work to create social change on behalf of the beloved community, despite all odds against them. Black women environmental justice activists experience encounters with the transcendent, then engage in reflection, and ultimately respond by taking action. This process is akin to what Thurman (1954) calls the inwardness and outwardness, exemplifying how black women environmental justice activists employ their faith in practice.

## REFERENCES

Bryant, B., & Mohai, P. (1992). *Race and the Incidence of Environmental Hazards*. Boulder, CO: Westview Press.

Bullard, R. D. (2000). *Dumping in Dixie: Race, Class, and Environmental Quality* (3rd ed.). Boulder, CO: Westview Press.

Bullard, R. D., & Johnson, G. S. (2000). "Environmental Justice: Grassroots Activism and Its Impact on Public Policy Decision Making." *Journal of Social Issues,* 56 (3), 555–78.

Cash, F. L. (2001). *African American Women and Social Action: The Clubwomen and Volunteerism from Jim Crow to the New Deal, 1896–1936.* Westport, CT: Greenwood Press.

Charmaz, K. (2002). "Qualitative Interviewing and Grounded Theory Analysis." In J. F. Gubrium & J. A. Holstein (Eds.), *Handbook of Interview Research: Context & Method* (pp. 675–94). Thousand Oaks, CA: Sage.

Clark, S. P., Brown, C. S., & Walker, A. (1986). *Ready from Within: Septima Clark and the Civil Rights Movement.* Navarro, CA: Wild Trees Press.

Collins, P. H. (1990). *Black Feminist Thought: Knowledge, Consciousness, and the Politics of Empowerment.* Boston: Unwin Hyman.

Collins, P. H. (2000). *Black Feminist Thought: Knowledge, Consciousness, and the Politics of Empowerment* (2nd ed.). New York: Routledge.

Crawford, V. L., Rouse, J. A., & Woods, B. (Eds.). (1990). *Women in the Civil Rights Movement: Trailblazers and Torchbearers, 1941–1965.* Brooklyn, NY: Carlson.

Daloz, L. A., Keen, C. H., Keen, J. P., & Parks, S. D. (1996). *Common Fire: Lives of Commitment in a Complex World.* Boston: Beacon Press.

Di Chiro, G. (1998). Environmental Justice from the Grassroots: Reflections on History, Gender, and Expertise. In D. J. Faber (Ed.), *The Struggle for Ecological Democracy: Environmental Justice Movements in the United States* (pp. 104–36). New York: Guilford Press.

hooks, b. (1990). *Yearning: Race, Gender, and Cultural Politics.* Boston, MA: South End Press.

Institute of Medicine. (1999). *Toward Environmental Justice: Research, Education, and Health policy needs.* Washington: DC: National Academy Press.

Langellier, K. M. (2003). Personal Narrative, Performance, Performativity: Two or Three Things I Know for Sure. In Y. Lincoln & N. Denzin (Eds.), *Turning Points in Qualitative Research: Tying Knots in a Handkerchief.* (pp. 441–68). Walnut Creek, CA: Altamira Press.

Mullings, L. (1997). *On Our Own Terms: Race, Class, and Gender in the Lives of African American Women.* New York: Routledge.

Peterson, E. A. (Ed.). (2002). *Freedom Road: Adult Education of African Americans* (Rev. ed.). Malabar, FL: Krieger.

Principles of Environmental Justice. (1991). First National People of Color Environmental Summit. Retrieved March 18, 2005, from: http://www.ejrc.cau.edu/princej.html.

Shockley, A. A. (Ed.). (1988). *Afro-American Women Writers, 1746–1933: An Anthology and Critical Guide.* Boston, MA: G. K. Hall.

Springer, K. (Ed.). (1999). *Still Lifting, Still Climbing: Contemporary African American Women's Activism.* New York: New York University Press.

Taylor, D. E. (2000). "The Rise of the Environmental Justice Paradigm: Injustice Framing and the Social Construction of Environmental Discourses." *American Behavioral Scientist, 43*(4), 508–80.

Thurman, H. (1954). *The Creative Encounter.* New York: Harper & Row.

Tisdell, E. J. (2001). "The Politics of Positionality: Teaching for Social Change in Higher Education." In R. M. Cervero & A. L. Wilson (Eds.), *The Jossey-Bass Higher and Adult Education Series* (1st ed., pp. 145–63). San Francisco: Jossey-Bass.

United Church of Christ-Commission for Racial Justice. (1987). *Toxic Wastes and Race in the United States: A National Report on the Racial and Socio-economic Characteristics with Hazardous Waste Sites.* New York.

# CHAPTER 3

# How Women Relate to the Evils of Nature

*Karen Baker-Fletcher*

We are living in a troubling but fascinating juncture in Western history. The United States, in particular, is caught in a cycle of destructive global economic policies in relation to North American land and the land of the so-called Third World that transcends political parties. Greed-induced Ponzi schemes, inflated house values, record high unemployment, home foreclosures, declining stock markets, and the recession of 2008 into 2009 reflect global economic demise. Even the election of the "audacity of hope" candidate, President Barack Obama, cannot substantively change the systemic, manifest-destiny mentality central to the sociocultural, political ethos of the United States of America since its inception. There are no political saviors.

Salvation in this life is found in communities of solidarity and resistance,[1] those who are faithful to realizing the positive side of the American dream in which all peoples and the entire earth might experience social, economic, and ecological justice without domination. This side of the American dream seeks to realize freedom and equality for an entire earth. In that part of the American dream, love for the land is realized more fully and Americans who claim to love God remember God's love not only for the people of the land, but also for the land in its own right. Here, there is understanding that this land is multicolored in its soil, waters, trees, vegetation, creatures, and humans from state to state, region to region.

What is our responsibility as people of faith for the land, for creation? Who is the God we worship? In American politics and faith, does the will to dominate the earth and its peoples compete with the will to mutual care, respect, justice, and liberation? Our task in this chapter is to make sense of alternative understandings of God in ways that voting people of faith might support. After examining biblical texts regarding creation, including notions of dominion, the essay continues with views of God; a poetic response to natural disaster; biblical theological reflections on creation and suffering; and a creative dance of the Spirit of God.

## IN THE BEGINNING, GOD

The creation account in Genesis 2 observes the fact that we humans, created from the dust of the earth and the breath of God, are deeply connected to the rest of creation. According to Ecclesiastes 3:19, animals and humans alike are made from the dust of the earth and will return to it. What befalls the beasts befalls humankind. They have all one breath so that a human being has no preeminence above a beast. In Genesis 1 and 2, God created human beings *last from the dust of the earth.* We are because of God, the dynamic creative power that is the source of life. "God is," in the words of Alfred North Whitehead, "that which inspires worship."[2]

According to Genesis 3, the desire among human beings to be like gods, possessing the knowledge of good and evil leads to discord in God's creation. Both men and women, represented by Adam and Eve, were culpable of the arrogance that they could be as knowledgeable and as powerful as gods. Knowledge is power. The desire to be like gods, then, is a desire for power to do what gods can do. It is a desire to possess a greater deterministic role in the nature of things.

To possess god-like power is to assume a greater share of power to determine the nature of things. What would human beings do, however, with such power? Divine creativity itself already is at work in the very nature of things, calling it into relationships of well-being. For human beings to possess divine power and knowledge of good and evil means human beings have the ability to manipulate the delicate balance of the cosmos. We see this happening worldwide with the encroachment of industry and technology employed unwisely against, rather than in cooperation with, the land.

Consider the news of what has been taking place in Kenya as reported in an article forwarded to the womanist network by the womanist poet, theologian, and biblical scholar Valerie Bridgeman. The article, titled "Nature, Nurture and Culture," is by Wangari Maathai. A 2004 Noble Peace Laureate, Maathai is Kenya's Assistant Minister for Environment, Natural Resources, and Wildlife and the founder of Kenya's Green Belt Movement. She writes:

Mount Kenya is a World Heritage Site. The equator passes right on its top, and it has a unique habitat and heritage. Because it is a glacier-topped mountain, it is the source of many of Kenya's rivers. Now, partly because of climate change and partly because of logging and encroachment through cultivation of crops, the glaciers are melting. Many of the rivers flowing from Mount Kenya have either dried up or become very low. Its biological diversity is threatened as the forests fall . . . Mount Kenya used to be a holy mountain for my people, the Kikuyus. They believed that their God dwelled on the mountain and that everything good—the rains, clean drinking water—flowed from it. As long as they saw the clouds (the mountain is a very shy mountain, usually hiding behind clouds), they knew they would get rain. And then the missionaries came. With all due respect to the missionaries (they are the ones who really taught me), in their wisdom, or lack of it, they said, "God does not dwell on Mount Kenya. God dwells in heaven."[3]

The missionary teachings resulted in tremendous cultural, ecological, and spiritual loss. Heaven on earth gradually began to disappear. For Matthai, people have been searching for heaven; including travel to the moon, yet heaven has remained unreachable in such a quest; for in reality, heaven is in this moment, here, now. This explains the beliefs of the Kikuyu people who claim God lives on the mountain. If we posit God as omnipresent, then clearly God exists on Mount Kenya. Matthai notes that if such a belief helps people to be good stewards and practice ecological justice by preserving and conserving Mount Kenya, then so be it. Such a belief would not allow destruction of forests through illegal clear-cutting or logging.

Matthai further considers the damaging effects that industry on Mount Kenya has had on the health of Africans. Prior to Europeans coming to Kenya, people drew from the environment, which shaped everything about them: values, bodies, minds, religious practices. Engaged in a sustainable spirituality in nature that also shaped their views of beauty, food, and inspiration, they had a good quality of life. These communities did not have things many in the West take for granted from salt, soft drinks, and cooking fat to daily meat. Communities who live close to nature, and treat their physical environment with respect are not yet industrialized. Their environments remain rife with rich animal and plant biological diversity.[4]

This does not mean, however, that some of the Kikuyu can expect to do better than others. Habitats that have not yet been affected are threatened by current global economic practices. Matthai notes that these environments are subject to the ills of "globalization, privatization and the piracy of biological materials found in them . . . causing communities to lose their rights to the resources they have preserved throughout the ages as part of their cultural heritage."[5] With the Bush administration, the fight for the people of

Mount Kenya was harder, because this administration tended to put corporations first, the land and its people last. The emphasis of that administration was U.S. control of global economic power. Nobel Peace Laureates like Matthai are not likely to draw a positive response from administrations whose objective is global economic control. The God of Matthai is not the God of that administration. We must ask what type of concept of God was represented by the former dominant party platform and its administration that was in place for eight years. Is it a God who desires the freedom and well-being of all creation? Or was the Bush administration's concept of God closer to that of God as tyrant, all-determining and controlling? Is this concept of God actually God, or is it an idol made in the image of corporate American interests?

## Views of God

In much of classical and modern Christianity, God is omnipotent. In such a worldview, Charles Hartshorne argues, one must logically conclude that God is a tyrant who determines every action. Yet, there is evidence of freedom in the universe. Freedom and absolute determinism negate one another. God, then, shares power with creation or there would be no freedom. God and creation exist in responsive relationship. Hartshorne, drawing on the work of his teacher and mentor Alfred North Whitehead, understands divine love as the "feeling of feeling."[6] In this understanding, God feels the suffering and joy of the land and its peoples. God *influences* creation, but God does not dominate and control creation. God persuades creation to participate in the infinite possibilities of creative becoming.

Who is the God of the Bush presidential administration? The God of that administration was not persuasive, but controlling. It manipulated Third World countries to its own economic desires with little regard for the well-being of other lands and peoples. That administration reflects the omnipotent God who is all-determining, all-controlling, all-powerful, and who negates the freedom of the land and its peoples. This God is neither biblically nor metaphysically sound. To use Joerg Rieger's language, this God is nothing less than the false God, Mammon. Millions of Americans have been seduced by Mammon.

The moderate and conservative Christians that I teach find most accessible a reinterpretation of dominion where the "dominion" over the earth that God gives to human beings in Genesis 1:26 is a trust that humankind, being in the likeness of God, will care for the earth as God, who is a community, cares for humankind. Human dominion is to reflect the realm of God, which seeks the well-being of creation. The earth and all its creatures have both intrinsic and instrumental value that is given to humankind's care as a trust. The term "dominion" is problematic for many who engage in spiritual striving for ecological justice today, but there are times when the environmental crises locally and the ecological crisis globally are such that it may be the better part of wisdom to reform understandings of the biblical language church folk cherish when there is resistance to changing the language. Sometimes we can change language. Sometimes at best, we translate and interpret the language of a religious culture more clearly in order to retrieve its healing, healthy, and loving core. What works in academia, I find, does not always work as well in the world of American faith and politics. May we continue in the struggle for ecojustice in the Spirit, seeking political common ground in our love for one planet. With that in mind, I proceed to what Catherine Keller calls "poetics" to offer a theological response to the events of Hurricane Katrina and its multidimensional aftermath, which affected the United States and the world physically, materially, and spiritually. Sometimes, it is helpful to apply theory regarding process theology and poetics to consider what a poetic theology may contribute:

## POETICS: THEOLOGICAL RESPONSE TO KATRINA AND ITS AFTERMATH

### Ha Shem

*Hurricane*
*Why*
*Hurricane*
*Sigh*
*A touch on*
*Our shoulders*
*In early*
*July*
*At first*
*So dry*
*Then so humid*
*Weather awry*
*The birds all timid*
*In shade of trees*
*Then diving like turtles*
*Without grace or ease*
*Dipping low*
*For dark and cool*
*Seeking oasis*
*In tepid pool*

*Past breeding*
*And nesting*
*Just wrestling*
*With heat*
*Past season*
*To Season*
*Black and*
*Orange*
*Webbed feet*
*Sense*
*Adam's empire is*
*The reason*
*For warnings*
*And warmings*
*In morning's*
*First "Hi"*
*Such sorrow*
*Little regret*
*For ignoring*
*Heaven's eye*
*Before emperors*
*In ties*
*Butt naked with lies*
*Muted earth's cries*
*In ascent to hell's throne*
*Deep in the bog of*
*Imperialist dung*
*Plaguing*
*Peasant*
*Pietas'*
*Hearts*
*All flung and wrung*
*By the tragic folly*
*Of empire's feast*
*With blasphemous prayers*
*Mocking the least*
*Hailing techno whizzers's of Oz*
*Flaccid grey-skinned priests*
*Passing numbers for gods*
*While laboring serfs grieve*
*The debris on God's altars*
*While creation groans*

*With constant plea*
*From bayou to bay*
*And from bay to the sea*
*And the winds prophesy:*
*What a meager repentance*
*Such blasphemous offerings*
*What mocking remembrance*
*Of secret waters rippling with mirth*
*Spirit hovering over depths meeting earth*
*Swirling wind and love*
*Coursing down from above*
*Panting, then pulsing, then hearing*
*Sophia's hymn*
*At the first cry of birth*
*I Am*
*Alpha*
*And*
*Omega*
*Thus breathes*
*Ha-Shem*[7]

## BIBLICAL THEOLOGY REFLECTIONS ON CREATION AND SUFFERING

*In the beginning, God created the heaven and the earth. And the earth was*
*without form, and void; and darkness was upon the face of the deep. And the*
*Spirit of God moved upon the face of the waters.*

(Genesis 1:1–2)

In Genesis 1:1–2, the Spirit of God hovers over the waters. The earth was
"without form." It was "void or empty." As I have stated elsewhere, on the one
hand, Jewish and Christian traditions emphasize the chaos or "deep" from
which our becoming was shaped. On the other hand, tradition claims that we
were created from nothing. The void, the formlessness, and the deep of Genesis are a remnant from the Babylonian *Enuma Elish*. They are a remnant
of the maternal in divine creativity—Tiamat, evident in the Hebrew *tehom*
or "the deep."[8] While the Hebrew scripture makes no explicit reference to a
matriarchal goddess, Bible scholar Susan Niditch notes that "if the Genesis
account lacks a matriarchal goddess, it also does not present the creation of
the world as dependent on her death or on a primal battle."[9] As I note in *Sisters of Dust, Sisters of Spirit*, a careful reading of Genesis does not associate
the formlessness, emptiness, darkness, the deep, or the waters with evil."[10]

The creation story in Genesis is a nativity story. The deep, the darkness, the waters dance in co-creative activity with the Spirit of God to bring the cosmos in which we find ourselves into processes of becoming.[11]

Catherine Keller finds *creatio ex profundus* (creation out of the deep) in Genesis 1:1–2.[12] *Creatio ex profundus* is undoubtedly an aspect of divine creativity; otherwise it is necessary to ignore Genesis 1:2. Tehom is not evil but is an intimate player in the creative processes of the world as we know it and the becoming of humankind. In Genesis 1 God calls God's creation—waters, land, sky, light, dark, vegetable, water-creatures, four-leggeds, two-leggeds, flying things, creeping things, and humans, male and female, "good." God views creation with unsurpassable, rigorous, and unconditional love as creation reflects God's own goodness. If God, the source of all life, created creation "good," then why do we experience evil and suffering?

During wheezing pants of wind in the unusually dry year of 2005 in North Texas, folk could feel something peculiar in the air of the spring and summer months. Clouds formed, heavy and gray; clouds blowing in and blowing right out of state with few moments of rain. Another drought, obviously, but things were strange this particular summer. Storm clouds coming in with the wind just blowing them hard away to rain some place else. God, please give us some rain, Christian communities prayed. God gave us a little bit, which kept things going; it wasn't as bad as it could have been. Still, even the ducks looked lazy in the reservoirs and lakes. The water was warm and even the tree shade was hot. The turtles weren't surfacing much, not where the children could see them. The children strained to get a good look at them in the tepid water, clouded by the murk of dust every little breeze blew in. Sometimes the air was just still. The egrets were still. The water looked still. The herons were still. The sighting of a lightning bug and the sound of a cricket at twilight were a brief reprieve from silence. It was too hot to swim. People of faith wondered what God was doing.

During the next year's drought, summer 2006, folk stopped asking so much about what God and nature were doing. They were loaded with facts, theories, and action plans that may or may not get enacted. For moderate skeptics and even for some died-in-wool conservatives, global warming was no longer something liberals made up. In fits and starts, a divided nation started wondering how to find some balance. Maybe it couldn't hurt to do something about global warming—even if it might just be a factor of the problem. A layer or so of the skins of apathy and denial had sloughed off, but not without resistance. Summer 2005 had brought on the slight shift in thinking. In summer 2005, nature had gotten too wild for the nation. It seemed all the rain that the drought-ridden regions had been praying for went to Louisiana, right in the middle of New Orleans, what nature left of it. Praying folk watched in horror. Folk who didn't believe in God watched in horror at what Hurricane Katrina throughout the gulf and broken down levees took down and left behind.

Rescue workers, pundits, scientists, politicians, celebrities, and intellectuals inharmoniously panicked while trying to keep victims, survivors, and an entire nation from panicking. Aid was slow, while the call for aid was gracious, pleading, demanding, and frustrated until finally language tainted by the excremental waters woke up the "who's who" of national and state bureaucracies. Conye West asserted, "George Bush doesn't like black people"; black psychologists protested; and former mayor of Atlanta and civil rights leader Reverend Andrew Young calmly and pastorally remembered poor Mississippi white communities and the black poor alike on cable network news. "It's class!" some argued. "It's race!" argued others. "It's race and class!" chimed in still more. "But why did they build there?" grumbled some. "They have a levee. Whose fault is it that the levee broke, hhnh?" demanded many. "Well, why didn't those people just leave when they were told?" vented the inconvenienced. "A lot of poor people don't have cars, you know," responded the social activists. "But those . . . people never . . . and they always . . ." "Who are you calling those people?" "I knew you would say that. You people all think alike!" "No, you people all . . ." "Let's all work together as a nation," interrupted the Red Cross, a president, governors, mayors, pastors. "We sent it—clothes, water, money, diapers, canned food," exclaim women, men, and children who gave from their pockets, bank accounts, overdraft accounts, social security checks, and piggy banks. "Why are they keeping the supplies from the victims? Why isn't the government letting the trucks through?"

Churches and convention centers in Texas, other neighboring states, and states as foreign to Louisiana natives as Massachusetts opened their doors. Gestures of liberty—"Give me your tired, your poor." The days were slow, people still left behind. "Stop shooting at us, we just want to cross the bridge, we want to get dry, we need to get warm, please get us out, feed our children, our babies are sick, our old one's are dying, clothe our loved ones—let the supplies through!" cried those struggling to escape the fecal odor of the corpse-filled city. . .

On NPR, news of leaders from other nations called the United States to order, each in their own way querying if we were in our right minds. "It looks like a Third World Country over there!" and "Your people are at war!" sounded shocked remarks from abroad. "These people are not refugees! They are Katrina victims!" Al Sharpton proclaimed. Thousands phoned in, emailed, walked in to shelters, wailed, "Have you seen my wife, my husband, my partner, my cousin, my child, my niece, my nephew, my friend . . .?" Some were found. Some were not. "Where is Aaron Neville's niece?" blared from television sets, until the answer, "They've found her. She climbed to a roof to sleep, after helping a lot of people. She took them in. It's who she is. She is so kind, so talented, and such a good heart. Some one raped her up there. She is alive." Such goodness. Such evil. Such grace. Such violence. Such love. Such hate. The mind of the United States was blown by the hurricane.

It is difficult to talk about Katrina. She was a force of nature! Was she a "she" a "he" an "it," gendered at all? Who do we blame and rant at? Us? Them? God? In such moments, human beings experience nature as evil. Where is God in the midst of it, some ask? "Nature fell when Adam and Eve fell," some Christians claim. "No, nature is just doing what nature does. It's all because of human fallenness; humankind has dominion over nature, but people were just too cheap and greedy to fix those levees right," retort others. "It's because that city has so much sin," the Super Christian says. "God is judging them. You know those people aren't Christian; they have voodoo . . . and they . . . do you know what all they do down their in New Orleans?! Sodom and Gomorrah!" Religion!!! "Forget God," say the theist and atheist ecologists alike. "We predicted this years ago! It's global warming! Listen to the scientists! Not the Washington scientists! The serious scientists!" "No, some bureaucratic "they" just didn't want to dole out the money to fix the levees!!!" Those who lost their homes and loved ones weep.

Their eyes were watching God? A lot of eyes were watching the president— or looking for him. Presidents are not God. Yet in America, where we can't pray in public schools, but where we can pledge allegiance to the flag—"one nation under God"— and where we can sing "America, America, God shed his grace on thee," presidents, like pastors, the logic seems to be, must be close to God. The president flew over New Orleans. It was on the news. But even those on the ground who looted television sets couldn't see him or hear him. There was no electricity. The rescue process moved in slow motion for days. Americans struggle not to expect a president to be their messiah. As if one man really rules this country. Governments are laden with red tape. Bureaucratic logic and illogic alike reveal themselves. There is always a fall guy, someone to blame. The public demands the sacrifice of some heretic in the system. In the wake of Katrina, the FEMA director's head began its slow roll toward resignation. A justified event, in most of our minds, satisfied our outrage for a moment. All the same, the clamor recalls the nation's Puritan beginnings: "Send him to the stockades!" We are not to blame, it is "him" or "her" or "them!"

Not everyone's eyes were watching God during and after the hurricane, like the characters in *Their Eyes Were Watching God* by Zora Neale Hurston. Her novel reflects another time, a time when folk heard God in thunder, saw God's mightiness in lightning, and felt God's presence in wind. African Americans, in particular, in those days, did not so easily separate nature and God. They knew God did everything for some purpose and that God was in, not just revealed in, but present in creation. God's voice was in the thunder. God's tears, salt-water and fresh, permeated rock, sand, and earth. God's presence was felt in every kiss of a breeze and every smashing gust of air. What God was doing in nature was God's business, a mystery, and a power not our own to respect. Some died in the midst and some lived to tell the story. No one knew why. It just was. Survival was important. You did your best to live. To find higher ground, strong shelter. You prayed for and sought those things. Folk could feel a storm coming on their skin; smell the scent of it in everything, grumbled about the pain of it in their bones. They sought safe cover when first seeing and hearing of the shelter-seeking behavior of birds, dogs, squirrels, cows, all manner of two-leggeds, four leggeds, flying and creeping things— signs of a bad storm coming; divine revelations in creation to find safe, strong, hiding places, something hard to find today. People helped one another. God, even in fierce gales and roaring thunder, inspired community.

For the folk of that generation, nature just was. Nature wasn't evil. God was not responsible for it. Death was not desired, but a natural part of life, a transition to life with ancestors and saints. For some, God was nature, impersonal, the traditional sky God of many indigenous cultures. For others, God was not nature; God was present in nature. God was present everywhere in all places, in the midst of good and evil rejoicing in all of creation's acts of creativity and lamenting creation's destructiveness, while embracing creation cycles of life and death by bringing forth new creation from the wreckage of the old. They did not worship nature. They worshipped God. They simply did not forget that God was present *in* the hurricane compassionately feeling the pain and hope of all creation. But those ways are un-remembered in urban contexts where even rural areas are urbanized with machines, industries, and toxic waste sites. Cities offer the cheapest land and most fragile shelter in the flood plains, hurricane alleys, tidal zones, buy or rent as is. Even if it weren't so, infrastructures shut down when the worst happens. Evacuation plans meant owning a car, having fare for an early flight, train, or bus ride out. The gulf-coast poor, many of them descendants of former slaves whose masters and descendants of masters or friends of those descendants of masters deemed them expendable and fit for flood land, could not get out. No free transportation was available. Still other descendants of poor white overseers, farmers, and laborers, also knew they, too, were deemed expendable and fit only for land the privileged did not want years long passed. Katrina exposed the source of New Orleans and Mississippi coastal blues in all their historical and present poverty. A city, a state, a nation were not prepared; embarrassment coloring the nation's capital a strange, nonpartisan shade of red. And, yes, we all, in spite of the best efforts of those of us who care and take seriously good stewardship of creation, have contributed to global warning. In the midst, however, divine grace is present. Human beings look to blame, while God, whose aim is always the well-being of creation, forgives, and calls creation to participate in resurrection hope.

## THE CREATIVE DANCE OF THE SPIRIT OF GOD

In the movement of the Holy Spirit, God in Genesis 1:1–2 is revealed as breath and life itself. The breath of God swirls dust and salt-waters into oases of life. But in the middle of a hurricane, wind and water look and sound like humankind's worst enemies. The event of Hurricane Katrina sent women, men, and children into a search for oases. We depend on nature for physical sustenance. Yet, nature takes the lives of human beings daily, sometimes en masse. God is Creator we learn in Genesis 1, who looks at creation and calls us, human and nonhuman good. Why then does God allow two sides to nature? Nature is benign on the one hand, truly good to us. Yet, nature has tremendous capacity to destroy. We are nature. We have the same capacity. Nature, like us, is free. We are human *creatures* who share capacity for creativity and destruction with the rest of nature.

We are made from springs of water mingling with the dust of creation and the breath of God. We are fragile, our bodies returning to earth when we expire. Yet, we are fiercely stubborn and unpredictable like Katrina herself. We trick ourselves into believing we have tamed the very elements of which we are made. If Katrina sinned, let one without sin cast the first stone. We are earth creatures and we are more. We do not understand our "more" very well, neglecting it, distorting it, turning away from it, denying it. We have imagined ourselves stronger than divine breath and natural wind. When God appears in the whirlwind, we dare not boast of our strength.

We remember who we are. We are not God. We are not stronger than the whirlwind. We did not create it and we can not control it. We have not even mastered self-discipline. Why then have we imagined we can master wind and sea? We are called to reflect God, not be God. God is divine community, three in one, lover, beloved, and spirit of love, mutually indwelling one another. Divine community calls us to live as inspired community in the world, loving beyond class, beyond race, beyond gender, beyond all manner of orientations, sexual or otherwise, and every kind of difference, to work as one creation for the well-being of all creation. We are not called to judge one another. We are called only to hear and discern the call of God, which is always the call to love God and our neighbors as ourselves. The neighbor is always the stranger, the one who has been struck down in the journey of life on this earth and in this cosmos, existentially and ontologically. The stranger is also the Samaritan, the one despised by the Super Holy, the Super Righteous, the Super Christian— the one who may be gay or lesbian, black or Appalachian white, Hispanic or Asian, Muslim or Buddhist, Jewish or Hindu, pagan or Christian, atheist or theist, agnostic or believer. But who is Katrina—stranger, neighbor, or enemy? Her winds clean the oceans and make new life possible, in an ideal world, the deep ecologists say. We've placed too much in her way and have failed to master plans for keeping us out of her way, the deep ecologist proclaims; therefore, we have forgotten how to love Katrina. It's not about loving Katrina, the pastoral counselors say; it is about not hating Katrina and accepting her. Sounds like Martin Luther King Jr.'s agape love, disinterested love that desires the well-being of the universe, one theologian said. Not exactly, say the pastoral counselors: "Katrina simply is. The frailty of life, the reality of destruction is something to accept not love."

The creation account in Genesis 2 observes the fact that we humans, created from the dust of the earth and the breath of God, are deeply connected to the rest of creation. According to Ecclesiastes 4:19, animals and humans alike are made from the dust of the earth and will return to it. What befalls the beasts, befalls humankind. They have all one breath so that a human being has no preeminence above a beast. In Genesis 1 and 2, God created human beings *last from the dust of the earth.* We are because of God, the dynamic creative power that is the source of life. "God is," in the words of Alfred North Whitehead, "that which inspires worship."[13]

If the Spirit of God is always present, if there is no hiding place where we can separate ourselves from the One who is Love and Life, if when we ascend to heaven the Spirit of God is there, if it is true that if we ascend to hell the Spirit of God is also there, if even the day and the night are alike to God, so that the night shines with a luminous darkness, then the Spirit of God was present even in Katrina. Like Job in the whirlwind, we may never understand. We know only that God, in Spirit and Word, hovering over the deep, created every creature and element of life in freedom to love God and one another—or not. We know only that God comes before us, with us, and after us, loving us, in all events.

Creation is called to participate in God's aim for the well-being of all creation in spite of the problem of evil. God will continue perfectly well without us if we refuse to enter renewal. God does not *need* us to further well-being, but God invites our participation in God's love for all of creation. We participate in this divine love not because we creaturely spirits can erase the problem of evil, but because we say yes to divine love for its own sake and become embodiments of love, like Jesus, in saying yes to the Great Lover of our bodies and souls.

## NOTES

1. See Sharon Welch, *Communities of Resistance and Solidarity: A Feminist Theology of Liberation* (Maryknoll, NY: Orbis, 1985), for a discussion of the "liberating strand" in Christian theology and the epistemological expertise of communities from below in her appropriation of Michel Foucault's "archaeology of knowledge." For more on Welch's understanding of community see her

more recent books: *Sweet Dreams in America: Making Ethics and Spirituality Work* (New York and London: Routledge, 1998) and *After Empire: The Art and Ethos of Enduring Peace* (Minneapolis, MN: Augsburg Fortress Press, 2004). For more on epistemology from the underside see Michel Foucault, *Archaeology of Knowledge* (New York and London: Routledge, 2002). For discussion of "solidarity" and *communidad*, I recommend Ada Maria Isasi-Diaz, *Mujerista Theology: A Theology for the Twenty-first Century* (Maryknoll, NY: Orbis, 1996) and idem. *La Lucha Continues: Mujerista Theology* (Maryknoll, NY: Orbis, 2004). For Welch, "community" is synonymous with "divinity." My own use of the term "community" is synthesis of the understandings Welch and Isasi-Diaz employ. Both agree, as do I, that there is no community without solidarity and that "God" or "divinity" is found in community. I, like, Isasi-Diaz and the Latina women with whom she writes in relationship, however, retain a strong understanding of the transcendence and immanence of God in my theological construction; such an understanding of the transcendence *and* omnipresence of God. In Welch's work I find an openness to both, however, along with emphasis on indigenous understandings that there is not a dualistic relationship between the spiritual and material. While our terminology is somewhat different, in that I generally write from a more explicit and traditional Christian, specifically Wesleyan perspective, I find resonances in Welch's understanding of divinity as community in traditional African, Native American, and African American religions. In such indigenous religions and cultures, the lines are blurred between transcendence and immanence, spirituality and materiality, leaving Western scholars divided as to whether such understandings are "pantheistic" (God is all creation) or "panentheistic" (God is in all creation), for the sake of academic clarity. At the same time, I find Western delineations an artificial imposition on non-Western structures of reason, a reluctance to honor the equality of cultural forms of reason that are different from Western forms of reason. I do believe that Western scholars are more capable of learning other forms of reason than some are wont to do, just as we are capable of learning multiple languages from diverse cultures. One does not know another language well enough to interpret adequately without versatility in cultural forms of reason. What is "blurred" and even "confusing" for Westerners who are not bicultural or intercultural in their reasoning is quite clear to those who employ a different and equally astute cultural form of reasoning. Sometimes, there simply is no adequate translation from one form of cultural reasoning to another, and we must accept that translation is always a matter of more or less adequate interpretation. My own conclusion is that indigenous understandings of so-called sacred and material realms are both pantheistic and panentheistic and neither pantheistic nor panentheistic. Yet, given that the guild of scholars remains predominantly Western in its cultural form of reason, I am willing to say that my own understanding is panentheistic. This does not mean that I think traditional African ways of thinking, like the Bantu Muntu or Ntu philosophy, for example, are pantheistic. Nor do I think they are panentheistic. To the contrary, I think that terms like "Muntu" or "Ntu" are not easily translated into Western languages and learned Western ways of thinking. This is similar to the situation in Buddhist-Western Christian dialogue and conversations between Western Christian dialogue and other Asian religions. In Christian tradition, Eastern classical theologians like Gregory of Nyssa, Pseudo-Dyonysius, and Maximus the Confessor make for easier conversation partners with and approaches to the world's religions. For more on my understanding of incarnation of divine community in earthly community see Karen Baker-Fletcher, *Dancing With God: A Womanist Perspective on the Trinity* (St Louis, MO: Chalice Press, 2006; 2007) and idem. *Sisters of Dust, Sisters of Spirit: Womanist Wordings on God and Creation* (Minneapolis, MN: Fortress Press, 1998).

2. Alfred North Whitehead.

3. Wangari Maathai, " The Cracked Mirror," *Resurgence,* November 11, 2004. http://www.greenbeltmovement.org/a.php?id=28; Viewed March 29, 2009.

4. Ibid.

5. Ibid.

6. One finds allusions to this key process theological concept of God in Charles Hartshorne, *Omnipotence and Other Theological Mistakes* (Albany: State University Press of New York, 1984), 27, 39 and 108 and Alfred North Whitehead, *Process and Reality: Corrected Edition,* ed. David Ray Griffin and Donald W. Sherburne (New York: Free Press, 1979), 343–44, 345, 351. Specific attention to "feeling of feeling" is found in Charles Hartshorne, *Whitehead's Philosophy: Selected Essays, 1935–1970* (Lincoln: University of Nebraska Press, 1972), 168.

7. Courtesy of Chalice Press, first published in Karen Baker-Fletcher, *Dancing With God: A Womanist Perspective on the Trinity* (St. Louis, MO: Chalice, 2006; 2007), Chapter 6, 117–19. See also Karen Baker-Fletcher, "Musings from White Rock Lake: Poems," in Laurel Kearns & Catherine Keller, ed., *Eco-Spirit: Religions and Philosophies for the Earth* (New York: Fordham University Press, 2007), 536–38 for an earlier version of this poem presented at the Fifth Annual Transdisciplinary Theological Colloquium (TTC) at Drew University in September 2005.

8. Susan Niditch, "Genesis," in *The Women's Bible Commentary* (Louisville, KY: Westminster John Knox Press, 1992), 13. Karen Baker-Fletcher, "Nativity and Wildness," *Sisters of Dust, Sisters of Spirit,* 25.

9. Ibid.

10. Ibid.

11. Karen Baker-Fletcher, "Nativity and Wildness," *Sisters of Dust, Sisters of Spirit,* 21–25.

12. Catherine Keller, *The Face of the Deep* (New York and London: Routledge, 2001).

13. Alfred North Whitehead, *Science and the Modern World* (New York: Macmillan, 1925), 129.

# PART II

# *Socioeconomics, Politics, Authority*

# CHAPTER 4

# Beyond Priesthood: Catholic Women Seek Empowerment in a Post-Vatican II Church

*Judith Johnson*

## THE FIRST WHISPERS

The Catholic women's ordination movement had a quiet beginning in the mid-20th century Euro-American world, when a female Swiss lawyer delivered a request to the world's Catholic bishops gathered for the Second Vatican Council: *Please ordain women.* That was the first time in modern history that a woman had ever presented a message to the Vatican requesting that women, herself included, become priests. But it was far from the last such "sign of the times." By the 21st century—even before its first decade has ended—that polite appeal in 1962 had evolved into a galvanized movement, crossing three disparate continents, seeking radically to transform the last of the Roman-medieval aristocracies into a renewed and egalitarian church.

The Swiss lawyer's request was followed soon by that of Dr. Ida Raming—one of less than a handful of women theologians in Catholic Germany at the time; she also appealed to the Vatican directly. Often cited among feminist church historians as the grandmother of the contemporary women's ordination movement, Dr. Raming guided the new activists through four decades of transformation and is, today, not only the fourth bishop ordained in the Roman Catholic Women priests' initiative, but an icon of the entire historical movement.

What was to become the RCWP initiative began as a modest step in June 2002, when Dr. Raming and her associate, Dr. Iris Mueller, stood with five other candidates (now known as the Danube Seven) on a riverboat somewhere in the waters separating Austria from the Czech Republic. They became the first ordained—and among the first excommunicated by the papal Magisterium[1]—but that is getting far ahead of our story.[2]

This chapter explores the move of Roman Catholic women to fight for ordination following the rubric of *aggiornamento*, a new wind blowing, following Vatican II. After reviewing the historic beginnings of this movement and the first Catholic women's ordination conferences, the chapter then: (1) examines the cultural and intellectual context of women's priestly ordination; (2) reflects on the birth of the Women's Ordination Conference (WOC); (3) explores the women's theological revolution related to ordination; (4) examines the gender war and the papal response; and (5) reflects on 21st-century milestones and the Danube Seven's ordination and excommunication.

## THE WOMEN PRIESTS MOVEMENT: SIGN OF THE TIMES

The global (and secular) call for women's liberation was arguably one of the major signs of the times prompting John XXIII to call the Catholic bishops of the world into a conciliar gathering (Vatican II) in the spirit of *aggiornamento*—that is, to update the Catholic Church. This call proved to be more of a catalyst for change than a cause of it. As they monitored the progress of Vatican II, alert nuns sensed their inherent dignity *as women* starting to mature before their own eyes. Only after the Council (but well before the Danube event) would the real *aggiornimento*[3] begin as women's past experiences *as Catholic* came under a more sophisticated microscope, as a basis for creating theology.

In late 1974, a small group of American Catholic laywomen gathered to interpret a shared vision of building an alliance to promote the ordination of women. While not the first such group, it would become the major activist force in the budding movement. With Christmas Eve only 10 days away, Mary B. Lynch of Denver gathered some 30 friends for a very unusual purpose. Since she had returned from the fall Synod of Bishops in Rome (1974), where she attended as a silent observer, she could not get the idea out of her head: *why not* ordain women as priests? Women had talked enough. It was time to raise the issue the bishops had refused to raise.

In response to Lynch's initiative, American and international Catholic women gathered for the First International Women's Ordination Conference (FIWOC) in fall 1975. They were part of a swelling global wave, cresting within the American church; here, a bishops' synod was urging all its "religious"—priests, bishops, brothers, and nuns—to join with lay Catholics in a call to action for a revolutionary synod of all the People of God,[4] to renew the church under the conciliar guidelines of Vatican II. The entire North American Catholic cosmos expected bold changes.[5]

The two initiatives (lay and cleric) combined—for the first time in Roman Catholic history—when the FIWOC opened its conference doors in late November under the theme *Women in Future Priesthood Now—a Call to Action.* Before 1200 participants, leading Catholic theologians, mostly women, mounted the platform to speak on an issue forbidden for two millennia. Although many vowed (and prominent) women religious[6] brought together the conference,[7] it was the *lay*women theologians, particularly Elisabeth Schüssler Fiorenza and Rosemary Radford Ruether, who were to become icons of the women's church-renewal movement. Schüssler Fiorenza, speaking over a year before the Pontifical Biblical Commission released its conclusion (agreeing with her), told her audience that it was "invalid" to deny women ordination on scriptural grounds. Ruether stressed women's ordination as a way to "overcome the idolatry of sexism."[8]

Despite the historic implications of the FIWOC gathering, in looking back, one can see only the sketchiest outline of a movement through a buoyant cloud of enthusiasm. Its premises and its ideology were only beginning to form. Only its goal of justice for women in a *service* priesthood and an appeal for a new look at the sacramental priesthood stood out clearly.

Its short-term goal—to form an executive committee for a permanent women's ordination movement—gave birth to the Women's Ordination Conference (WOC), which would become the global voice for women called to priestly ministry. It also delegated a task force to dialogue with the bishops and paved the way to a consultation process with them. The bishops—perhaps slightly overwhelmed by the success of the FIWOC—called for the Catholic Church's first lay synod, the Call to Action (CTA) conference, held the following October in Detroit. What the bishops did not anticipate was that their initiative would lay the seeds of a progressive revolution in American Catholicism, going way beyond priesthood issues. "For the first time, laywomen and men, sisters, priests, bishops, archbishops and cardinals" came together, spoke together, and actually *listened* to each other as they projected, together, a vision of the future Church.[9]

Yet, the truth of the matter was, the American bishops' romance with Catholic women died soon after the first dialogue. The CTA synod in October 1977 merely alerted the papacy to stymie the progressive movement altogether. Already in late 1976, an aging pope, Paul VI, was setting into stone (on the Rock of St. Peter) the final version of *Inter Insignores*—the papacy's first encyclical devoted to repressing the People of God's move toward ordaining women.[10] But before we can explore the issue into the 21st century, we must look back at the historical context that created the cultural and intellectual soil out of which the issue of women's priestly ordination has arisen.

## THE VATICAN AND THE "TWO PRIESTHOODS"

Impelled by the clear evidence in the "signs of the times," the Second Vatican Council had redefined "Church" as the People of God, that is, as all baptized laity. To supplant antiquated ideas of women's subordination, the papacy would develop a more nuanced concept of "complementarity"—a concept which literally held the devil in its details. Complementarity came to define men and women as existing in a "mutually dependent relationship" which could arguably be called equal but different. However, the vivid head-and-body metaphor was never washed off the papal palette.

Although the Vatican documents never cite the inherent *maleness* encoded into the *ordained* priesthood, they do identify two priesthoods (of "vital difference"), derived from two sacraments: one from a *common* baptism and one from the anointing of Holy Orders.[11] The crux of the matter rested on the hierarchy's uncontroverted need to maintain a special, *ordained* caste to preside over the Eucharist; behind the need lay the latent fear that women might see the entire People of God as *sharing* in the *one* priesthood in Christ—with the right to consecrate the Eucharist—*even without ordination.*

Two decades later this linguistic parsing led to feminist bumper stickers saying "Ordain Women or Stop Baptizing Us."

The heirs of the medieval papacy were ill-prepared for the women-priest evolution. From the start of the 1970s, with Episcopalians illicitly ordaining women and the Leadership Conference of Women Religious (LCWR) calling for women's ordination, the pope felt pressed to announce, in *L'Osservatore Romano*, the official Vatican newspaper: "Jesus does not call women to the ministry [and] does not communicate to women the message he received from the Father. It is a fact, and we are bound to recognize it."[12] That was only the beginning. Toward the mid-70s, when it was clear to the papal *Magisterium*[13] that even bishops (mostly North American) were supporting the dissident nuns, Cardinal Joseph Ratzinger's Congregation for the Doctrine of the Faith (CDF)—the leading secretariat of the papal court—was quietly assigned to write an encyclical on the subject, to be known as *Inter Insigniores*.

Vatican II had not anticipated the questions to come later, principally from women, regarding the all-male priesthood: are we not *all* Other Christs by baptism? Even the Pontifical Biblical Commission (PBC) could churn up no solid biblical basis to justify the male-only tradition, beyond its unacceptable subordination theories. Finally, in *Inter Insigniores* ("Declaration on the Admission of Women to the Ministerial Priesthood"), the CDF reified two images used by the Council, one on women (as a "complementary" body)[14] and one on priests *acting* in *"persona Christi."* In doing so the Vatican would return to prominence the symbolic head-body distinctions between men and women (as symbolic of the church/Christ dynamic), making it a fact of so-called Christian or theological anthropology: by *acting* in the person of Christ, the priest was *being* the image of Christ. And since Christ was a *male,* only males could become other Christs.[15] If that was not enough to humble women, the CDF scraped the paint off its medieval palette to say: man (like Christ) is the Head, and woman, like the Church, is *never the Head.*[16] *That* only God could change. And, since God is changeless, don't expect much.

Thus, on that November day in 1978 when WOC Baltimore began, the battle lines were set, the core issues posted—and the gestation period before the birth of a truly genuinely global women's ordination movement was almost over. To begin the birthing process, one woman's button said it all: "Question Authority."

## WOC 1978: New Woman, New Church, New Priestly Ministry

Behind a banner proclaiming "New Woman, New Church, New Priestly Ministry" hundreds of women marched from the historic Baltimore waterfront to the City's Civic Center, underscoring the historic significance of WOC coming to Baltimore, the seat of the first Catholic diocese in America, to re-birth the Church. It was an exuberant but relatively quiet march. One could hear the inchoate chant of the chains keeping beat with the marchers whom they linked together, repeating a rhythm of clattering metal that, like a ghost's rattle, echoed the convention theme: "We Burst the Chains that Oppress—and Forge the Chains that Free,"[17]

As keynote speaker, Elisabeth Schüssler Fiorenza,[18] led a strategic attack on the Vatican. Not perhaps, since St. Catherine of Siena, had a woman castigated the papacy in such a public and theological context as when Fiorenza said, "the Vatican Declaration *and* its theological defenders risk Christological heresy in order to maintain the present sexist church structures and ideologies." She chastened a hierarchy that "degrades these sacramental actions to the level of juridical magic," and censured *Inter Insigniores* for declaring that only a man can image Christ. She rebuked the hierarchy for insisting "on the magic-religious character of the sacraments" as "male rituals of birthing" and boldly asserted: "Christology has become *androlatry,* therefore idolatry."[19]

## THE FIRST WOMEN'S THEOLOGICAL REVOLUTION

By the end of 1978, it appeared that a dramatic change was awaiting the Roman Catholic Church. It was then that Karol Wotijla was installed as John Paul II. Within his first months in office, he would not only have to deal with the first major WOC congress, but also with a diminutive Catholic nun, standing alone before him—and the television cameras of the world.

> Sister Theresa Kane, a Sister of Mercy and a leader of the LCWR, knew that standing before the newly elected Pope John Paul II publicly, to present him a message from American women, was an awesome obligation rather than a privilege. Yet she spoke out boldly: "As women," she said, "we have heard the powerful messages of our church addressing the dignity and reverence for all persons. As women, we have pondered these words, [leading] us to state that the church . . . *must respond* by providing the possibility of *women as persons* being included *in all ministries* of our church."[20]

After the Baltimore WOC Conference, Ruth Fitzpatrick, the first national WOC director, and others such as Ruether, began a decade-long dialogue with the National Council of Catholic Bishops. By the time WOC held its 1983 symposium, Schüssler Fiorenza had published her classic *In Memory of Her: A Discipleship of Equals,* and Rosemary Radford Ruether had written *Sexism and God-Talk. God-Talk* would later become the name of a national radio show that allowed women to speak out about their religious experiences and prophetic visions of the future of Christianity. The world of Catholic women was in high gear.

By March 1983, the Bishops had produced their first draft of "Partners in the Mystery of Redemption" with no direct input from women—a draft left largely on the cutting-room floor for another decade. By the end of the year, the 1983 Code of Canon Law appeared,[21] drawing fine lines between the *function* and *office* of ministries. For example, while priests held the "sacred office," girls could only be "deputized" as altar servers, as functionaries, but not hold the position permanently, as an "office." Even canon lawyers objected that this magisterial insertion violated Canon 208 (on the equality of the baptized). One other very important door did open, largely because of the verbiage in Canon 517, which said that a "dearth of priests" could allow for the pastoral *care* of a parish to be delegated to a "person who is not a priest." It said nothing about being male. *However, this was not the transfer of a sacred office.* It became a veritable "Pandora's box" (as well as a stop-gap solution) for the hierarchy as it allowed for "female leadership at the parish level."[22] Women began swelling the ranks of parish administrators. These women would come en masse to the 1995 WOC conference, calling for a resurgence of appeals to the hierarchy for the admission of women to the priesthood.

## THE FIRST GENDER WAR IN THE CATHOLIC CHURCH BEGINS

If one were able to gather up the bytes within Pope John Paul II's mind in 1988, one would find most of the pieces merging into the image of an Iron Curtain shaking under global pressures. At the far side of his envisioned puzzle, the women's ordination issue would appear as a gnat gnawing its way under the papal skullcap. With the Iron Curtain about to split wide open, John Paul had little time and less patience to deal with women who still did not know their place. Yet the 1987 (worldwide) Synod of Bishops, unable to come up with any solutions of their own—it had burned all its drafts on "women's issues in the church"—now urged the pope to do it for them. Seeing women as the opposite of priest, John Paul decided to address both his clergy and women, in two letters, setting forth his version of Paul VI's "Christian anthropology," thus continuing the message of *Inter Insigniores*.

First, the pontiff wrote to his worldwide clergy about the persona of the priest as mother, about a "spiritual fatherhood" that, like an earthly mother-hood, needed feminine "characteristics" such as docility and receptivity.[23] A woman gave earthly birth, a priest spiritual birth, the papal letter said—a frontal assault on Catholic feminists such as Schüssler Fiorenza, who had stressed women's nurturing qualities to justify women priests. Now the Vatican would turn real maternal attributes into a surreal male Medea.

Four months later, John Paul followed up with *Mulieris dignitate* ("On the Dignity and Vocation of Women"), where he merged the Adam-and-Eve myths with the nuptial analogy of bridegroom/bride (from Ephesians 5:22–23). Women, stunned into silence, soon realized that the armor of met-aphor staved off all rebuttals from reason. (In the "Christian anthropology" of John Paul II, woman came into the world solely to be man's helpmate. She is the vessel for his seed; he is the one who generates. She models the figure of Mary, Christ's mother, the model of priesthood who, humbly, never seeks priesthood. It is her divinely selected *male* progeny, the image of Christ, who is invited to priesthood. Even when woman images the Church, the Bride of Christ, she is not alone; for the Church is not *only* female. *Every* baptized Christian can be "bride" but, in John Paul's theological-anthropological view, only a male can image Christ, can absorb his sacred power, can become priest-as-mother, pulling the nuptial analogy into a union within himself, in which he is both bridegroom and bride.[24]

Thus, John Paul dumbfounded less biased theologians and prelates.[25] When biology became the source of women's dignity, *her* sacred "office" became maternal by divine mandate, the source of her limited but God-given *natural* power.[26] For the most discerning observers, the pontiff's agenda was clear: although women could produce the "royal priesthood" of believers—they could not *image* Christ. In as much as men cannot *function* as birth-givers, so too women cannot [be allowed to] *function* as priests.[27]

Despite Christian anthropology's roots in a long-outmoded Platonic-Aristotelian metaphysics, John Paul's "theology of the body" presented a logic-free pseudo-theology that was dissonant not only to feminist thought (and common sense) but to Catholic tradition and progressive theology. Oblivious to the fatal flaw in its allusive apologia, the Vatican could not detect the subliminal andolatry (as Schüssler Fiorenza had interpreted it) in its assumptions. Catholic women felt the cage again closed around them. As Marie Bouclin, a Canadian scholar in the abuse of women by priests, points out: John Paul was exploiting women through use of the iconic image of Mary; he was using a seductive ploy in overvaluing the ideal of motherhood. Women familiar with how a dysfunctional system operates began to see through the subversive strategy.[28]

The pen of *Mulieris dignitatem* had barely been put down when the Berlin Wall began to crack. *The Vatican's most well-guarded secret was about to emerge* from the papal Pandora's Box, from under the folds of the falling curtain. In early 1990, a small Austrian press, *Kirche Intern,* had followed up on a lead that several women had been ordained in the underground church of Czechoslovakia during the Soviet occupation. The Vatican could not continue to suppress the story once the *New York Times* broke the story in the United States (December 8, 1991) followed (December 20) by the *NCR (National Catholic Reporter).*[29] Yet with bishops cautiously denying the story's validity, it made few waves, even in pro-ordination circles. But it did in the Vatican; the pope knew that at least *one bishop* (with the knowledge and tolerance of Paul VI) had ordained a woman. And he would have to be defrocked, discredited completely.[30] The national coordinator of WOC was another exception: Ruth Fitzpatrick spent several sleuthing months tracking down the allusive woman-priest in the Czech Republic—and by summer in 1992, she and a few other WOC board members were knocking at the door of Ludmila Javorova, in the small city of Brno.

Ludmila Javorova was not quite ready to declare her ordination to the world; by now, virtually all her fellow (male) priests shunned or reviled her. She would make one more appeal to the Vatican. She would do whatever the church asked—but she knew in her heart that the Curia would lend a deaf ear to the saga of her years as (a *female*) Vicar General for her bishop. The entire underground ministry and its persecutions, she knew, would be trivialized. *She wanted mostly for Christ to tell her what to do.*

The WOC contingency pretty much kept its word,[31] although they could apply no damage control to what the *New York Times* and *NCR* had done. They had to plan WOC's 1995 20th anniversary celebration without even a mention of Ludmila Javorova. Instinctively, it appeared, they knew that American Catholic women were, for the most part, not ready to hear the repressed news. On the other hand, the reality of *knowing* that, in their day, a live Catholic woman-priest existed, that *it had happened*, energized WOC like nothing else could.

When, in 1994, Anglican prelates accepting women's ordination and even his own Canadian bishops boldly asking the Vatican to consider the issue, John Paul knew that the mania had to stop; even the German youth were demanding women priests. And there was that persistent little matter of Ludmila Javorova, who insisted on believing she was a valid Roman Catholic priest. *If she and her message were not suppressed*—but that was already too late. John Paul II put his hand to pen for one final swat at the gnats' nest.

## ORDINATIO SACERDOTALIS

Perhaps the most remarkable aspect of *Ordinatio Sacerdotalis* ("On Reserving Priestly Ordination to Men Alone") was its length: only five pages, offering no new arguments and few old. Rather than present theological or biblical apologies,[32] the pontiff opened the door to legal questions. And even if the cryptic document had shed the metaphoric approach of preceding bulls, its lament had roused more resistance than assent from Catholic and Anglican readers. The new directive was an "action of authority born of irritation."[33] His "because-I-said-so" approach had inflamed the issue. In the last paragraph John Paul II had written:

> Wherefore, in order that all doubt may be removed regarding a matter of great importance, a matter which pertains to the Church's divine constitution itself . . . I declare that the *Church has no authority whatsoever* to confer priestly ordination on women and that this judgment is to be *definitively held* by all the Church's faithful.[34]

If women fell silent (momentarily) to the issue of ordination, it was the silence of shock rather than obedience as progressive Catholics riveted attention on the explosive use of the word *definitive*. The pope signed this letter on May 22, 1994, the feast day of St. Rita, patroness of hopeless marriages and, in this instance, the Brides of Christ were indeed finding conditions hopeless. How did the pontiff himself interpret *definitive?* Was it merely "*Roma locuta, causa finita*": Rome has spoken, "case closed"? If "definitively" meant infallibly, where was the consultation with the bishops beforehand, "*ex cathedra*"?[35] Liberal Catholics, male and female, waited without an umbrella for the next rain of words; this was a mandate that needed ignoring until it was *defined*. Its unpersuasive arguments, resting solely on papal authority, were soon being examined as heretical by Catholics who had never before put the words "pope" and "heretic" together in the same sentence—and still lived.

Just as the doors opened on WOC 1995—with over a thousand attendees flowing into the Washington, DC, area—Cardinal Ratzinger told the world, in only one-hundred-fifty words, that *Ordinatio Sacerdotalis* had indeed elevated the issue of a male-only priesthood to the level of divine truth, incapable of being changed by any future world synod or pontiff or even divine intervention. In that short but traditional form, a response to doubt (*Responsum ad dubium*)[36] the word *definitive* was elevated to mean *infallible*.


## THE LAST SALVOS OF THE 20TH CENTURY

Rather than penning courteous letters, ordination activists took to their feet, in low-keyed, in-your-face demonstrations-without-confrontation, witnessing before bishops' meetings and cathedrals, especially during male ordinations, starting what WOC would later call its "ministry of irritation." Under the umbrella of its own *sensus fidelium*, a wiser, more mature women's ordination movement emerged worldwide. By fall 1996, the *Wir sind Kirche* (We Are Church) phenomenon in Central Europe had mushroomed into a super-caucus of over two million Germans and Austrians who signed a mass referendum for widespread church reform. One demand read: "We believe in a church with equal rights for women," in which women fully participate in all the "official decision-making," which "welcomed" women to "all ministries, including the deaconate and the ministerial priesthood"—a church of celibate *and* non-celibate clergy, a church that "affirms people rather than condemns them."[37]

The time for obsequious appeals was over. Germany's Maria von Magdala group, founded by Ida Raming, planned its 10th anniversary celebration—its Initiative for Equality of Women in the Church—to demand that women *once again* be ordained as deacons. In 1997, England's Catholic Women's Ordination, allied with other reform groups, promoted its own (British) Roman Catholic Declaration—and, at its first Worldwide Day of Prayer, members of Women's Ordination South Africa (WOSA) washed each other's feet, to signify parallels between apartheid and the church's ban on ordaining women. The Europeans were again leading the charge. And when Europe rises up, the Vatican listens—but it rarely capitulates.

Within three years, WOC's national coordinator, Andrea Johnson—a mother who felt called to priesthood—joined with like-minded supporters from Ireland, England, and continental Europe (especially IMWAC[38]) to plan the first international conference of Women's Ordination Worldwide (WOW). However, Andrea, Maureen Fiedler, and fellow WOC board member Dolly Pomerleau had an even more crucial reason for coming to Europe: to meet with Ludmila Javorova. Pomerleau had been with Ruth Fitzpatrick in Brno in 1992—when Fitzpatrick had first found Ludmila—and now she would return with the new WOC leaders to Brno, the Czech village of Ludmila. Perhaps they could convince her that the time had come to release herself from her self-imposed silence. Had they not kept their promise and revealed nothing of their first visit? ("Imagine!" Maureen Fiedler wrote a few weeks later, "a woman priest who has already celebrated her silver jubilee!")

Ludmila appeared to have gained strength over the past five years, Pomerleau observed. Although she declined to attend WOW-Dublin, she strongly supported women called to priesthood. She had made public her own ordination solely because the world needed to know there *were* Roman Catholic women priests.[39] But America intrigued her; she would go there—with no press, just quietly speaking with women called to priesthood. And the following year, she did.

## MOVING INTO PRIESTHOOD

I remember well[40] that June evening in Dublin, the night before the opening of the First International Ecumenical[41] Conference of Women's Ordination Worldwide (WOW 2001). Conference events were to be rather low-key, coming in under the Vatican's radar. That evening, WOC invited its Irish and English hosts to its hospitality suite in student housing at University College Dublin. Curiously, the London-based coordinator, Sister Myra Poole, did not show—and the main organizer from Ireland, Soline Vatinel of B.A.S.I.C.,[42] literally burst into the WOC suite shouting, "The Vatican has cancelled our main speaker!" She went quickly into details: the Vatican had informed the World Council of Churches in Geneva that if they allowed Aruna Gnanadason[43] even to attend, that would force the end to all Vatican negotiations[44] with the WCC. Aruna cancelled her reservations and gave no welcoming address.

The Vatican had also locked its radar on two other major speakers—women from religious orders, Myra Poole and Joan Chittester. The 21st century, for progressive Catholic women, was opening with a double WOW.

About six weeks before the conference opened its doors, Myra Poole's provincial leader in Rome, head of the Sisters of Notre Dame worldwide, wrote Myra a letter she had hoped never to send. Enclosed were copies of three letters she had received from the Vatican, each consecutive letter more severe, signed by leading hierarchs within the Curia's Congregation for Consecrated Life and Societies of Apostolic Life (CICLSAL), which governed the lives of religious orders of women and men. The first letter demanded that Poole resign from her position with WOW; the second, bearing the added signature of a curial canon lawyer, ordered her Notre Dame provincial to forbid her to travel to Ireland. The third letter—bearing a *third* signature, that of the Cardinal Prefect heading the Congregation—demanded that Myra be placed under an order of "formal obedience" (which, if disobeyed, would require her dismissal from her community, her home, and the life she had chosen to lead for over four decades). Myra's provincial was beyond distraught: dare she endanger her community's hard-earned Constitution, their very way of life? There was neither time nor a process by which to garner a consensus from her Notre Dame sisters in the global community.[45]

Myra wrestled with the issue as if wrestling with the devil himself, sharing her torment with few. As she made it quietly to Dublin, her paralyzed conscience frayed. Her loyalty to her communal sisters, her sense of commitment grabbed at her heart. *But part of that commitment was there in Dublin.* On Saturday afternoon, with the International Panel about to begin its session, Myra appeared, as if rising from the middle of the standing crowd.[46] *We seemed to feel her presence before we saw her, before she reached the platform where a microphone slipped into her hand. I am sure I was not alone in feeling that history was being recorded in that microphone, that maybe Myra was really the re-visioning of Hildegard of Bingen or Catherine of Siena rising before papal power. I just hoped she wasn't about to become our Joan of Arc.*

Yet it was an American Benedictine nun, Joan Chittester, with her keynote address later that day, who would cause the bigger stir. She would stir her audience, stir up the press, and make her biggest stir with the papal palace: "So if a Church preaches equality but . . . lives an ecclesiology of superiority, it is close to repeating the theological errors that underlay centuries of church-sanctioned slavery." Truly the clarion-prophet of the Catholic women's movement, Joan Chittester set before the assembly what its future would be, beyond priesthood. Discipleship "cut a reckless path" she said, yet we were to take our discipleship "seriously." Persons with "high need of approval, social status and public respectability need not apply."[47] Although we were unaware as we listened, she too had been put under orders of "formal obedience"; she too was treading on the hot coals of martyrdom, 21st-century style.

Joan's prioress at the Erie (Pennsylvania) Benedictine Abbey, had boldly taken a copy of Joan's talk with her to Rome *even before* Joan set off for Dublin. She would meet the Secretary and Prefect of the Congregation for Consecrated Life on the Vatican's own turf.[48] Perhaps if they read the outline of Joan's talk (and no more, of course), they would see the innocence in speaking of *discipleship* in the third millennium. As for Joan herself, she could not force her to *obey.* Benedictine women were *guided* into making mature decisions according to the dictates of their own consciences. They were never forced. She would tell that to the prelate—or to the pope, if it came to that.

In Rome, the prioress from Erie simply refused to be the follower. She refused to punish Joan for her "formal" disobedience, then handed the pontiff a referendum signed by 127 of 128 of her community's nuns, all declaring that if Joan were cast out of the Order, they would follow.[49] The world presses would later quote her as telling the pontiff:

> Benedictine authority and obedience are achieved through dialogue between a member and her prioress . . . . Sister Joan . . . must make her own decision based on her sense of Church, her monastic profession and her own personal integrity. I do not see her participation in this [WOW] conference as a "source of scandal" to the faithful . . . I am trying to remain faithful to the role of the 1500-year-old monastic tradition *within the larger church.* Benedictine communities of men and women were never intended to be part of the hierarchical or clerical status of the church, but to stand apart from this structure and offer a different voice. Only if we do this can we live the gift that we are for the church.[50]

In a distinctly separate decision, the Superior of the Sisters of Notre Dame announced that Sister Myra Poole would remain (unpunished) with her community in England. For the first time in the history of the Roman Catholic Church, two women, both religious-community leaders, had forced a pontiff—in a move beyond and outside of priesthood—into a checkmate position. Yet both Myra Poole, SND, and John Chittester, OSB, knew all too well the price their communities would, in time, pay for their boldness and obduracy.[51]

WOW 2001 did its best to ignore Rome as it attempted to prevent potential clashes from within its own subgroups. Disputes over the visions and goals of its 370 attendees (from 26 countries) could easily have fractured WOW's very tenuous unity. To resolve potential discord, the WOW-Dublin schedule alternated prominent speakers—such as Sister Joan and Nobel Peace Prize recipient, Mairead Corrigan Maguire[52] of Northern Ireland—with quiet gatherings for informal dialogue among the attendees to share their incongruent views and to reach a consensus in two days. To most, their call to priesthood was like a voice beckoning them into a fog, impelling them toward ordination, but not showing them where or how that could happen *without leaving the church.*

One such woman, an Austrian leader in IMWAC, was strategically planning to bring those forbidden ordinations about. Well into her own secret preparation for priesthood, Christine Mayr-Lumetzberger had professed she would not leave the Roman Catholic Church—so, the conservative wing of WOW loved her. And since she proclaimed that she would overcome all obstacles to be ordained *soon,* the progressives too loved her. Few had heard of her, but within months she would carve out for her group a rather elevated niche in the yet-unwritten history of the worldwide women's ordination movement.

After WOW-Dublin, the activism of women seeking Catholic priesthood became a global media magnet, pulling the press into each conference, in wait for stirrings from the waking giant in Vatican City.[53] The second volley in the gender war was about to burst forth.

## NEW MILESTONES FOR A NEW MILLENNIUM

With WOW 2001, women-priest advocates from around the globe began to experience a psychological shift in their interpretation of what it meant to be Catholic and female. The living spirit of a discipleship of equals, breathed into life by Elisabeth Schüssler Fiorenza, had reached a more practical level of maturity with Joan Chittester; but could it take on a structural form? It would have to evolve from somewhere, some community or branch of the faithful, just as the Benedictine women had from the Desert Mothers of Egypt 15 centuries earlier.[54]

Christine Mayr-Lumetzberger, a former member of the Benedictine order, was about to keep her promise to remain *within* the Roman church, even as she is ordained. What Christine and those joining with her would do next would literally spark a revolution *within the Catholic tradition* (at this writing). While Christine was preparing to attend WOW 2001, a kindred spirit called upon her to come to a most unusual meeting. That kindred spirit would introduce her to a select few women whom she felt would become—*should* become—the first female priests in over a millennium of recorded church history.[55] This group included philosopher Dr. Gisela Forster of Munich,[56] who, with Christine, agreed to develop a formation program for women seeking priesthood, a type of women's home-study seminary. For Christine and Gisela, planning, promoting, and monitoring the three-year *Weiheämter* program[57] was the easier part; finding a Roman Catholic bishop who would ordain them at the end of the three years was hidden some-where behind a very fragile, fading rainbow, bent, and twisted under the shackles of Rome.

Finally, these kindred spirits managed to stir up a Roman Catholic bishop out of favor with Rome, who would later, with a little luck and the backup of another bishop or two—be able to ordain the women in the traditional rites prescribed by the Vatican. Exactly one year after WOW-Dublin, seven prepared women would present themselves to receive the Roman Catholic sacrament of Holy Orders, while floating up the Danube (Danau) River.

## THE DANUBE RIVER UPRISING

On June 29, 2002, the feast of Sts. Peter and Paul, a vested Christine Mayr-Lumetzberger of Austria walked into "apostolic succession" with six select shipmates aboard a German day-cruiser. After their years of stress-filled, clandestine study, the women prostrated themselves before two controversial Catholic bishops on the mildly rocking floor of the MS Passau somewhere in so-called international waters of the Danube (between Austria and Germany),[58] to begin a life that would never see placid waters again.

Besides Mayr-Lumetzberger and Gisela Forster there were Germany's feminist theologians, Drs. Ida Raming and Iris Mueller, joined by a fourth German, Pia Brunner; an Austrian nun, Sister Adelinde Theresia Roitinger; and an Austrian-American under the pseudonym of Angela White.[59] Together they would become known as the "Danube Seven."

The women, plagued by intense fear of retribution and retaliation at each step of preparation, had invited three, rather than two, bishops. Both bishops and candidates knew that the risks were far from over; but they also knew the time had come for women to be anointed priests within the penumbra of the Roman Catholic Church, even if it was in a type of Stygian darkness that forebode a dismal rather than a reassuring future.

The way the ordination evolved that day would jar not only the Seven, but even their guests. Bishops Romulo Braschi of Argentina (with Ferdinand Regelsberger of Austria)—both married and out of favor with Rome—followed the Roman ritual of Holy Orders vigilantly—too vigilantly for the ordinands, who had expected more female-friendly inclusive language. And the absent third bishop appeared to have dropped off the planet; none of the ordinands (as of that moment) had any idea of his whereabouts.[60] A rumor would later leak out that the *intended* ordaining bishop, in "good standing" with Rome, sat locked in a hotel room not far from the port, under (it is said) a Vatican imposed guard.

Some groups, such as WOC in the United States and CANWE in Canada, espoused the ordination. For WOC, the Danube event was a major leap of faith into a future it had resisted supporting.[61] In England, CWO (Myra Poole's Catholic Women's Ordination group out of London) assessed the ordination as spiritually an answer to a divine call, but the New Wine movement and even John Wijngaard's women's ordination Web site, pulled back from applauding an ordination by a bishop "not in good standing," but offered empathy. The Austrian *Wir sind Kirche,* had discreetly distanced itself from Mayr-Lumetzberger's decision to be ordained, as did Germany's "Church from Below," yet members attended with hope-filled optimism for their German friends.[62] Yet even their strongest supporters knew that the canonical validity of their ordination—hence, of their entire initiative—rested on the validity of Braschi's episcopacy, which rested on the validity of the bishop who had ordained him.

As the Danube Seven became the first Catholic women to publicly, before a global press, dissent from the dictates of Canon Law 1024 (by receiving Holy Orders), the Vatican, within days, shot its own cannon, with a white flag attached: if the women repented by July 22, the order of excommunication against them would be rescinded. The women thought it appropriate and prophetic that, after being warned about an ordination on the feast of Sts. Peter and Paul, the apostles who had founded the church in Rome, they would have until the feast day of Mary Magdalene to repent.[63] They were dissenting from a bad law; they would repeat again and again. At the moment, they had no prophetic understanding of what a global impact their historic dissent would make—nor of the quick, public ferocity of the papal response that would follow, nipping at their heels.

## THE TRIPLE-CROWN EXCOMMUNICATION

The Danube ordinands, strengthened by the subliminal message contained in the *date of their deadline*—the feast of St. Mary Magdalene—allowed the designated time of grace to elapse and, on August 5, the CDF issued its final decree of excommunication, a cautionary "Warning Regarding the Attempted Priestly Ordination of Some Catholic Women."[64] Its preface focused on Archbishop Braschi's previous excommunication and cited him as "the founder of a schismatic community," to dispel any "doubts" of his lack of canonical status[65]; then, in one short paragraph, we read: "this Dicastery . . . declares that [these women] have incurred excommunication *reserved to the Apostolic See* with all the effects established by Canon 1331 of the Code of Canon Law."[66]

This excommunication process set an interesting precedent; in most cases where individuals seek ordination outside the Roman Catholic fold, such as in an Anglican, Lutheran, or "Old Catholic" communions, the Vatican considers them as having severed their Catholic connection in order to affiliate with a non-Roman Catholic sect outside Vatican jurisdiction. They would have, in Rome's terms, "excommunicated themselves." The Danube Seven saw it differently; in their own eyes, they had entered into a *contra legem* situation[67]: (1) they had carefully orchestrated their ordination rite, including seeking out a bishop who would ensure their "apostolic succession"; (2) they sought solely to receive the sacerdotal ordination (albeit *contra legem*), not to start a new church; (3) they had deliberately invited excommunication *from Rome*; and they were well aware that this type of active female dissent had never occurred before.

The dicastery apparently also felt impelled to scold the women for their very "unwomanly" behavior, an "affront to the dignity of women" whose divine role was "distinctive" from the priesthood, and, above all, their action was solely a "simulation of a sacrament," not a sacrament at all. The women promptly sent their own sparse and straightforward reply: they had committed no offense punishable by excommunication,[68] they stated, adding on a note of crescendo that the dictum of male-only ordination in itself contradicted the "very principles of Catholicism."

Six silent weeks later the Danube Seven filed for "recourse" under canons §§1732–1739.[69] Using Vatican terms, they would cite their own ordinations as *valid* but "illicit," that is, *contra legem*—against the law of Canon 1024—a Latin phrase that would became part of the ordination advocates' everyday vocabulary, alongside *Ordinatio Sacradotalis.*[70]

Just before Christmas 2002, the papal court issued a third document, the last of the three orders covering the women's excommunication. The 15 examiners that Ratzinger assembled[71] had reached the "collegial decision" that recourse was out of the question. The Supreme Pontiff had declared the *doctrine* banning women's ordination as "definitively proposed"—and against the pope "there was no recourse."[72] Again, that should have been the end. Again, it was only the beginning. Yet, the Danube Seven had achieved most of the goals they had set for themselves. The fact that the pope had taken up the issue himself fortified the women in their sense of prophetic destiny; his actions said implicitly to them that they were still considered Catholic.[73]

Rome may never hand its women a key to the papal palace, but women have already carved a deep fissure into the core of grassroots Catholicism. Nevertheless, the papal palace, by the act of issuing its excommunication orders against the Danube Seven (the initial core of the group that has become known as the Roman Catholic Womenpriests)has recognized them *as dissenters still within the fold.*

Although the RCWP by the end of the first decade of the 21st century had become the largest of the groups of Roman Catholic women practicing a "Catholic" priestly ministry, it is not alone. Catholic women have developed a range of sacramental (or priestly) ministerial models of faith. While seeking to move "beyond" priesthood—to redefine, if not undermine, a monarchical-hierarchical model still entrenched in feudal norms—they have set in place a sprawling mosaic of Catholic-rooted ministries thriving beyond, or beneath, papal pillars.

Catholic women, in their new roles as priestly ministers, may well have, I believe, initiated a movement as revolutionary as the 16th-century Protestant Reformation.

Upon coming to the United States in spring 2008, Pope Benedict XVIII was immediately bombarded with questions of why he would excommunicate women who seek ordination—and not pedophile priests, who abused children. Certainly, the pedophiles were worse sinners. Benedict told the press that the pedophiles are sinners who can be forgiven, but the women seeking priesthood were "undermining the very structure of the Church."[74] Benedict is correct—in this sense: the *institutional* church, in as much as it rests upon the "structure" of a divinely mandated all-male descent line, cannot bend any more than the "rock" that represents it can. It can only crumble. This has nothing to do with doctrine. It is this structure—its descent line from a male Christ to an exclusively male 12 apostles to an exclusively male line of bishops—that must be preserved. If women become priests, it disappears.

## NOTES

1. *Magisterium,* the (Latin) name given by the Church to its "teaching authority" is also the name given to the papal offices or congregations, principally the Congregation for the Defense of the Faith—the old Office of the Propagation of the Faith or, still earlier, that Office of the Inquisition.

2. Long before either one (or any other woman) was allowed to receive her doctorate in Sacred Theology from a European university, Raming and Mueller began their lifetime study of woman and the Catholic priesthood. They would expand their concise document, *The Exclusion of Women from the Priesthood: Divine Law or Sex Discrimination?* (Metuchen, NJ: Scarecrow Press, 1976). This study appeared in 2005 in a (two-volume) history of the women's ordination controversy in the Roman Catholic Church.

3. Pope John XXIII's purpose in calling the Second Vatican Council into session was to bring the church up-to-date, to open windows on the modern world.

4. In its primary definition of "church," Vatican II had used the term "People of God," thus defining the church as primarily all Christians; the clerical-episcopal/papal *institution* became only a secondary definition of "church." This is what Dominican Sister Nadine Foley meant when she opened the conference, cautioning women: "We come together . . . not to confront the Church, not to act in defiance of the Church, but to *be* Church" (Fitzpatrick, p. 77).

5. For details, see Nadine Foley, OP, "Who are These Women?" in *Women and the Catholic Priesthood: An Expanded Vision.* Proceedings of the Detroit Ordination, ed. Anne Marie Gardiner SSND, My references derive from a short, unpublished, history of women's ordination by longtime WOC leader, Ruth Fitzpatrick.

6. The term "women religious" (rather than *religious* women) is an ecclesial term to define women in religious orders, contemplative and active, vowed canonical and (as we shall see) unvowed lay.

7. Opening the event, Marie Augusta Neal, SND, called for a "new model of priesthood" that would be accountable "to the people." Keynote speaker

Elizabeth Carroll, a Sister of Mercy (RSM), set the prophetic tone with a warning to her fellow sisters against getting too caught up in "hierarchical clericalism." Like Neal, Carroll was a university professor, had held the presidential post in the Leadership Conference of Women Religious (LCWR), and was serving on a federal committee (Fitzpatrick's notes, pp. 78–79). Another LCWR leader, Sister Mary Daniel Turner, SNDdeN, served on the advisory board of a national American Jewish Committees.

8. Fitzpatrick's notes, pp. 78–79.

9. The first CTA conference actually spawned the organization, called Future Church, which operated on the borders of the official hierarchy for three decades by Sister Christine Schenk, SND—a Notre Dame nun who (post-2005) has been pushing the envelope of women's official ordination as deacons in the Roman Church. In 2007, Future Church was officially ousted its (symbolically appropriate) home in the basement of a Catholic Church in Cleveland. Sister Christine's long struggle for Future Church to function within a diocesan umbrella ceased—primarily over her strengthening boldness in support of women's ordination.

10. The Vatican's "Commentary on the Declaration" (of Women to the Ministerial Priesthood), January 27, 1977, states that it first became alert to the issue with the decision of the Swedish Lutheran Church in 1958 to ordain women. The immediate cause of the 1977 commentary, however, was the illicit Episcopal ordination of 11 women in Philadelphia in 1974.

11. Holy Orders, the Council said, had the power to "configure the priest to Christ," empowering him to act "in the *person of Christ*," (Taken from the Congregation for the Clergy's "The Priest: Pastor and Leader of the Parish Community, reprinted in *Origins* 32, n. 23, November 14, 2002, pp. 375–78). This was excerpted in Deborah Halter's *The Papal No* (pp. 16–17). NOTE: Up to the 12th century, ordination was never (as we know it) a permanent anointing: it assigned a church function. It took over two centuries more, until the Council of Florence (1439), before ordination (as Holy Orders) was decreed to be a sacrament.

12. Deborah Halter, *The Papal No* (New York: The Crossroad Publishing Company, 2004), p. 216.

13. As noted earlier, the capitalized Magisterium denotes the teaching authority of the papacy, actualized in the official duties of the Congregation for the Doctrine of the Faith, the office that decides which theologians are heretics, when a bishop should be censures, etc.

14. The papal court fell back on to its "theological anthropology," with its Aristotelian-based theory that woman actually had a different "nature" than man: women and men mutually *completed* each other, but in distinctly different ways.

15. The Council had said, in its official document *Presbyteronnan Ordinatio* ("A Decree on the Ministry and life of Priests") that, by the "sacramental "grace" of Holy Orders, priests acted "in *persona Christi.*"

16. This makes perfect sense if one thinks in the philosophical terminology of ancient Greece—as the Vatican was doing. In that era, the male represented

the fullness of a human being; we could say that 'A' stood for the "alpha" male, the full human being, and the female was never able to reach even A-minus quality in this lifetime. This defines an entirely different paradigm of male-female humanity than today's concept that A (male) and B (female) are equally human on Nature's balance scale. Thus "complementary" (and even Paul's statement in Corinthians—"an entirely different meaning when arrived at from differing premises. Consequently, if *in nature* the Alpha-male represents the fully human being, Christ had to be born a male, and "other Christs" had to be males.

17. *The Church World*, November 30, 1978.

18. Like Raming and Mueller, Schüssler Fiorenza fought the all-male caste of German theologians in order to get her doctoral degree in theology. But unlike them, she left Germany to teach at the University of Notre Dame and later at Harvard Divinity School.

19. Elisabeth Schüssler Fiorenza's speech, "Too Comfort or to Challenge," in the *New Women, New Church, New Priestly Ministry: The Proceedings*, p. 49.

20. McNamara, p. 633 (quoting from Barbara Ferraro and Patricia Hussey, with Jane O'Reilly, *No Turning Back: Two Nuns' battle with the Vatican over Women's Right to Choose*, p. 153.) Italics are mine.

21. The long-awaited revised Code of Canon Law was well received among women more for what it did not say than what it did: The long, repressive references to women's dependency in marriage had been deleted.

22. Quotations are from Halter, pp. 65–67.

23. Halter, pp. 74–78.

24. Deborah Halter, *The Papal No*, gives an insightful yet concise summary of *Mulieris dignitate*. See especially pp. 76–81.

25. Bishop Ray Lucker (then the bishop of America's smallest diocese, New Ulm, Minnesota) once observed: "Cardinal Ratzinger has said we have the conclusion, now we need the reasons. When we face that, we realize we have very serious problems. How can we support that which has no reasons?" (Halter, p. 126.)

26. In a *third* letter—this time to all the laity—John Paul affirmed that women's "rightful presence," her *meaning as a person* rested upon her existence in "mutual complementarity" with men. (Pope John Paul II, *Christifideles Laici*, Para. 50, as contained in Halter, p. 82.) Italics are mine.

27. Progressive Catholic information channels and journals have a proliferation of articles on *Mulieres dignitatem*. Halter, pp. 76–81, contains an excellent and concise analysis. See also Richard McBrien's *Catholicism*, p. 776 for a concise summary of topic.

28. Marie Evans Bouclin, *Seeking Wholeness: Women Dealing with Abuse of Power in the Catholic Church*, pp. 47–48.

29. See Tim McCarthy, "Married Priests among Slovak Church's Woes," *NCR*, September 21, 1990. NOTE: The Vatican had its own approach: *all* clerics from the underground chain would be cast under the cloak of papal suspicion, so that the very bishops who had ordained them could be removed.

30. Bishop Felix Davidek, long imprisoned by the Czech communists, had built up one of the strongest Catholic underground "church" wings behind the Iron Curtain. Had he not ordained women, he most likely would have become a candidate for sainthood rather than psychologically persecuted.

31. WOC board member, Dolly Pomerleau, an early organizer of WOC, returned from Brno to the Quixote Center in Hyattsville, Maryland, to write about Ludmila in "Journey of Hope: A Prophetic Encounter in Czechoslovakia," for a small Catholic audience.

32. (I use the term apology in its scholastic sense: answers to arguments.) The pontiff's argument was that *maleness* was identified as integral to the "substance" of the sacrament—which was the priest himself.

33. British Vatican-watcher Peter Hebblethwaite is quoted in Halter, p. 94.

34. *Ordinatio Sacerdotalis* ("Apostolic Letter on Reserving Priesthood to Men Only," *Origins* 24, n. 4, June 9, 1994, May 22, 1994, p. 5. See assessment in Halter, p. 213).

35. "Ex-cathedra" means "from the [papal/St. Peter's] chair; that is, before a doctrine is officially declared "infallible" in the Roman Catholic Church (according to Vatican I, 1869–70) it must be a matter of "faith and morals," taught by the pope *and* the *whole* body of worldwide bishops, and be assented to *beforehand* as a universal belief of the whole body of the faithful (referred to as the *sensus fidelium*).

36. The *Dubium*, or doubt, was about whether the church has "any authority whatsoever" to confer priestly ordination on women [as presented in *Ordinatio Sacerdotalis*]. Was this to be understood as belonging to the deposit of the faith? The *Responsum* answered in the affirmative. The teaching requires definitive assent since 1) the teaching had been "constantly preserved" in the Church's "tradition" and 2) it has been set forth infallibly by the ordinary and "universal Magisterium" [meaning, the teachings of the world's bishops as recorded in the documents of Vatican II]. Where they did this, except in their silence, I do not know.

37. Maureen Fiedler, "A Visit with Ludmila Javorova: A Woman Priest" in *New Woman, New Church* (WOC Publication, Washington, DC) Summer 1996, p. 4. Information also derives from Dolly Pomerleau's privately published recollections in "Journey of Hope: A Prophetic Encounter in Czechoslovakia."

38. IMWAC: The International Movement of We Are the Church, which became global.

39. See Fiedler, pp. 4 and 11.

40. As a member of the national board of the Women's Ordination Conference (WOC), I was one of the minor coordinators of the WOW 2001 conference.

41. The word "ecumenical" in the title was somewhat of a misnomer, since virtually all the attendees were Roman Catholic, with a few very supportive Anglican women priests. The word was added to soften (to conservative ears) the fact that some attendees would actually promote women's ordinations in

"schismatic" communities rather than solely with papal permission, within the magisterial church.

42. B.A.S.I.C. stands for Brothers and Sisters in Christ, an Irish Catholic organization seeking equal dignity for women in the Church and its ministry.

43. Under pressure from World Council leaders (but not obliged to "obey"), Aruna Gnanadason, a native of India, was wary that she could harm the work of the Council if she attended WOW-Dublin. A key expert on women's ministries worldwide, she had first met WOW leaders at the First European Synod of Women at Gmund, Austria, in summer of 1996, when WOW 2001 was first planned.

44. The Vatican did not grasp that WCC could only request, not force, Gnanadason to cancel her plans. Its second demand—that WCC pull back its considerable donation to WOW's travel fund for "third-world" attendees—was, for ethical reasons, flatly rejected.

45. See Myra Poole's reflections in *Making All Things New: Women's Ordination—A Catalyst for Change in the Catholic Church,* co-written by Dorothea McEwan and Myra Poole, pp. 75–79.

46. This is as I recollect it, from where I had stood, at the edge of the room.

47. From my notes; also in McEwan and Poole, p. 79. The full address can be found in *Women's Ordination Worldwide First International Congress—Text and Content,*(Eamons McCarthy, ed., pp. 15–20.

48. This was not the first time Joan *and* the Benedictine women had stood on the firing line of a papal inquisition. Usually the Vatican would work more stealthily, through the advocacy of a local ordinary. This time it was *she* who would go directly to Rome.

49. Rome would later claim (through press releases) that the Vatican authorities "never considered taking disciplinary measures" if the Benedictine sisters did not "discipline" Sister Joan. (See full article in *The Tablet,* London, July 14, 2001.) (The Benedictine Order was not notified of this; see full story in McEwan and Poole, pp. 71–79.)

50. McEwan and Poole, pp. 72–73, quote from McCarthy, pp. 83–84.

51. Over the years following WOW 2001, Joan Chittester's speaking engagements with Catholic groups were quickly cut off by diocesan bishops. Her books were not as easily banned—or her spirit.

52. Maguire surprisingly stressed that *religious* persecution (like that against women priests) was worse than physical persecution (such as her country's women had endured for decades).

53. Articles and (many later) opinion/editorial pieces appeared in the *Irish Times,* the (London) *Times,* the *New York Times,* the *Chicago Tribune,* the *Cleveland Plain Dealer,* the *Boston Globe*—and around the globe.

54. Although the monastic communities in the Benedictine movement go back to the Rule of St, Benedict of Nursia (c. 550), Benedictines, both male and female, will often cite the roots of their lifestyle (and Rule) as lying with the desert fathers and mothers. (Richard P. McBrien, ed.), *The HarperCollins Encyclopedia*

*of Catholicism,* refers to this tradition; see p. 153. Laura Swan's book, *The Forgotten Mothers: Sayings, Lives, and Stories of Early Christian Women* (Mahwah, NJ: The Paulist Press, 2001) is one of few works on the desert "mothers."

55. Archeological and other suppressed records had shown that women had served in priestly capacities in the Catholic tradition from the earliest centuries.

56. Gisela, with her husband Anselm, had studied and taught philosophy with their close friend, John Ratzinger, before he went to the Curia where he now headed the former Office of the Holy Inquisition—the CDF (the Congregation for the Doctrine of the Faith).

57. *Weiheämter* stands for (preparation for) the official priestly ordination.

58. As an ordination "at sea," outside a measurable location, the illicit ceremony came under Vatican jurisdiction rather than the jurisdiction of a local bishop, perhaps to the eternal gratitude of at least two bishops.

59. Facing the very public wedding of her daughter later in the summer, the seventh Danube ordinand waited three months to drop her pseudonym; she was Dagmar Celeste (the former wife of the ex-governor of Ohio, Richard Celeste).

60. The Danube Seven has never publicly identified the Czech bishop who had secretly ordained them temporary deacons, but later press reports (and rumors over the next few years) identified the missing prelate as a "practicing priest" from the Czech Underground Church, who, like Ludmila Javorova, had been ordained a bishop by Felix Davidek. (Some of my brief description comes from Howarth's account.)

61. The WOC board, in giving a cautious support to the ordination, moved into an entirely new direction and awaited a deluge of angry membership mail—which never came.

62. Much of my description comes from Rea Howarth's account in "Witness to Her Story: Seven Women Ordained on the Danube River," in *Speaking Out: The Newsletter of CSO,* Summer 2002, p. 2.

63. For yearly ordinations, Catholic dioceses often select June 29th, the feast of the two "apostles" cited as the major founders of Christianity—honoring Peter, especially, as the head of the "line of apostolic succession".

64. My copy of the "Warning" derives from Halter, Document 10, *The Papal NO,* p. 235.

65. Braschi, according to a release issued by Gisela Forster later, had been a Brazilian priest who had fallen from episcopal grace when he had opposed the military juntas (1976–1983). Ordained a bishop in a breakaway church, he was later re-consecrated a bishop by Roman Catholic bishop Jeronimo Podesta in 1999 (and produced a notarized affidavit attesting to it, which satisfied Forster).

66. Canon 1331 forbids excommunicated persons from celebrating, conferring, or receiving the sacraments or functioning in an ecclesiastical office; and any sacramental actions performed by them are null and void.

67. *Contra legem* means "against the law" of (in this case) Canon 1024. This canon, which states that only males may be ordained priests, was put into the 1983 Code of Canon Law unchanged from the 1917 Code.

68. WOC had disseminated its own critique of the "warning" before the imposed excommunication was published, stating that among the "nine offenses for which excommunication could be imposed" women's ordination was never mentioned. See "The Vatican, Women, and Excommunication: Actions Contrary to Teachings," August 2002, as well as *The Code of Canon Law: Text and Commentary,* ed. James A. Coriden, et al. (The Canon Law Society of America, 1985), 932.

69. These canons governed appeals to the Code; while the canon could not be challenged, the *use* of a particular canon in a particular case could be.

70. By stressing the illegality of the act, the Danube Seven (and the women priests to follow them) are implicitly pointing out that this is a *legal action,* not a doctrinal matter, a matter of belief. Laws, even in the Catholic Church, can (and do frequently) change.

71. The decree noted that a *Sessione Ordinaria* of the CDF had examined the request, including Joseph Ratzinger, and the CDF's Prefect, Archbishop Tarciscio Bertone, and 13 other high-ranking church officials, several of them affiliated with Opus Dei. See Halter, pp. 237–39 for a copy of the decree.

72. Statements partially quoted as in Halter, pp. 148 and 238.

73. Excommunication does not mean one is kicked out of the church; on the contrary, one is "merely" cited as being in "grave error" and may not receive the sacraments; such persons, however, are still required to attend Mass regularly and practice the tenets of the Catholic faith.

74. See the archival records of romancatholicwomenpriests.org, May 2008.

# CHAPTER 5

# Gender and Society: Competing Visions of Women's Agency, Equality, and Well-being

*Pamela K. Brubaker*

The United Nations affirmed "the equal rights of men and women" in the preamble to its 1945 Charter, as part of a reaffirmation of "faith in fundamental human rights, in the dignity and worth of persons." As is evident in the Charter, a belief in human dignity and worth, a foundational moral norm shared by religious and secular people, grounds human rights. Christian women's activism on gender and society in the post–World War II period offers competing visions of the meaning of equality between the sexes, women's moral agency, and well-being. These three interrelated themes resonate with the themes of this section: socioeconomics, politics, and authority. Although well-being is an expansive concept, socioeconomic conditions are vital to its attainment. Equality is primarily a political issue in that equal rights are established and their meaning negotiated through political processes. Moral agency can be understood as a question of authority: who is authorized to act? On what grounds?

This chapter explores women's political activism in relation to United States' Christian and interfaith organizations: the Roman Catholic Church, the World Council of Churches, and through transnational feminist networks. The first section examines conservative and progressive advocacy in the United States for and against equal rights for men and women, grounded in competing visions of gender roles. Conservative Christians contend that equal rights, especially reproductive rights, weaken the traditional family. Liberal and progressive Christians support equal rights, but not all advocate for reproductive choice. Those who do so claim that reproductive rights are essential to women's well-being. The second section discusses Roman Catholic and ecumenical activism in international arenas on issues of gender and society. An exploration of how Christian beliefs and practices are drawn upon to limit or enhance women's moral agency and their socioeconomic activity informs this discussion. The third section explores faith-based transnational feminist networks' advocacy and activism. These networks draw on human rights discourse to advocate for women's well-being, understood in part as freedom from domestic violence and impoverishment. A feminist analysis of neoliberal economic globalization undergirds their work. The conclusion analyzes the possibilities and limitations of the Millennium Development Goals to promote women's well-being, from the perspective of these networks.

## CHRISTIAN WOMEN'S ACTIVISM IN THE UNITED STATES AND BEYOND

### CONSERVATIVE CHRISTIAN ACTIVISM

We begin with Christian women's activism in the "religious right" in the United States. This movement first brought Christian women's activism into a prominent role in the political arena in the post–World War II period. Conservative women began to organize in response to the proposed Equal Rights Amendment (ERA), which Congress finally approved in 1972 for ratification by state legislatures, and the 1973 Supreme Court decision legalizing abortion. These women acted politically as moral agents to protect the gender roles that they believe are ordained by God. In their judgment, equal rights would undermine the sacred calling of motherhood.

In 1972 Phyllis Schafly, a Roman Catholic and political conservative, reorganized the work of her Eagle Forum to defeat the Equal Rights Amendment. The mission of the Eagle Forum "is to enable conservative and pro-family men and women to participate in the process of self-government and public policy making so that America will continue to be a land of individual liberty, respect for family integrity, public and private virtue, and private enterprise." The Eagle Forum is not explicitly religious; but its Web site does post this Bible verse: " *They that wait upon the Lord shall renew their strength, they shall mount up with wings as eagles, they shall run, and not be weary; and they shall walk and not faint.*' Isaiah 40:31." Schafly became a prominent leader in what she and others call the "pro-family" movement, and they have been influential in keeping the ERA from being ratified as part of the U.S. Constitution.[1]

Beverly LaHaye founded Concerned Women of America (CWA) in 1979, after hearing a television interview with Betty Friedan (a founder of the National Organization of Women). CWA states that it is based on "biblical values" and works to defend the traditional family. Other Christian conservative groups that identified as "pro-family" also organized in the late 1970s, including the American Family Association (Rev. Donald Wildmon) and Focus on the Family (James Dobson). The Council for National Policy (CNP), founded in May 1981 by the Rev. Tim LaHaye (Beverly's husband), T. Cullen Davis, and Nelson Bunker Hunt, is an umbrella group for religious conservatives, economic conservatives, and foreign policy conservatives. The CNP is committed to making the member's "shared moral values" dominant in domestic and foreign policy. One of the six permanent standing committees is "Family," co-chaired by James Dobson and Phyllis Schafly. Some studies indicate that religious conservatives are overwhelmingly women.[2] A survey by the Christian Coalition, founded in the late 1980s by Reverend Pat Robertson, indicated that about 62 percent of its membership in the 1990s was women, usually educated and middle class.[3] Women play active roles, both as leaders in the movement and as candidates for public office.

Most religious conservatives believe that the two-parent heterosexual family with children, husband as breadwinner, and wife as homemaker, is ordained by God. Thus homosexuality and abortion, two primary targets of religious right political activity, are morally wrong as they subvert this model of gender and family. Sociologist Kristen Luker points out that "abortion strips the veil of sanctity from motherhood." If pregnancy is discretionary, "then motherhood has been demoted from a sacred calling to a job."[4] The traditional family is also a "kind of linchpin between Christian discipleship and American citizenship," according to Suzanne Holland, who interviewed members of Focus on the Family. The traditional family is a story with which religious conservatives can identify, sustain affective allegiance, and from which they can oppose the direction of society. Coherent stories are necessary for preserving faith and culture, and the traditional family serves this purpose for religious conservatives.[5]

Political scientists Mark Rozell and Clyde Wilcox state that the Christian Coalition achieved an unprecedented amount of power and legitimacy in U.S. politics after the election of a Republican majority in Congress in 1994. This transformation created problems for the religious right as it attempts to expand its appeal and keep its base politically mobilized, and for the Republican party, which needs to integrate social conservatives with libertarian members.[6] These difficulties have been apparent in recent elections, particularly when the Democrats regained the majority in Congress in 2006 and the 2008 presidential election. The religious right no longer seems to have the political clout it once did, although its agenda has made gains at local, state, and national levels. (There are also similar organizations in other countries, such as Australia and New Zealand.) Schafly and the Eagle Forum and LaHaye and Concerned Women of America are still active around these issues.

## LIBERAL AND PROGRESSIVE RELIGIOUS ACTIVISM

Religious groups that organized to counter the religious right—Call to Renewal and the Interfaith Alliance, among others—supported equal rights for women and men, egalitarian marriages, and single-parent families. The work of feminist and womanist theologians was influential for some members of these organizations. Feminist theologians such as Elisabeth Schüssler Fiorenza and Rosemary Radford Ruether had demonstrated that there is not one biblical model of the family, and that a few passages in the New Testament even seemed to be antifamily. Womanist theologian Delores Williams challenged those who call themselves Christian to be in solidarity with suffering black people who struggle for survival/quality of life, including those "living in dire poverty, the poverty-stricken single parent trying to raise children."[7] However, these progressive groups did not address reproductive issues since members did not agree on them.

The Religious Coalition for Reproductive Choice (RCRC), an interfaith organization based in Washington, DC, was founded in 1973 after the bishops of the Roman Catholic Church pledged to overturn the *Roe v. Wade* Supreme Court decision legalizing abortion. Its founders included prochoice clergy who had first organized in 1967 as the Clergy Consultation Service on Abortion. RCRC's motto is "pro-faith, pro-family, and pro-choice"; one of its campaigns is called "Trust Women." In addition to advocacy to "preserve reproductive choice," RCRC offers faith-based sexuality education for youth and compassionate clergy counseling. Since abortion continues to be controversial in many Protestant congregations, some of the RCRC members are women's caucuses from denominations who are not pro-choice. RCRC is also an interracial organization and has an ongoing "Black Church Initiative."[8]

Beverly W. Harrison, a feminist Christian ethicist, argued in her 1983 book, *Our Right to Choose*, that women's ability to control their reproductive power, including access to legal abortion, is foundational to women's well-being and full life. Harrison pointed out that those who opposed legalized abortion were once again challenging "women's competence as moral decision makers." She declared that although all should honor the principle of respect for human life, we need to recognize that frequently this principle conflicts with other applicable moral values when making actual decisions. Other concepts are needed in facilitating decision making between two intrinsic values: prenatal or fetal life and the pregnant woman's life.[9] Harrison concludes that although procreative choice is a moral good, resorting to abortion—although permissible—is never a desirable means of expressing procreative choice. Thus social policies that reduce the need for abortion, including access to safe, effective, and affordable contraception, are advocated. This position is shared by RCRC and CFFC.

Catholics for a Free Choice (CFFC), also based in Washington, DC, emerged out of a 1970 New York lobby group—Catholics for the Elimination of All Restrictive Abortion & Contraceptive Laws. Three women—Joan Harriman, Patricia Fogarty McQuillan, and Meta Mulcahy founded CFFC. Joseph O'Rourke, its first president, was expelled from the Jesuits and the priesthood in 1974 for his involvement in CFFC. He continued to serve as president until 1979. Frances Kissling served as president for a quarter of a century (1982–2007). She was instrumental in helping found reproductive rights organizations in Latin America (Catolicas por el Derecho a Decidir [CFCC-CCD], in Bolivia, Brazil, Mexico, Colombia, Chile, and Argentina) and having *Our Right to Choose* translated into Spanish. Catholic feminist theologian and activist Rosemary Ruether writes that CFCC-CCD is a network of mostly Catholic women inspired by a feminist rereading of Catholicism "who critique the dominant sexual ethics of the Catholic church, and lobby for legalization of abortion, accessible family planning, sexual education, and reproductive health."[10] Their journal, *Conscience*, and its independent Spanish-language counterpart, *Conciencia*, deconstructs patriarchal sexual oppression of women and offers a vital understanding of healthy sexuality and just human relationships. The CFCC-CCD network is a good example of transnational religious activism. The next section explores Roman Catholic and ecumenical transnational activism in relation to women's moral agency and socioeconomic well-being.

## TRANSNATIONAL RELIGIOUS ACTIVISM ON GENDER AND SOCIETY

In his book *Global Religions*, sociologist Mark Juergensmeyer helpfully explains that religion is "the cultural expression of people's sense of ultimate significance," that these cultural elements move as people move, and that they intermingle and evolve over time just like people do. He identifies three types of global religions—global diasporas like Judaism and Hinduism, the religion of globalization and plural societies, and transnational religions such as Buddhism, Christianity, and Islam. Transnational religions are open to converts and spread with the transnational acceptance of their religious ideas. An examination of the relationship of these religions and state power suggests that the same Christianity, Buddhism, and Islam that legitimates a supportive ideology for some rulers serve as resistance or rebellion for others.[11] Organized religions have provided infrastructure and funds to facilitate development of transnational networks. Religious traditions also provide cultural resources for social movements—identity, sense of community, narratives, music—as was evident in the U.S. civil rights movement.

In this section we examine how Christianity both legitimates and resists certain gender identities and economic policies in the international arena. As we will see, United Nations conferences have been a primary site for contesting different visions. As case studies, our focus is the Roman Catholic Church, the world's largest Christian denomination with over one billion members around the globe, and the World Council of Churches, the world's largest ecumenical organization with over 340 member denominations representing over 560 million Christians from 110 countries. To understand their involvement in international political activism adequately, one needs a grasp of the structure and polity of these organizations.

The World Council of Churches [WCC] is a "fellowship of churches" established in 1948 and based in Geneva, Switzerland, whose members are from Orthodox, Protestant, and Pentecostal traditions. (Although the Roman Catholic Church is not a member, it works cooperatively with the WCC on some programs.) A Central Committee, made up of representatives from its member churches, governs the WCC. The supreme legislative body is the Assembly of delegates from member churches, held every seven years for program review, policymaking, and worship. The Assembly elects the Central Committee and the presidents of the WCC. The Central Committee appoints the General Secretary. The WCC has consultative status at the United Nations.

The Roman Catholic Church, a much older body, structured differently, is hierarchical and patriarchal. The Pope, who is also the Bishop of Rome, is the highest visible authority in matters of faith, morals, and Church governance. Governing bodies include the College of Cardinals, who elect the pope; regional and national conferences of bishops; and councils called by the pope. The most recent council was the Second Vatican Council (1962–1965). The Pope appoints cardinals and bishops from the priesthood, which is limited to men. Since the Vatican (the location of the papacy) is a state, it is eligible to be a member state of the United Nations—but chooses instead to have permanent observer status, with voice but not vote. The Vatican has played a leading role on family and reproductive issues in this arena. However, Catholic networks like CFFC-CDD have advocated for women's reproductive rights and the Center for Concern (discussed later) has advocated for women's concerns on human rights and socioeconomic issues. Both are nongovernmental organizations (NGOS) with representation at the United Nations.

## ROMAN CATHOLIC PAPAL TEACHING

Modern Catholic social teaching originated with the Papal Encyclical *Rerum Novarum* (The Condition of Labor) issued by Pope Leo XIII in 1891. Affirmation of equal dignity of women and men has been part of this teaching since Pius XI (1930s), yet never without qualification. Kathryn Pauly Morgan, a Canadian philosopher, identifies four "maneuvers" in ethical theory and moral practice which limit women's moral agency and are helpful for reflecting on Catholic thought. The first questions women's capacity for full moral agency through analyses of the concept of human nature. Theories are generated "about the nature of women which claim that women differ from men either in degree or kind such that women are not entitled to full moral agency."[12] This maneuver is common in Catholic teaching on the family. More recent teaching has moved beyond the difference in degree characteristic of Thomas Aquinas, who claimed that "woman is defective and misbegotten" and therefore "naturally subject to man, because in man the discretion of reason predominates."[13] However, claims continue to be made about the special vocation of women to motherhood. Pope John Paul II issued *Mulieris Dignitatem* (On the Dignity and Vocation of Women) in 1988; in it he maintains a difference in kind which tends to deny women full moral agency.

A brief review of some of the main points of this papal letter illustrates this maneuver and more clearly shows how notions of femininity limit women's moral agency. John Paul affirms the mutuality and equality of male and female, but he also maintains the notion "that dignity and vocation result from the specific diversity and personal originality of man and woman." "Consequently, even the rightful opposition of women to what is expressed in the biblical words 'he shall rule over you' (GN 3:16) must not under any condition lead to the 'masculinization' of women." John Paul defines femininity as *receiving* so as to *give* of self, always in response to the love of God or of husband. (This understanding of femininity and motherhood as "receiving" also informs Catholic teaching against artificial contraception.) John Paul also claims this notion as the basis for denying women ordination to the priesthood, as they cannot represent Christ who *first* gave of *himself*.[14] Interestingly, both Jesus and women give of themselves but since John Paul focuses on the maleness of Jesus, he insists that men are to take initiative, as Jesus did. Women give, as Jesus did, but since they are female, he asserts that they are not to take initiative. Thus, women's full moral agency is limited due to her "difference in kind" from men.

CATHOLIC WOMEN'S ACTIVISM

Although some Catholic women accept this view of femininity and mother-hood, other Catholic women are challenging the denial of their full moral agency and personhood. A group of Peruvian women spoke out on the occasion of the visit of John Paul II to Peru. They represent many other women when they insist that:

> A woman's dignity resides in the fact that she is a human being, graced by God with the potential for realizing herself fully as a person. This self-realization must not be limited to her maternal role. The very fact that we can be mothers demands that we be given every opportunity to develop ourselves as persons.[15]

These women also called on the church to challenge patriarchy and sexism: being faithful to a commitment for the poor, the church must speak out about women's great suffering and exploitation The church must deal with the sins of patriarchy, controlling rule over women, sexism, and bias against women because they are women, which touches upon societal structures, one's interpersonal relationships, and the church's institutional shortcomings with the Christian commitment for human liberation.

The reflections of these Peruvian women are an example of what Rose-mary Radford Ruether calls "small alternative networks that are often critical of the dominant tradition, yet also envision a liberating rereading of it." Ruether notes that religion inspires these women to resist oppression and create alternatives. The CFFC-CDD network discussed earlier is one example Ruether gives, as are the members of religious orders in Latin America who are inspired by liberation theology to help create cooperatives. This form of activism is not oriented toward politics and public policy but creating socioeconomic alternatives to enhance well-being. Ruether writes from her own experience in Central America about Nicaraguan women who formed cooperatives like the Association of Rural Women Workers of Chinandega and the Multiple Services Cooperative of Masaya. These cooperatives provide credit and other services, such as land titling and the teaching of organic farming methods. The leaders bring together Catholic and evangelicals, although the groups claim no official religious identity. Both Catholic and Protestant groups "sympathetic to liberation thought" have been helpful. For instance, in many regions of Nicaragua, Maryknoll nuns live in small communal groups and help poor women launch small cooperatives for natural medicines, raising chickens, and so forth. Ruether notes that help from outside groups—international NGOs and church-sponsored groups—who provide starter funds, skill training, and technical aid, is essential. They create a network of mutual aid and help make it possible for local cooperative leaders to attend international meetings like the UN Women's conference in Beijing in 1995.[16]

The Global Women's Project of the Center of Concern (COC) in Washington, DC, has also played an important role in bringing women's perspectives to United Nations' conferences. The Center itself was founded as a joint initiative of the U.S. Conference of Catholic Bishops and the Society of Jesus (Jesuits) after the 1971 Rome Synod of Bishops issued "Justice in the World." COC is international in perspective, ecumenical and interfaith in outlook, and autonomous in structure. COC studies issues relating to development, justice, and peace from a Christian perspective and works with various UN agencies. The Global Women's Project was started in 1974, under the leadership of Maria Riley, to prepare for the 1975 UN International Women's Year Conference. The project is committed to analyzing current economic policies critically and advocating for changes that are more socially just, with an emphasis on women's human rights and equity. The Project engages in research, theological reflection, outreach, advocacy, popular education, and coalition building. In 1999, COC helped launch the International Gender and Trade Network, whose research and advocacy has been crucial for the global justice movement. COC is a good example of how some religious organizations use their networks and resources to support the growth of transnational feminist networks.[17]

## WORLD COUNCIL OF CHURCHES SOCIAL TEACHING

The World Council of Churches (WCC) is a transnational religious community, whose members share a broad religious tradition. With the formation of the WCC in 1948, women's participation in the ecumenical movement became an agenda item. However, it was presumed in the Council's early social teaching that economic reality was the same for both women and men and that the normative changes toward economic justice would affect them equally. Thus any roots of women's oppression in her capacity to bear children or the assumed "naturalness" of childrearing and domestic labor as women's role were not analyzed. Consequently, women's double work day, occupational segregations, and other specific aspects of women's economic vulnerability were not addressed. These presuppositions distort women's moral agency through the invisibility of moral domains, another maneuver identified by Kathryn Morgan. She points to maternal practice and domestic labor as two of the domains in women's lives, arenas rarely respected as having moral value and import.[18] Women's experience remained invisible in social teaching until the 1968 assembly, when discrimination against women was first acknowledged in a social justice context.

Some Protestant and Orthodox churches sacralized traditional family relations, as did papal teaching. There was a tendency not to treat family relations as an arena of justice. For Protestants, this is grounded in a private/ public dichotomy characteristic of liberalism. In this view, the public sphere is the realm of justice, the private the realm of love. This dichotomy results in a romanticization and mystification of the family. This is a variation of another maneuver Morgan describes, that of assigning women to "the private sphere" and then asserting that "the public sphere" is the sphere of true morality. (The Council seems to presume this, rather than directly asserting it.) Further, until the emergence of feminist theology, theological anthropology, a religious understanding of what it means to be human, was grounded in male experience.

## WOMEN'S ACTIVISM IN THE WCC

A WCC consultation on "Sexism in the 1970s: Discrimination against Women" was held in 1974, with 170 women from 50 countries participating. This event brought feminist theologies into the life and work of the WCC. The findings and recommendations of the consultation were brought to the 1975 WCC Assembly in Nairobi, Kenya. The Assembly described sexism, racism, and economic structures as structures of injustice which must be changed. The actions of the Assembly had also been influenced by work begun during the UN International Women's Year in 1975.

The WCC participated in the activities of the UN Decade for Women (1975–85), launched during International Women's Year. The Decade themes were equality, development and peace—principles which the WCC also supported. At the 1985 End-of the-Decade Conference and Forum in Nairobi, Kenya, the WCC hosted a hospitality center. They also sponsored a workshop on "Women and World Religions" and published a book with chapters written by women scholars from these religions. All the scholars found liberatory aspects in their traditions early on, followed by patriarchalization—that reinstated the rule of men over women.

The Ecumenical Decade for the Churches in Consultation with Women (1988–98) was launched as a follow-up to the UN Decade. Its goals were:

1. Empowering women to challenge oppressive structures in the global community, their country and their church
2. Affirming—through shared leadership and decision-making, theology and spirituality—the decisive contributions of women in churches and communities
3. Giving visibility to women's perspectives and actions in the work and struggle for justice, peace, and the integrity of creation

4. Enabling the churches to free themselves from racism, sexism, and classism [acts of oppression due to race, gender, and lack of status/wealth]; from teachings and practices that discriminate against women
5. Encouraging the churches to take actions in solidarity with women[19]

Regional consultations were held during the decade; international teams also delivered "Living Letters" to most regions.

The decade culminated with a celebration in Harare, Zimbabwe, in November of 1998, preceded by "Women-to-Women" visits to several African countries. Over 1,000 women and about a dozen men participated in the event. Plenary sessions included a hearing on violence against women within churches. Participants wrote and sent a letter to the upcoming WCC Assembly, which identified areas of concern they wanted the Assembly to address. The letter began with a statement of commitment: "Together we seek to live out the biblical affirmation that we are created in the image of God, male and female (Gen 1:27), and the baptismal vision that 'There is no longer Jew or Greek, there is no longer slave or free, there is no longer male and female, for all of you are one in Christ Jesus'" (Gal 3:28). Among the requests to the Assembly were that it announce "to the world that violence against women is a sin," demand the cancellation of the debt of the poorest countries, "maintain a strong commitment to eradicate racism," and work for "the creation of just economic systems and just structures in church and society so that women and men together may know the blessings of justice, equal pay for equal work, sustainable and livable wages, and honourable labour practices."[20] The WCC continues to work on these issues through various programs, including "Women in Church and Society."

## Ecumenical Association of Third World Theologians (EATWOT)

A critical evaluation of scripture, theology, ethics, church history, ministry, liturgy and other areas of religious teaching and practice from a gender perspective was first undertaken in the 1970s and 80s by feminist and womanist scholars and activists from the global north, including ones mentioned in this chapter. Women theologians and activists from the global south also began to meet together and publish their work. Women from Africa, Asia, and Latin America met with the Ecumenical Association of Third World Theologians (EATWOT).

EATWOT describes itself as an association of men and women committed to the struggle for the liberation of Third World peoples, by promoting new models of theology for social justice, religious pluralism, and peace. EATWOT members take their third-world context seriously, and do theology "from the vantage point of the poor seeking liberation, integrity of creation, gender co-responsibility, racial and ethnic equality and interfaith dialogue."[21] EATWOT began in 1976 in Tanzania, when 22 representatives from Africa, Asia, and Latin America, and one black theologian from the United States met at Dar-es Salaam for an "Ecumenical Dialogue of Third World Theologians" to share theological efforts in their denominations—Catholic, Orthodox, and Protestant.[22]

EATWOT women held their first intercontinental conference in the late 1980s and claimed theologizing as a way in which women struggle for their right to life, to liberation from oppression. "Spiritual experience rooted in action for justice" is an integral part of their theologizing. The conference's final document focuses on life and merits citing rather fully:

> The passionate and compassionate way in which women do theology is a rich contribution to theological science. The key to this process is the word LIFE. We perceived that in the three continents women are deeply covenanted with life, giving and protecting life. . . . In doing theology, we in the Third World find ourselves committed and faithful to all the vital elements that compose human life. Thus without losing its scientific seriousness, which includes analyzing the basic causes of women's multiple oppression, our theologizing is deeply rooted in experience, in affection, in life. We as women feel called to do scientific theology passionately, a theology based on feeling as well as knowledge, on wisdom as well as science, a theology made not only with the mind but also with the heart, the body, the womb.[23]

The goal of theologizing "is to bring a new dimension to the struggle for justice and for promoting God's reign."[24] Their profound insights were a significant contribution to the development of a spirituality and theology of life, which was also developed by the World Council of Churches. Mercy Amba Oduyoye was a leader in both EATWOT and the WCC.[25] The EATWOT women's intercontinental conference is an example of a transnational feminist network. The next section examines networks that primarily draw on human rights discourse to advocate for women's well-being.

## TRANSNATIONAL FEMINIST (AND OTHER) NETWORKS

According to Valentine Moghadam, transnational feminist networks (TFNs) are structures that bring together women from three or more countries targeting shared agendas; for example, violence against women, women's human rights, and women's reproductive health and rights. TFNs work with each other and with other transnational organizations focused on labor, human rights, social justice, and the environment to bring a feminist perspective and to influence policy-making. Moghadam suggests that TFNs' call for gender and economic justice, along with taking seriously gender relations when opting for an alternative macroeconomic framework, is a distinct contribution. Moghadam describes the work of these networks as beginning with formation or activation of or joining with global networks to organize pressure outside state structures and then to participate in intergovernmental and multilateral political arenas. TFNs interact with these organizations to bring up new issues, particularly gender perspectives on trade and macroeconomics, and women's human rights, and also to impact policy.[26] In this section the focus is Christian women's participation in TFNs working on women's rights and socioeconomic issues.

## Human Rights Activism

After the conclusion of the UN Women's Decade in 1985, some TFNs focused their activism in international forums on gaining recognition that human rights are women's rights and women's rights are human rights. The 1993 World Conference on Human Rights issued the Vienna Declaration, which was a major milestone for women's human rights activists. Article 18 declared that "The human rights of women and of the girl-child are an inalienable, integral and indivisible part of universal human rights." The conference also recognized violence against women as a violation of human rights. This recognition resulted from the efforts of many women's organizations that brought petitions from 124 countries bearing half a million signatures demanding that gender violence be recognized as a violation of human rights. Various religious organizations contributed to this effort. For instance, the World Council of Churches sponsored a meeting of Asian lawyers and human-rights activists which pressed for an Asian Commission on Women's Human Rights to offer a feminist perspective on women's human-rights violations, including domestic violence and the impoverishment of women.[27]

Akua Kuenyehia, dean of the Faculty of Law at the University of Ghana, points out that the struggle for basic needs and subsistence is the struggle for dignity of the great majority of African women. This struggle is firmly situated in a context of cultural and economic domination and within an international system whose allocation of resources is unjust and inequitable. She argues that issues such as poverty and disease must be addressed within the context of human rights discourse. Furthermore, she points out that structural adjustment programs violate the social and economic rights of women. For example, Article 25 of the 1948 UN Declaration of Human Rights states, "Everyone has the right to a standard of living adequate for the health and well-being of self and family, including food, clothing, housing, medical care and necessary social services." Kuenyehia concludes that strategic alliances with other regional groups in the global women's movement have been very beneficial in the effort to challenge these rights violations.[28]

Structural adjustment programs were on the agenda of the 1985 UN Women's Conference and Forum. In the workshops on development, women from Africa, Asia, and Latin America reported how these programs that had been imposed by the World Bank and International Monetary Fund (IMF) as conditions for loans were increasing the suffering of people in their countries. A typical program required countries to orient their agriculture and other production for export. This ensured that countries would earn foreign currency to repay their loans. But it also meant that land, previously used for domestic food consumption, was now used to grow crops like coffee and cocoa for export. Countries were also required to open their markets to international corporations and change trade policies which favored their own producers. This requirement contributed to job loss, as it was difficult for local producers to compete with large foreign corporations. Another requirement was the privatization of state owned concerns, which meant that income from these industries now went to private corporations rather than the public budget. Deregulation—removing worker and environmental protections—was also required. In addition, countries were required to cut social spending on education and health care.[29]

These policies led to dramatic drops in living standards. Malnutrition and child mortality rates increased. Health care was unaffordable for many families. Children—particularly girls—left school as their families could not afford the fees. Women's burdens increased as their hours of unpaid work lengthened to help their families survive. These economic policies, often called neoliberalism, dominate the process of economic globalization. Neoliberalism looks to private capital and free markets to allocate resources and promote growth. Overall, these policies have widened the gap between the wealthy and poor both within and between countries, exploited the earth's resources at an unsustainable rate, and increased pollution and social exclusion. A sobering statistic is that the income of the richest 1 percent of the global population is equal to that of the poorest 57 percent, and at least 26,000 people die every day from poverty and malnutrition.[30] The International Monetary Fund, World Bank, and the World Trade Organization—key actors in setting the rules for the global economy—contend that they are not bound by Conventions on Human Rights. The global justice movement and transnational feminist networks charge that this stance undermines commitment to and enforcement of human rights and are campaigning for these organizations to recognize their obligation to adhere to human rights agreements.

## WOMEN AND GLOBALIZATION PROJECT (WCC)

Economic globalization has been a particular focus of the World Council of Churches since 1998, when delegates to the WCC Eighth Assembly called on the ecumenical community to address and remedy the suffering globalization was causing their communities. The WCC held several regional consultations on economic globalization, in conjunction with the World Alliance of Reformed Churches and Lutheran World Federation. The consultations included representatives from member churches, other religious traditions, and experts from transnational global justice organizations focused on trade and debt. This process—Alternative Globalization Addressing Peoples and Earth—culminated in the *AGAPE Background Document* and the *AGAPE Call to Love and Action*, which articulated a theological rationale based on the central concern for social justice in Jewish and Christian scriptures. The document also presented elements of a life-giving economy: just trade and finance; debt cancellation and reparations, support for and development of alternatives based on cooperation.[31]

The Women and Globalization Programme (WGP) was established in 2002, to bring women's perspectives to WCC work on economic globalization. This program held several consultations with representatives from member churches and transnational feminist networks. Athena Peralta, an economist and staff for the WGP, produced a document, *A Caring Economy: A Feminist Contribution to Alternatives to Globalization Addressing People and Earth,* which drew on these consultations to present a vision, analysis, and strategies. Peralta demonstrated that women are disproportionately burdened by negative impacts of neoliberal economic globalization, which exploit the underpaid market labor of women and their unpaid domestic work. She noted that a crucial methodological principle of feminist economics is that this unpaid domestic labor, which maintains human life outside of the market, is vital to any economic system. The document presents principles of a caring economy articulated by feminist theologians, economists, and activists during a 2003 consultation. These include "provision of basic needs for all, women and men"; "caring and care work are made visible, (re)valued, (re)affirmed, (re)produced and (re)distributed equitably by both women and men"; and "an economy where all human rights—including women's economic, social and cultural rights—are upheld and protected." Peralta concludes that "the major challenge for churches and feminist movements is not only to make the care economy visible and valuable, but also, and more importantly, to make justice, sustainability, and caring for life the starting point for economic theory and practice."[32]

The Women and Globalization Programme cohosted an "Ecumenical Women's Forum for Life-Promoting Trade" (Protestant, Orthodox,

Catholic) in conjunction with the World Trade Organization Ministerial Meeting in Hong Kong, December 2005. The 70 participants came from 27 countries and from various faith communities and traditions. This forum was a part of the "People's Action Week on WTO—Ensure People's Livelihood, Security, and Dignity." Thousands of people—farmers, students, workers, human rights advocates, and religious activists—came from around the world for education, advocacy, and action against unjust trade rules. The International Gender and Trade Network was heavily involved in the week's activities. Several IGTN members also spoke at the Ecumenical Forum. Since it was first organized in 1999, the IGTN has produced in-depth analyses of trade policy from a gender perspective and advocates for more just policies at WTO Ministerial Meetings and other trade negotiations.

Forum participants wrote and sent a letter to Pascal Lamy, World Trade Organization Director-General, dated December 15, 2005, that begins by affirming that their Christian identity and commitments view social justice as crucial. They then address various trade rules and negotiations—the Agreement on Agriculture, the General Agreement on Trade and Services—drawing in part on the work of IGTN. This is followed by a critique of WTO trade rules:

> Driven by the free market ideology and the profit imperative, the WTO's trade rules shrink democratic space and processes leading to growing trade inequalities as well as widening social disparities. Market contracts are superimposed on social contracts and corporate interests are translated into international law which has become increasingly de-linked from human rights. Thereby, the WTO undermines the fullness of life for all. It denies the theological covenant among peoples, communities and the earth, serving instead the interests of transnational capital and corporations.[33]

The letter concludes with a statement of faith: "We believe that God created all human beings with dignity, respect, and equality. We uphold the principle of life-promoting trade, which is in harmony with social justice and the empowerment of peoples and respects the diversity of global communities."[34] During demonstrations, forum participants carried a colorful banner they had made, which portrays a world filled with life and the words "No to the WTO! Yes to Life!" superimposed on it. This banner reflects the spirituality and theology of life first articulated by EATWOT women at their intercontinental conference some years earlier. Transnational feminist networks continue to nurture and support each other in the struggle for gender and social justice.

## CONCLUSION: GENDER AND THE MILLENNIUM DEVELOPMENT GOALS

The Millennium Development Goals (MDGs) are the focus of international efforts to reduce poverty, disease, and environmental degradation in the 21st century. Several of the goals directly or indirectly affect women's equality, agency, and well-being and thus are of concern for Christian women; notably the teachings of Jesus to feed the hungry, clothe the naked, and provide shelter for the homeless; the edict to love thy neighbor, and the Golden Rule. The goals were issued by the Millennium Assembly, held at the United Nations in September 2000, the largest gathering of world leaders in history with 189 countries present. The Millennium Declaration stated eight goals. The first goal is to reduce by half the proportion of people living in extreme hunger and poverty by 2015, with 1990 levels as the baseline. The other goals are to achieve universal primary education, promote gender equality and empower women, reduce child mortality, improve maternal health, combat HIV/AIDS, malaria and other diseases, and ensure environmental sustainability—all through creating "a global partnership for development."[35] The MDGs have been endorsed by many churches and ecumenical agencies, including the National Council of Churches of the USA. Aruna Gnanadason, former director of the WCC women's program, has pointed out that the goals directly or indirectly affect women and are worthy of support. However, some Christian women activists see a need for expansion and critique of the MDGS, particularly since they have become the central focus for gender and social justice work.

Critics have pointed out that there is no mention of jobs or livelihoods as part of the goals, which is rather surprising with the emphasis on reducing extreme poverty. This lack is of concern to the Women and Globalization Programme of the WCC, which draws on the work of international organizations and feminist economics for its criticisms and constructive proposal. The International Labour Organization reported in 2005 that "global economic growth is increasingly failing to translate into new and better jobs that lead to a reduction in poverty."[36] There is a growing campaign to focus alternative economic policies on "decent work" for all who want it. Decent work includes adequate remuneration, dignity, security, and social protection. Diane Elson, a feminist economist and member of Women in Development in Europe, proposes expanding the idea of "decent work" to "include unpaid, non-market work and to address the obstacles that women with caring responsibilities face in taking up opportunities for decent paid work."[37] Unpaid, non-market work includes care work and subsistence agriculture—most of which is done by women, often included in the concept of social reproduction. "Decent jobs, emancipated work, and people's livelihoods" are among the actions advocated in the WCC AGAPE document. The WGP's proposal for a caring economy (discussed in the previous section) advocates for recognition and valuing unpaid care work, grounded in feminist theological and ethical perspectives.

The International Interfaith Network for Development and Reproductive Health, organized by Catholics for a Free Choice (CFFC), raised other concerns about the MDGs in a pamphlet: "A Faith-Filled Commitment to Development Includes a Commitment to Women's Rights and Reproductive Health: Religious Reflections on the Millennium Development Goals," which was prepared for the 2005 World Summit. The Network strongly endorses the MDGs and offers support from the world's faiths and traditions for each of the eight goals. (Liberal and progressive Christian activism is often carried out as part of interfaith networks when addressing international issues.) However, it notes that there are limits to the MDGs and asks whether cutting poverty in half and achieving universal primary education are "really enough." They point out that "the role that peace and anti-militarism play in the struggle against poverty" needs attention since "too much of the world's resources are consumed fighting unjust wars." The main concern, though, is evident in the title of the reflections: women's rights and reproductive health. The Network is committed "to the inclusion in the MDG mindset of universal access to freely chosen reproductive health services, and . . . *the right to determine freely and responsibly the number and the spacing of children.*" The statement recalls that this human right was articulated at the 1969 International Conference on Human Rights in Tehran and restated at the 1994 International Conference on Population and Development (ICPD) in Cairo.[38]

The aforementioned 2005 statement notes that the MDGs do not speak about family planning or reproductive health and rights, which are of immense significance for poverty reduction and of special concern to faith and traditional communities. Although the statement does not explicitly analyze the sources of this silence, it is clear that it comes mainly from the opposition to reproductive rights of (1) the Roman Catholic Church, which, as the Vatican state, is a permanent observer with voice at the United Nations; from (2) some Muslim countries (although contraception is not prohibited in Islam); and (3) from Christian conservative religious activists discussed earlier. The "Religious Reflections" statement does note that although religions and traditions are not monolithic, they share a common moral concern for the most vulnerable. It regards religion as a positive force which can promote peace, justice, and human rights, but also recognize that religious extremism can be a force to crush peace, justice, and human rights. Religious conservatives would likely reject the implicit charge that they are religious extremists.

Clearly there continues to be competing visions of women's equality, moral agency, and well-being. The Equal Rights Amendment to the U.S. Constitution has failed, primarily because of conservative Christian opposition. Reproductive rights, particularly legalized abortion, are still a contentious issue in the United States and internationally as is evident in their absence in the MDGs. Roman Catholics and other Christians base their opposition to reproductive rights on the authority of scripture and tradition. Those who support women's equality and reproductive rights offer different interpretations of these sources. They also ground their support in human rights discourse, where authority is based on philosophical reasoning and democratic political processes. The debate on how to promote socioeconomic well-being is unsettled. The worldwide financial and economic crises, which began in late 2008, may undermine support for neoliberal economic policies. Those who advocate socioeconomic alternatives are hopeful that a space has opened for consideration of their proposals. Although many men are suffering from these crises, there is solid evidence that women, and by default, often their children, around the world bear the brunt of the burden of providing for the well-being of their families through their underpaid and unpaid labor.

There is an emerging consensus among many scholars and activists that women's equality and rights promote not only women's well-being but also that of families and communities around the globe. Maria Riley of the Center of Concern Global Women's Project expressed this perspective eloquently in 1988: "Our only hope for a transformed and whole/holy humanity lies in the ability of our creative imaginations and political wills to develop a world structured on the mutuality of all human persons, women and men together."[39]

## NOTES

1. Eagle Forum Web site, www.eagleforum.org, accessed May 20, 2008.

2. Skipp Porteous, "Reshaping America: CNP Instrumental in Government Shutdown," *Freedom Writer Magazine,* Institute for First Amendment Studies, 1996; Council for National Policy, Sourcewatch: A Project of the Center for Media and Democracy, http://www.sourcewatch.org/index.php?title=Council_for_National_Policy, accessed May 20, 2008. According to this Web site, Schafly was one of the speakers at the 2006 CNP meeting. The CNP is a private organization and seldom releases information about its membership or activities.

3. Ralph Reed, *Politically Incorrect: The Emerging Faith Factor in American Politics,* Eagen, MN: Word Publishing, 1994, 225.

4. Kristen Luker, *Abortion and the Politics of Motherhood,* University of California Press, 1984, 205. Luker found that some of the women who participate

in the anti-abortion movement are motivated by a concern for maintaining their ability to rely on men (husbands) to support their social roles as mothers.

5. Suzanne Holland, "Discipleship and Citizenship in the Religious Right: Family as Linchpin," Unpublished manuscript, delivered at the Society for the Social Scientific Study of Religion, October 29, 1995.

6. Mark J. Rozell and Clyde Wilcox, "Second coming: The strategies of the new Christian Right," *Political Science Quarterly* (Summer 1996), 271–94.

7. Delores Williams, *Sisters in the Wilderness: The Challenge of Womanist God-Talk,* Maryknoll, NY: Orbis Books, 1993, 201. Schüssler Fiorenza and Ruether have written many articles and books; two classic texts are Elisabeth Schüssler Fiorenza, *In Memory of Her: A Feminist Theological Construction of Christian Origins,* Crossroad, 1983, and Rosemary Radford Ruether, *Sexism and God Talk: Toward a Feminist Theology,* Boston: Beacon Press, 1983.

8. Information from RCRC Web site, www.rcrc.org, accessed May 21, 2008.

9. Beverly W. Harrison, *Our Right to Choose: Toward a New Ethic of Abortion,* Beacon Press, 1983; Beverly W. Harrison with Shirley Cloyes, "Theology and Morality of Procreative Choice," *Making the Connections: Essays in Feminist Social Ethics,* ed. Carol S. Robb, Boston: Beacon Press, 1985, 115, 128, 132.

10. Rosemary Radford Ruether, *Integrating Ecofeminism, Globalization and World Religions,* New York: Rowman and Littlefield, 2005, 159.

11. Mark Juergensmeyer, *Global Religions: An Introduction,* Oxford: Oxford University Press, 2003, 3, 5, 8.

12. Kathryn Pauly Morgan, "Women and Moral Madness," *Canadian Journal of Moral Philosophy,* Supplementary Volume 13: 201–26, nd, 204.

13. Thomas Aquinas, *Summa Theologica* I. 92. 1 and 2, ed. Father of the English Dominican Province, London: Burns, Oates and Washbourned, Ltd., 1914.

14. *Mulieris Dignitatem* (On the Dignity and Vocation of Women), August 15, 1988, para. 10, 11, 26–7, in *Origins* 18 (1988). This is similar to some conservative Protestant teaching. For instance, the Southern Baptist Convention amended its statement of faith to declare that wives are to gracefully submit to their husbands. In contrast, a statement by the U.S. Catholic Bishops called for mutual submission, a stance which was explicitly rejected by the Southern Baptist Convention.

15. "Reflections of Peruvian Women on the Occasion of the Visit of Pope John Paul II" (approved English translation), *Women in the Church,* The New LADOC 'Keyhole' Series, no. 2, Lima, Peru: Latin American Documentation, 1986, 2–3.

16. Ruether, 157–58. According to Ruether, the official Catholic Church of Nicaragua "has been of little help to the poor" and is tied to the neoliberal policies of post-Sandanista governments.

17. Information from the Center of Concern Web site, www.coc.org, accessed May 20, 2008.

18. Morgan, "Women and Moral Madness," 221.

19. Sub-unit on Women in Church and Society, *Ecumenical Decade 1988–1998: Churches in Solidarity with Women*, Geneva, Switzerland: World Council of Churches, 1998, 1.

20. The author participated in this event. "From solidarity to accountability," Letter to the Eighth Assembly of the World Council of Churches from the women and men of the Decade Festival of the Churches in Solidarity with Women, November 30, 1998, available at http://www.oikoumene.org/en/resources/documents/assembly/harare-1998/30-11-98-from-solidarity-to-accountability.html.

21. Information on EATWOT from their Web site, www.eatwot.org, accessed May 22, 2008.

22. Ibid.

23. "Final Document: Intercontinental Women's Conference," Virginia Fabella and Mercy Oduyoye, eds. *With Passion and Compassion: Third World Women Doing Theology*, Maryknoll, NY: Orbis Books, 1988, 186.

24. Ibid.

25. Mercy Amba Oduyoye, *Beads and Strands: Reflections of an African Woman on Christianity in Africa*, Maryknoll, NY: Orbis Books, 2004.

26. Valentine M. Moghadam, *Globalizing Women: Transnational Feminist Networks*, Baltimore, MD: John Hopkins University Press, 2005, 4, 13–14; the third activity of TFNs is to "act and agitate within states to enhance public awareness and participation," 14.

27. *Ecumenical Press Service*, Year 56/issue 03 (January 16–20, 1989) no. 51.

28. Akua Kuenyehia, "Economic and Social Rights of Women: A West African Perspective," *Common Ground or Mutual Exclusion: Women's Movements and International Relations*, eds., Marianne Braig and Sonja Wolte, 160–70, London: Zed Books, 2002.

29. Pamela K. Brubaker, *Globalization at What Price: Economic Change and Daily Life*, Cleveland, OH: Pilgrim Press, 2007, 33–35.

30. Branko Milanovic, *Economic Journal*, The Hunger Project, The United Nations, January 18, 2002.

31. *Alternative Globalization Addressing Peoples and Earth AGAPE: A Background Document*, Geneva, Switzerland: World Council of Churches, 2005.

32. Athena Peralta, *A Caring Economy: A Feminist Contribution to Alternatives to Globalisation Addressing Peoples and Earth*, Geneva, Switzerland: World Council of Churches, 2005, 55, 44, 50, 57; The Project on Global Working Families recently published the results of a decade of research that documents how serious the issue of care has become. They found that "[a]round the world, families are increasingly living on the edge" because of deteriorating working conditions. It has become increasing difficult or impossible for employed adults "to care for themselves and their families' health and well-being." (Jody Heymann, *Forgotten Families: Ending the Global Crisis Confronting Children and Working Families in the Global Economy*, Oxford: Oxford University Press, 2006, 189–90).

33. Ecumenical Women's Forum for Life-Promoting Trade, "Letter to Pascal Lamy, WTO Director, December 15, 2005, author's files. The author was a participant in the Forum.

34. Ibid.

35. UNDP, *Human Development Report 2003: Millennium Development Goals: a compact among nations to end poverty*, Oxford: Oxford University Press, 2003.

36. ILO Press Room, "Globalization Failing to create new, quality jobs or reduce poverty," December 9, 2005. According to its Web site, The International Labour Organization (ILO) is the tripartite UN agency that brings together governments, employers and workers of its member states in common action to promote decent work throughout the world, www.ilo.org.

37. Diane Elson, "Alternative Feminist Economics," WIDE-Network Women in Development, WIDE Annual Conference 2005, www.eurosur.org/wide/Structure/Elson.htm. "Full and productive employment and decent work for all" was eventually added to the targets for the goal of reducing extreme poverty and hunger. (United Nations Development Programme, *Millennium Development Goals*, http://www.undp.org/mdg/goal1.shtml, accessed August 20, 2009.) There is no mention, though, of including unpaid, nonmarket work as suggested by Elson.

38. International Interfaith Network for Development and Reproductive Health, "A Faith-Filled Commitment to Development Includes a Commitment to Women's Rights and Reproductive Health: Religious Reflections on the Millennium Development Goals," prepared for the 2005 World Summit, September 14–15, 2005, available at http://www.un-ngls.org/un-summit-interfaith.pdf. Catholics For a Free Choice acted as the secretariat for the International Interfaith Network for Development and Reproductive Health. The author of this chapter signed this statement but had no role in helping prepare it.

39. Maria Riley, "Women and Work: Linking Faith and Justice," *Women, Poverty and the Economy*, Geneva, Switzerland: World Council of Churches, 1988, 8.

# CHAPTER 6

# Oppression and Resistance: The Church, Women's Work, and the Struggle for Liberation

*Joan M. Martin*

For two millennia, Christian faith, teaching, practice, and tradition have been formidable forces in shaping women's experiences of work in the home and family, and labor in the marketplace. In every era, her place in society has structured her work from midnight to midnight in service to the family and market economy. In working in either sphere, women's demeanor and roles were circumscribed in patriarchal pronouncements by ecclesiastical authorities and the political-economic development of the times. These two dimensions have been intertwined through the ages: religious practice and theology, and the structuring of society.

This chapter broadly discusses the nature of women's moral agency as they have experienced work in sustaining livelihood for themselves, their families, and their communities. To do this, a Christian womanist/feminist ethic provides a methodological framework to privilege and centrally located women's lived experience of work and labor as the basis of this analysis. At the heart of discussion is the recognition that a Christian womanist/feminist ethic is a justice-seeking ethic. Further, this essay articulates notions and principles of a moral framework in solidarity with women's lived experience in the struggle for justice and dignity in work. In this context, "work" and "labor" are used as synonymously overarching terms for women's livelihood in the family, church, and society. The concept of "toil" underscores the nature of work, paid or unpaid, when it is invisible, unrecognized, unvalued, exploitative, and robs women of their full human equality and dignity in relation to the work of men.

## THE FOUNDATIONS OF MORAL AGENCY

Moral agency is one of *the* most important humanlike capacities: "it is the capacity to determine the quality and character of choices made in light of our understanding of what is good and right, bad of wrong."[1] Because moral agency assumes that morality is *always* a social activity—a dynamic between one's self and others—it is never a private or isolated activity, but decision-making and action by persons-in-community. This is why moral agency occurs as an organic dynamic involving all the elements of familial, religious, racial or ethnic, socioeconomic, political, gendered, educational, and cultural influences that shape who a person is and what she does in community; the community being the "place" where worldviews and perceptions (the shared values and corporate existence) give one the sense of "self, nature, the universe, and what we know constitutes 'truth, knowledge, and reality'"[2] For women, as for all people, moral agency and what it means is formed in the web of subjective experience that takes place in relation to objective, historical, structures and their operation. Moral agency is never abstract, but always concrete. Thus, this chapter will focus on women's work experienced in the family and marketplace.

### THE BIBLICAL WITNESS

For women in Christianity, the concept of the Bible as sacred scripture and a closed canon in Western Christendom has dominated interpretation and instruction in ethics, moral behavior, and notions of women's being and purpose; and has attested to principles of women's normative roles and expectations in the human community. As a patriarchal gendered, historical, and cultural production, the Bible has had the power to name the nature of women's moral being and action as being God-ordained and revealed in, and as, sacred scripture. In doing so, the multiple voices of women in the text were narrowly constructed, interpreted, and in many instances absent along with their moral agency. From diverse kinds of feminist/womanist voices, the challenge has been to wrestle with textual and theological processes of deconstruction, necessary retrieval of women in the text, and reconstruction of theologies and ethics from which to see women's moral agency in their lived experience. In seeking to understand the structural framework of women's work and labor, womanist/feminist ethics have had to develop appropriate tools for the hermeneutical task of presenting alternative ethical readings and strategies in making Christian ethics more fully faithful in light of women's experience as human experience.

In opposition to traditional interpretations of Christian biblical faith that begin with Creation as the ground for understanding the nature of God, human beings, and work, reconstructive traditions often begin with events of liberation. In asserting that black women bring lived experience to reading and interpreting Christian faith, womanist theologian Delores S. Williams argues that a critical point of liberation is the narrative of Hagar, the Egyptian slave to barren Sarah and concubine to Abraham. By doing so, moral agency is revealed in the "lived experiences of relation, loss, gain, faith, hope, celebration and defiance."[3] The text excavates the interlocking power of oppressive relations in the two narratives—difference in relations between women's work and women's social statuses in a conventional slave culture, difference in skin color and ethnic origin, difference in religious traditions, difference in relations to patriarchal power, and difference in the epiphanies of God that occur (Gen.16, 21). Resistance or 'push back' comes in black women's interpretation of Hagar, showing Hagar's moral agency of resistance in the narratives. Hagar's actions are for the survival of herself and her son. Williams's reading of Hagar thus counters, enriches, and stands as a corrective to the normative reading of the Exodus liberation struggles interpreted by black male hermeneutics as the dominant liberation tradition (led by Moses). Similarly, Williams's reading is also a critique of white Christian feminist readings that focus on Sarah. For Williams, this process is a deconstruction of normative readings that focus on either Abraham or Sarah and permits the retrieval of Hagar's experience, not only for "black women's discourse in black churches, but also [for bringing] black women's experience into the discourse of *all* Christian theology from which it has previously been excluded."[4] In Williams's reading of Hagar, God becomes known in an act of defiance, in the struggle to maintain a more sustaining quality of life and future for her son.

For ecofeminist theologian Dorothee Soëlle, liberation in Exodus precedes the Genesis 2 creation myth in order to draw a difference in the relationship between God the Creator, the earth creation, and humans, the created. Soëlle understands the Exodus tradition as the normative historical event that defines the nature of God, freedom, and liberation, and of the human experience of oppression and liberation. Her point is to challenge the traditional rendering that Genesis is the principle narrative signifying the absolutely transcendent God as Lord and subject while human beings are objects made from dust, Genesis 2. From this point of view, God's act in freeing the Israelites becomes the primary collective memory that always calls Israel back to be faithful in the Hebrew Scriptures. Soëlle, Carter Heyward, and other Christian feminists point toward a theology of "power-in-relation" where the normative affirmation of the split between God's absolute transcendence from human beings, and the creation is cast in a different light.[5] God, humans, and the creation participate together in doing the work of love, continuing liberation and creation begun in Exodus. Freedom comes with a call from God. Only from the point of view of Israel's memory of liberation, particularly when confronted with the Babylonian creation myths during its exile, can the people understand and create the myth of the one God's creation of the world and of humans, wherein "work" is a partnership with God, the meaning of the Latin term, "vocation."

Renita Weems reads the story Ruth and Naomi as a story of friendship between a younger and older widow, related by marriage and both bereaved; a rare and "welcome contrast to the more usual stories that portray women at odds with one another" or those of male friendships. Together, Ruth and Naomi struggle to determine how they will respond to the customs and conventions of their respective people regarding the fate of widowed women. They choose and act on a principle of female friendship. Yet, from a patriarchal worldview, Ruth and Naomi's friendship and the ethics therein, are only the prologue for the real business of survival in service to a customary patrimony and marriage that can be instruments later used in the fulfillment of divine promise. Finally, the "Virtuous Wife" (Prov. 31) is normatively portrayed as the ideal woman who can achieve everything at home and be an effective woman in commerce because she is filled with wisdom. Instead, some womanist/feminist scholars[6] explore the meaning that the woman is "Ruah" or "Sophia" that is, Wisdom, the female dimension of the divine in Hebrew Scripture and the Holy Spirit of the New Testament respectively. Interpreting "The Virtuous Wife" as such renders the Spirit of God, and therefore part of God's self and nature, as part of the divine image of God. Hence, the near absolute image of "God the Father" is transformed.

The traditional patriarchal reading of "women's work" in the New Testament depicts the conflict between Martha's preparing the house for Jesus's arrival and her sister Mary's intention which is to learn from Jesus (Luke 10). However, women do exhibit quite a deal of moral agency and leadership in the gospels as well as in the New Testament. Consider how the ritually "unclean" woman (Mark 5:25; Luke 8:43), who had been hemorrhaging for 12 years, inserted herself into the crowd of disciples around Jesus, and touched his clothes and was healed. This woman had been socially ostracized by her illness, but was willing to take risky action in approaching Jesus and stand up to claim responsibility for her actions. The "sinful" woman who appointed Jesus while he was at the Pharisee's home (Luke 7:36ff) and the Samaritan woman at the well (John 4) were among many women who took fearful yet bold action in encounters with Jesus. In these instances, Jesus reminds the disciples of the faith demonstrated and courage revealed by these women that cause them to act, and he unconditionally accepts.

In the earliest narratives of the Church, Christian faith and practice in homes were often depicted under the leadership of women such as Lydia, a businesswoman and worshipper of God, who deals in purple cloth, indicating that women attracted to the faith were dealers and traders in the marketplace (Acts 16); Nympha of Laodicea (Col. 4:55), and Euodia and Syntche who "labored with Paul" (Philipp. 4:2ff). The Apostle Paul praises women's leadership for their proclamation and fledgling church organization. For example, Prisca and her husband, Aquila, are instrumental in the correction of Apollos of Alexandria who sought to be a knowledgeable follower of Jesus (Act 18), and again in 1 Corinthians 16. Phoebe of Cenchreae is said to have been a deacon, in the manner of a preacher or minister as Paul calls himself, and not a deaconess (Rom. 16). Yet much scholarly debate and congregational preaching today still argues the meaning of "Women should be silent in the churches (1 Cor. 14) and the Household Codes that provide ethical instruct for social authority and obedient love" (Eph. 5; Cor. 3; Col. 3f; 1 Pet. 2). However, where women were granted teaching roles in the earliest Christian communities, these roles were eliminated in the era of the Church Fathers (the theologians of the Early Church and post New Testament period until the fifth century CE). Throughout most of scripture, women's actions as moral agents are the exception.

## BACKGROUND IN CHRISTIAN TRADITION

In the New Testament, God had become "embodied," in Jesus of Nazareth, a man whose ordinary everyday livelihood was that of a carpenter who lived "vocation" in mutual relationship with God and humankind. Again, God called people to faith most intimately and freely through Jesus. Yet the other powerful pull was the Greek worldview. In the gospels, the New Testament writers and the Early Fathers lived in a world dominated by the pervasive Greek dichotomy of mind and body, and by notions of work as a "curse," upon human life exemplified in the writings of Aristotle, Plato, and the Stoics. "The contemplative life of the mind—the most excellent and noblest of human potential—was the way in which humans came closest to the true form of the divine form. Work, the endless cycle of activity humans needed to preserve embodied life and existence, was the work of slaves, artisans, farmers, women, and children."[7] These two opposing views would reside in the Church until the Reformation, with the contemplative, "religious view" of calling or vocation being the priestly and monastic life, and the cycle of work necessary for bodily existence to become the life of work of the laity.

The view of women's nature as subordinate in church and society has been the dominant worldview. This "nature" has been viewed as fundamentally reproductive—in childbearing and rearing, in domicile caretaking (her own or that of another woman), and in feudalism's subsistence agriculture in the West. Yet part of the struggle to resist the demeaning and subordinate nature assigned to women was for women themselves to develop gradually and participate in sex-segregated ascetic and monastic movements, beginning in approximately in the fourth century.

To assist in understanding the relationship of this Christian tradition to the work and labor of women, the work of Christian feminist ethicists is instrumental in addressing the interrelated religious and social value-laden assumptions in Christian social ethics, social theory, and economic theory. Feminist ethicist Mary E. Hobgood examines the social [theory] models in Catholic thought[8] beyond those found within Scripture. The "natural law" tradition (theologically, God is the source of the moral law which governs the universe, God's will through God's revelation, nature, and human life) adapted from Stoic philosophy posits the existence of a universal and eternal law deducible from the operation of nature and available to all persons through the human "Reason."[9] "Reason" provides the means by which humans can discern the ethical framework present in the laws governing the natural world. This governing order offers a model for human social life. Translated, within the Church and Aquinas's thought, this model was an "organic" social theory based in natural law. It reasoned that "God intended the property and goods of the earth to be held in common by all people, although in reality the Church institutionally wanted more power over the rule of feudalism."[10] In its own way, fealty—loyalty sworn to a feudal lord by a tenant—was a common good structure of reciprocity and protection, although unequal and hierarchical in which women were socially and religiously subordinate.

This is a philosophical tradition that the Church imbued with a theological interpretation based on its understanding of eternal, divine revelation. Aquinas makes four presuppositions (among others) about women cogent to this discussion. First, Aquinas believes that the intentions of nature originate in God, who is its Creator, and as such when God created nature, God made not only the male but also the female. In Aquinas's words, "The principle constituent of God's image in man, mind (intellect) is to be found in both male and female. Created, male and female are made in God's image."[11] Second, Aquinas asserts that woman was necessarily created as a "helper" to man in the work of generation [of the species]. Interestingly enough, woman is not a "helpmate" to man. The "helpmate" role is reserved for other men since they can be more efficient in helping other men than can women.

Third, Aquinas insists that male and female both have reason or intellectual faculties because intellect is primary to the nature of God. However, man [the male] has greater reason and will than woman because woman was created for man, and not man for woman.[12] Here is Aquinas's biological hierarchy where woman, although created *imago dei*, is created with inequality that is intended by God to have been perfected in her reproduction purposes prior to the Fall. Based in part on this biological hierarchy, Aquinas makes the correlation that society is "hierarchically organized . . . *paternalistically benevolent* [italics mine], socially cooperative, and committed to the common good demanded by [feudal] hierarchy."[13]

There are two major figures of the Protestant Reformation, Martin Luther and John Calvin, in the 16th century, whose theology proposes an original, full equality between women and men. This made women "essentially" equal in human nature so far as the *imago dei* is concerned. Susan Parsons asserts, however, that for Luther and Calvin, sin resulting from the so-called Fall, which is really an expulsion, made full equality impossible.[14] She sees the difference in the two reformers' position hinging on the impact that the Fall had for the experience of women and men. "For Luther, woman's subjugation to man in the social world is justified as punishment for her sin; for Calvin, structures of subordination are ordered by God as the appropriate social order for a fallen world."[15]

Parsons recognizes the problem this creates in the Christian tradition for understanding women's nature, and therefore her role in society and her ability to be a moral agent. From Aquinas's viewpoint, marital companionship, love, and procreation "has an impact on her human nature, through obedience and biology, but simultaneously destroys the offensive aspects of her being a full human being—reason and free will."[16] Luther and Calvin suggest that "the norms for woman's life are to be found in obedience to divine will, in either accepting justified punishment or in conformance to the divine orders of creation."[17]

Jane Dempsey Douglass wants to modify this view of Calvin's thought, seeing Calvin as a leader knowledgeable of the Church's theological tradition who knew "the divine subordination of women did not fit either the totality of the biblical texts nor the social realities of the sixteenth-century world around him." Douglass further argues that "inferiorities in women's status . . . seem to be considered by Calvin to be matter of human historical judgments,"[18] as he wrestles theologically with the meaning of Paul's writings on women's status in God's image, her role in the Church, and the meaning of Christian freedom. Hence, Calvin presents a very traditional, but mixed view on women's subordination that remained wedded to the notion that Christian society was an integration of religion, culture, and the state.[19]

## WOMEN'S WORK AND LABOR FROM THE
## 17TH THROUGH 19TH CENTURIES

The rise of colonialism, particularly in the North American British colonies, brought a nascent diversity of labor for women and men in pre- and early capitalist labor structures. Teresa L. Amott and Julie A. Matthaei, describe this development pointing to multiple forms of labor-related groups that emerged. There was the free white European American family economy in which women and all household members worked together to meet family needs and earn income through craft-related activities, in part because there were few avenues of wage labor. Second, as colonization grew for primarily economic expansion (and not religious freedom) whites that had wealth or large land holdings could create additional systems of labor, bringing labor from various different parts of the globe. Indentured servants (including a relatively small number of women) worked for masters for specific numbers of years before either selling their labor for wages or creating a free family economic unit. Contract labor workers were free when they met the terms of masters' specific labor obligations.[20] After fulfilling the terms of the contract, they too could hire out their labor and/or more readily engage in a family farming economy, trading, or exploration. Under chattel enslavement, Native peoples were first sought but proved elusive for the purpose of long-term or life-long servitude. It was African enslaved people who became literally chattel, that is, property owned—bought, bred, and sold for life—by others.

The enslavement of Africans and African Americans was another labor form in the United States. For the vast majority of African American women, enslavement meant that they worked in the fields alongside African American men. Other women worked in the slave owner's home as nursemaid, domestic, gardener, and cook. Generally, fieldwork wasn't particularly gendered, and enslaved women who were pregnant were given no respite in light of their condition. Women plowed fields, split rails, and drove teams of horses. This work gives dynamic meaning to work as "toil." Moreover, childbearing and childrearing were generally viewed as assets for the slave master. The most problematic nature of this work for enslaved women was a three-fold nightmare of being bred to produce increasing numbers of slaves for the home plantation or for sale at auction; the ever-present danger and humiliation of rape by slave owners, overseers, and male slaves; and the sale of women's family members. Women dangerously resisted in a variety of ways that were intended to thwart this oppression. Many women attempted to escape but were caught and returned to their owners with dire punishment accompanying their return. Many did not try to escape because their families were present on one's plantation or nearby plantation, but did often hide for days in the deepest woods, if available, to get some respite from the plantation regime, and to attend to self-care. Some women who had access to the slave owner's table would attempt poisoning masters and mistresses to make them sick but not die. Perhaps most important were the root medicines created as abortifacients to deny pregnancy and birth of children.[21]

Christianity and slavery had a complex relationship for the nearly 250-year history of the institution, first in the British colonies, and later in the life of the republic. When the Atlantic slave trade began, "the conversion of the slaves to Christianity was viewed . . . as a justification for slavery,"[22] in order that they not die as pagans. Nevertheless by the mid-1650s, there was considerable concern among slave trader and owners that upon receiving instruction and baptism, Christianity would emancipate slaves to the detriment of the profitability of the slave trade and the plantation labor system. Six North American British colonies "enacted laws by 1706, denying that baptism altered the condition of the slave 'as to bondage or freedom.'"[23] During the Great Awakening, beginning in 1740, blacks were among those most affected by the new revivalist power, with their numbers of conversion increasing each decade. In part, this was affected by the emotional and spiritual content and environment of revivals, while also enabling slaves to integrate Christian faith (not necessarily doctrine) with dimensions of African traditional religion in its many forms. The question of utilizing "slave preachers" also became a point of concern for state legislatures after the Revolutionary War and into the 19th century as to the slave preacher's role in the community of slaves. The issue remained a potent one for planters, as enslaved women and men participated in rebellions led by black preachers such as the following three rebellions: the "Gabriel" Rebellion in Richmond in 1800; the revolt implicating the Reverend Denmark Vesey in Charleston in 1822; and the worst slave revolt in U.S. history, the Reverend Nat Turner Rebellion in 1831, in Southampton, Virginia.[24] Religious conversion and instruction by pro-slavery Christian apologists remained an important part in the perpetuation of this labor system, but under much closer scrutiny and restrictions. An example of the question-and-answer response in "slave catechisms" (summaries of Christian principles for slave instruction) was the following: "Q: What did God make you for? A: To make a crop."[25] Further, enslaved women's narratives depict Sunday evening church services on plantations where white ministers or docile slave preachers exhorted, "Servants, be obedient to them that are your masters according to the flesh, with fear and trembling, in singleness of your heart, as unto Christ" (Ephes. 6:5).

From 1619 to 1865, enslaved women had their own responses to the harsh and dehumanizing structures of chattel slavery. Moral agency and resistance took shape in everyday life and activities. Customs, rituals, religious festivals, harvest times, and self-determined patterns of organization within the plantation system helped enslaved women discern and self-define the meaning of their human nature, critical truths and realities of life, and alternative forms of "family," "personhood," and worldviews. Suspicious of the pro-slavery white Christian community, the enslaved community's religious ceremonies were often hidden from the eyes of slave masters and mistresses, creating cultural spaces for the practice of African religious customs integrated together with Christian ones. It was called "slave religion."[26]

In work and labor, enslaved women provided moral instruction to children about survival when questioned by overseers about missing livestock, in clandestine literacy lessons when possible, and folk medicine and culinary skills that assisted enslaved communities retain and create necessary cultural supports for survival. Enslaved women, together with men, created alternative family forms since most slave states prohibited legal marriage between slaves, and when there were no possibilities of escaping north, women hid enslaved people in flight North in the places of worship deep in woods away from the knowledge of overseers and owners. These and other means sustained African and African American culture-continuation, resistance, and in the extreme, individual acts of liberation in which the enslaved community of women lived out subversive and daily forms of moral agency.

In the 19th century the roles of white women were being shaped by both religion and society. Socioeconomic class relations also defined the impact of these two influences on the changing nature of women's roles. "The disestablishment of religion in the U.S. Constitution at the end of the prior century made religious life a private concern, especially in Anglo-Saxon Protestantism, wherein religion and domesticity worked to make the private sphere of women also the 'feminine' sphere. As normative notions, they further reinforced the view that women were domestically religious and men were occupied in the secular, real world."[27] According to Rosemary R. Ruether and Rosemary S. Keller, "Piety, domesticity, and submissiveness were seen as essential to woman's nature and contrary to man's. The key Christian ingredients necessary to identify women's "femininity" were sacrificial love, servanthood, altruism, and redemptive grace.[28] These characteristics reinforced female dependency, subordination, and motherhood as the central features of the Christian woman. Her task was to make sure her home provided the necessary moral training appropriate for husbands, boys, and girls.

The counterpoint for the changing roles of these class-identified women was the rise of various forms of religious and social movements, and biblical justification for human liberation. Religion could feminize women into what became "True Womanhood,"[29] and it also could open women to new leadership roles in utopian movements, the Abolitionist Movement, evangelism, missionary work, and social reform. Women such as Elizabeth Cady Stanton and Lucretia Mott, activists in the abolition movement, begin to consider a women's rights movement while at the 1840 World Anti-Slavery

Convention in London, England. Eight years later, Stanton, Mott, and other women (many of whom were Quakers) held the Seneca Falls Women's Rights Convention in July 1848 and passed the "Declaration of Sentiments."[30] The Declaration was modeled on the Declaration of Independence, and nearly a dozen specific resolutions drafted by Stanton were included. In tandem with the Anti-Slavery Movement and later Reconstruction, women's organization of missionary societies and social reform clubs began addressing the needs of women more forthrightly. Women moved into positions formerly held by men in the pre–Civil War era, becoming teachers, secretaries, and those with means, successful entrepreneurs. Black women were building such organizations as well, particularly through the theme of "racial uplift" in the Reconstruction and Jim Crow eras after the Civil War, in the black churchwomen's missionary organizations and club movements.[31]

The women's rights feminist movement, women's missionary societies, and social reform clubs labored throughout the mid- to late 19th century often having strong disagreements concerning women's nature. Utopian and perfectionist streams of thought (deeply embedded in religious sentiment) asserted different forms of the notion that women were the complementary, redemptive uplift in home and society of the "carnal masculine gender."[32] Many in this argument asserted women's superiority to men and argued that, through the promulgation of perfectionist reform, womanhood would lift the race. Liberal feminism, sometimes associated with secular views of human nature, believed in the equality of the sexes. For them, women had the same capacity to do most kinds of work men did because they had the capacity for reason and conscience.[33] Both streams had much more complexity and different class representation than presented here. Important as were these ideas and actions, women social reform movements saw women wage earners as women to be redeemed so that such women would become civilized and able to approach the moral standards of the women's rights/feminist movement of the time.

The 19th century was also the age when women's "putting out system" of spinning and weaving thread left the home as an income-earning women's activity and became the purview of the industrial factory dominated by men.[34] First young New England mill girls moved into the factories (often moving away from their rural homes), working as much as six days a week for 12 hours a day and wage labor.[35] Conditions in many of these factories were wretched, and as the industrial factory spread through the Northeastern United States, women wage-earners, both native- born and the increasing number of European immigrant women, began to organize against the oppressive working conditions. Deeply embedded in religious sentiment, immigrant women became factory workers but also worked for a pittance in urban slums, and served as paid and unpaid domestic labor, outside and inside their homes. Like black women, immigrant women did not have the means to participate in the ideology of "true womanhood" through domesticity, although they were judged by those moral standards even as they worked in public by day and at home by night. The nature and course of women workers' resistance, to the middle- and upper-class moral and religious notions of femininity, and the demeaning nature of wage labor created alternative forms of moral agency. Mill girls and later garment workers began the long struggle of labor organizing, albeit in sex/race segregated unions and reform organizations.[36] The solidarity in labor organizing was not based on theological or humanist ideologies, but on the concrete conditions of their lives and workplaces, both of which could be described as "toil." As such, they struggled for a different kind of dignity than did women in the feminist movements."[37] Lowell, Massachusetts, was the organizing area for early work stoppages by the Factory Girls' Association in the 1830s and again after 1842, when female workers formed the Lowell Female Reform Association, after refusing to trust the supposed benevolence of their male supervisors and factory owners."

By the end of the late 19th century, immigrant women wage earners were the backbone of the garment industry,[38] making dresses, serving as seamstresses and collar makers, artificial flower makers, and laundry workers. Others worked in the developing manufacturing industries. Women factory wage earners grew to include not only European women, but Russian Jewish women as well. As a result and where possible, women learned the skills of speaking in public as well as organizing, on occasion formed alliances with white middle- and upper-middle class women, and supported male workers doing dangerous work. Thus women wage earners would become a permanent part of the U.S. labor movement into and throughout the 20th century.

It is critical to understand three points in light of these labor systems regarding women's work. First, the theology and ethics of the predominant churches of the times sanctioned these labor systems (including the women in their memberships) without much question until the 19th century abolition movement, women's rights movement, Civil War, women's missionary societies, and social reform clubs. Second, women and men of the same racial/ethnic group did similar work in these systems although the social roles of women and men were unequal. Lastly, with emerging capitalism and further development of men's wage labor, women's work in the family and in reproduction was still generally invisible, expected, and not respected as legitimate work and livelihood. Thus, after working all day in the factories, women came home and toiled. What did change was that the "rise of capitalism drew people out of pre-capitalist labor systems, and into wage labor . . . depending upon gender, race, ethnicity, and class."[39] As women entered wage labor as a result of industrial capitalism in the mid-19th through 20th centuries, race, class, and gender would shape the nature of women's unpaid work in the family and paid labor in the market.

## THE CHURCH AND WOMEN LABOR—PAID AND UNPAID

Pamela K. Brubaker's work, *Women Don't Count: The Challenge of Women's Poverty to Christian Ethics,* outlines the responses of Roman Catholic social teachings and ecumenical councils in Protestantism to the economic structure of industrial capitalism influencing workers in the late 19th century and into the 20th century. Catholic social teachings and ecumenical social ethics take two different trajectories in their presuppositions about worker justice and women's status in the workplace as well as the home. Brubaker makes it clear that women's unpaid work in the family and economic status in poverty and wage labor was not, however, on the agenda of either tradition when they addressed economic ethics and the rights of workers.

For Brubaker, the significant shift slowly took place in the ecumenical arena as challenges to liberal social theory and neoclassical economics were made in successive assemblies, consultations, and reports. She notes that beginning with the 1937 Oxford Conference "the growing emancipation of women is identified as a particular instance of a beneficial consequence of the breaking up of tradition[yet] . . . there is no analysis of women's participation in the economy."[40] By this time, the industrial capitalist economy has begun to produce goods and services changing the nature of women's unpaid work in the home. Depending on socioeconomic class and race, women's ability to purchase commodities changed the nature of housework with the use of appliances and food processing to more efficient management of the home. Growing consumerism increased the need for more wage labor, and along with women entering the workforce in World War II, women had been integrated into the wage labor force. That integration was differently structured and often segregated by occupation and wage, and according to race, gender, and class, giving rise to the struggle of women within trade unionism.

Under the reign of John XXIII, the Catholic Church becomes somewhat more open to women's paid work and presence in the public sphere. Yet, speaking about women, the pope is clear in saying that "women must be wise in all their undertakings and find the resources to face their duties as wives and mothers . . . to make their homes warm and peaceful after the tiring labor of the day."[41] Issues of structural economic injustice for the "global south" (formerly termed, the Third World or Two-Third's World) come to the fore in Catholic social thought when the Church is faced with Latin American liberation theology in 1968.[42] Using radical economic social theory models, these theologians and some bishops challenge the Church to examine its theological and social presuppositions about the nature of capitalist development and its impact on workers. Concerns for justice for workers become enfolded in a broader notion of social justice encompassing human liberation and economic development. Still, Catholic social teachings continue to understand the status of women and the mutuality and equality of women and men in limited notions.

Arguably, it was not until women's participation in the civil rights and antiwar movements that the advent of the second wave of the women's movement occurred in the mid-60s, demanding the equality of women and men and the end of discrimination against women in all social institutions. By the World Council of Churches (WCC) 1975 Nairobi Assembly, Brubaker sees that economic social ethics in the council had been shaped by the women's movements in both church and society, and had begun to change with women's insistence that the WCC make connections between its analysis of "just economic criteria, foundational human rights, and women's disadvantage worldwide in light of poverty and sexism as unjust structural issues. Women also insisted that they could "make a special contribution regarding participatory decision-making because of their experiences of oppression and liberation."[43] By the WCC Ecumenical Decade of the Churches in Solidarity with Women (1988–98) there is affirmation for "women's empowerment to challenge oppressive structures, participation and leadership in decision-making in the struggles for justice, peace and the integrity of creation, and a call for the churches to take actions in solidarity with women."[44] Women's human dignity, however, remains misunderstood and embedded in universalisms about "the human," based on male experience, and the domain(s) of women's moral agency in both public and private spheres continued in invisibility and marginality.[45]

## OUR CONTEMPORARY SITUATION

Although the structure of work is rapidly changing in the global economy of capitalism, for women who are economically poor, nearly every hour of each day is consumed with the work of survival for self, family, and community whether the work is paid or unpaid labor. Arguably, the work that women do in subsistence activity (considered "nonmarket") is economic production, although not recognized as such in the market economy.[46] Women's work for survival and human flourishing *is* moral work as women struggle to become economically secure, self-determining, and in control of their labor and their bodies.

The United Nations Development Programme has reported that

discrimination against women is a fault line running through every society in the world today, varying only by degree. . . . Women are constantly paid less than men, have a weaker political voice, often have access to fewer educational opportunities, and few resources. According to [the United Nations'] statistics, 200 million women entered the global workforce in the decade before 2003, and 60 percent of the one billion poorest people are women. Further, in the global economy, women perform 60 percent of the under-protected and unpaid informal jobs, even when unemployment rates are low.[47]

When the AFL-CIO made its 2008 Annual International Women's Day Statement it asserted that, "there are 1.2 billion women in work today—about 40 percent of total world employment—yet globally, women still:

- earn 12–60% less than men, even in occupations such as nursing and teaching; in the United States, women are paid 77.6% of men's hourly earnings;
- make up 60% of the 550 million working poor;
- are concentrated in low-paid, unprotected, temporary, or casual work;
- lack maternity protection rights and face violence and sexual harassment at or near the workplace; and
- do not enjoy the same level of social protection as their male counterparts[48]

These figures suggest that women's work in the global and domestic economy is a "fault line," continuing to deny women of livelihood and moral agency in support of their families and communities.

At present, there are two phenomena dramatically increasing women's vulnerability as even low-wage and subsistence workers in the United States and abroad. The first dynamic is that of migrant-worker women and global migration that also engages critical economic and political issues in relation to the United States' role in the global economy and the status and conditions of such workers. Economic processes of globalization impact the movement of capital and of people in the production of goods and services for increasing consumerism globally. For various reasons and as a result of complex forces, migration is the movement of people *created, increased, accentuated, and propelled* by those practices. Moreover, some migration and immigration result from high unemployment in countries whose populations must move to find work because of loss of traditional lands or the change from subsistence production to privatization. The rising indebtedness of countries in the global industrial north (the developed nations of Western Europe, North America, and Japan) as well as of those countries in the global south (undeveloped or underdeveloped nations) is also a critical factor in migration for work between nations. Due to these practices and forces, immigration and notions of sovereignty have become complex and problematic for the United States at nearly every level of society—employment and wages, social services and taxation, public education, and immigration policy and law (federal and state), trade, and foreign aid. In this mix, women migrant workers are severely impacted.[49]

The second phenomenon is the driving down of wages and increase in low-wage jobs in employment sectors such as industrial and commercial cleaning, food processing, entertainment, retail sales, unskilled manufacturing, healthcare, farm labor, and contingent work. Women of every background in the United States are affected by the driving down of wages, particularly women of color and white women of the working poor and impoverished classes. As a result, they are economically (materially), physically (in terms of healthcare for themselves and their children), subject to physical/sexual abuse, spiritual abuse, and have few marketable skills that would increase their earning power. Caught in these conditions of work and toil, women's moral agency becomes very limited. Here are some examples.

The National Farm Worker Ministry (NFWM) began in 1920 as a ministry of charity and service farm workers, and then transformed itself from charity to justice-making, working with César Chávez of the United Farmer Workers' Union in the 1960s. Still a vehicle for people of faith to respond to the call for justice, NFWM women struggle to support domestic and undocumented women farm workers such as Josefina San Juan from Mexico, whose story they publicized two years ago. *The Bradenton (FL) Herald*, on October 30, 2005, headlined a page 1, article, "Women of the Fields"[50] about undocumented migrant farm worker women. It related the plight of a Latina woman, Josefina San Juan from Mexico, who had been raped four years earlier by another migrant worker as she showered in the facility provided for the farmer workers. "There were no locks on the bathroom doors," San Juan told the *Herald* staff writers. She had been in the United States only fifteen days before the rape occurred. She did not speak much English, had no relatives for support, and no place to go if she was thrown off the Manatee County farm where she worked. Moreover, she was terrified and felt ashamed. San Juan said that at the time, "I didn't tell anyone."

Jameela Washington (not her real name) is a security officer in Philadelphia, Pennsylvania. She says that "because I'm often relieved from my shift late, I don't get to [go] home in time to get my kids ready for school. If I could save money, I'd put it aside for my kids to go to college, but my salary is not even enough to go from paycheck to paycheck."[51] Like Jameela, most security workers make a median wage of $9.00 per hour, which over the course of a year, puts her $17.00 below the federal poverty threshold of $19,157, for a family of four. Jameela is one of the African American women security workers whose moral agency is demonstrated by her involvement in the struggle to unionize in several major U.S. cities to improve their earnings and to receive minimum benefits.[52] In doing so, she runs the risk of losing her job.

There are also struggles that end in justice. Women are working to regain and retain skills they and their families once had as family farmers. Expanding the notion of family farming, is the concept of nontraditional women in agriculture. For example, three black women from Smithville, Georgia, own and operate a Pecan Plant in Leslie, Georgia, having formed a co-op. The women take the pecan through a tedious process of removing the shell, sorting, cleaning and soaking them as any other pecan processing would do. They add value to their product by removing the shells and selling pecans in halves and pieces, and they can even sell the shells which are finely ground into a product called "meals". The co-op also sells pecan candy; adding more value to pecan halves and pieces.[53] In an era when small family farms are disappearing, in particular African American family farms, New Women In Agriculture and ventures like them are resisting the encroachment of corporate agribusiness and becoming models of women's moral agency.

## A Framework in Solidarity with Women's Lived Experience as Moral Agents in the Struggle for Dignity in Work

A Christian womanist/feminist ethic of justice and dignity for women's work begins with the principle that women are fully human beings, created *imago dei*. Whether seen through Christian natural law ethics or Christian womanist/feminist liberation ethics, women are reasoning persons with the freedom and "capacity to determine the quality and character of choices and actions." In light of God's freedom and call to a redemptive partnership with God, women share vitally in the vocation of continually creating, sustaining, and loving God, God's earth creation, and humankind. In part, this vocation is lived through work, and not toil, that recognizes, values, and respects the worth of women's work as livelihood for sustaining self, family, and community. This means that moral agency is a gracious gift from Jesus who gives women and men the power of "right relationship" and moral authority to seek justice and receive the fruits of our labor in and through good work, not only for the present generation but future generations of earth creation and human well-being.

First, such an ethic calls for economic institutions and political accountability that fosters women's ability to integrate self, family, community, and livelihood.[54] Because women's work, paid (including wage labor) and unpaid (in the home and in voluntary association) has been historically, economically, politically, and theologically devalued, the result has been that women's work has remained fragmenting, alienating both at home and in the workplace. Further, it has often been a source of individual and communal internalized oppression and coerced sacrifice, to the detriment of herself, family, and relationships with others. In response to the structural dehumanization of women's work, the Church's vocation is nothing less than to theologize new understandings of work that prioritize the vocation of all humans as a vocation of justice, right-relationship, and sustainability of earth and human community through human labor, including women's labor. Therefore, the Church sees its participation in God's mission as the critique of every political economy that places wealth accumulation and exploitation over human need and the common good, and takes moral action to be faithful to its vocation.

Second, such an ethic calls for women to have the moral authority over and human right to her own body and person as women determine their accountabilities to and with their intimate partners, children, and community. Abuse and/or intimidation at home or in the workplace is a violation of that authority and fundamental right. The essentializing of woman's nature (nature as based on biology) on the basis of gender, race/ethnicity, culture, class and physical ability makes women of all backgrounds vulnerable to abuse in every sphere of life, injuring her spirit, and demeaning her in the eyes of her children and community. Thus, resistance to abuse is exercising the agency to live into God's vision of full humanity. The Church is called participate with God and in solidarity with women in prophetic witness to just public policy, pastoral care that embodies restoration of right relations beginning with the healing of abused women and children, and the building of communities of equality between women and men.

Third, such an ethic calls women of every background and condition to work in solidarity with other women and men to dismantle the human constructions and structures of oppression. This acknowledges that women can, at different times and in different circumstances, be the target group of oppression and the untargeted group of unearned advantage and privilege based on power—personal, interpersonal, institutional, and cultural forms of power. Further, it calls for women to receive, use, and share in the distribution of society's good, its decision-making processes, and in its accountability for the common good of all. Moreover, it calls for the sustainability of the earth as both a gift from God, and the foundation of the material life of all its creatures including ourselves. In this respect, the Church is God's instrument of God's providence and love.

Fourth, but not last, such an ethic calls for the integration of virtues of care, justice, and love be shared by women and men alike for the benefit and betterment of community. Women and men together can and must learn the virtues of care and love, in particular, as both feminine and masculine virtues because they are the nature of God implanted in humanity through the *imago dei* as much as are justice and righteousness. The Church vocation and work is to equip women and men in its communities for ministries of care, nurture, and love, with the same agency that its vocation is to equip persons for faithful justice-making. Thus, the Church's two-millennium history of shaping women's work and labor no longer needs to lean primarily toward oppression and exploitation. Rather, its third millennium can be a forceful *metanoia* (a turning around) of repentance and righteousness.

## NOTES

1. Joan M. Martin, *More Than Chains and Toil: A Christian Work Ethic of Enslaved Women* (Louisville, KY: Westminster/John Knox Press, 2000), pp. 39–40, as quoted from Peter J. Paris, *The Social Teachings of the Black Churches* (Philadelphia, PA: Fortress Press 1985), p. 60.

2. Martin, *More Than Chains*, p. 40; Paris, *Social Teachings*, pp. 57–61.

3. Delores S. Williams, *Sisters in the Wilderness: The Challenge of Womanist God-Talk* (Maryknoll, NY: Orbis Books, 1993), p. xiv.

4. Ibid., p. xiv.

5. Dorothee Soëlle with Shirley Cloyes, *To Work and To Love: A Theology of Creation* (Philadelphia, PA: Fortress Press, 1984), pp. 26–27.

6. Sue Cady, Marian Ronan, and Hal Taussig, *Sophia: The Future of Feminist Spirituality* (Minneapolis, MN: Winston Press, 1986). See Cady, Ronan, and Taussig's work for a full discussion of *Ruach*, Sophia.

7. Lee Hardy, *The Fabric of This World: Inquiries into Calling, Career Choice, and the Design of Human Work* (Grand Rapids, MI: William B. Eerdmanns Publishing Company, 1990), pp. 11, 7–8.

8. Mary E. Hobgood, *Catholic Social Teaching and Economic Theory: Paradigms in Conflict* (Philadelphia, PA: Temple University Press, 1992), p. 4.

9. Ibid., p. 4. Also see Chapter 2 for a fuller explanation of Aquinas on private property.

10. Thomas Aquinas, *Summa Theologica,* a concise translation, ed. Timothy McDermott (Notre Dame, IN: Christian Classics, 1991), p. 143.

11. Ibid., p. 144.

12. Ibid., p. 144.

13. Hobgood, *Catholic Social Teaching*, p. 4

14. Susan Frank Parsons, *Feminism and Christian Ethics* (Cambridge, MA: Cambridge University Press, 1996), pp. 226–27.

15. Ibid., p. 227.

16. Ibid., p 227.

17. Ibid., p. 227.

18. Jane Dempsey Douglass, *Women, Freedom, and Calvin* (Philadelphia. PA: The Westminster Press, 1985), p. 45. All of this is a much more complex

argument that Dempsey articulates, taking into account Calvin's commentaries and sermons.

19. David J. O'Brien and Thomas A. Shannon, eds., *Catholic Social Thought: The Documentary Heritage* (Maryknoll, NY: Orbis Books, 1991), p. 4.

20. Theresa L. Amott and Julie A. Matthaei, *Race, Gender and Work: A Multicultural Economic History of Women in the United States* (Boston, MA: South End Press, 1991), p. 292.

21. Eugene D. Genovese, *Roll Jordan, Roll: The World the Slaves Made* (New York: Vintage Books, 1974), pp. 496–97.

22. Albert J. Raboteau, *Slave Religion: The "Invisible Institution" in the Antebellum South* (New York: Oxford University Press, 1978), p. 96.

23. Ibid., p. 99.

24. Ibid., pp. 147, 163–64.

25. *Christian Advocate and Journal*, February 12, 1836, p. 98, as quoted in Donald G. Matthews, *Slavery and Methodism: A Chapter in American Morality* (Princeton, NJ: Princeton University Press, 1965), p. 78.

26. Raboteau, *Slave Religion*, p. x.

27. Rosemary Radfor Ruether and Rosemary Skinner, eds. *Women and Religion in America*, Vol. 1. The Nineteenth Century (New York: Harper and Row Publishers, 1981), p. ix.

28. Ibid., ix.

29. Carolyn De Swarte Gifford, "Women in Social Reform Movements, in *Women and Religion in America*, Vol. 1. The Nineteenth Century, ed. Rosemary Radford Ruether and Rosemary Skinner Keller (New York: Harper and Row Publishers, 1981), p. 295.

30. "The Seneca Falls Convention, July 19–20, 1848," http://www.npg.si.edu/col/seneca/ senfalls1.htm; accessed: 02/27/09.

31. Evelyn Brooks Higginbotham, *Righteous Discontent: The Women's Movement in the Black Baptist Church, 1880–1920* (Cambridge. MA: Harvard University Press, 1993), pp.13–18.

32. Ruether and Keller, eds., *Women and Religion in America*, p. xiii.

33. Ibid., p. xiii.

34. Amott and Matthaei, *Race, Gender, and Work*, p. 100.

35. Ibid., p. 101.

36. Ibid., p. 101.

37. Ibid., p. 101.

38. Ibid., p. 115.

39. Ibid., p. 296.

40. Brubaker, Pamela K. *Women Don't Count: The Challenge of Women's Poverty to Christian Social Ethics* (Atlanta, GA: Scholars Press, 1994), p. 121.

41. Ibid., p. 72.

42. Ibid., p. 92.

43. Ibid., p. 147.

44. Sub-Unit on Women in Church and Society, "Ecumenical Decade (1988–1998): Churches in Solidarity with Women" (Geneva: World Council of Churches, 1980) p. 1 as quoted in Brubaker, *Globalization at What Cost?*, p. 156.

45. Ibid., p. 159.

46. The discussion regarding whether or not to define women's subsistence activity as production and as part of nations' GNP is a long discussion. See Ester Boserup, *Women's Role in Economic Development* (New York: St. Martin's Press, 1970), and Derek W. Blades, *Non-Monetary (Subsistence) Activities in the National Accounts of Developing Countries* (Paris: OECD, 1975), as reported in Lourdes Benería, *Gender, Development, and Globalization: Economics As If All People Mattered* (New York: Routledge, 2003), p. 137.

47. Pamela K. Brubaker, *Globalization At What Cost? Economic Change and Daily Life* (Cleveland, OH: The Pilgrim Press, 2001), p. 27.

48. AFL-CIO Executive Council Statement, International Women's Day: "Decent Work, Decent Life For Women," March 5, 2008, San Diego, CA, http://www.aflcio.org/aboutus/thisistheaflcio/ecouncil03052008.cfm; accessed 05/15/2008.

49. For an in-depth discussion of what can be called "the de facto transnationaling of immigration policy," see Saskia Sassen, *Globalization and its Discontents* (New York: The Free Press, 1998), especially chapter 2.

50. Laura Figueroa and Richard Dymond, "Women of the Fields" (*The Bradenton Herald*, Bradenton, FL: October 30, 2005), front section, p. 1A, www.bradenton.com/news/local/13033270.htm; accessed August 21, 2008 from http://www.nfwm.org/, "Women Farm Workers Face Special Challenges."

51. Interfaith Worker Justice Report, "In Whom Do We Find Our Security? Finding Justice for Security Officers" (Chicago: Interfaith Worker Justice, 2005), p. 3.

52. Ibid., p. 3.

53. Unitarian Universalist Service Committee, and the Presbyterian Church Self-Development of Peoples Fund, http://www.uusc.org/content/women_and_girls_informal_economy; accessed 02/13/09.

54. My own adaptation of a principle from Gloria H. Albrecht, *Hitting Home: Feminist Ethics, Women's Work, and the Betrayal of "Family Values"* (New York: Continuum International Publishing Group, 2002), p. 149.

## References

AFL-CIO Executive Council Statement, International Women's Day: "Decent Work, Decent Life For Women," March 5, 2008. San Diego, CA, http://www.aflcio.org/aboutus/thisistheaflcio/ecouncil03052008.cfm; accessed 5/15/2008.

Albrecht, Gloria H. *Hitting Home: Feminist Ethics, Women's Work, and the Betrayal of "Family Values."* New York: Continuum International Publishing Group, 2002.

Amott, Theresa L. and Julie A. Matthaei. *Race, Gender, and Work: A Multicultural Economic History of Women in the United States.* Boston, MA: South End Press, 1991.

Aquinas, Thomas. *Summa Theologica.* A Concise Translation, ed. Timothy McDermott. Notre Dame, IN: Christian Classics, 1991.

Brubaker, Pamela K. *Globalization At What Cost? Economic Change and Daily Life.* Cleveland, OH: The Pilgrim Press, 2001.

Brubaker, Pamela K. *Women Don't Count: The Challenge of Women's Poverty to Christian Ethics.* Atlanta, GA: Scholars Press, 1994.

Cady, Susan, Marian Ronan, and Hal Taussig. *Sophia: The Future of Feminist Spirituality.* Minneapolis, MN: Winston Press, 1986.

Douglass, Jane Dempsey. *Women, Freedom, and Calvin.* Philadelphia, PA: Westminster Press, 1985.

Figueroa, Laura and Richard Dymond. "Women of the Fields." *The Bradenton Herald* (Bradenton, FL), October 30, 2005, front section, p. 1A, www.bradenton.com/news/local/13033270.htm; accessed August 21, 2008, http://www.nfwm.org/, "Women Farm Workers Face Special Challenges."

Gifford, Carolyn De Swarte. "Women in Social Reform Movements." In *Women and Religion in America.* Vol. 1. The Nineteenth Century. ed. Rosemary Radford Ruether and Rosemary Skinner Keller. New York: Harper and Row Publishers, 1981.

Hardy, Lee. *The Fabric of This World: Inquiries into Calling, Career Choice, and the Design of Human Work.* Grand Rapids, MI: William B. Eerdmanns Publishing Company, 1990.

Higginbotham, Evelyn Brooks. *Righteous Discontent: The Women's Movement in the Black Baptist Church, 1880–1920.* Cambridge. MA: Harvard University Press, 1993, pp. 13–18.

Hobgood, Mary E. *Catholic Social Teaching and Economic Theory: Paradigms in Conflict.* Philadelphia, PA: Temple University Press, 1992.

Interfaith Worker Justice Report. "In Whom Do We Find Our Security? Finding Justice for Security Officers." Chicago, IL: Interfaith Worker Justice, 2005.

Martin, Joan M. *More Than Chains and Toil: A Christian Work Ethic of Enslaved Women.* Louisville, KY: Westminster/John Knox Press, 2000.

Matthews, Donald G. *Slavery and Methodism: A Chapter in American Morality.* Princeton, NJ: Princeton University Press, 1965.

O'Brien, Savid J. and Thomas A. Shannon, eds. *Catholic Social Thought: The Documentary Heritage.* Maryknoll, NY: Orbis Books, 1991.

Paris, Peter J. *The Social Teachings of the Black Churches.* Philadelphia, PA: Fortress Press, 1985.

Parsons, Susan Frank. *Feminism and Christian Ethics.* Cambridge, MA: Cambridge University Press, 1996.

Raboteau, Albert J. *Slave Religion: The "Invisible Institution" in the Antebellum South*. New York: Oxford University Press, 1978.

Ruether, Rosemary Radford and Rosemary Skinner Keller, eds. *Women and Religion in America*. Vol. 1. The Nineteenth Century. New York: Harper and Row Publishers, 1981.

Sassen, Saskia. *Globalization and Its Discontents: Economics as If All People Mattered*. New York: Routledge, 2003.

"Seneca Falls Convention, July 1929, 1848," http://www.npg.si.edu/col/seneca/senfalls1.htm; accessed 02/27/09.

Soëlle, Dorothee, with Shirley Cloyes. *To Work and To Love: A Theology of Creation*. Philadelphia, PA: Fortress Press, 1984.

Unitarian Universalist Service Committee, and The Presbyterian Church (United States) Self-Development of Peoples Fund, http://www.uusc.org/content/ women_and_girls_informal_economy; accessed 02/13/09.

Williams, Delores S. *Sisters in the Wilderness: The Challenge of Womanist God-Talk*. Maryknoll, NY: Orbis Books, 1993.

# PART III

# *Body, Mind, Spirit*

# CHAPTER 7

# Spirit Matters: Body, Mind, and Motherhood

## Jean T. Corey

*The questions that we have to ask and to answer about that procession during this moment of transition are so important that they may well change the lives of all men and women forever. For we have to ask ourselves, here and now, do we wish to join that procession, or don't we? On what terms shall we join that procession? Above all, where is it leading us, the procession of educated men?*[1]
—*Virginia Woolf*

In her groundbreaking book *Of Woman Born*, Adrienne Rich writes that we would all be spiritually malnourished, had it not been for the research and scholarship of "childless" women like Charlotte Bronte, Jane Austen, and Virginia Woolf.[2] Certainly, Virginia Woolf's fiction and essays shaped important conversations about motherhood, body, mind, and spirit for most of the 20th century. Well before the 20th century, advocates for women's rights were already challenging Christianity's assumptions about women's roles, particularly the assumption that a woman's primary role was to be fruitful and multiply—to mother—enabling men (apparently white men) to have dominion over all the earth. Though their rhetorical approaches often evidenced decidedly different assumptions about women's bodies, many feminists agreed that the Bible was used all too often to keep women in their place.

While Christianity declared that both scripture and nature's law affirmed men's roles as active creators and women's seemingly passive role as nurturer, men in the sciences were busy confirming white men's superiority with biological explanations for the inferiority of "others" (those who were not white and not male). Victorian physicians and anthropologists (all white males) determined that women's capacity to conceive and bear children diverted energy from their brain's creativity, and women's bodies, in fact, distorted their ability to reason and write well. This chapter explores the intersections and shared relationships between mothering and body, mind and spirit, for women of faith. By examining how health, faith, and motherhood challenge and extend one's understanding of body, mind, and spirit, the chapter: (1) explores motherhood in a society that divides public and private spaces based upon gender; (2) examines women's experience to offer a new reading of the significance of connecting body, mind, and spirit framed by history, public, and private experiences; (3) uses Patricia Hill Collins's term of motherwork to analyze a spirituality of resistance against and growth of women's lived experiences of disempowerment and dehumanizing situations; (4) ponders the impact of religion and culture regarding experiences of want, grief, anguish, and survival; (5) reflects on the spirituality of those mothering through adoption and caring for those with HIV; and (6) concludes by envisioning a new world of mothers, othermothers, and their children. This chapter moves toward a generative epistemology or way of knowing which allows women to think back through othermothers and engage in the kind of motherwork necessary for envisioning a new world.

## MOTHERHOOD AND THE GREAT DIVIDE

Over the course of her short life, as science and technology gained authority in the dominant culture, Woolf watched her middle-class European world become more and more secularized. Theories about the human body and sexuality were accompanied by questions about the validity and necessity of faith at all, particularly a faith that centered on bodily mysteries such as a virgin birth and resurrection of the dead. Most advocates for women's rights believed that decentering the *authority* of the church held great promise for women's access to the public sphere, but in *Three Guinea*, a prophetic Woolf warns that women should enter "the procession of educated men" with caution.

The "procession of educated men," Woolf explains is a consuming force, which wears a different dress in its various venues of authority, whether academic, political, commercial, or religious: our brothers, educated in public and private schools and universities, go up the steps, through doors, upward and onward to pulpits, "preaching, teaching, administering justice, practicing medicine, transacting business, making money."[3]

For the first time in history, a woman had the option of joining the *procession*, or, at least, "traipsing along at the tail end."[4] How shameful it would seem for her to forgo that opportunity. Woolf, however, warns women that this process would change their realities. They would leave home early and get back late, thus leaving little or no time for mothers to be with their children. Further, this process is a lifetime undertaking, from early twenties to mid-sixties, and in the process, a woman loses precious time that will thwart and limit options for "friendship, travel, or art"; the work may be awfully barbarous, and sometimes the cost is the loss of one's senses: sight, sound, speech all go; "[t]hey have no time for conversation. They lose their sense of proportion—the relations between one thing and another. Humanity goes."[5]

As Woolf moves back and forth between the facts of the public world and the emotions of the private sphere, she makes a compelling argument that regardless of the gender of its participants, the procession is irretrievably headed for war. She concludes the lengthy argument with this warning: "If in the 'immensity of public abstraction,' men forget the private world, or if in 'the intensity of our private emotions,' women forget the public world, [b] oth houses will be ruined, the public and the private, the material and the spiritual, for they are inseparably connected."[6]

Almost 50 years later, Ursula LeGuin reflects on her own negotiations of a divided and gendered world in her commencement address to women at Bryn Mawr College. She tells the graduates she has learned three languages throughout life, all of them English. Her first language was the language of home—the mother tongue, the language of relationship, and connection. LeGuin's second language is the father tongue, the language of power, which seeks objectivity by creating distance between subject and object, self and other. Though many would like to claim the father tongue as the voice of reason, LeGuin assures them that reason is far more than objective thought, and when "either the political or the scientific discourse announces itself as the voice of reason, it is playing God, and should be spanked and stood in the corner."[7] And, in fact, as evangelical Christianity was busy making Christianity more believable, more reasonable to the dominant culture, white feminists did just what LeGuin recommended—they spanked God and put "him" in 'the corner." The third language, which LeGuin notes is almost hardly ever spoken is that of one's native tongue, where public discourse meets private experience, a merging of beauty and power, reasoned dialogue or discourse, where "dancing is the body moving as art."[8]

My experience as an undergraduate student in the late 1970s resonated with LeGuin's observations. I had not grown up in the church, but had a conversion experience shortly before I went to college. Anxious to serve God, I decided to pursue nursing—caring for sick people seemed a natural. Tucked away in the corner of campus, the nursing school was the only building on Vanderbilt University's campus where you could find a critical mass of women professors (all of them white). Our subject matter was caring for the body. And while our efforts were aimed at *life*, our speculative tool was the *dead* body—Vanderbilt's nursing school prided itself as being the only nursing school in the country with its own cadavers. I thought of the nursing school's physical location years later when reading Hélène Cixous' essay "Laugh of the Medusa": "Men say that there are two unrepresentable things: death and the feminine sex. That's because they need femininity to be associated with death. . . ."[9] In the corner of campus with our dead bodies, our task as nursing students was to memorize, *never* to think, to theorize, to create, or imagine. These were the domain of the liberal arts. The few liberal arts courses required for the nursing program, however, gave me enough of a taste to know that I found these enterprises far more rewarding. I loved the world of texts, the making of meaning. Though I distrusted my mind's ability to join the conversation of the all male professors in the school of liberal arts, I wanted to at least to listen in. With the nursing school's blessing, I transferred to the school of liberal arts and became an English major. In my new major, bodies, dead or alive, were no longer the subject (or object) in the classroom. In fact, at the time, Vanderbilt's English department was still heady from the success of the New Critics, and the body had no place at all. My professors were white men; the texts we read were overwhelmingly written by white men, and though I too was white, it was clear to me that as a 20-year-old woman, my own experiences as woman, and as a Christian, had nothing to offer the interpretive process. To be taken seriously in the classroom, I knew I would have to become a disembodied reader and knower.

A self-described white, lesbian, Jewish mother and poet, Adrienne Rich argues that women's fear and hatred of our bodies "has often crippled our brains." Trying to "think from somewhere outside their female bodies," women are "still merely reproducing old forms of intellection."[10] Rich attributes women's uneasy relationship with their bodies to the overlapping patriarchal institutions of motherhood and religion. She poignantly argues that unless women commit themselves to exploring and understanding the spiritual and political significance of their bodies, women will continue to be cut off from their own innate brilliance.

Rich understands that while the patriarchal definition of motherhood has personal psychic and spiritual implications, the political implications are near lethal. Western culture has limited the definition of motherhood. As a result, it has split women off from the dominant culture. "[I]n so doing it has also split itself off from life, becoming the death-culture of quantification, abstraction, and the will to power which has reached its most refined destructiveness in this century."[11] Rich believes a new world will be possible when women free themselves from the patriarchal institution of motherhood, repossess their own bodies, and claim their rightful place as subjects. Only then can women truly "create new life, bringing forth not only children (if and as we choose) but the visions, and the thinking, necessary to sustain, console, and alter human existence—a new relationship to the universe."[12]

Nancy Chodorow agrees that forced heterosexuality has limited women's ways of being in the world: "Biological sex is organized in terms of heterosexual marriage which gives men rights over their wives' bodies and their children."[13] Using object relations theory, Chodorow illustrates that that in our industrialized world where production depended on the division of labor, mothering necessarily reproduced itself. While sons are taught to perceive themselves as individual selves, whose task in life is *to separate* from their mothers, daughters are taught to connect to mothers, their selves determined *in relationship* to their mother. In short, women's mothering as part of the oppressed side of the division of labor is destined to reproduce its own oppression.

But Barbara Katz Rothman suggests that because historically feminists, women who seek to empower women, often failed to question the interlocking ideologies of patriarchy, technology, and capitalism that informed their theorizing, women's struggle for rights often extends the mind/body dualism they are challenging. Rothman defines the ideology or principles of patriarchy as a kinship system that revolves around the concept of men's seed growing within women's bodies. Rothman goes on to show that while American liberal philosophy wedded with capitalist ideology of ownership has been invaluable for women's rights—rights to their own bodies and rights to their children, these rights perpetuate an ethos of individualism. Rothman acknowledges that this model has been helpful for empowering women to choose if and when they become mothers, but offers little empowerment *to* mothers. At the intersection of these three ideologies, children have become a high commodity. Rothman observes that while women can now own their own bodies, mother's bodies which are invested in the menial labor of mothering are not a very high commodity in a patriarchal system.[14]

Rothman dreams of a world "beyond mothers and fathers," where parenting is no longer conceived as a gender-based activity. In our efforts to revise parenting as a social relationship of nurture and care, Rothman cautions that "we must not recreate endlessly separate worlds of power and care."[15] A well-warranted concern, but are separate worlds of power and care inevitable without decentering our notions of power altogether?

## REREADING POWER: CONNECTING BODY, MIND, *AND* SPIRIT

In her essay "Laugh of the Medusa," French feminist Hélène Cixous tells us that women must end this "biological and cultural confusion." Women's real lack of power is their inability to connect with their spiritual selves. Claiming the woman and lesbian identities that had been used to exclude her from the public sphere, Cixous explores women's fragmentation in the midst of multiple and interrelated cultural practices of sexism, racism, forced heterosexuality, and colonization: unjust practices due to gender, race, sexual orientation, and imposed seizure of land. With language as her speculative tool, Cixous attempts to rescue women from a "phallogocentric," world, a world which privileges men's experience. In such a world, women's position is only, always object and Cixous seeks to restore her as subject. Cixous encourages women to inscribe their own texts with milk and blood, the stuff of life which men have deemed unfit for a public world. Putting themselves "into the text—as into the world and into history," women will discover their deep resources.[16] Unlike subjectivity that is constructed in a world of male domination, woman as universal subject understands herself as "both the force which produces, and is produced . . . by the other—in particular, the other woman . . . the mother who makes everything all right, who nourishes and who stands up against separation; a force that will not be cut off but will knock the wind out of the codes."[17]

Two weeks before I began my first graduate school class at Duke University, an interdisciplinary class taught by ethicist Stanley Hauerwas, I gave birth to our third child. Between changing diapers and nursing, I read and wrote responses to Aristotle, Aquinas, and Meilander. And, I was always sure to nurse our daughter one last time before rushing off to class—this was to save my husband from a miserable evening with a crying baby, and to save me from the embarrassment of leaking milk in the middle of a debate on epistemology, or the study of how we know things. Even with all my precautions, I spent much of the class red faced, fearful that I would be discovered bringing blood and milk, the messy fluids of life, into the sacred world of Duke's divinity school. Oddly enough, though my postnatal body gave me great anxiety in the classroom, I had a heightened sense of my participation in the making of meaning going on in the classroom. Certainly in the few years that had passed between my undergraduate and graduate school experience, the rules for making meaning had changed. Readers now had more authority, even readers such as me, who had previously been excluded from the academy. But I think my participation had more to do with an internalized sense of power than with Stanley Fish's work on reader-response theory, the theory which gives readers the power to determine the meaning of a text. Cixous tells us the "taboo of the pregnant woman," is clear proof of her power "because it has always been suspected, that when pregnant the woman not only doubles her market value, but—what's more important takes on intrinsic values as a woman in her own eyes and undeniably, acquires body and sex."[18] Little wonder women are more likely to experience domestic violence or be murdered when pregnant.

In my own case, the social and intellectual disembodiment I had been schooled in by my mother at home was no longer a possibility; I had undeniably acquired body and sex. Remembering my experience years later, I realized that the source of life and energy for my baby daughter at home, gave me the creative power to begin humanizing my work in the academy.

Black, feminist, lesbian poet Audre Lorde tells us there are many kinds of power, "used and unused, acknowledged or otherwise," but ". . . to perpetuate itself every oppression must corrupt or distort those various sources of power within the culture of the oppressed that can provide energy for change."[19] As a result, women are taught to distrust the power of the erotic, which Lorde describes as "a resource within each of us that lies in a deeply female and spiritual plane." While many white feminists agree with Lorde's assertion of spirit and spiritual as a creative and generative force, many (most?) are careful to make distinctions between spirit and any sort of belief or faith in a divine being. Perhaps they take this stance because they believe "spirit" and "spiritual" had too long been the domain of faith and religion; perhaps some have seen too much hurt in the great temples, mosques, synagogues and cathedrals of faith and religion.

Historian Gerda Lerner observes that in the rise of feminine consciousness in Western culture, women argued for emancipation for spiritual reasons long before they began to negotiate independence through political solutions.[20] She points to the faith of women as the single most powerful force against patriarchy in history. Although patriarchy often co-opts religion, if we consistently lump God-centeredness with male-centeredness in our analysis of women's experience, we are not only unobservant, but unwise in our stewarding of a critical source of women's power. Certainly this is true for women of color, locally and globally.

Sociologist Patricia Hill Collins observes that white middle-class feminist theorists fail to acknowledge that they "are rooted in specific locations, and that the specific contexts in which they are located provide the thought-models of how they interpret the world."[21] As a result, though their theories "appear to be universal and objective," they provide only "partial perspectives reflecting the white middle class context in which their creators live." In the end, "large segments of experience, specifically those of women who are not white and middle-class, have been excluded." Certainly this would be true for white feminists theorizing about the relationship of women's body, mind, and spirit, and motherhood.

While patriarchal assumptions about white women's bodies may have led to repressed sexuality and *dis*/embodiment for white women, those same forces present very different problems for women of color, whose bodies have been exploited and often abused. bell hooks explains that with the institution of slavery, the same forces that had placed white women on a pedestal, simultaneously defined black women as oversexed whores. Such devaluation of black femininity justified white men's exploitation and rape of black women—a reality that exists to this day.[22] Womanist sociologist Cheryl Townsend Gilkes suggests that there is such a "history of ambivalence" about the physical appearance of black women that self-hatred and cultural humiliation continually "assaults" contemporary African American women, undermining their capacity for "self-love."[23] Lynne Westfield poetically describes black women's efforts to re-member their bodily selves: "so many parts are missing faded damaged/it is difficult/to re-member my whole/danceable self."[24]

Such different bodily experiences, of course, render very different mothering experiences for women of color. hooks challenges white feminists' assumption that motherhood is the primary source of women's oppression: "had black women voiced their views on motherhood, it would not have been named a serious obstacle to our freedom as women. Racism, availability of jobs, lack of skills or education would have been at the top of the list—but not motherhood."[25]

Womanist theologian Kelly Brown Douglas asserts that because slavery was built on oppressive *racial* hierarchies, within their families and communities, enslaved women shared "reciprocal relationships of mutuality," with their men.[26] In her widely acclaimed book *Sisters in the Wilderness*, Delores Williams observes that "Even though their sexuality has been completely brutalized and exploited by white men of every social class," slave mothers' narratives reflect a "vigorous spiritual self-confidence."[27] The institution of slavery determined certain fixed roles for slave mothers. Among these roles were labor, reproduction, and nurturing. Often the roles of motherhood and nurture included "the tasks of protecting, providing for, resisting oppression and liberating."[28] Williams goes on to explain that for black mothers the overlapping institutions of motherhood and the church were actually sites of empowerment. During and after slavery, roles for black woman's motherhood became established within the system of slavocracy. Negatively called mammy, this place for women became reinstitutionalized in some African American denominational and nondenominational churches as church mothers, or mothers of the church. Antebellum white family life provided mammies an environment with a great deal of authority. The African American church provides a context where mothers of the church have tremendous power and receive tremendous respect. These mothers experience similar power in communities where they reside.[29]

In *Black Feminist Thought*, Collins suggests that even today, traditional black church services reflect "the interactive nature of black women's epistemology," which she describes as an emphasis on personal accountability; the belief in experience as a source of wisdom and knowledge; a commitment to dialogue as a tool for exploring differences; and an ethic of empathy.[30] White women, Collins explains, also have experiences and emotions to draw from; however, with the exception of the family, few white controlled U.S. social institutions validate these ways of knowing. Black women, on the other hand, "have long had the support of the black church, an institution with deep roots in the African past and a philosophy that accepts and encourages expressiveness and an ethic of caring."[31]

In her essay "Shifting the Center: Race, Class, and Feminist Theorizing About Motherhood," Collins looks closely at how differences like these distort white women's theorizing about motherhood. Because white feminists are not asking questions about the survival of their children or their racial ethnic communities, their assumptions about power and identity do not fit black women or other women of color's experiences as mothers. In light of this difference, Collins offers the term motherwork: "to soften the existing dichotomies in feminist theorizing about motherhood that posit rigid distinctions between private and public, family and work, the individual and collective, identity as individual autonomy and identity growing from the collective self-determination of one's group."[32] And, I would add to Collins's list of dichotomies sacred and secular.

### SHIFTING THE CENTER: MOTHERWORK AS RESISTANCE AND GROWTH

> Resistance begins with people confronting pain, whether it's theirs or somebody else's, and wanting to do something to change it. And it's this pain that so much makes its mark in daily life. Pain as a catalyst for change, for working to change.[33]
>
> —bell hooks

While Woolf, LeGuin, Rich, and Cixous gave me language for my own experience as a white middle-class woman who longed for relevance in a male dominated world, their spirituality, like my own, was informed more by an ethos of individual autonomy at odds with the ethic and needs of the community. I found a different, and in some ways more satisfying, spiritual nourishment in the writing of women of color. Toni Morrison, Alice Walker, Gloria Naylor, Louise Erdrich, Gloria Anzaldua, and Maxine Hong Kingston acknowledge and affirm a world where motherhood and "spirit matters"[34]—a world where grace is embodied "not in abstraction like virtual reality, but in tangible things—in real bodies and real gatherings. Sacramental experiences are experiences of persons' bodies, emotions, intellect, and will coming to deeper knowledge and love of God."[35] But more importantly, the narrative style and technique of these women allowed me to *experience* an "other" spirituality, a spirituality informed by the "S/spirit who works body divinely."[36]

In "Diverting Mothering," Sau-ling C. Wong writes about white women like me who are inspired by the spirituality in the mother-daughter stories of women of color, but often ignore "elements of cultural resistance and survival, of self preservation and community-building." Wong describes a "psycho-spiritual plantation system," in which perceived or actual "spiritual superiority" of caregivers (in this case mothers) of color "functions mainly as a *resource*, subject to appropriation to salve the insecurities of the master/ mistress."[37] But I believe closer attention to this misreading of spirituality has potential to make visible white middle-class women's assumptions about mind, body, spirit, and motherhood.

According to Judylyn Ryan, spirituality is the foundation of many black women writers' visions of empowerment and their characters' knowledge of self and strength. Ryan explains that this spirituality is informed by an African religious cosmology "characterized by interconnectedness."[38] This spirituality is not limited to the confines of a particular religion or institution; but neither is it *opposed* to religion. In fact, Ryan believes that black women artists are committed to "dismantling" what she calls a "paradigm [model] of resistance," which defines subjectivity in oppositional terms. It is reactive, pointing always to oppositional relationships. Instead the artists embrace a "proactive paradigm of growth," which provides "a multidimensional interpretive lens that recognizes interdependent relationships."[39] Unlike a paradigm of resistance, which conflates power and privilege, a paradigm of growth differentiates power and privilege by "defining power both as coercive/oppressive and as creative/righteous agency."[40]

This paradigm of growth is reflective of womanist spirituality, a spirituality which "seeks to grow into wholeness of spirit and body, mind and heart—into holiness in God," according to womanist theologian Emilie Townes, who defines womanist spirituality as a profound kneading of humanity and divinity into oneness: one breath, hope, vision of living and witness toward spanning the vast chasm of prejudices, hatreds, and oppressions into a magnificent, richer divine love we know with Jesus in our lives. This love for self and others holds together each person and community amidst relationship.[41]

Like white feminists, womanists are deeply aware of how a culture of domination and subordination has (mis)used the Bible to disempower and dehumanize not only women, but other bodies as well, including men of color, gays, and lesbians. Womanists also know the power garnered by their foremothers' and fathers' active interpretation of both the word and the world. Once again women of colors' different social-cultural locations and interpretive frameworks result in different relationship with scripture. Womanist theologian Renita Weems suggests that because the bible's portrayal of human relationships resonates with the experience of African American women, they "find the bible especially meaningful because it reflects a distinctive way of living that African American women have valued and continue to advocate with great energy."[42] But because they are marginalized by gender, race and often class, African American women are particularly sensitive to oppression found in the biblical narrative. Rather than rejecting the biblical canon, however, womanists seek to "supplant the biblical account of salvation history altogether with extrabiblical accounts that help provide a fuller, more egalitarian reconstruction of biblical history."[43]

Delores Williams points out that Alice Walkers' *Color Purple* is peopled with mothers and othermothers who nurture amidst "a host of destructive domestic and social forces." Protagonist Celie dutifully mothers her step husband's children, while her sister Nettie, a "childless" missionary living in Africa, mothers the biological children Celie conceived via her rape by her stepfather. Unjust laws demand that Sophia mother the children of her white mistress, while her biological children, due to her unjust imprisonment, are mothered by her husband Harpo's second wife. And Shug nurtures and mothers all of the characters, as well as herself. Liberated, women and men love self and other, wholly and holy. Ultimately, they remember a world where the "nurturing of the children is the task of the entire black community—male and female."[44]

Three years ago, my husband and I spent the year in Kenya adopting our now four and five year old children, Maya Achieng and Robert Baraka. We loved our time in Kenya, but when our adoptions were finally approved, we were anxious to return home to our four older biological children and our respective jobs, to begin a life of "normalcy" with our new family. At the end of my first week back at work, I received a phone call from my physician telling me I had been diagnosed with uterine cancer. While attending an academic conference a few months later, I recounted my experiences of adoption and cancer to my friend and colleague, Dee James. Dee is also a mother, and had been struggling with multiple life-threatening illnesses during the two years since we'd seen each other. As Dee and I discussed the ways we felt betrayed by our own bodies, Dee reminded me of Baby Suggs sermon in Toni Morrison's novel *Beloved*:

> She did not tell them to clean up their lives or to go and sin no more. She did not tell them they were the blessed of the earth, its inheriting meek or its glory bound pure . . . She told them the only grace they could have was the grace they could imagine. That if they could not see it, they would not

have it. "Here," she said, "in this here place, we flesh; flesh that weeps, laughs; flesh that dances on bare feet in grass. Love it. Love it hard. Yonder they do not love your flesh. They despise it. They don't love your eyes; they'd just as soon pick em out. No more do they love the skin on your back. Yonder they flay it. And O my people they do not love your hands. Those they only use, tie, bind, chop off and leave empty. . . . Love your hands,! Love them. Raise them up and kiss them. Touch others with them, pat them together, stroke them on your face 'cause they don't love that either. YOU got to love it, YOU! . . . This is flesh I'm talking about here. Flesh that needs to be loved . . ." She stood up then and danced with her twisted hip the rest of what her heart had to say . . . Long notes held together until the four-part harmony was perfect enough for their deeply loved flesh.[45]

Uninterested in their personal behavior, Baby Suggs empowers her congregation to "claim" themselves. Critiquing the lingering effects of slavery, Baby Suggs warns them of the lingering psychic and spiritual forces that continue to imprison their freed selves, but at the same time she reminds them of their own life-giving power to love themselves and one another. A sermon that is not limited to words, Baby Suggs's distorted and broken body continues to speak hope and life to her congregation, and through their worship in the clearing, their physical, mental, emotional, and spiritual selves are re-membered, the congregation is re-membered to one another.

Last year, I received a reflective essay titled "Mothers" from a young woman who has been both student and teacher to me, as well as one of the best conversation partners I know of. Prompted by her recent re-reading of Walker and Morrison, Tanya Lane wrote about her own mother:

I remember . . .
Smelling the cocoa butter from her glowing skin, feeling her blue and flower checked dress against my arm, agreeing with her as I pray to receive the Holy Spirit.
I remember . . .
Hearing her ask again and again, "Have you found a church yet?" Searching for an answer, I wonder at her persistence.
I remember . . .
Sitting in the sermon where the Spirit is moving, listening to her hum and then affirm—Yes Lord!—and then speak in tongues as others join her in worship. I remember my mother as a woman who could turn nothing into plenty. Her marginalized position as a low-income, black woman in a middle class predominantly white church, seemed at odds with the multitude of people who would seek after her for guidance. At first I thought this was peculiar, but as I plunge into the spirituality of African American literature, I usually find Black women in the thick of things. These women

are not powerful in the traditional sense, and oftentimes are rightly described as "de mule(s) uh de world" (Hurston, 29). This degrading position stands in ironic juxtaposition to many authors' use of these women as a conduit to the deep and terrible mysteries of God.[46]

Tanya's mother embraces a generative spirituality which empowers her with a righteous agency that resists the forces of this world that would marginalize her.

## RE-MEMBERING: DESIRE AND LAMENT AND SURVIVAL

*He and his boys up there were keeping it new, at the risk of ruin, destruction, madness, and death, in order to find new ways to make us listen. For, while the tale of how we suffer, and how we are delighted, and how we may triumph is never new, it always **must be heard**. There isn't any other tale to tell, it's the only light we've got in all this darkness. And this tale, according to that face, that body, those strong hands on those strings, has another aspect in every country, and a new depth in every generation.[47]*

—James Baldwin

Virginia Woolf says that a woman thinks back, if she thinks back at all, through her mother. Certainly, for the first four decades of my life, my own understanding of body, mind, faith, and motherhood were largely informed by my mother, who read the world through the eyes of her mother. Both women were incredibly strong, brilliant, and vibrant women who knew something about survival. At age 16 my grandmother's mother died, leaving my grandmother the sole survivor of her family. My own mother discovered she had aggressive breast cancer shortly after the birth of her fifth child. In spite of the cancer that quickly ravaged her body, she looked death in the eye for six painful years and said "not yet." But my family knows little about what my mother or grandmother experienced or felt in the face of death and great loss—because in our middle-class white world, these stories, stories of longing and lament, words and experiences expressing grief, were private stories a woman learned to keep to herself.

The truth is, desire and lament are not peculiar to a particular gender, sexuality, or ethnicity. They are the emotions that distinguish humans from all other earthly creatures, the image of God in each one of us. And while many communities acknowledge and affirm the important work of othermothers, patriarchal Christianity assumes biological mothers are the "real deal"—a reality that continues to be a source of pain for many women, regardless of their cultural context. Many of my single women friends and colleagues in the United States tell me that they find church to be a particularly lonely place for them. African theologian Mercy Oduyoye writes about the many ways African tribal communities and Christian churches continue to stigmatize childless women. Recounting her own experience as a single, childless woman of faith, Oduyoye describes her painful struggle to resist the feelings of inferiority associated with childlessness and her search for "models of faith who had not biologically increased and multiplied but who participated in glorifying God.[48]

Oduyoye explains that while African culture continues to inform religious and cultural norms for community life, it simultaneously constricts women. Even in Africa, where most societies have historically been matrilineal, mothering, what Oduyoye defines as "the determination to see another person become human," has become increasingly devalued as Western culture intensifies its claim to be legal and ethical standards bearer for the rest of the world. In the face of HIV/AIDS, violence against women, extreme poverty, and warfare, Oduyoye found her theological work to be irrelevant to the life of the community. In response to this disconnect, she gave birth to "The Circle of Concerned Women Theologians."[49]

It is not only theologians who are paying attention to the intersection of religion and culture in the life of African women. NGOs and academic-research teams in sub-Saharan Africa are also beginning to understand the rich fund of knowledge possessed by mothers committed to the survival of their children and their communities. As chair of University of Nairobi's department of oral literature, Peter Wasamba explains that the disciplinary research teams he has been involved in understand that mothers possess promising knowledge for scholarship aimed at sustainability and growth.

Like Oduyoye, Wasamba is intimately familiar with the personal anguish found at the intersection of traditional cultural practices and contemporary Christianity. I first met Wasamba at a gathering of adoptive parents in Kenya. As he spoke to the group, he acknowledged the humility he and his wife Dolphine experienced because of their inability to conceive a child. After several years of marriage and no children to show for it, many elders in the community were advising Peter that it was time for him to look for another "fertile" wife—which was the customary response to infertility in their local community. The Wasambas crossed many cultural and ethnic barriers when they decided to adopt their son Timothy, a child from a different ethnic group. When asked about how they negotiated this decision, Peter explains that though many perceive adoption as a "foreign idea," brought by Westerners, "adoption" for the Wasambas has reminded them "of a time when Kenya understood children were God's gift to us . . . and when we look at our son, we are able to remember the love that was before," before, before the forces of colonization, neocolonization, globalization, to a time when Kenya considered *all* children a blessing, a sign of hope for the future.[50]

## Mothering in the Borderlands

*Beading and weaving continue as if in preparation for our puberty rights for our new woman beingness. As African women, Akan and Yoruba, we work to shape our new work. Like our weaving and our beadwork, we bring it into being as we create new patterns of life based on the old.*

—Mercy Oduyoye[51]

Adoption is the subject of much heated debate right now, particularly adoption across racial, ethnic, and national lines. While it is certainly a topic that warrants careful thought, it is beyond the scope of this essay. The reality is that the number of children orphaned by AIDS continues to grow (UNAIDS estimates that by 2010 there will be 20 million children in sub-Saharan Africa alone orphaned by AIDS),[52] and in the midst of this crisis othermothers, mostly women, but some men, all people of deep faith, are determined to "answer life with life."

One beautiful example is Zam, a young wife and mother who works with mothers and children who are suffering with HIV/AIDS. Living in the slums of Kibera, the epicenter of Kenya's 2008 postelection conflict, Zam tells countless stories of women crossing traditional ethnic and religious borders in order to care for the many who are infected with and affected by AIDS and poverty. When asked about how her work has shaped her understanding of body, mind, spirit and motherhood, like most Kenyans, Zam answers with a story. She tells me about a young neighbor of hers who was forced to leave her home and community after her husband died of AIDS. Facing death just a few months later, the young woman had no one from her own tribe or religious community to keep watch with her. Zam explains in that moment, "I had to be a Christian for her." In the face of great pain and loss, Zam, a Nubian and Muslim who had always been "the other" to this young women, chose to become "other" to herself, so she could comfort and care for her neighbor. Surely, this is an example of Christ's call to love one's neighbor as oneself.

On the shores of Lake Victoria in Kisumu, Kenya, Prisca Adeche and her husband John are focusing their efforts on the most vulnerable in society, the orphans. They, too, are working to transform Africa "from a hostile space into a nurturing womb and cradle provided by God."[53] Having parented close to 600 babies (including my son Robert Baraka), their journey has not been an easy one. Many times the political environment has threatened the viability of the home. A "visionary pragmatist,"[54] or down-to-earth person, Prisca recalls one crucial moment when they were tempted to throw in the towel, and to return their respectable and stable jobs at the bank and the hospital:

We closed the door and fasted—I lay flat on the floor. I dreamt I had a baby on my back, three in my lap and babies on top. I've seen the hand of God.

I grew up with a heart for protecting young children. And it is best to obey what is bodily inside of us.[55]

At the moment John and Prisca are providing a home for 60 children; among them are children whom society has named "abandoned," "taboo," or "HIV positive." Upon their arrival at the home, Prisca holds each infant, often through the night, praying, singing, and envisioning how God will use the child to restore hope to their people, and the world. By sunrise, the child has been given a new name that reflects the dignity and worth of the child—Favor, Moses, Wisdom, Precious, or Desmond Tutu.

Like the African women Mercy Oduyoye describes in her essay "Spirituality as Resistance and Reconstruction," Zam and Prisca are one of the countless mothers and othermothers struggling to "build and maintain life giving and life enhancing [communities]." Resisting the global and economic forces that would name them "developing," "poor," "HIV positive," they are transforming "death into life" and opening "the way to the reconstruction of a compassionate world."[56]

In fact, the motherwork of women like Zam and Prisca extends beyond the continent of Africa. They are teaching white women here in the United States much about our innerconnectedness. I just returned from a trip from Kenya with my sisters-in-law Susan and Lannie Thompson. Like Oduyoye, Susan and Lannie have known their own share of pain in a family and community fixed on fertility. Seventeen years ago Lannie and my brother John courageously "stepped out of the procession," and adopted my niece Jackie. One of the most deeply spiritual moments of my life was when I went with Lannie and my brother John to meet and receive their second daughter (eventually named Jean) into our family. As Jackie, Jean, Lannie and my other sister-in-law Susan have come to know and love their five Kenyan nieces and nephews, they have put their shoulder to the wheel. Using beautiful beads made by single, Kenyan women, they create and sell jewelry to raise funds for the othermothers in Kenya who are working to create a space where the next generation of children can grow up with hope and dignity.

## ENVISIONING A NEW WORLD THROUGH MOTHERS, OTHERMOTHERS, AND OUR CHILDREN

I believe in the Spirit . . . in the just peace that can be created, in the possibility of meaningful life for all humankind . . .

—Dorothee Soelle[57]

A few weeks ago my grown biological son, Ben, spent a week with us before he began his new job teaching high school biology. Over the course of the week my son cooked, cleaned, and cared for the children while my husband worked on the house and I wrote about motherhood. Occasionally, I would take a break to go for a walk or a swim with my son. As we walked or swam, Ben recounted his own painful history of identity and belonging. Growing up as a gay young man in an intolerant and homophobic small town in the South gave Ben plenty to talk about. Each conversation sent me back to my writing with one more discovery about the relationship of body, mind, spirit, and motherhood. One night at dinner we all listened in as Ben discussed his and his partner Jory's dreams to adopt children of their own. As we were cleaning up after dinner, five-year-old Robbie walked into the kitchen with a pensive look on his face. "Mommy, when two men get married, who will be the mommy and who will be the daddy?" My son Ben and I looked at each other and burst out laughing. This was the million dollar question.

Even at his young age, Robbie has been asked enough questions about his relationship with his family to know that most people assume that a woman becomes a mommy when a baby grows in her tummy. But he also knows that he and his sister Maya did not grow in my tummy, and still I am their mommy. I pointed out to Robbie that some say that a mommy is the one that takes care of the house and of the children, but everyone in the family is well aware that my husband does far more of this work than I. So, neither definition of "mommy" worked for our home. When we got to this point in the conversation, my husband, who happened to be listening into our conversation in the next room, popped his head in and commented that the explanation seemed to be missing a testicular highway. The truth is, biological categories of identity are far more fluid than they were when Woolf, LeGuin, Rich, and Anzaldua were publishing their important critical work. In fact, with the miraculous help of science and technology, a man gave birth to a baby this year.

Several years after she co-edited *This Bridge Called My Back*, a collection of essays by lesbian writers of color, Gloria Anzaldua reflects on her younger self's understanding of identity. Written just after she was diagnosed with terminal cancer, Anzaldua's introduction to *This Bridge We Call Home: Radical Visions for Transformation* reflects on the limitations of a politics of identity. While it had been an important avenue in her empowerment as a younger, lesbian, woman of color, Anzaldua now realizes that by resisting those identity boxes that defined her only in bodily terms, that is her race, ethnicity, and sexuality, she has discovered ". . . another tribe, a different story (of mestizaje), that enables [her] to re-think [herself] in global-spiritual terms." In this new story, "national boundaries dividing us from the 'others' are porous, and the crack between worlds serve as gateways." Anzaldua describes a new identity which has "roots [we] share with all people and other beings—-spirit, feeling, and body compose a greater identity category."[58]

Mercy Oduyoye too believes we need a new myth, which "focuses on human interconnectedness as a part of becoming human," new myths which "mirror our new vision of the earth as a home for a single human race, interconnected and of equal value."[59] In a recent collection of essays in Mercy's honor, Kenyan theologian Nyambura Njoroge writes about Oduyoye's willingness to name her pain of childlessness, modeling for other African women theologians "a theology of lament," a theology which Njoroge believes calls for real celebration.[60] White feminist theologian Letty Russell encourages *all* women to follow Oduyoye's lead by resisting the patriarchal assumptions of hierarchy found in the gospel narratives and "seek other ways to understand and interpret the story of the birth of this Jewish child to Mary."[61]

Certainly, we must continue to resist those narratives of motherhood that reinscribe oppressive dichotomies, splitting us off from our physical, mental, emotional and spiritual selves, as they split us off from the dominant culture. But in our search for more generative symbols and texts, we might be better off looking beyond those narratives embedded in patriarchal assumptions about genetic-based parenting. In fact, as we strive to create spaces free of hierarchy, we might best be served by claiming our identity as "adopted children."

A good friend and colleague, Emerson Powery, a father and biblical scholar committed to creating and nurturing environments which call students, men, and women to engage in resistant and generative reading which leads to the "holistic liberation of [all] humankind."[62] While most marginalized readers find Paul particularly antagonistic, Powery offers Paul's interpretation of Spirit in Romans 8 as an unlikely, but potential site for liberatory reading. Paul reminds the Roman Christians of their status as adopted children, "the Spirit, as subject, 'bears witness' to those who are true 'children'" (v. 17) Powery suggests that Paul's description of the Spirit's groaning and sighing through all creation reflects two important things about suffering: 1. Though our adopted nature calls Christians to be co-sufferers with Christ now, this suffering compares minimally to the glory and hope of the day to come; and 2. the Spirit's sighing and groaning through all creation reflect our interconnectedness to each other and to "the entire ecological system: *all* creation groans."[63] Powery goes on to explain that situated in the middle of Romans 8, Paul's explication of Spirit is a catalyst for practical (sociopolitical) action. Our identity as adopted children allows us to function as both parent and child, as we await the fullness of our adoption, like the Spirit, we too "groan inwardly" with the sighs of childbirth (v. 23).[64] As "adopted children," each one of us, women *and* men, are called to participate with the Spirit, answering life with life, working for the future of our children and other children, and for those children yet to be born.

In the process of adopting our children, my cousin, a lawyer in the United States, advised my husband and me to be sure to secure the death certificate of our daughter's birth parents. Though we spent much time going back and forth with elders of the community, we were only able to track down the birth mother's death certificate. Our social worker assured us the mother's death certificate would suffice. On the day of the hearing, a distant relative of our daughter's mother agreed to come to court to assure the judge that our daughter had not been given up in coercion. When we left the judge's chamber, I thanked the relative for all her help. Commenting on the father's missing death certificate, I asked her when the father had died. "1998," she replied. This was confusing to me as our daughter was born in 2002. My concern must have shown, because the relative quickly leaned over and explained, "we think her mother had a friend."

It pains me to think how many times I've repeated this story to friends in the United States. My rendering of the story always alluded to my daughter's Kenyan relative confusion about things. It never dawned on me that I might be the one confused, that perhaps my daughter's Kenyan relative didn't share my ideas and experiences about what it means to be a mother and what it means to be a child. Two years later, I returned to Kenya to research the "rhetoric of engagement" among Kenyan women living with HIV/AIDS. Only then did I realize that when a person is born into a matrilineal society, it does not matter who the father is; my daughter *belonged* to her biological mother, who in turn belonged to her community.

I know that as I strive to imagine the world through the eyes of others, even my own children, biological or adoptive, gay or straight, sons or daughters, my older, white, female, heterosexual skin will always obscure what I can see and not see.[65] But through my children, I am learning to listen closely to those stories of desire and pain behind and in front of us. My Kenyan children come from a world where death does not separate family or the tribal community: "the temporal movement of human life is a continuous cyclical process from the realm of spirit to that of history."[66] Now, as I think back about my mother and those other women and men who have nurtured my body, mind, and spirit, I am learning also to envision a world, through my daughter's first mother, as well as the millions of other mothers who continue to answer life with life, working to create a world where bodies, minds, and spirits do matter, a world where each child cannot only survive, but can grow to love and serve God with dignity and hope.

## NOTES

1. Virginia Woolf. *Three Guineas*, 62.
2. Adrienne Rich. *Of Woman Born : Motherhood as Experience and Institution*, 252.
3. Virginia Woolf, *Three Guineas*, 61.
4. Ibid., 61.

5. Ibid., 72.

6. Ibid., 163.

7. Ursula LeGuin, *Dancing at the Edge of the World: Thoughts on Words, Women, Places,* 149.

8. Ibid., 151.

9. Hélène Cixous, "Laugh of the Medusa," 403.

10. Adrienne Rich, *Of Woman Born,* 284.

11. Ibid., 285.

12. Ibid., 286.

13. Nancy Chodorow, *The Reproduction of Mothering : Psychoanalysis and the Sociology of Gender,* 19.

14. Barbara Katz Rothman, "Beyond Mothers and Fathers: Ideology in a Patriarchal Society," 151.

15. Ibid., 156.

16. Hélène Cixous, "Laugh of the Medusa, 402.

17. Ibid., 396.

18. Ibid., 403.

19. Audre Lorde, *Sister Outsider: Speeches and Essays by Audre Lorde,* 53.

20. Gerda Lerner, *Creation of Patriarchy,* 11.

21. Patricia Collins, "Shifting the Center: Race, Class and Feminist Theorizing About Motherhood," 61.

22. bell hooks, *Ain't I a Woman? Black Women and Feminism,* 51–86.

23. Cheryl Townsend Gilkes, "The 'Loves' and 'Troubles' of African-American Women's Bodies," 232–34.

24. N. Lynne Westfield, *Dear Sisters: Womanist Practice of Hospitality,* 98.

25. Quoted in Andrea O'Reilly, *Toni Morrison and Motherhood : A Politics of the Heart,* 4.

26. Kelly Brown Douglas, "To Reflect the Image of God: A Womanist Perspective on Right Relationship," 75.

27. Delores S. Williams, *Sisters in the Wilderness,* 40.

28. Ibid., 39.

29. Ibid., 35.

30. Patricia Hill Collins, *Black Feminist Thought,* 221–38.

31. Ibid., 264.

32. Patricia Hill Collins, "Shifting the Center," 37–38.

33. bell hooks, *Yearning,* 215.

34. bell hooks, *Teaching Community: A Pedagogy of Hope,* 83.

35. Lynne N. Westfield, *Dear Sisters: Womanist Practice of Hospitality,* 81.

36. Luke Powery, *The Holy Spirit and African American Preaching,* 32.

37. Sau-ling C. Wong, "Diverted Mothering," 82.

38. J. S. Ryan, *Spirituality as Ideology in Black Women's Film and Literature,* 11.

39. Ibid., 8.

40. Ibid., 17.

41. Emilie Townes, *Embracing the Spirit,* viii.

42. Renita Weems, "African American Women and the Bible," 58.

43. Ibid., 69.

44. Delores S. Williams, *Sisters in the Wilderness*, 54.

45. Toni Morrison, *Beloved*, 103–4.

46. Tanya Lane, "Mothers," 8. Courtesy of Tanya Lane-Albala.

47. James Baldwin, "Sonny's Blues," 198.

48. Mercy Oduyoye, "A Coming Home to Myself: The Childless Woman in the West African Space." In *Liberating Eschatology: Essays in Honor of Letty M. Russell*, 117.

49. Isabel Apawo Phiri and Sarajini Nadar, eds., *African Women, Religion, and Health: Essays in Honor of Mercy Amba Ewudziwa Oduyoye*, 2.

50. Conversation with Peter Wasamba, June 25, 2008, Nairobi, Kenya.

51. Mercy Oduyoye, *Beads and Strands: Reflections of an African Woman on Christianity in Africa,* 103.

52. UNAIDS, "Children Orphaned by AIDS in Sub-Saharan Africa, http://data.unaids.org/publications/Fact-Sheets03/fs_orphans_africa_en.pdf.

53. Mercy Oduyoye, "Spirituality of Resistance and Reconstruction." In *Women Resisting Violence: Spirituality for Life*, 65.

54. Patricia Collins, *Black Feminist Thought*, 175.

55. Conversation with Prisca Adeche, June 28, 2008, Kisumu, Kenya.

56. Mercy Oduyoye, "Spirituality of Resistance and Reconstruction," 162.

57. Dorothee Soelle, *Against the Wind: Memoir of a Radical Christian,* 40.

58. Gloria Anzaldua, *This Bridge We Call Home: Radical Visions for Transformation,* 5.

59. Mercy Oduoyoye, *Beads and Strands,* 107.

60. Nyambura J. Njoroge, "Let's Celebrate the Power of Naming," 62.

61. Letty Russell, "Mercy Amba Ewudziwa: Wise Woman Bearing Gifts," 49.

62. Emerson Powery, "The Groans of 'Brother Saul: An Exploratory Reading of Romans 8 for Survival," 319.

63. Ibid.

64. Ibid., 320.

65. In "Notes toward a Politics of Location" Adrienne Rich writes about how her white skin limits what she sees and knows.

66. Peter Paris, *The Spirituality of African Peoples: The Search for a Common Moral Discourse,* 52.

## REFERENCES

Anzaldua, Gloria. 2002. *This Bridge We Call Home: Radical Visions of Transformation.* New York: Routledge.

Baldwin, J. 1998. "Sonny's Blues." In Ford, R. (Ed.), *The Granta Book of the American Short Story* (pp. 170–99). London: Granta Books.

Carr, Anne E., Elisabeth Schüssler Fiorenza, and Philip Hillyer. 1989. *Motherhood: Experience, Institution, Theology (Concilium)*. Edinburgh: T&T Clark.

Chodorow, Nancy. 1978. *The Reproduction of Mothering : Psychoanalysis and the Sociology of Gender*. Berkeley: University of California Press.

Cixous, Hélène. 1976. "Laugh of the Medusa." In DeShazer, M. K. (Ed.), *The Longman Anthology of Women's Literature* (pp. 390–405). New York: Longman.

Collins, Patricia Hill. 1994. "Shifting the Center: Race, Class and Feminist Theorizing about Motherhood." In Glenn, E. N., Chang, G., & Forcey, L. R. (Eds.), *Mothering: Ideology, Experience, and Agency* (pp. 45–65). New York: Routledge.

Collins, Patricia Hill. 2000. *Black Feminist Thought : Knowledge, Consciousness, and the Politics of Empowerment*. Rev. 10th anniversary ed. New York: Routledge.

Douglas, K. B. 1995. "To Reflect the Image of God: A Womanist Perspective on Right Relationship." In Sanders, C. J. (Ed.), *Living the Intersection: Womanism and Afrocentrism in Theology* (pp. 67–80). Minneapolis, MN: Fortress.

Gilkes, C. T. 1993. "The 'Loves' and 'Troubles' of African-American Women's Bodies." In Townes, Emilie M. (Ed.), *A Troubling In My Soul: Womanist Perspectives on Evil and Suffering* (pp. 232–34) Maryknoll, NY: Orbis Books.

hooks, bell. 1981. *Ain't I a Woman: Black Women and Feminism*. Boston, MA: South End Press.

hooks, bell. 1990. *Yearning*. Boston, MA: South End Press.

hooks, bell. 2003. *Teaching Community: A Pedagogy of Hope*. New York: Routledge.

Kyung, Chung Hyun. 1991. *Struggle to Be the Sun Again: Introducing Asian Women's Theology*. Maryknoll, NY: Orbis Books.

Lane, Tanya. 2004. "Mothers." Unpublished essay.

LeGuin, Ursula. 1997 [1989]. *Dancing at the Edge of the World: Thoughts on Words, Women, Places*. New York: Grove/Atlantic Press.

Lerner, Gerda. 1987. *The Creation of Patriarchy (Women and History)*. Oxford, UK; Oxford University Press.

Lorde, Audre. 1984. *Sister Outsider. Speeches and Essays by Audre Lorde*. Berkeley, CA: Crossing Press.

Njoroge, Nyambura J. 2006. "Let's Celebrate the Power of Naming." In Phiri, Isabel Apawo and Nadar, Sarojini (Eds.), *African Women, Religion, and Health: Essays in Honor of Mercy Amba Ewudziwa Oduyoye* (pp. 59–76). Maryknoll, NY: Orbis Books.

Oduyoye, Mercy Amba. 1996. "Spirituality of resistance and reconstruction." In Mananzan, Mary John; Oduyoye, Mercy Amba; Tamez, Elsa; Clarkson, J. Shannon; Grey, Mary C.; and Russell, Letty M. (Eds.). *Women Resisting Violence: Spirituality for Life*. (pp. 161–72). Maryknoll, NY: Orbis Books.

Oduyoye, Mercy Amba. 1999. "A Coming Home to Myself: The Childless Woman in the West African Space." In *Liberating eschatology: Essays in Honor of Letty M. Russell*. Louisville, KY: John Knox Press.

Oduyoye, Mercy Amba. 2004. *Beads and Strands : Reflections of an African Woman on Christianity in Africa.* Theology in Africa Series. Maryknoll, NY: Orbis Books.

O'Reilly, Andrea. 2004. *Toni Morrison and Motherhood : A Politics of the Heart.* Albany: State University of New York Press.

Paris, Peter J. 1995. *The Spirituality of African Peoples: The Search for a Common Moral Discourse.* Minneapolis, MN: Fortress Press.

Phiri, Isabel Apawo and Sarojini Nadar, eds. 2006. *African Women, Religion, and Health: Essays in Honor of Mercy Amba Ewudziwa Oduyoye.* Maryknoll, NY: Orbis Books.

Powery, Emerson. 2004. "The Groans of 'Brother Saul': An Exploratory Reading of Romans 8 for 'Survival.'" *Word & World* 24/3: 315–22.

Powery, Luke. 2007. *The Holy Spirit and African-American Preaching,* Unpublished doctoral dissertation, Toronto, Canada: University of Toronto Press.

Rich, Adrienne Cecile. 1995. *Of Woman Born : Motherhood as Experience and Institution.* New York: Norton.

Rich, Adrienne Cecile. 2001. "Notes toward a Politics of Location." In DeShazer, M. K. (Ed.), *The Longman Anthology of Women's Literature* (pp. 1095–1106). New York: Longman, 2001.

Rothman, B. K. 2004. "Beyond Mothers and fathers: Ideology in a Patriarchal Society." In Glenn, E. N., Chang, G., & Forcey, L. R. (Eds.), *Mothering: Ideology, Experience, and Agency* (pp. 139–60). New York: Routledge.

Russell, Letty M. 2006. "Mercy Amba Ewudziwa: Wise Woman Bearing Gifts." In Phiri, Isabel Apawo and Nadar, Sarojini (Eds.), *African Women, Religion, and Health: Essays in Honor of Mercy Amba Ewudziwa Oduyoye"* (pp. 43–58). Maryknoll, NY: Orbis Books.

Ryan, Judylyn S. 2005. *Spirituality as Ideology in Black Women's Film and Literature.* Charlottesville: University of Virginia Press.

Smith, Sidonie. 1993. *Subjectivity, Identity, and the Body: Women's Autobiographical Practices in the Twentieth Century.* Bloomington: Indiana University Press.

Soelle, Dorothee. 1999. *Against the Wind: Memoir of a Radical Christian* (trans. Barbara and Martin Rimscheidt), Minneapolis, MN: Augsburg Fortress.

Townes, Emilie Maureen. 1997. *Embracing the Spirit: Womanist Perspectives on Hope, Salvation, and Transformation.* The Bishop Henry McNeal Turner/ Sojourner Truth Series in Black Religion, v. 13. Maryknoll, NY: Orbis Books.

Weems, R. 1991. "African American Women and the Bible." In Felder, C. H. (Ed.), *Stony the Road We Trod* (pp. 57–77). Minneapolis, MN: Augsburg Fortress.

Westfield, N. L. 2001. *Dear Sisters: Womanist Practice of Hospitality.* Cleveland, OH: Pilgrim Press.

Williams, Delores S. 1993. Sisters in the Wilderness: The Challenge of Womanist God-talk. Maryknoll, NY: Orbis Books.

Wong, S. C. 1994. "Diverted Mothering: Representations of Caregivers of Color in the Age of "Multiculturalism." In Glenn, E. N., Chang, G., & Forcey, L. R. (Eds.), *Mothering: Ideology, Experience, and Agency* (pp. 67–94). New York: Routledge.

Woolf, Virginia, Jane Marcus, and Mark Hussey. 2006. *Three Guineas.* A Harvest Book. Annotated ed., 1st ed. Orlando, FL: Harcourt, Inc.

# CHAPTER 8

# Spirituality, Love, and Women

*Soyoung Baik-Chey*

## QUESTIONING OUR EXISTENTIAL REALITIES: "MOM, WHY ARE YOU ALWAYS SICK?"

For young girls, the world can be experienced as filled with "curious" and "wondrous" things. To me, the world was a huge question mark. From waking up in the morning until bed time, I kept asking questions about the wonderland. "Why does that leaf suddenly turn red?" "Does this ant go to heaven when it dies? Is 'ant heaven' separated from human heaven?" "When did I start to be myself?" Sometimes laughing, sometimes perplexed, sometimes tired, but usually with sincerity and smile, mom, my first teacher, provided the best and most thoughtful answers to the girl of curiosity.

Of the never-ending questions, the most curious one was why my mom had always been sick. Getting up late in the morning, walking slowly without vivid energy, and lying down often, she seemed to be seriously ill. I did not know what was wrong with my mother in those days. When I came to know the answer for that question, I was a 35-year-old married woman, mother of a three-year-old son, and just experiencing miscarriage in the 12th week of pregnancy.

As a Korean woman and Christian, I encountered so many cultural and religious assumptions regarding allegedly "natural" occurring things, as wife, mother, and a daughter-in-law. When I started writing my doctoral dissertation in Boston, I naturally moved to Dallas, my husband's first working site, having been taught that a virtuous wife has to follow her husband. I naturally became a full time caregiver to my son, given my strong belief in maternal self-sacrificing love. However, I still wanted to continue my academic program. As a full- time housewife, I could not find extra time for my study. An INS officer questioned once whether my immigrant status was as a full-time student or a full-time housewife, when being interviewed for achieving my green card; I was both. Facing a clash between the natural duty of motherly self-giving love and the eagerness to continue my study, I felt I was divided into two pieces. Yet, I tried to do both because both were equally important to me. Radically reducing sleeping time, I overworked and lost my unborn child in my 12th week of pregnancy. Hearing that I was selfish and lacking agape, a Christian self-denying love, by pursuing my egoistic desire of continuing my own work, I felt guilty. I became seriously ill. I could barely move; it was even hard to breathe.

For a long time, I did not realize that it was not my fault; nor a matter of my selfishness denying agapic love of a Christian mother, even while witnessing so many Korean Christian women suffering the same malady. There is something seriously wrong with a system which makes women sick. Such an oppressive system blocks the breathing between dynamic relational communication of women's physical experience with their spiritual and mental desires. Created in the image of God, all human beings are capable of being creative and self-expressive. Being creative and self-expressive is not only a human capacity but a human obligation and a right, as the children of God created *imago dei*. When cultural and religious systems condemn women's self-expression and creativity as selfish, wicked, and wrong and block routes for women to express their creativity, they become sick: their cultural presuppositions oppose their ontological capabilities.

This chapter analyzes how historical construction as opposed to natural instinct leads Korean Christian women to struggle with incongruence between their ontological capabilities and their cultural presuppositions. As Korean Christian women, we have internalized cultural-religious teachings in two major patriarchic heritages, Christian and Confucian. These two traditions teach that women are bodies and vessels, which restricts women to being repositories for their male partners for reproduction, requiring them to practice a self-sacrificing, self-denying devotion to benefit their husbands and their children. These male-made teachings on women estrange women's spiritual-and-mental capability and desire from their physical realities. In the first part of this essay, I provide an in-depth analysis describing details about Confucian and Christian cultural-religious heritages, which have led Korean Christian women to internalize as natural the self-giving, self-denying love of a mother and a wife. I especially pay attention to the historic process of institutionalizing Confucian cultural values in Korea since these Confucian values are intertwined with Christian values, governing contemporary Korean Christian women's consciousness and unconsciousness. Questioning androcentric Christian and Confucian interpretations on women and love (agape in Christian terms) as problematic, in the following section, this essay, based on the perspective of a Korean Christian woman, suggests a theological rethinking of body, mind, and spirit in a harmonious and integrated way of being and loving.

## Christian Heritage Defines Women

### Female Body as Deficient, Carnal, and Demonic

Where does Korean Christian women's tragic reality of incongruence between cultural presuppositions and their ontological capacities come from? The incongruence firstly comes from Christian stories of women observed and written through male theologians' distorted eyes. Throughout the history of Christianity, male theologians, as reflected below, have addressed that a female body, ontologically carnal, is far from spiritual salvation and sober mentality. To achieve spiritual salvation and sober mentality, a female needs to sanctify her body either through keeping her virginity or practicing extreme ascetic attitudes to the extent of denying female bodiness. Being a saint implies a certain understanding that a pure body evidences a pure spirit, proclaiming the image of holiness as the status of virginity. The Virgin Mary was an archetypal woman who is holy in this first way. Androcentric Christian tradition praised Thecla, a companion of Paul's apostolic mission, as another representative stereotype of the holy woman who keeps physical virginity as the evidence of devoted mind and pure spirit. Having listened to St. Paul's Christian message, she refused to marry her fiancé and devoted herself to becoming a pure bride of Jesus the Christ. She was sentenced to death and set on fire in the center of the Colosseum, yet heavy rains came from heaven extinguishing the fire. Her second danger involved possibly losing her virginity when she met Alexander, the powerful Roman officer in Antioch, who was fascinated by her beauty. As the result of refusing his request and insulting him in public, he forced her to stand before hungry wild animals. However, a female lion protected her, fighting against other wild animals. Witnessing heavenly protection of Thecla from the attack of a furious ox, Alexander gave up persecuting her. Her last threatening moment of losing her virginity occurred when theologians of Cellucia, who were jealous of her 72 years of celibacy, her successful ascetic life and outstanding sermons— sent some gangsters to rape her. She prayed hard for the protection of her physical purity and suddenly a rock was cracked to let her hide inside, and this became her dwelling place till her death.[1] It seems to me ridiculous, however, that the body as sinful and unworthy becomes the single crucial medium to acquire saintness of the self.

Under this tradition of celebrating virginity as the methodological way to stay ontologically holy, the early Christian fathers recommended celibacy to Christian women as the best way to achieve holiness. Jerome the Early Church Father said: "Eve in Paradise was a virgin: it was only after she put on a garment of skins that her married life began . . . the gift of virginity has been poured most abundantly upon women, seeing that it was from a woman it began.[2]

If the first way of maintaining virginity does not work, in androcentric Christian discourses, the second best is still left, that is, to deny the female body and practice an extravagant ascetic life. To be holy, female sexuality and its attractiveness need to be denied, making it logical that negation of female bodiness is the route to achieve spiritual pureness. The negation sometimes results in giving up female sexual identity itself. More often, female ascetic Christians who internalized the teaching of the early Christianity tended to identify their body with male bodies as seen in the exemplary story of Pelagia, who was once a famous and gorgeous actress in Ethessa and then known as "Pelagius" after her conversion to Christianity. Covered with jewelry and shiny decorations, whenever she demonstrated her beauty in public, even many Catholic fathers could hardly focus their stirring minds. Nonnus the Catholic father, who had a revelationary dream to sanctify Pelagia, however, was not tempted, and eventually taught and baptized her. With Pelagia's deep repentance, she chose the way of hidden ascetic monasterial life in Jerusalem. Nonnus called her Pelagius, and people around her thought she was a male monk. Due to her long-practiced fasting and ascetic lifestyle, even Jacob, who used to know Pelagia the actress, could not recognize her at first sight. When people came to know that such a famous and faithful Pelagius was a female, while cleansing her dead body, they praised God saying that she is the real treasure of God who voluntarily takes on male appearance negating female bodiness.[3] This episode indicates that holiness has been often regarded as identical to the negation of female body and living as a male body.

Maria of Egypt was also a representative to achieve the second way of being holy through the negation of female bodiness. *From the Great Canon, the Work of Saint Andrew of Cretem* includes an oral tradition about her as stated by Zosimas, a prominent Catholic leader regarded as an ideal ascetic Christian. Zosimas confessed that he thought he did not have any ascetic practice that he had not accomplished until he met Maria of Egypt, whom Zosimas first thought to be a thing, not a human, almost burned by strong sunlight. Maria, with a naked, dark-skinned, and white-haired body, told her story to Zosimas about how she practiced a 47-year-long extreme ascetic life as the evidence of receiving divine forgiveness.[4]

As such, the early Christian tradition has praised women who internal-ized and practiced the negation of bodily desire as the way to achieve spiritual purity and sober mentality. This tradition had stably developed in the history of Christianity mainly due to two reasons: the first one is the intellectual influence of Hellenistic dualism that dichotomizes body and spirit, placing the latter on a higher and nobler status; the second one, central to this article, is male theologians' fear and ambiguous feelings about the female body that transcends their capabilities and experiences. Recent feminist observe that this idea has developed because of men's dubious feelings about the female body. According to Rosi Braidotti, female sexuality, which has both the power of giving life (reproduction) and the power of death (abortion), created men's perspective on women as "ambiguous" and "fearful." Since male thinkers define their ontological entity as "normal" based on their experience of being a man, they interpret femininity pejoratively as "abnormal." They have viewed being woman and mother as "monstrum," something different, and otherness as "morphologically dubious."[5] They regarded women's otherness character-istics such as reproduction and physical attraction to male partners as both "sacred and soiled, holy and hellish, attractive and repulsive, and all powerful and therefore impossible to live with."[6]

Such subtle, ambiguous, and complex feelings toward female body has led androcentric Christian writers, along with other male-centered thinkers, to conclude that the female capacity of reproduction is "natural" given by God, but "passive" and only "physical" in principle as a mere container or incubator that preserves life essence provided by male body. Greatly influ-enced by Aristotle who taught that female body is a "defect," something failed in the developing process of being human, early and medieval Chris-tian fathers interpreted female as mutant, abnormal, and inferior to male.[7] No wonder that Augustine, a child of a Hellenistic Christian intellectual inheritance, said reproduction is the single purpose of woman's creation. Although Augustine permitted sexual intercourse, he interpreted it as sin-ful, only a "forgivable" sin because it participated in the reproduction of the Christian generation. He says marriage is where men and women unite for procreation and do not defraud one another. Non-Christian men can experi-ence this blessing of nature, but it becomes sinful because they do not pro-create in faith. Sexual intercourse with a whore involves a culpable nature. Augustine sees any use of the body in ways not intended as prohibited and against nature.[8]

Compared to Augustine, Thomas Aquinas evaluated sexual intercourse in a more positive sense. He thought it belongs to a realm of divine ordina-tion, saying that "generation by coition is natural to man by reason of his animal life, which he possessed even before sin."[9] Nevertheless, mainline Christian belief in abhorrence toward bodiness or the body subordinated to spirit exists in Aquinas, who agreed with Augustine's suggestion to practice sexual intercourse only for the spiritual purpose of producing the children of God. Aquinas along with the citation from Augustine admonished that Christians should perform their physical love without "the ardor of desire and restlessness of mind."[10]

Unlike Catholic fathers, Martin Luther, with his other Protestant associates, saw human bodiness as "divine" and "good" as the creation of God, but he was not a "protestant" in terms of his focus on reproductive functions of the female body as the major role of women. Luther asserted that God divided humanity into two groups or classes (Genesis 1:27), and God saw this reality as a good creation (Genesis 1:31). Neither woman nor man should be abusive or disrespectful to the other. Both should honor the good creation and *imago dei* that pleases God. After their creation, God tells humanity to reproduce (Gen. 1:28). This divine statement needs to be honored by humanity.[11]

Luther, who regarded reproduction as a "divine" Christian vocation, did permit only exceptional cases of religious genius such as Paul and Jeremiah who could beget spiritual children of God to choose celibacy as vocation.[12] To Luther, reproduction of the children of God was so important as a divine mission that it became a sort of Christian obligation and vocation that Christians should complete to glorify God.

Luther's positive approach to a human body as "good" and marital relations as "divine" are a developed idea in comparison to the early and medieval assertion of woman as a necessary evil or a mere container for reproduction. He also preached equal and mutual sexual sincerity and parental devotion both to the husband and the wife.[13] Nevertheless, Luther still regarded a wife's divine vocation as fulfilled exclusively in the private realm of her home, where she tends and cares for children, engages household duties, and obeys her husband: noble and important works.[14]

Luther also admonished that another major role of a Protestant wife was to become "an antidote against fornication" and to be "obedient" to her husband. Luther's interpretation of marital life was not much different from Paul's. In his *Lectures on Genesis*, Luther asserted that women are to be in charge of household management. Based upon Paul, women are also to be the antidote or medicine against sin (1 Col. 7:2): to avoid fornication, every man ought to have his own wife. After all, God has favored men by saving women for them, protecting men from fornication and providing for procreation.[15]

Staying in a private family institution, to Luther, the wife's major work is to take the role of reproduction partner and serve as an antidote against fornication of the husband. Under such logic, the wife hardly pronounces the subjectivity of her own sexuality. Luther and some other Protestant thinkers' understanding of female bodiness as good and divine overcomes pejorative interpretations of bodiness in early and medieval Christianity. Nevertheless, it is still androcentric. A Christian female's body is good and divine only when it functions as the reproduction and nursing instrument and an antidote for her husband's fornication. Such social teaching has been a major idea in Christian churches until now. With the rise of Christian fundamentalism in the 21st century, now more than ever, many Christian women have internalized these teachings as a spiritual and divine calling.

How ironic, that androcentric Christian thinkers' statements of subordination of body to spirit andor divine use of the body to complete one's intellectual, mental, and spiritual achievement are contradictory to their other teachings. These thinkers also taught that the body is sinful and shameful, not worthy to preserve, so thus needs to be denied. Sometimes they admonished that the body, which always pursues physical and selfish desires, cannot communicate with one's spirit that is eager for divine desires. How can a body be a crucial instrument of or route for achieving spiritual holiness and/ or divine vocation when it is neither equal nor communicative to one's spirit and mind?

A fear of erotic power of a female body in male-biased Christian tradition has created an awkward belief that a female body is so sinful that it must be negated, rejected, and even tortured to reach the higher level of mental and spiritual achievement; At the same time, a woman's body can be a divine tool if it is sexually protected and preserved as virgin, if it functions as the womb for bearing children, and serves as an antidote against the husband's possible fornication. If a body is not related and communicative with one's spirit/ mind, why can't her spiritual and mental holiness be sustained when she fails such bodily obligations? To me, such an approach seems erroneous.

The most notorious case of an erroneous and deranged interpretation of the female body might be witch-hunts in the Middle Ages. *Malleus Maleficarum*, the work of two male Dominican monks of unhealthy mind and spirit, invoked the dwellers of Christendom to torture innocent women's bodies calling them "demonic." Sprenger and Kramer noted that women are witches more often than men, because the fragile, female sex is mentally and physically weak. With spiritual and intellectual things, women are different from men; they are more carnal. Even scripture notes that women have little discretion, particularly given that they come from the bent rib of a man. An imperfect animal, women are naturally deceitful and wicked, thus more apt to dabble in witchcraft.[16]

Their strong abhorrence of the female body led Sprenger and Kramer to conclude that Eve's carnal lust, which precipitated Adam's sinful deed, proves a female's physical propensity to practice witchcraft.[17] Judged by such morbid messages, many faultless women, from 1570 to 1630, were accused of being "adulteresses," "fornicatresses," and "the concubines of the Great

[Satan]."[18] In terms of the religious eagerness to eliminate witchcraft, Protestants paralleled Catholics. They tortured the female body in the name of sanctification. The procedure to sanctify a witch started with removing all hairs from her body, cutting off finger nails, baptizing her with sanctified water, and getting her dressed in salt-soaked clothing. Then torture started:[19] her accusers forced a woman to disrobe and stand naked before strange males called professional examiners. These examiners put sharp pins on her body, especially in sensitive areas such as the breast, nipples, and other genital areas. Sometimes her torturers burned her on these sensitive places or soaked her entire body under water. They even cut off genital areas and eventually raped these alleged witches.[20] Such erotic torturing procedures ended only when a woman—shameful, embarrassed, abused, battered, and almost dying—confessed, "I am not sure, but I think I am a witch."[21] Following this public excursion the witch was commonly set on fire. Sometimes they removed her internal organs from her body and then put her to death by hanging, by blowing her up with an explosive powder, or by burying her alive.[22]

Thus during major moments of Christian history, the female body has been denied, controlled, and sometimes tortured because it was regarded as carnal, dangerous, and demonic. Regarding femaleness as passive and obedient as ordained by God, major male theologians taught Christians that a woman does not have the right to control her own body, "because female was created from man" not vice versa (I Cor. 11:8). From Paul to the 20th-century pope (in 1941) who proclaimed a wife's obedience to her husband as divine rule, to an Anglican Church bishop (in 1987) on a radio program who denied the possibility of women's ordination—concerned that female clergy might evoke male clergy's sexual instinct,[23] we Christian women have heard and internalized male theologians' sermons which provide divine legitimacy to degrade, devalue, insult, and sometimes torture female bodies for almost 2,000 years.

## CHRISTIAN VIRTUES AS SELF-GIVING AND SELF-SACRIFICING

Western male theologians, who thought they had exclusive authority and legitimate power to interpret divine and secular matters, drew sharp hierarchical distinguishing lines between agape as the self-sacrificing spiritual love and eros, the sensual desire to achieve and assert the self. They provided the cross of Jesus Christ as the single and best evidence to practice agapic love. Applying the ancient Hebrew religious symbol of *hattat* to the death of Jesus, major Christian theologians praised the self-sacrificing love of giving one's own life to others as "salvific." Apostle Paul once said a Christian of such love endures pain, does not search for her own benefits, forgives and covers all sinful actions done by others to the self, is always calm and kindful, and never shows anger to others.(I Cor. 13: 4–7). Early fathers also recommended that Christians practice agapic love. According to Augustine, self-love is the principle of the earthly kingdom, which often results in the denial of God; while self-denying love is the principle of the heavenly kingdom, which often results in the denial of the self and self interests. Wisdom, Courage, and Justice could be "splendid vices" if these are pursued from the motivation of self-love and for self-development.[24] St. Francis proclaimed one-way directed love to serve others without any expectations of returns.[25]

Modern theologians have inherited such a simplified, dichotomized contradiction between "divine" agape and "immoral" eros. Anders Nygren, for example, did not admit eros as a righteous form of Christian love. To him, streams of Christian love flew toward two directions; toward God and to the neighbors. He pinpointed characteristics of Christian love as selflessness and disinterest in self. Self-love, to Nygren, was the enemy which sincere Christians had to struggle with and finally overcome.[26] To Reinhold Niebuhr, perhaps one of the most influential theologians in the modern Christian church—the cross, the symbol of the self-sacrificing love, was the completion of humanity in history. Jesus's life purpose was to be united with agape, divine love. Niebuhr saw the cross as the symbol antithetical to self-assertion. In human history, God's agapic love was seen as absolutely powerless because it denied demonstrating the use of power in this world. It is not identical to eros, which Niebuhr interpreted as the love of rational, calculative, self-interest and mutually expected. Agape completes eros, imperfect and inferior to agapic love in Niebuhr's eyes. Eros is natural desire but agape is noble and religious because it has divine origin.[27]

How frustrating that Reinhold Niebuhr, who saw structural evil in dualistic modern civilization, failed to see that the actual implication of his double standard could work negatively to Christian women who mainly stayed in private realms. Niebuhr, a Christian realist, admitted an ethical dualism based on the matter of possibility. Niebuhr defined as "ideal" and "salvific" the practice of agapic love, the love of listening to and of self-giving to others. One can realize such love in private realms where personal relationships interact, on the one hand. On the other, he saw that it was "impossible" to apply such agapic love to public realms where rational and calculative competitions are the rule of survival.[28] In spite of his realistic and practical approaches, Niebuhr seemed to overlook two realities: that those who are mainly in a private realm, where such self-sacrificing agapic love is exclusively recommended, are women; and that the husband and children, who are in the world of competition where they should be self-interested for survival, cannot immediately give up such a self-interested attitude once they enter home and become agapic. These realities drive a Christian woman to become a single person who practices such "salvific" love to the rest of family members who request it, against her own benefits. Considerable human experience relies on interaction between cultural-religious expectation and societal members' internalization. In a patriarchal society, getting married, for a woman, does not mean starting a new life but finishing or completing her life. Her battlefield is not a world of history. She does not participate in creating a better world order. Instead, she struggles with dust everyday at home. The purpose of motherhood (often romanticized as constructive, meaningful, and participatory work to make a good society) is, however, to raise children to establish independent identities and finally to transcend their mother. Her happiness or feelings of satisfaction are mostly dependent on others: her husband's success or children's healthy growth. By being women, their existential realities and cultural lives are often already sacrificial and salvific without such an application of the religious virtue of agapic love.

## KOREAN CONFUCIAN HERITAGE DEFINES WOMEN

By being Korean Christian women, we have another androcentric tradition, Confucianism, which has controlled and institutionalized women's body, mind, and spirit as men wish and desire. An interesting observation is that Confucian moral teachings are consolidated in the Korean churches while they are weakened in secular society as Korean society is modernized. Affinities between male-centered Christian and Confucian social teachings on women (passive, physical, self-denying and self-sacrificing being) strengthen each other and put heavy cultural pressure on the majority of Korean Christian women. Ironically, Korean churches, once regarded as the forerunners of modernization in Korea, have now become the furious preservers of conservative Confucian-Christian moral values. Witnessing such a phenomenon, what I want to pinpoint here in this section is that just as androcentric Christian tradition was a historical construction, Confucian tradition is also male-made. The fact that both Christian and Confucian interpretations on women and love are historic, neither natural nor divine, provides Korean Christian women with possibilities to create a new social teaching in our religious tradition from women's perspective.

Not until the mid-Chosŏn dynasty (the 16th century) was Korean society institutionalized based on male-centered Confucian values. Pre-Chosŏn Korea had been "maternal" in some aspects. "Changga rŭl ganda" (going to wife's house), for example, has been a common expression of "get-married" which is still used in modern Korea. This customary verbal expression exemplifies an age-old custom of the bridegroom staying at his father-in-law's house ever since he married his fiancé, which is quite different from Chinese patriarchal traditions of the bride's living at an in-law's house right after the marriage (which is called *ch'inyŏngje*). This Korean custom is called *sŏryu puga* (husband stays at wife's parents' house), common in pre-Confucian Chosŏn society. The staying period varied from 3 years to 24-years,[29] so the couple usually raised their children and let them be married at the wife's parents' house.[30] Children could choose either their father's surname or mother's surname according to their preferences and beneficial conditions.[31] The pre-Chosŏn family did not adopt a male for social and economic succession. Unlike Chinese culture, where patrilineal inheritance laws were established in an early period, daughters and her sons (grandsons) in pre-Chosŏn society could equally inherit a parent's or parents' possessions, not only property but also social status such as kingship and administrative positions. *Ŭmsŏje* (giving beneficial advantages to offspring of contributed officers) was applied not only to sons and grandsons but also to daughters' husband and her sons.[32]

Chosŏn governmental rulers, however, intentionally attempted to reconstruct societal institutional structure based on Confucian moral/social teachings. To enfeeble preexisting social structure, as the necessary procedure to establish the stable base for the new emerging dynasty, the Chosŏn governmental rulers, by having taken Chu-His's Confucianism as the national ideology, presented institutional reformation in Korean society, in public and private domains.[33] By the late 17th century, due to centrally and systematically controlled governmental efforts, the entire Korean society became Confucian at last. Along with the elimination of *sŏryu puga* in marriage customs, people started to regard daughters as *"ch'ulga oein"* (the one who has left the father's home permanently and regarded as a stranger). Patrilineal inheritance law was also established as the result of consistent governmental effort to implant Confucian institutional orders to Chŏson society. As patrilineal institutions settled into the society, the first son in charge of the ancestors' worship service (*chesa*) became the major heir, inheriting considerable portions of his father's property.

To build Confucian Chosŏn systems both in family and in society, Chosŏn governors distributed to Korean families Chinese Confucian texts such as the *Yegyŏng* (Book of Rites) and *Chuja charye* (Family Ritual of Master Chu Hsi), which provide a moral evaluation on women under the polarized category of two groups of women, *dŏgnyŏ* (women in wisdom) and *agnyŏ* (wicked women). According to these books, wise women are those who take care of and perform all housework so their husbands do not need to worry about family matters and can concentrate fully on public matters.[34] Meanwhile, *agnyŏ*, immoral women, are those who interfere in their husbands' public works.[35]

The Confucian system divided social institutions into two distinguishing realms, that is, public and private. The dichotomized realms of *nae* (inside, private) and *woe* (outside, public) were exclusively designed according to gender. The system created *naewoebŏp* (laws regarding *nae* and *woe*), which prevented female and male members from participating in each other's business. This dichotomized realm-setting restricted gender roles: males cannot stay inside while females cannot stay outside; males go on the right side of the road while females go on the left side of the road; males answer immediately while females hold back quick responses. From the age of seven, boys and girls could not sit side by side in the same space.[36]

House structure was designed to promote the *naewoebŏp*, dividing the building into two spaces, *anch'ae* (inside house) and *sarangch'ae* (detached building from *anch'ae*). Between *anch'ae* and *sarangch'ae* there was *chungmun*, a middle gate that divided these areas from each other.[37] Chosŏn *yangban* (scholar-officers) class rulers started to use palanquins for women to let them consistently stay "inside." The Chosŏn government gradually reinforced *naewaebŏp* so Chosŏn women could not go outside without covering their faces. Also, women in Chosŏn could not continue the long-time tradition of flower festivals in spring, natural power worship ceremonies, and other outdoors activities. They were not allowed to go to Buddhist temples without strict guidance. Buddhist monks could not visit their houses, especially *yangban* widows' houses. If it happened, an official authority would strike about 100 blows with a club as the punishment.[38] These restrictions became "taken for granted" to *yangban* women by the 17th century and common to most members of Chosŏn society by the 19th century.

Applying *yin* and *yang* principles in neo-Confucian thought and the polarized distinction between "essential" Confucian thought and "inessential" folk beliefs to the project of constructing Confucian society, Chosŏn male scholars taught people the passivity and dependency of female inessential *yin* character to *yang*, the essentially perfect male character of being. The principle of *yin* and *yang* is that they generate and develop the life of myriad things. *Yang* is a tendency of males characterized as heavenly, divine, elevated, lofty, sincere, moving, active, great, and strong; *yin* is a tendency of females characterized as low, meek, passive, obedient, calm, and weak.[39] The Confucian scholar-official class emphasized these characteristics as a "natural" and "heavenly" order that generates and develops all myriad things in the world.

In the Confucian system, women's most honorable purpose was to become *hyŏnmo yangch'ŏ* (the wise wife and a good mother). Many Confucian writings described the way of *hoynmo yangch'ŏ* as: completing filial piety to one's own parents before marriage and to in-laws after the marriage; serving her husband as her sole "heaven"; always being obedient and keeping sexual sincerity exclusively to him; and raising her children to preserve and enhance her husband's family fame.[40] This is called *samjong chido,* Confucian women's three ways of subordination: to subordinate to the father, to the husband, and to the grown-up son.

Demonstrating her own opinions and failing to excel in the reproduction function of childbearing were regarded as "vices," which became major reasons for being divorced. In those cases of divorce, the women could not have any constitutional and societal protections and rights to reject the unequal treatment. She would live with shame as the daughter who disgraced her in-law family and her own family as well. Otherwise, she would commit suicide.

Since the patrilineal family tree had to be maintained, the Confucian Chosŏn system did not allow Chosŏn women to get remarried if her husband died before her. Chosŏn government prevented the children of remarried women from applying for public examinations to acquire an official position in bureaucratic Chosŏn governmental system. This law was not familiar to pre-Chosŏn customary thought so even considerable numbers of scholar-officers did not agree on its practice because widows in many cases could not afford their physical survival without a male partner's support in the marriage system. Nevertheless, King Sŏngjong established *chaega kŭmjibŏp* (legal prevention of remarriage) in 1477, proclaiming that "to starve to death is a small thing but to lose her chastity is a great matter."[41] More than often, this *chaega kŭmjibŏp* forced women in Confucian Chosŏn society to commit suicide in order to make their husband's family "honorable." Their deaths, I submit, were cultural deaths caused by internalized and manipulated cultural pressure. A woman named Park during King Sukjong's reign, for example, was praised and recorded as the model of honorable Chosŏn woman for her continuous attempts at suicide following her husband's death, and her final success of suicide by completely not eating. Being starved to death, without energy left in her body and dressed in purely white clothing, she bowed four times before her husband's photo and died.[42] Just as many Christian women in the European Middle Ages chose cultural death by performing extreme ascetic practices, regarded as expressions of religious sincerity, Chosŏn women also chose cultural death by performing the Confucian way of being a wise and moral woman.

To reinforce and preserve the system, the Chosŏn government provided financial, legal, and societal benefits to male members in the family of *yŏllyŏ,* a woman of sexual sincerity, who mainly died following the death of her husband or committed suicide under the threatening moment of losing her chastity by rape. A monument in remembrance of *yŏllyŏ* was built before the house; grains and other prizes were provided to her remaining family members; the children of *yŏllyŏ* received beneficiary favors from community and government; and even the family members were exempted from conscription of public compulsory labors. A widow did not have any alternative when the death of her single life could provide the entire family members with opportunities to enjoy commonwealth given from the government. Reinforced by cultural presuppositions and members of society who took for granted those cultural values, countless numbers of Chosŏn women committed suicide.[43]

In contrast to the sanctification of *yŏllyŏ*, Chosŏn laws were cruel to a woman who lost her chastity by having sexual intercourse with someone other than her legal husband. Culturally agreed upon and practiced punishment was the display of her naked body in public places, such as the market place, for three days, followed by cutting off her head; or, they would "draw and quarter" her body by ripping her body apart while she was still alive by pulling from four directions. Her children's names were recorded in the record of the name of fornicating women, and they were blocked from applying for official positions.[44]

Under this strict cultural pressure, various stories about *yŏllyŏ* were recorded and delivered in oral traditions.[45] By the late Chosŏn time, this cultural value system of *yŏllyŏ* penetrated most ordinary families, as well as the ruling scholar-officer class. During war times such as *Imjin waeran* (1592–1598, wars caused by Japanese military invasion) and *Byŏngja horan* (1636–1637, a war caused by Chinese military invasion) almost four hundred women were prized as *yŏllyŏ* for their suicide that allowed them to refuse foreign soldiers' sexual violence. Women who preserved their lives and lost their sexual purity were called *hwannyang nyŏn* (originally meaning "women who returned home" but implying "women of disgrace who preserved their own life despite losing their chastity"). Most husbands who encountered their disgraced wives upon their return from war divorced them.[46] As seen above, the Confucian system and its cultural presuppositions forced Korean women to the lowest, most powerless, self-denying, and self-sacrificing status.

## BODY, MIND, AND SPIRIT DANCE IN DIVINE LOVE

When does a paradigm shift? It is when the paradigm fails to explain existing phenomena in the world with the rationale the paradigm generates. The paradigm shifts when increasing numbers of people say that they cannot find meaningful, plausible, and acceptable interpretations in that existing paradigm. Recognizing that the cultural-religious heritages that we used to consider as natural and even divine are male-centered interpretations of women and love, incongruent with our ontological and existential realities, I question that if one takes an experience of being Korean Christian women as a perspective and a starting point for doing theology, to what extent would the theological interpretations and applications of Christian love be different from those driven from an androcentric experience and perspective? If the male-centered interpretation of agape is not appropriate to Korean Christian women's experiences, and if that interpretation has led Korean Christians to accept, endure, and even voluntarily pursue unreflected self-sacrifice in their lives, generating their physical, mental, and spiritual illness, then the paradigm should be changed.

Since half a century ago, Western Christian women from a feminist perspective have demonstrated the inappropriateness of androcentric interpretation of agape as self-sacrificing/self-denying love and its superior position to eros—here I use the term meaning not only sensual and physical love but also the self-love that pursues nourishment and achievement of the healthy self-oriented desire. By the 1980s, Christian feminist theologians started to produce theological articles and books that deconstruct androcentric interpretations of agape and that reconstruct correlational and holistic understandings of love as the divine sensuous life-energy to sustain and nurture righteous and passionate relationships among all living things. Carter Heyward and Beverly Harrison, for example, were leading feminists who beautifully reconstructed theological interpretations of Christian love as "mutual," "righteous," "passionate," and "sensuous" love that embraces characteristics of agape, philia, and eros in traditional categorical distinction. What they found "problematic" in androcentric "love" interpretations was the one-way direction from God to Christians who were unworthy to receive such a great love, and from Christians to neighbors who were usually unworthy to receive such a self-giving sacrificial love. Harrison and Heyward found the stoppage of the dynamic stream of love. Harrison correctly saw that, traditionally, theologians contrast agape, disinterested love, with eros as egotistic passion, even though not all egoistic passion is sexual or erotic. Further, these types of love are traditionally held in conflict, and concepts of self-assertion and self-denial are deemed irreconcilable realities in the world.[47]

Love is ontologically relational. Women's experiences reveal that love influences both the lover and the loved, making them grow and change as the result of loving interactions. In fact, our ontological and existential reality is relational in itself. My body is not a separated husk that cannot communicate with my mind and spirit. As children of God, confessed in the symbol of a Trinitarian God, our reality of being *imago dei* can be also interpreted in a "trinitarian" way. It is my confession based on my intellectual and daily experiences, that if God the trinitarian deity is a symbol of God's spiritual freedom, Christ's physical involvement in history, and the Holy Spirit as the Sustaining Power's mental desire to sustain Her beloved world, the mystical entity of Her children' body, mind, and spirit can be also understood in a "trinitarian" way. Just as God, Christ, and the Holy Spirit are not independent, separated

selves but one entity in three persons, a human being is also the one self as
the dynamic association of nonhierarchical, interrelational, and interpersonal
body, mind, and spirit. Elizabeth Johnson in her outstanding work *She Who
Is: The Mystery of God in Feminist Theological Discourse* describes dynamic,
relational existence of a Trinitarian God in the concept of "perichoresis." She
puts it:

> As its most basic the symbol of the Trinity evokes a livingness in God, a
> dynamic coming and going with the world that points to an inner divine
> circling around in unimaginable relation. God's relatedness to the world in
> creating, redeeming, and renewing activity suggests to the Christian mind
> that God's own being is somehow similarly differentiated . . . a relational,
> dynamic, tripersonal mystery of love—who would not opt for the latter?[48]

Criticizing the traditional image of a trinitarian God as a "static," "monolithic"
kind of unity,[49] with the "exclusive use of male imagery,"[50] Johnson recon-
structs a trinitarian God as "dynamic," "communal," and "equal." Extending
Edmund Hill's dynamic interrelation in Trinitarian doctrine by adopting the
Greek word *perichoreuo*, "an eternal divine round dance,"[51] Johnson suggests
a metaphor of "a tripe helix," "one of the most mysterious, powerful shapes
in all creation."[52] According to her, "the strands of the helix do not originate
from each other but are simply there together, not statically but moving in a
dance of separation and recombination, which creates new persons."[53] Life-
giving, life-generating, life-sustaining, and life-recovering movements are
dynamically interpenetrated in such an ongoing conversing and dancing of
three "persons" of one God.[54]

   The God, who is in a dynamic relation in three persons, is also relational
with Her creations. Carter Heyward rewrote the first chapter of Genesis
from her experience and perspective of being a woman: "In the beginning,
I AM WHO I AM created everything that lived and grew and changed and
wondered and tried and stretched and cuddled and recoiled. . . . The Creator, I AM WHO I AM, could find no adequate word for this process except
'love.'"[55]

   From a woman's experience, Heyward knew that love means "changing and becoming something new."[56] Our Korean female ancestors in pre-
Chosŏn times also knew that they grew, changed, and became a new being in
the process of the interaction of body, mind, and spirit of themselves, of the
divine, and of all myriad things. The *Mago* myth, for example, is the creation
myth in which the three female gods who are in ontological continuity and
harmony performed major works in creating and sustaining human beings
and the world. How sad that the androcentric Korean ruling class oppressed
and covered up life-giving female traditions, official history books, ignoring

this myth, starting from the *Tangun* myth that has a male founder. The *Mago* myth only survives in a family secret document called "Pudoji" which Pak Chae-sang (363–419?) wrote in the Silla kingdom.[57]

Since our ontological and existential reality is relational, our love is also relational. It also delivers and shows a mystery of being in a dynamic trinitarian symbol: our love is "agapic" for its divine origin which leads a lover to transcend the self; it is "philia" that concerns our mutual-regard, mutual-respect, and mutual acceptance to make the partner change and grow; and it is also "erotic" in terms of its incarnated, embodied, felt, and touched characteristics. And these characteristics of love are not separated from each other. A body can remember how her mother's, her lover's, her friend's deep spiritual and mental cares are embodied on her body cells, and how spiritual fulfillment and mental happiness give physical energy to "live out" in the world. These physical remembrances are vital energy sources for the self to have spiritual and mental happiness, too. We don't need to choose one mode among such mystical dynamic existences of our being and our loving. It is because they are "dancing" in one.

The cross of Jesus, which male theologians interpreted as the apex of sacrificial love, can also be reinterpreted in such a dynamic relational ontology of "trinitarian" God and human love. As Harrison reinterpreted the cross from a feminist perspective, Jesus died not because of his irrational eagerness to complete selfless love but because of his persistent "radical love" which never stopped in dynamic relation with his Hebrew friends under Roman colonialization, which we call "injustice." She notes that Jesus's radical nature pertains to his concept of the power of mutuality. Thus, his death signals his refusal to desert that radical activity of love, of embodied communal reciprocity and solidarity. Believers are also called to such radical aliveness. Jesus accepted his call to radical love by accepting his sacrifice toward creating right relationships as justice-making.[58] We can accept the self-sacrificing love. It is not because, however, it is a universal, absolute, and divine Christian virtue, but because it is the case of improving our existential realities in the process of relational being and loving. Our body can talk the spiritual and mental dimensions of our being and loving.

Created as relational, a body shares feelings, intellectual learnings, spiritual awakening with mind and spirit. And it creates a new way of being and loving every time in the process of its encounter with the divine, the other human beings, and all the myriad things in the world. Our "trinitarian" way of being and loving does not try to possess something exclusively as "mine" nor to isolate something as "otherness." Instead, in the relational way of being and loving, we try to share and grow together. We refuse, deny, and fight against any attempt to make it separate from our connected reality of being and loving.

## NOTES

1. Ra Ŭn-sŏng, *Wuidaehan yŏin dŭl ui palchach'ui* [Heroines in the Early Church History] (Seoul: Korean Institution of Church History, 2005), 18–34.

2. Jerome, Letter 22, "To Eustochium: The Virgin's Profession," *Selected Letters of St. Jerome*, trans. F. A. Wright (Cambridge, MA: Harvard University Press, Loeb Classical Library, 1933), recited in *Women and Religion: A Feminist Sourcebook of Christian Thought*, ed. Elizabeth Clark and Herbert Richardson (New York: Harper & Row Publishers, 1977), 60.

3. Sŏ Wŏn-mo, Pang Sŏng-gyu, Yi Chŏng-suk, Sŏ Hyŏn-sŏn, eds. *Yŏsŏng kwa ch'ogi Kidokgyo* [Women and the Early Christianity] (Seoul: Chrisitandigest, 2002), 115–27.

4. Ra Ŭn-sŏng, *Wuidaehan yŏin dŭl ŭi palchach'ui* [Heroines in the Early Church History], 302–25.

5. Rosi Braidotti, *Nomadic Subject* (New York: Columbia University Press, 1994), in *Writing on the Body: Female Embodiment and Feminist Theory*, ed. Katie Conboy, Nadia Medina, and Sarah Stanbury (New York: Columbia University Press, 1997), 64.

6. Ibid., 65.

7. Ibid., 63.

8. Augustine, "On Marriage and Concupiscence," *Augustine: Anti-Pelagian Writings; Nicene and Post-Nicene Fathers*, 1st ser., vol. 5, ed. Philip Schaff (New York: Christian Literature Society, 1893), in Clark and Richardson, *Women and Religion: A Feminist Sourcebook of Christian Thought*, 72–77.

9. From Thomas Aquinas, *Summa Theologica*, ed. Fathers of the English Dominican Province (London: Burns, Oates and Washbourne, 1914), in Clark and Richardson, *Women and Religion: A Feminist Sourcebook of Christian Thought*, 92.

10. Ibid., 93.

11. Martin Luther, "The Estate of Marriage," *Luther's Works*, vol. 45, *The Christian in Society* 2, ed. Walther I. Brandt (Philadelphia, PA: Muhlenberg Press, 1962), in Clark and Richardson, *Women and Religion A Feminist Sourcebook of Christian Thought*, 134–36.

12. Ibid., 138.

13. Ibid.

14. Ibid., 140.

15. Martin Luther, "Lectures on Genesis," *Luther's Works*, vol. 1, ed. Jaroslav Pelikan (St. Louis, MO: Concordia Publishing House, 1958), in Clark and Richardson, *Women and Religion: A Feminist Sourcebook of Christian Thought*, 143–45.

16. J. Sprenger and H. Kramer, *Malleus maleficarum*, trans. Montague Summers (London: The Pushkin Press, 1948), in Clark and Richardson, *Women and Religion: A Feminist Sourcebook of Christian Thought*, 121–23.

17. Ibid., 124–125.

18. Ibid., 125.

19. Guy Bechtel, *Le Quattro donne di Dio*, trans. Chŏn hye-jŏng (Seoul: Yŏsŏng sinmunsa, 2004), 222.

20. Ibid., 226–36.

21. Ibid., 232.

22. Ibid., 237–39.

23. Anthony Giddens, *Sociology*, trans. Kim Mi-suk et al. (Seoul: Eulyoo Publishing Co. Ltd., 2003), 481–82.

24. From Augustine, *The City of God*, recited in *Christian Ethics*, Waldo Beach and Reinhold Niebuhr, trans. Kim Chung-gi (Seoul: Taehan kidoggyo ch'up'ansa, 1985), 129–35.

25. *The Little Flowers of St. Francis of Assisi*, trans. Dom R. Hudleston (London: Burns Oates, 1953), recited in Beach and Niebuhr, *Christian Ethics*, 145.

26. Anders Nygren, *Agape and Eros* (Philadelphia, PA: The Westminster Press, 1953), 217.

27. Reinhold Niebuhr, *The Nature and Destiny of Man*, vol. 2 (1943), trans. Yi Sangsŏl et al. (Seoul: Minjung Publishing Co., 1958), 89, 94–95, 105–14.

28. Reinhold Niebuhr, *Moral Man and Immoral Society* (1932), trans. Yi Hanwoo (Seoul: Munye Publishing Co., 1992), 277–78, 280, 284.

29. Koryŏsidaesa yŏngyhoe [Association of Study in Koryŏ History], *Koryŏin dŭlŭi saranggwa kajok, kŭrigo munhak* [Love, Family and Literature of Koryŏ people] (Seoul: Sinsŏwŏn, 2006), 103.

30. Yi Pae-yong, *Hanguk yŏksa sok ŭi yŏsŏngdŭl* [Women in Korean History] (Seoul: Wŏjini, 2005), 18–19.

31. Koryŏsidaesa yŏngyhoe, Love, Family and Literature of Koryŏ people, 125.

32. Ibid., 129.

33. On this particular topic, see Chai-sik Chung[Chŏng], *A Korean Confucian Encounter with the Modern World Yi Hang-no and the West* (Institute of East Asian Studies, Berkeley: University of California Press, 1995), esp. 9–21.

34. *The Book of Yu*, in *The Chinese Classics*, vol. 3 *The Shoo King or the Book of Historical Documents*, trans. James Legge (London, Hong Kong: Henry Frowdge, Oxford University Press Warehouse, 1865), 84–85.

35. Pak Yŏng-ok, *Han'guk yŏsŏng kŭndaehwa ŭi yŏksajŏk maengnak* [A Historical Context of Modernization of Korean Women] (Seoul: Chisik sanŏpsa, 2001), 28.

36. Ibid., 53.

37. Yi, Women in Korean History, 26.

38. Ibid., 27–29.

39. I paraphrase and shorten the contents of the *Book of Changes* recited in Pak Yong-ok's work, 31.

40. Yi, Women in Korean History, 37–38.

41. Peter H. Lee et al., *Sourcebook of Korean Civilization*, vol. 1 *From Early Times to the Sixteenth Century* (New York: Columbia University Press, 1993), 563–65.

42. Yi, Women in Korean History, 30.

43. Ibid., 31.

44. Ibid.

45. Ibid., 33.

46. Ibid., 33–34.

47. Beverly W. Harrison, "Sexism and the Language of Christian Ethics" in *Making the Connections Essays in Feminist Social Ethics*, ed. Carol S. Robb (Boston, MA: Beacon Press, 1985), 28.

48. Elizabeth Johnson, *She Who Is: The Mystery of God in Feminist Theological Discourse* (New York: Crossroad, 1996), 192.

49. Ibid., 220.

50. Ibid., 193.

51. Ibid., 220.

52. Ibid., 221.

53. Ibid.

54. Ibid., 220.

55. Carter Heyward, *Our Passion for Justice Images of Power, Sexuality, and Liberation* (New York: The Pilgrim Press, 1984), 43.

56. Ibid.

57. Based on this Mago myth in a further study, I plan to develop a theological reflection of trinitarian goddess from a Korean perspective.

58. Harrison, "The Power of Anger in the Work of Love: Christian Ethics for Women and Other Strangers," in *Making the Connections Essays in Feminist Social Ethics*, 18–19.

# CHAPTER 9

# What the Mind Forgets the Body Remembers: Women, Poverty, and HIV

*Linda E. Thomas*

We have come a long way from assuming that HIV/AIDS is only a gay disease and shunning its carriers. We have come a long way, in the United States at least, from the many years when thousands were dying from HIV/AIDS and President Ronald Reagan would not even speak of the disease publicly. The red ribbon is no longer an anomaly. Even a few churches—here and there—speak and teach about the reality of HIV/AIDS (at least on the single Sunday in December that is World AIDS Day).

Yet, beyond that single Sunday, churchgoers in the United States still rarely enter into frank discussions with one another about sexual practices and sexually transmitted diseases. We do not unearth on Sunday mornings the centuries and millennia worth of theological principles that govern sexual choices, gendered realities, or concepts of sexual power in relationships. Only once in a while—mostly in private with doors closed or in times of crisis—do discussions ensue about one of life's fundamental components: sex.

How often do we hear of, or converse about the fact that women are the fastest growing population in the United States being infected with HIV, primarily through heterosexual intercourse? I posit that seldom does that make it into our public or private discourse.

How often do we talk publicly about a sexual reality that will affect or is affecting approximately 50 percent of persons living in the United States; that is, one of every two of us living in the United States has or will have a sexually transmitted disease or sexually transmitted infection in our lifetime?[1] How often do we talk together in church or in structured public discourse about the inequitable power dynamics that receive support from religious teachings? Such teachings tell heterosexual women that our role is to please, accept, and submit to our male partners' sexual dominance. How often do we talk about the problematic underlying ideology and the very real, unhealthy, and, to be honest, less pleasurable consequences that result from it?

This chapter examines HIV/AIDS, African women, and the Bible in conversation with related realities in the United States. I engage statistics and realities in the United States as a preface to my topic that focuses on issues surrounding HIV/AIDS in South Africa for two reasons. First, we are a part of this story, this crisis, and this epidemic. HIV/AIDS affects us all: it is born, in part, from our very own religious and cultural traditions in the United States. Second, I write this article in honor of Mother Christina Nku, a proto-womanist and founder of St. John's Apostolic Faith Mission in South Africa, and I use the South African context as a case study, interwoven throughout. If anyone is squirming, even just a little bit, at this notion, which freely broaches the topic, I rest my case. Here, in the much enlightened United States, we still have a long way to go in dealing together with sexuality in an effectively public way.

## THE CONTEXT AND MY PERSPECTIVE FOR VIEWING THE PANDEMIC

I have no doubt that HIV/AIDS is a part of the lives of some of those reading this article, particularly those of us who are African American. Of all persons living in the United States with HIV/AIDS, a full 44 percent are indeed African American.[2] Furthermore, African American and Latina women, who only account for about 25 percent of the United States female population, constitute a striking 79 percent of HIV/AIDS cases among women.[3] Clearly, we all live with both the heritage and the physical reality of HIV/AIDS.

Second, I am often struck by the ease with which issues can be dissected, analyzed, mused about, considered, and pondered, from afar. Those in the Christian tradition have long looked to the other, the outsider, as the one in need of healing. We view the other and often see that their problems need fixing. Such othering is a tradition as old as the first attempts to Christianize the continent of Africa and as ingrained as the continued attempts to place blame, send moral critique, or purport that the other need only to learn about Jesus, as we have done, for their lives to be more fulfilled, more morally righteous—in short, more like us. I will not do that in this article.

I am part of the heritage and history that infiltrated and continues to penetrate the lives and ideologies that influence the ways that HIV/AIDS is transmitted and managed. While I explicate and share the realities of women in South Africa who live with HIV/AIDS, I do not do this to suggest that the problem is "over there" in some distant land or only affecting "those people." My intent for this chapter, while focusing on South Africa, is to be enlightening about the particularities of women living in South Africa. However, my ultimate aim is for us to listen and know that many of the same issues, in varying degrees or with situational differences, affect our very lives and the lives of those with whom we live, work, and encounter daily—our bodies, minds, and spirits. South Africa forms a frame and the women who live with HIV/AIDS are particular. They are not, however, the other; the issue is not only out there, over there, or only with them. The issue is both global and local, here and there, right now.

I am a North American womanist scholar. That, at first glance, causes me to appear to be somewhat of an outsider among the South African women about whom I write. When I speak, however, I do so as a long time researcher with deep personal and professional relationships among the particular community at St. John's Church in South Africa. I am writing of a community that I have witnessed and stood with for many years as they live with, manage, survive, and thrive amidst the gendered reality of HIV/AIDS in South Africa. I share their reality, aware that their challenges are faced in circumstantially different but ideologically similar ways by communities in my neighborhood, at my own church, and among my students, colleagues, and friends in Chicago, in the United States, and in many pockets across the world.

I begin with the basics, the things we know but which require repetition until they cease. Even those nation-states like the new South Africa whose constitutions speak of a nonracist, nonsexist society continue, in practice, to perpetuate patriarchal control of women. Just as women in the United States are far more often forced to live in poverty with the lowest wage-earning jobs, women in South Africa are trapped by the dual cuffs of patriarchy and poverty. Add to that the entrenched reality of racism and we have the infamous and insidious triplet: the intersection of race, gender, and class that brings unduly difficult burdens for women to survive in South Africa. The penetration of HIV/AIDS has raced in to create a fourth point of capture that dominates the lives of women in South Africa.

Here are the statistics: In 2006 the Health Department of South Africa reported that over 4,000,000 persons were living with HIV/AIDS. By comparison, that number in the United States, as reported by the Centers for Disease Control (CDC) in 2005 was less than 450,000. Among those in South Africa over the age of two, girls and women in virtually every age group are definitively more likely than their male counterparts to live with HIV/AIDS. Indeed,

UNICEF reports that among adolescents, girls are five times more likely than boys to contract HIV/AIDS.[4] Of South Africans ranging from 20–24 years of age, 6 percent of men live with HIV/AIDS, compared to 24 percent of women. Of those who are 25–29, the numbers are equally staggering: 12.1 percent of men and 33.3 percent of women live with HIV/AIDS.[5]

The sheer percentages of persons living with HIV/AIDS are enough to demand a closer look. Yet, it is the divide among women and men that brings me to this discussion. I intend to explain some of the reasons that women are disproportionately affected by and infected with HIV/AIDS. And I will bring to light at least some of the reasons that 29.1 percent of pregnant women in South Africa are living with HIV/AIDS.

The reasons are simple to name. We speak about them in classrooms and from pulpits with great regularity—or at least we purport to. While easy to name, harder to say, and incredibly complex to solve, the main reasons are: patriarchy, sexism, poverty, and religion. Most major disciplines could point to a contributing factor. Basically, the confluence of a myriad of "ologies" (studies/teachings) that perpetuate oppressive practices are killing girls and women disproportionately. UNICEF says it plainly: the dramatic disproportion of females living with HIV/AIDS is due to sex and gender inequities.[6]

Women's vulnerability to HIV/AIDS infection is particularly heightened by their economic dependence on men, lack of access to education, poverty, sexual exploitation, coercion and rape, as well as by their engagement in informal and commercial sex work. Women face additional and more acute discrimination when they are identified as being HIV positive. Because they are often first to test positive through prenatal testing, they are branded as the spreaders of the virus. Once their HIV-positive status is revealed or disclosed, women face being physically abused, losing access to important economic resources, and the threat of being chased from their homes.[7]

The result is this: honestly and terribly, in this time of HIV/AIDS, African women and their children die first. They die without equal rights, without access to power, without power of influence, without access to education, and with religious beliefs that support and are complicit in male dominance. South African scholar Mpine Qakida asserts that South Africa's women's rights are inherently nonexistent and that the male-dominated South African society perpetuates the current AIDS crisis.[8] Research bears out that the majority of African cultures judge women as inferior to men, and consign them roles considered of less importance in the private realm of life. Males are the power brokers in the private and public sphere when it comes to decision-making, and this is very important to consider in the private sphere of sexual practices in an HIV/AIDS era. As South African theologian Beverly Haddad writes, "Women experience great difficulty in negotiating sexual practices in their relationships. Because of their subordinate cultural status, it is accepted that women's role is to please men sexually, and they have little say over the kinds of sexual practices they engage in."⁹ This type of reality is the experience of many poor women throughout the world.

## IMPACT OF THEOLOGY AND ECONOMICS ON THE HIV/AIDS PANDEMIC

All theological reflection related to the HIV/AIDS pandemic on the continent of Africa needs to incorporate an analysis of the unequal power relations between women and men. Moreover, we must be mindful that the political economy on both macro- and micro-levels further marginalize women, particularly those women who are "infected and affected" by the HIV/AIDS virus. Indeed, "poor and marginalized women are severely discriminated against in macro-social and economic policies resulting in this group continuing to bear the brunt of poverty in South Africa."¹⁰ As such, African women are situated in a micro-political economy that is adversely influenced by globalization. As Professor Musa Dube asserts, "Globalization as an anti-social force worsens poverty, escalates mobility, the trafficking of women and girls, and sex work, thereby creating fertile ground for the spread of HIV/AIDS."¹¹

If a globalized economy is a primary macro force at work that allows HIV/AIDS to breed, the places where that insemination occurs are in the so-called private sphere of personal heterosexual relationships. Across the variety of cultures on the continent of Africa, marriage and patriarchy are norms that together subordinate and create the conditions for the spread of HIV/AIDS. In sub-Saharan Africa the "culture of marriage" is the primary vehicle through which African women contract HIV/AIDS. By "culture of marriage" I mean the folkways and mores out of which African men and women live daily. In other words, marital sexual intercourse is the cradle in which the disease is rocked.

Practices such as *lobola* (bride-price) and strict biblical interpretation contribute to women's cultural vulnerability to HIV/AIDS. Husbands often treat their wives as if they are owned because the men paid *lobola* in order to marry. This proprietary treatment extends to the couple's sexual relationship, with the husband expecting sex on demand. Requesting the use of a condom often evokes anger and suspicion, and surely there is no need for male compliance since the husband is the head of the household, as St. Paul, St. Peter, and other biblical authors remind us in Genesis, Ephesians, Colossians, and I Peter. The result is deadly for women, since condoms are the single most effective way to prevent the spread of HIV/AIDS. Yet, women have no power to insist on condom use during intercourse and thus women contract HIV/AIDS at unacceptable rates because of it.

Women do not discuss safer sexual practices with their husbands/partners because it is not culturally or religiously appropriate for females to have such an exchange with the males who are infecting them. Professor Mpine Qakida notes that women are not able to discuss safe sex practices with their respective partner because women will be looked upon as sexually promiscuous.[12] In other words, to talk openly about sex is uncommon for African women, so to speak directly about a sexual practice infers licentiousness on the part of the woman. This implication is not incredibly different in this place, the United States, that many of us call home and certainly not different for those of us who were trained in traditional Christian social norms.

Of course, religion is not the only source for norms that inhibit open discourse about sexuality or the only source for the norms that rip away a woman's control over her own body. Culturally, the misinformed belief of HIV-positive males that having sexual intercourse with a female virgin will cure them of the disease still persists. Layered onto that is a culturally rooted dilemma for unmarried women suggesting that female virgins who consciously decide to refrain from sex are considered sexually unendorsed by men, untested, and possibly incompetent at pleasuring a male partner. However, sexually experienced women can and are viewed as sexually promiscuous—an equally problematic stigma. Men expect women to have experience in pleasing them sexually yet reject women who seem too experienced. The entire perception of the situation is driven by the male sexual partner, and the woman is in a vexing catch-22.[13]

For those of us trained in the Christian tradition, it is not a difficult step to see how Christian teachings about sex/gender relationships and the glaring, gaping lack of open discussion in churches about healthy sexual activity makes the Christian influence one that ultimately perpetuates the spread of HIV/AIDS among women. Not surprisingly, it is the concerted governmental and nongovernmental, largely secular awareness and education campaigns that are breaking the silence, according to Haddad. She concludes with a familiar refrain that the "church continues to be slow to speak openly about the subject, which is so closely tied to issues of sexuality."[14] Again, the metaphor of Dr. Martin Luther King Jr. resounds with grave clarity, that the religious community functions as "a mere taillight behind other community agencies rather than a headlight"[15] in this issue that is about life and death.

## THROUGH THE EYES OF BIBLICAL INTERPRETATION

Surely, the predominant literalistic biblical interpretations imposed on existing patriarchal African cultures reinforce the subordinated position of women and tie them down for further slaughtering by HIV/AIDS. As long as this is the case, the disease will not be controlled.[16] In all likelihood, the church will not intervene because many African cultures are firmly rooted in the church. Progressive theologians are trying, however, to bring a liberationist rereading of texts to combat the entrenched and dominant historical readings. Whether or not it is an effort that succeeds, time will tell. At the least however, and gratefully, there is an effort underfoot and across the ocean.

New Testament scholar Dr. Musa Dube underscores the gendered face of HIV/AIDS and promotes a gender-sensitive multisectoral approach to the pandemic. She urges people to read HIV/AIDS into biblical texts to expose the social injustices visited upon African women. She claims that much biblical interpretation supports patriarchal customs in ways that "increase the likelihood that women will become HIV positive."[17] She further argues that "texts of terror" that posit God's punishment upon people living with HIV/AIDS must be reevaluated in order for fresh and hope-filled readings to come forth for those living with and dying from HIV/AIDS. Her edited book, *Grant Me Justice: HIV/AIDS and Gender Readings of the Bible*,[18] offers a method for communities to reread the Bible for liberation amidst the HIV/AIDS struggle in Africa. Given the matrices of oppression that cultivate the spread of HIV/AIDS, *Grant Me Justice's* main concern is with providing a culturally sensitive tool that recognizes the layered nature of African male-female relations as they are tied to race/ethnicity, gender, sexuality and class. Furthermore, the authors write in a manner that suggests they believe that the Bible and faith offer liberating models that can provide hope in ominous times. The book's goal is to advocate for justice and to empower women living on the continent to address the HIV/AIDS pandemic by being resilient and by persistently fighting injustice. The volume judiciously provides a rereading of key biblical texts, making it useful for a broad audience.

Part 1 of *Grant Me Justice* focuses on the Hebrew Bible, HIV/AIDS, and gender, with Denise Ackermann and Johanna Stiebert reinterpreting significant texts on women and sexuality. Ackermann rereads the story of the rape of Tamar as the story of violence against women in South Africa. According to Ackerman, the Tamar narrative offers the "bleak immensity" of HIV/AIDS on continental Africa. Yet, she claims that there are traces of resistance and hope in the passage, positing that the subordination of women is a virus more deadly than HIV/AIDS.

The story of Tamar, of course, has been reinterpreted by womanist and feminist theologians, with some degree of success, as a story of survival and a strategy of brokering power in an inequitable patriarchal world—as have the other dozen or so stories focusing on women that are sprinkled throughout the Christian canon. For those living within the Christian tradition, without question, these rereadings provide a glimpse, and sometimes, even a name to which women may look for inspiration, affinity, or strength. I would not wish to take that away or diminish it in any way; nevertheless, with complete respect, I will posit a question and concern.

Even with this liberating interpretation, I wonder if it is reasonable to place hope in scriptures to reshape patriarchy when the Bible overwhelmingly buttresses it.[19] There is no question that the dominant, pervasive, and penetrating social standard throughout the biblical tradition is one of a male-dominated patriarchy where women primarily serve and are eternally cursed, since a woman allegedly was the one who first brought sin and death into the world. In this tradition, are women not destined to be either temptresses or very minor characters at best? Do the Christian tradition and its teachings, by their nature or at their core, fall into support of patriarchy? As an ordained woman in the Methodist tradition, I do not ask these questions lightly. And in light of the continued oppression of women throughout the so-called Christian nations where the church almost always functions as a taillight, and when South African women and children are dying in part because of my tradition, it must be asked.

As if that is not enough to ask, I have another question and concern, of equal importance. For the most part, even among womanist and black theologians, there exists a basic assumption that the Christian canon has universal application. With the use of reinterpretation, the entire canon has been taken as an authoritative and foundational theological source that may be transported anywhere to anyone with equal validity and authority. And so I ask, are we to be sure that a so-named sacred text written in the ancient Near East in early antiquity speaks with any universal or God-given authority to the women living with and dying from HIV/AIDS in South Africa?[20]

It gives me some measure of comfort to know that there are others who are asking the question and actively seeking to claim authority from other sources. While Dube and the other authors who are members of the Circle of Concerned African Women attempt to reform interpretations of the Bible, South African theologian Tinyiko Sam Maluleke and Hebrew Bible scholar Sarojini Nadar offer stories about women and violence from their personal lives to illustrate the ways that the "unholy trinity—religion, culture and gender socialization"[21] perpetuates aggression against women. They claim, frankly and unapologetically, that the Bible is the primary source used by Christians to propagate violence against women as God's will through divine design. Patriarchal and misogynistic biblical interpretation supports the belief that God bestowed upon men power and authority over women. This belief, held by both women and men, supports the regularity of the subordination of and violence against women, which in turn maintains an HIV/AIDS deathtrap for women. Given the statistics, it is difficult to rely on the limited stories of female strength in light of the thousands of pages that teach otherwise in the biblical texts.

And so the question remains: Can the Christian Bible be seen as the authoritative and most life-giving text for women living with HIV/AIDS? Is knowing Jesus and following his life of sacrifice, his relinquishment of power, and ultimately his glorified, unjust death the most positive message for women forced into sexual relationships without power where they contract a disease that kills them? Is it the best resource for their survival? I do not know if this is the message that will grant women any legitimate power over their situations, especially when even the Jesus story takes place in a patriarchal world governed by men. I do not think that this is the most helpful message in a place where the sacred and secular crash into one another. Despite the comforting notion of a loving God who understands pain and injustice and who promises redemption, such a God existing in a world consumed with patriarchy, the messages of submission, and the model of women predominantly presented in the Christian scriptures is discomforting in the lives of African American and South African women, especially those who are infected with HIV/AIDS because of forced submission, sacrifice, and patriarchy.

## Breaking the Cycle of Poverty and HIV/AIDS

Now that we have explored the pockets of traditional theology that are trying to make sense of and find life in the Christian scriptures, what are other methods of survival that can and do bring life to women affected by HIV/AIDS? First, lives can be changed through the eradication of poverty. If churches spent more energy on eradicating poverty and less on preaching condemnation, then the Christian community would be bringing a life-giving message to women in South Africa. The political economy of HIV/AIDS determines who lives and who dies of this disease; and while HIV/AIDS does not discriminate between the rich and the poor, it is the poor who are most adversely affected by the disease and who die at the highest rates.

African scholar Eunice Kamaara claims that HIV/AIDS has such a negative impact upon the poor that it plays a significant role in the advancement of poverty. She writes: "While HIV is not just confined to the poor, poverty contributes enormously to the spread of HIV and to the development from HIV to AIDS. On the other hand, HIV/AIDS contributes enormously to poverty. This means that a vicious circle exists where poverty contributes to HIV/AIDS and vice versa complicating the situation."[22] UNAIDS Associate Director for Policy, Strategy and Research, Robert Hecht, speaking at the World AIDS conference held in Durban, South Africa, in 2000, supports Kamaara's thesis. He writes, "Breaking this cycle will require not only increased investments in more effective HIV prevention and care, but also more effective measures to combat poverty."[23]

Of course, not unlike virtually all patriarchal nation-states, poverty dis-proportionately affects women. Due to laws that restrict the land and inheri-tance rights of women and their access to education and healthcare, it is mostly women in South Africa who bear the burden of living with poverty while living with HIV/AIDS. Land is transferred upon a husband's death not to his wife, but to a male relative who has no obligation to allow the woman and/or her children to remain there. Even so, she has far less access to jobs that pay enough to maintain land or a home at the same level as she could with her husband.[24] Further, illiteracy rates are as high as 50 percent in rural areas. And hospitals and clinics are virtually nonexistent or ill-equipped in poor communities.

Apart from religious ideology of any kind, there are tangible ways that religious communities can provide the services and education necessary to remove one of the barriers to women's health and life. As education and income increase, HIV/AIDS decreases. This we know. A major goal of reli-gious communities must be to do something with the knowledge without spreading the word of patriarchy. These are things those among us with resources can do to save the lives of women forced to live with HIV/AIDS.

## FROM IMPOSING AND THEORIZING TO INQUIRY TO WITNESS: ENGAGEMENT IN SOUTH AFRICA

However, there is one final thing we can do, an approach we can take, and model from which we can learn. We Westernized theologians and scholars can abandon our academic and religious approaches to this problem. We can stop theorizing, planning, and imposing our solutions on the people of South Africa. Instead, we can simply be quiet; well, almost completely quiet. We may ask for an invitation to witness the ways in which South African com-munities are developing survival and healing strategies. We can be blessed by watching, observing, and seeing the solutions designed by those who know far more about living with HIV/AIDS in epidemic proportions.

This is what I have chosen to do. Rather than go to bless, impart, or teach, I go to South Africa, to the St. John's community, and I am blessed. I learn. I see how those who live daily in communities rife with poverty, patri-archy, and poisoned by HIV/AIDS have developed ways to heal, to care, and manage to get by in situations where most of us, myself included, would have no idea where to begin.

St. John's takes an approach that is multifaceted. First, in partnership with community organizations, they are asking questions about the larger social implications of land distribution. Then, with the help of community activists, the congregation builds homes for members with needs. Sometimes they build homes for members who are certainly near death from HIV/AIDS related causes. Due to the aforementioned issues of sexual discrimination in land reassignment, this leaves the question of who should rightfully inherit the land and the home and what should happen when there are children in that home. Traditionally, the land would pass to a male relative, who might or might not care for or allow those orphaned or widowed to stay in the home.

Leaders and members of St. John's are beginning to see that long-term, this tradition does not work, for it results in more poverty and in more orphans and widows without adequate shelter who are living under the power structure of male relatives. Although it will take time to change the power structures, St. John's is beginning to ask fundamental questions about the ways in which its own community's traditions may be contributing to poverty and the resultant exposure to HIV/AIDS.

As U.S. citizens, we must take note that St. John's first examined its own implications in the epidemic. The problem is not "out there" with "others" for St. John's. Nor is the problem primarily theological. The problem is practical, structural, and something that they are seeking to change about themselves first. May we follow suit and question the ways that our traditions within our communities contribute to the spread of HIV/AIDS and the ways we fail to bring life to those living with HIV/AIDS.

Second, and related, St. John's actively seeks out people in the surrounding community who are living with HIV/AIDS. They do not just hang a sign outside of the church that reads, "All are Welcome," and they do not place the burden on ailing persons to find the community. Instead, the church finds those in need. Its members get people to clinics. They share information. They actively pursue those who are alienated. In short, they do not simply claim that all are welcome; St. John's truly meets people where they are—on their own doorstep, not the church's.

Finally, St. John's offers sacramental healing within the walls of the church. Mother Gomba is the female head of the congregation, which in and of itself is a powerful statement in a land of male dominance. I have witnessed the congregation's life-giving power of ritual healing. Mother Gomba and her ministerial leaders have developed a fourfold ritual for anyone who is living with an ailment or disease. The ritual combines traditional elements of African religion with some Christian elements in a very embodied ritual that physically and symbolically renews the person living with a disease of any kind. Notably, and intentionally, HIV/AIDS is not singled out as different, not given a special ribbon or scarlet letter, not made out to be a "special" or marked disease. The lack of singling out HIV/AIDS is not an attempt to hide or mask it, but rather a way of normalizing it so that persons affected need not feel set apart, as often happens negatively outside of St. John's. Whatever the ailment or disease, care is given indiscriminately.

First, the priest/healer "prophets" the person. With the Bible in hand and the person who has requested healing present, the priest/healer opens the text (to no specific place), fixes her/his eyes upon a passage, reads it out loud and begins to talk to the person about her/his life. Two things happen— first, the person typically hears something about her/his life with which she/ he resonates. There may be elements shared that are in fact true. Second, the person hears what will happen to her/him in the future. This may or may not be positive.

Whatever the prophecy, the person has some sense of what she/he can and must do. This gives the person motivation and restores in her/him a sense of ability to "do something." The specifics of the "something" matter, to be sure. However, equally, if not more powerfully, the person regains a sense that she/he actually can do something: she/he can and must actively take part in her/his own healing.

What follows the "propheting" session is a ritual bath. The priest/healer draws water into a bath tub and adds an ash/salt mixture. Sunlight Soap, which the adherent supplies to the minister, is also used. Again, the adherent supplying the soap functionally makes the person an active participant in her/his healing. The adherent takes the bath, washing herself/himself seven times. Then she/he emerges from the bath water and puts on clothes without drying her/his body. The full physicality of the ritual places the person firmly in her/his body, where the disease still lives, but does so in a way that embraces and reclaims the corporeal as worthy and capable of being healed. The healing is not a simple prayer. It involves active body movement.

The adherent then goes to the church sanctuary with the minister who is vested in a blue-and-white stole and a shepherd's staff. The adherent stands on a white cross that is etched in the floor in front of the altar and the priest/ healer, using holy water and the blue and white stole that he wears, submerges his hands in the holy water and places the stole upon the adherent's head and shoulders while saying a prayer. Holy water is then sprinkled upon the person who desires healing. Here, the connection physically is made between priest/healer and adherent. The stole, warm from the body of the priest/healer, is transferred to the body of the one who seeks healing. The stole does not come from a pristine box. It is given directly from the body of one to another, making a ritualized connection between embodied members of a community.

This initial healing session is followed by three other sessions over a period of a month in which a healing team assists the person in other visceral and corporeal rituals that involve vomiting (after ingesting a very large volume of water), followed by an enema and a concluding bath employing the same elements used in the first session. The final element is, indeed, more theological, involving participation in community worship services throughout

the month-long ritual process, which allows the adherent to engage in a com-
bination of private and public sacramental acts.

While the physicality may seem unfamiliar to our notions of ritual in
the United States, for St. John's, the ritual process markedly and intentionally involves the entire body. Precisely by treating the body without shame,
with touch, with the most fundamental human bodily functions, and without
holding back or buttoning up, the St. John's rituals honor, give esteem to, and
renew the bodies of those who otherwise would spend their days and nights
allowing themselves to be sapped of life's energy and ability. When I am with
St. John's religious community, I am struck immediately and surely blessed
by the ways that one community, surrounded by patriarchy, poverty, and
disease—all of epidemic proportions and each as insidious as the other—has
found ways to heal individuals, seek out those who may not otherwise find
a clinic, and at the same time work to change the systems within their own
community and culture that contribute to the spread of HIV/AIDS.

I close with the questions asked earlier and with some new ones to pon-
der: Does or should or can the Christian Bible serve as the ultimate source
of authority in the lives of South Africans living with the HIV/AIDS epidemic? Is it the Christian Bible that gives the St. John's religious community's priests/healers the authority to take care of people among them? Is the
message of a sacrificing Jesus who promises some other worldly existence the
central message necessary for full and complete wholeness? Is the message
of a sacrificing, servant model a healthy one for subjugated women?

I do not know the answer to these questions, but now is the right time
and place to begin asking them, perhaps as we learn from St. John's and ask
first of our own communities, "How does our theological and religious community contribute to the spread of HIV/AIDS?" The problem of HIV/AIDS
is linked to poverty and to its confluence with heterosexual norms that are
supported by biblical teachings that continue to be taken literally in South
Africa and around the world. May we continue the conversation until we are
no longer a taillight but the headlight that searches within and ultimately
shines and exposes those things that we can stop, start, and change here, in
our own selves, our own homes, and our own communities.

Whether we talk about HIV/AIDS in South Africa or in the United States
we can say confidently that wherever HIV/AIDS is, women are the people
affected by it the most adversely. Moreover, we can conclude that wherever
poverty is most entrenched and paired with Christianity, we have a formula
for a deeply embedded HIV/AIDS problem. This is a disease that attacks
the body, creates a crisis in the mind, and devastates the spirit of person and
nations. Even in regions of the world where medicine makes living with HIV/
AIDs relatively easy, creating an ambiance for the mind to forget or deny one's
reality, the body remembers what the mind forgets. The body remembers

because it is the place that stores knowledge; it holds the inscribed text that women across the globe have been taught about the superiority of males and inferiority of females. The Spirit of women is then compromised and it is only the mother god, women, and proactive women-friendly and invested males who help turn the tide of the theological and anthropological issue of HIV/AIDS.

## NOTES

1. American Social Health Association, "Learn about STDs/STIs," American Social Health Association, Inc., http://www.ashastd.org/learn/learn_statistics.cfm (accessed September 15, 2007).

2. Dob Noble, "United States HIV & AIDS statistics summary," AVERT, http://www.avert.org/statsum.htm (accessed September 16, 2007).

3. Ibid.

4. UNICEF, "UNICEF South Africa—HIV and AIDS—Gender-based Violence," UNICEF, http://www.unicef.org/southafrica/hiv_aids_729.html (accessed September 15, 2009).

5. Ibid.

6. Ibid.

7. Ibid.

8. Mpine Qakida, "Let's Talk About Sex: Reaching Young People Through the Media in the Age of AIDS," *Journal of Theology for Southern Africa* 14 (November 2002): 83.

9. Beverly Haddad, "Reflections on the Church and HIV/AIDS: South Africa," *Theology Today* 62 (2005): 35.

10. Beverly Haddad, "Theologising Development: A Gendered Analysis of Poverty, Survival and Faith," *Journal of Theology in Southern Africa* 110 (July 2001): 6.

11. Musa W. Dube, "Theological Challenges: Proclaiming the Fullness of Life in the HIV/AIDS & Global Economic Era," *International Review of Mission* Vol. 91 No. 363 (2003): 536.

12. Qakida, 83.

13. Ibid.

14. Haddad, "Reflections on the church and HIV/AIDS," 32.

15. This quote comes from Martin Luther King Jr.'s "Letter from a Birmingham Jail." See Martin Luther King Jr., "Articles: Letter From a Birmingham Jail—Historical Text Archive," Historical Text Archive: Electronic History Resources, http://historicaltextarchive.com/sections.php?op=viewarticle&artid=40. The full quote is "So here we are moving toward the exit of the twentieth century with a religious community largely adjusted to the status quo, standing as a tail-light behind other community agencies rather than a headlight leading men to higher levels of justice."

16. Isabel Apawo Phiri, "HIV/AIDS: An African Theological Response in Mission," *Ecumenical Review* 56 (2004): 426.

17. Letty M. Russell, "Re-Imagining the Bible in a Pandemic of HIV/AIDS," in Dube, Musa W. and Kanyoro, Musimbi, eds. *Grant Me Justice! HIV/AIDS & Gender Readings of the Bible* (Pietermaritzburg, 3200 South Africa: Cluster Publications and Orbis Books, 2004), 202–3.

18. Musa W. Dube and Musimbi Kanyoro, eds., *Grant Me Justice! HIV/AIDS & Gender Readings of the Bible* (Pietermaritzburg, 3200 South Africa: Cluster Publications and Orbis Books, 2004).

19. I wish to acknowledge Monique Moultrie, a PhD student at Vanderbilt Divinity School for helping me to frame this question in my Womanist Theology class in the fall of 2005.

20. I thank Adam Wright, a Masters Degree student at Vanderbilt Divinity School for raising the question in my Theologies of Women of Color class in the fall of 2007.

21. Tinyiko Sam Maluleke and Sarojini Sadar, "Breaking the Covenant of Violence Against Women," *Journal of Theology in Southern Africa* 114 (November 2002): 14.

22. Eunice Kamaara, "Stigmatization of Persons Living with HIV/AIDS in Africa: Pastoral Challenges," *African Ecclesial Review* (2004): 38.

23. Ibid.

24. Haddad, "Theologizing Development," 9.

## References

American Social Health Association. "Learn about STDs/STIs." American Social Health Association, Inc. http://www.ashastd.org/learn/learn_statistics.cfm.

Dube, Musa W. "Theological Challenges: Proclaiming the Fullness of Life in the HIV/AIDS & Global Economic Era." *International Review of Mission* Vol. 91 No. 363 (2003).

Dube, Musa W. and Kanyoro, Musimbi, eds. *Grant Me Justice! HIV/AIDS & Gender Readings of the Bible*. Pietermaritzburg, 3200 South Africa: Cluster Publications and Orbis Books, 2004.

Haddad, Beverly. "Reflections on the Church and HIV/AIDS: South Africa." *Theology Today* 62 (2005): 29–37.

Haddad, Beverly. "Theologising Development: A Gendered Analysis of Poverty, Survival and Faith." *Journal of Theology in Southern Africa* 110 (July 2001): 5–19.

Kamaara, Eunice. "Stigmatization of Persons Living with HIV/AIDS in Africa: Pastoral Challenges." *African Ecclesial Review* (2004): 35–54.

King, Martin Luther, Jr. "Articles: Letter From a Birmingham Jail—Historical Text Archive." Historical Text Archive: Electronic History Resources. http://historicaltextarchive.com/sections.php?op=viewarticle&artid=40.

Maluleke, Tinyiko Sam and Sarojini Nadar. "Breaking the Covenant of Violence Against Women." *Journal of Theology in Southern Africa* 14 (November 2002): 5–17.

Noble, Rob. "United States HIV & AIDS Statistics Summary." AVERT. http://www.avert.org/statsum.htm.

Qakida, Mpine. "Let's Talk About Sex: Reaching Young People Through the Media in the Age of AIDS." *Journal of Theology for Southern Africa* 14 (November 2002): 79–92.

Phiri, Isabel Apawo. "HIV/AIDS: An African Theological Response in Mission." *Ecumenical Review* 56 (2004): 422–31.

Russell, Letty M. "Re-Imagining the Bible in a Pandemic of HIV/AIDS" in Dube, Musa W. and Kanyoro, Musimbi, eds. *Grant Me Justice! HIV/AIDS & Gender Readings of the Bible*. Pietermaritzburg, 3200 South Africa: Cluster Publications and Orbis Books, 2004, 201–10.

UNICEF. "UNICEF South Africa—HIV and AIDS—Gender-based violence." UNICEF. http://www.unicef.org/southafrica/hiv_aids_729.html.

# PART IV

*Sex, Power, Vulnerability*

# CHAPTER 10

# Sexual Violence: A Sin against Women

*Marie M. Fortune*

Sexual violence is a sin. What is sexual violence and what is wrong about it? Why is the sin of sexual violence at times so difficult to perceive? How do we speak ethically of justice in relationship? Why have Christian ethics and pastoral writings often avoided or misunderstood the justice issues inherent to sexual violence? How does the Bible discuss sexual violence and what can we learn from it?

In Christian scripture, in both the Good Samaritan story (Luke 10:25–37) and in Jesus's reminder that as we do to the least of our sisters and brothers, we do also to him (Matthew 25:40), we find a generic mandate to give aid to the injured. However, this mandate is not sufficient when we are faced with a lack of clarity as to who is the injured, what is the injury, and who caused the injury. Such is the case with sexual violence. While this generic mandate may call forth a response of compassion, what in the Christian tradition challenges us to a response of justice? How are we to understand and interpret sexual violence as an experience of suffering in light of our faith? How does the relationship between sexuality and sexual violence affect our understanding of Christian sexual ethics? How has our understanding of Christian sexual ethics contributed to our unresponsiveness to sexual violence? This essay examines these questions regarding sexual violence and the dynamics of an appropriate Christian sexual ethics. After reflecting on the violence and violations of sexual violence, the essay then: examines the witness of Hebrew scripture and the issue of sexual violence as property crimes; explores child abuse and incest; analyzes sexual harassment and exploitation

203

of vulnerability; and investigates contemporary Christian traditions regarding sexual violence.

## THE VIOLENCE OF SEXUAL VIOLENCE

Sexual violence is, first and foremost, an act of violence, hatred, and aggression. Whether it is viewed clinically or legally, objectively or subjectively, violence is the common denominator. Like other acts of violence (assault and battery, murder, terrorism), there is harm of and injury to victims. The injuries may be psychological and/or physical.[1] In acts of sexual violence, usually the injuries are both.

The word "rape" is from the Latin root *rapere*, "to seize." The focus in English is "to seize and carry away by force" and/or "to force another person to engage in sexual intercourse." The contemporary legal and applied definitions are gender neutral and clearly indicate that either rapist or victim can be of either or the same gender. Thus rape is the *forced* penetration of the mouth, anus, or vagina by a penis or an object regardless of gender. However, because of the social inequities imposed due to gender, race, age, and sexual orientation, the most likely victims of rape are women and children of all races and nondominant men.

Although legal definitions of rape vary, the most comprehensive definition refers to forced penetration by the penis or any object of the vagina, mouth, or anus against the will of the victim. Lesser forms of forced sexual contact are dealt with as assault and battery. This legal definition represents a significant improvement over earlier rape laws which only specified vaginal intercourse forced by a male on a female. Rather this contemporary definition describes what actually happens in rape situations and does not limit rape to penis-vagina intercourse. The current inclusive definition provides for oral or anal sex against the will of the victim. In addition, it does not specify the gender of the victim or offender as the previous laws did. Thus male-male rape can be prosecuted as rape rather than under the old sodomy laws which made male rape of a male an illegal *sexual activity* rather than an assault.[2] Rape by a female offender would include using an object or fingers to penetrate a victim.[3] The more recent laws place the emphasis on the assaultive aspect rather than on the sexual nature of the act.

Rape can be categorized according the relationship between the rapist and victim. *Acquaintance rape*, the most common, describes an assault against someone who is known to the assailant, usually friend, coworker, neighbor, and so forth. *Date rape* specifically describes an assault against one's dating partner.[4] *Marital rape* describes an assault against one's marriage partner or intimate. *Stranger rape,* the least common, occurs when a rapist attacks someone who is a stranger. (This would also include acts of rape carried out in wartime as acts of terror against a community.) Rape is an act done *to* a victim, against her/his will. Rape uses sex as a weapon to do injury to another person. The fact that the sexual contact is inflicted against the will of the person and causes injury to that person makes rape a violent act.

## THE VIOLATION OF SEXUAL VIOLENCE

As a sin against a person, sexual violence violates the bodily integrity of another, thus denying a person the choice to determine her/his own boundaries and activities. Sexual violence violates another's personhood because it objectifies the other, making them a nonperson. By rendering a person powerless, that is, by taking away her/his resources, agency and sense of self, sexual violence creates a victim, that is, someone who experiences her/his environment as unsafe and is never allowed to feel safe within her/his own body. A victim also suffers the physical, emotional, and spiritual consequences of violence.

Though often it is hard to recognize this, sexual violence is also a violation of relationship. The sexual offender betrays trust in a relationship, which destroys the possibility of relationship between people. As an extension, sexual violence also destroys community, creating an atmosphere of fear and distrust among family, friends, coworkers, and acquaintances.

That a child will respond with fear when confronted by physical force from a stranger is not surprising. These are the consequences of a violent act. But with someone known and trusted, the child is overwhelmed, confused, overpowered, and terrorized even without overt physical force. In addition to the terror that comes from the experience of coercion and force, the child may experience the betrayal of a family relationship.

For many, the realization that sexual violence is a sin has been difficult to accept. For years, the myths have proliferated of rapists who simply cannot control themselves and victims who really want to be raped. In these erroneous stereotypes, the agency of the rapist and the victim status of the victim are reversed or even disappear completely. It is an old viewpoint, one for instance portrayed in the classic movie *Gone With the Wind,* in which Rhett Butler forcefully carried a resisting Scarlett O'Hara up the stairs to a bedroom rape from which she awakens happily the next morning, smiling. This now classic image continues to inform each generation anew.

## THE WITNESS OF HEBREW SCRIPTURE

Hebrew scripture tells the story of sexual violence in multiple forms. As such, it is a powerful witness to the victim's experience and to the difficulty that family and community had in responding. It also offers some specific ethical guidelines for how the community understood and responded to rape. (Scriptures based on NRSV translation.)

## PROPERTY CRIMES

The Hebrew scriptural laws (Deuteronomy 22:23–28) address three specific situations of sexual assault and deal with them depending on the circumstances of the situation and the marital status of the victim.

- If a man "lies with" a betrothed virgin in *the city*, both shall be stoned to death: the woman because she did not cry out and the man for violating his neighbor's wife (v. 23–24).

The assumption here is that if the victim was in the city and cried out, someone would have intervened and prevented the attack. There is no recognition that force or fear may have prevented her screams or that her screams may have gone unheard. So if the attack was carried out without someone intervening, the victim must not have cried for help. This means that she must have eagerly participated in a sexual encounter and thus deserved to die because she "belonged" to another man.

- If a man seizes and "lies with" a betrothed virgin *in the country*, only the man shall be killed because although the woman cried out for help, there was no one to save her, "for this case is like that of someone who attacks and murders a neighbor." Only here is the violent nature of the crime emphasized (v. 25–27).
- If a man encounters a virgin not engaged and ". . . seizes her and lies with, *and they are caught in the act*" (v. 28).

The man must give *the father* of the woman 50 pieces of silver and *marry her (and may never divorce her) because he has violated her.* The rapist's punishment is to be married to his victim for the rest of his life.

All of these laws address the sexual assault of a woman as a property crime against the man to whom the woman "belonged," husband, or father. Consequences for the victim depended on the locale of the crime and disregarded the actual circumstance. If the woman was a virgin and still "belonged" to her father when she was assaulted, the assailant had to pay the *father* restitution and *the victim was condemned to marriage* to her assailant. Consistently these laws regarded rape as a property crime. The one exception is the reference to the analogy between the rape and murder of a neighbor. Unfortunately, this assessment of the seriousness of rape is overshadowed by the other references.[5]

In all of the scriptural examples which refer to acts of sexual assault and abuse, the authors are concerned with the offense as a violation of male property rights.[6] We can only assume that the authors' attitudes reflect the views of the community.[7] The irony is that even though rape as a property crime completely ignored the well-being of the victim, it did carry with it a response exacting accountability from the rapist and often severe punishment as well, including capital punishment.

Needless to say, framing rape as a property crime against an owner ignores the real victim and her experience of violence and violation of personal autonomy. Rape as a property crime isn't about women at all but in fact about men's relationships with other men as they jockey for social, political, and economic power.

The first story of rape in Hebrew scripture appears in Genesis 34.[8] We are introduced to Dinah, daughter of Leah and Jacob, on her way "out to visit the women of the region." While she was visiting, Shechem, son of Hamor, saw her; he then "seized her and lay with her by force" (v. 2).[9] Apparently, the outrage is that Shechem "lay with" Dinah, that is, he, an uncircumcised male, had sexual contact with her, not that he attacked her.

If we were to derive an understanding of sexual violence based on this passage from Genesis, we would say that sexual violence is wrong because it violates the property rights of men. At no point is the reader provided with any information about Dinah's experience or reaction to the assault.

The sexual attack on Dinah is the dramatic backdrop for the struggle between Jacob's and Hamor's families. The attack is not acknowledged as an offense against Dinah herself, but as a property violation against Jacob and his sons. The response to this violation was collective, vengeful violence. The emphasis in the description is on the sexual nature of the violation: he "lay with her," "defiled her," and treated her as a "whore."

The first lesson we draw from this example is that rape is often misunderstood and misattributed. We often see rape not through the perspective of the victim but through the perspective of those around her, or from the perspective of the attacker. And the response—that Dinah might marry her rapist—places this passage squarely in a contemporary dynamic of the confusion of sexual activity and sexual violence.

## CHILD SEXUAL ABUSE AND INCEST

Generally, child sexual abuse is divided into incestuous abuse in which a child is sexually abused by a member of her/his family or child molestation in which a child is sexually abused by a friend, an acquaintance or a stranger. This abuse may involve an adult or older teen touching the child sexually or getting the child to touch the adult or teen sexually. It may also include taking photos of the child in sexualized poses (which often is linked to the child pornography industry) or prostituting the child (i.e., forcing a child into prostitution for the commercial benefit of the adult). Trafficking and child prostitution are very serious global problems: the popularity of sex tourism, combined with the fear of AIDS, creates a high demand for child prostitutes.[10]

While rape usually represents a clearly assaultive situation, that is, physically forced, child sexual abuse is more often coercive than assaultive. The offender—whether a stranger, someone known to the child, or a family member—takes advantage of the vulnerability of the child and coerces her/him into sexual activity. Therefore, the term "abuse" rather than "assault" is a more common designation. However, as in rape, child sexual abuse is a form of violence, for it results in both psychological and physical injury to its victim.

Legally, child sexual abuse is described using various terms. Sexual abuse may be considered rape if physical force is used and penetration takes place, or statutory rape if force is not used but the victim is underage and thus unable to give legal consent.[11] Sexual abuse without penetration (touching, fondling, masturbation, etc.) usually is defined as "indecent liberties."

Clinically, child sexual abuse is the sexual exploitation of a child who is not developmentally capable of understanding or resisting the contact, and/or who is psychologically and socially dependent on the offender.[12] There are two criteria which provide the parameters for understanding child sexual abuse as a form of violence and aggression. The first (as in rape) is the lack of consent on the part of the victim. However, in the case of child sexual abuse, the lack of consent is a given. Children, by definition, cannot give or withhold consent when approached sexually by an adult because they are immature, uninformed, and usually dependent on the adult. Consequently, they lack the real power to resist.[13] Therefore, any sexual contact between an adult and a child is abusive. The second criterion for understanding child sexual abuse has to do with whose self-interest is being served by the sexual contact and who is injured. Child sexual abuse describes "contacts or interactions between a child and an adult when the child is being used for sexual stimulation of that adult or another person."[14] The sexual *use* of a child disregards the child's welfare. The child becomes an object exclusively to meet the needs of the offender. The act is exploitative and, consequently, damaging to the child.

While the particular behaviors which constitute sexual violence or abuse remain the same, the context is an important part of comprehending the experience. Thus incestuous abuse (as described above) takes place in the family which shapes the dynamics of the abuse, often limits its disclosure, and determines any forthcoming intervention.

In II Samuel 13, we find the story of incest in the royal family. Although the victim is a young adult and not a child, the family dynamics are similar. Tamar is a full sister of Absalom and a half sister of Amnon; all are children of David. In the story, Amnon tricked Tamar into coming to see him; then he grabbed her and told her to lie with him. She refused saying: "do not force me; for such a thing is not done in Israel; do not do anything so vile" (v. 12). Tamar reminded him that she would be shamed and he would be a scoundrel. She told him to speak to King David who "will not withhold me from you" (v. 13). Ignoring her suggestion and "being stronger than she, he forced her, and lay with her" (v. 14).

As with the Rape of Dinah, we are again told the story of a rape, but this time not only rape, but incestuous assault, that is, sexual violence done by a family member. Yet, the violation portrayed in the text is still one of property. At that time, it was possible for a man to marry his half-sister, a practice which was later forbidden under the law (see Leviticus 18:9). Yet, Amnon refused to request permission from David to marry Tamar, perhaps fearing that the request would be denied. The folly and shame result from Amnon's rape of Tamar without David's permission. In this story, the reader is provided with Tamar's reaction and reminder that she will bear the shame of this attack.

After the rape, Amnon's feelings shifted dramatically to hatred and he sent Tamar away. She confronted him saying that sending her away is an even greater wrong than the assault. Again he ignored her and put her out. Tamar, as a virgin daughter of the king, was wearing a long robe with sleeves. She rent the robe, put ashes on her head, and went away crying. When Absalom saw her he asked if she had been with Amnon. Because it was true, Tamar remained in despair in Absalom's house. When King David heard what happened, he was very angry, "but he would not punish his son Amnon, because he loved him . . ." (II Sm 13: 21). We are not told what David felt for Tamar. Absalom hated Amnon for what he did to Tamar. Absalom killed Amnon and afterwards fled while David grieved for his son, Amnon. Some of King David's rogue troops kill Absalom as he hangs from a tree where his hair was caught on low branches (II Sm. 18:9, 14–15). David mourns for the loss of Absalom, the son he told his soldiers to keep safe (II Sm. 18:5, 33; 19:1–4).

Tamar's reaction to her rape is one of public grief and desolation. While this is a common victim reaction to rape, Tamar grieves because she has lost her virginity without gaining a husband to care for her. Because of the property violation, she is left without provision; she becomes damaged goods. In fact, as she points out, Amnon does have a responsibility for her. Yet, he refuses to take that responsibility and thus leaves her in shame. This is the essence of the offense described here. In this situation, sexual violence is seen primarily as sexual activity and a property crime; and the real offense against Tamar—tricked into a situation she could not control—is overlooked, disregarded. The primary story is the conflict between brothers. The text only allows us to hear Tamar's perspective on the experience in relationship to this primary story; and so, the sexual assault of a woman is incidental. The reaction of her brother Absalom is the traditional act of revenge ending in murder.

While the story makes it clear that the incestuous abuse was destructive to Tamar, her family, and the community and that such a thing should not have been done to her, this judgment is based on the violation of her father's property rights rather than the violation of her bodily integrity. The community *never* attends to the victimization of Tamar *per se* but rather focuses on the economic injury done to her father and brother.

## SEXUAL HARASSMENT AND EXPLOITATION OF VULNERABILITY

There are numerous situations where someone is vulnerable because of the inequality of power in a relationship. Under these circumstances, the person with greater power may take advantage of the one with lesser power, for example, a teacher and student, therapist and client, pastor and parishioner, or boss and employee.

Sexual harassment generally refers to conduct which takes place in the workplace between a supervisor and employee or between coworkers. It is "the use of one's authority or power, either explicitly or implicitly, to coerce another into unwanted sexual relations or to punish another for his or her refusal; or the creation of an intimidating, hostile or offensive working environment through verbal or physical conduct of a sexual nature."[15] Specifically, when someone takes advantage of her/his role as minister, teacher, coach, therapist, and so forth to cross sexual boundaries, it is a form of sexual abuse.

In II Samuel 11–12, the story of David and Bathsheba, we find a story which epitomizes the betrayal of trust by one who has power. David, the most powerful King of biblical Israel, was attracted to Bathsheba and finally had her husband sent to the front lines of battle where he was killed so that David could have Bathsheba to himself. Nathan, David's advisor, came to him and told him a story about a rich man who takes a lamb from a poor man for the rich man's own use. David reacted with outrage saying that the rich man deserved to die and that he should restore the poor man fourfold. Nathan then said, "You are the man!" and proceeded to delineate the ways that David had betrayed the trust that so many, including Nathan, had placed in him. Nathan named the abuse of David's power as king to have what he wanted and so to compromise his moral authority. In scripture, David was chastened and sobered and acknowledged Nathan's naming of his sin and betrayal of trust. He accepted the consequences which included the loss of his firstborn son. He went on to be Israel's greatest king.

In these biblical stories, we see the wide variety of sexual offenses that constitute sexual coercion and/or force used to establish and maintain control over another person. The only thing that victims/survivors have in common at the time of the offense is their vulnerability. Vulnerability is often heavily determined by social location and experiences in the context of the public or private spheres. Power vis-à-vis vulnerability is the framework within which we must consider the sin of sexual violence.

## THE CONTEMPORARY CHRISTIAN TRADITION ON SEXUAL VIOLENCE

To comprehend the impact of the Christian tradition on our understanding of sexual violence, we must examine the ways that the tradition addresses sexual violence historically and contemporarily.

Most contemporary Christian ethicists who do address sexual violence at all do so in a cursory yet revealing manner. Here we often find a contradiction of constructive ethical insight and traditional ethical confusion. For example, in an article on sexual ethics (1981), John T. Noonan Jr., described rape as

> the most universally abhorred sexual act; . . . it inflicts fear, bodily harm, and psychological trauma; . . . it creates the possibility of conception; . . . it invades the victim's privacy; . . . it expresses hatred. . . . It is the touching of the genital zone accompanied by animosity, threat and trauma which makes rape *repulsive* [emphasis added].[16]

He identifies rape as an abhorrent *sexual* act but then describes a *violent* act. "Repulsive" is an unusual adjective to use to assert an ethical norm.

In his discussion of sexual sins, Karl Menninger devotes one sentence in his book *Whatever Became of Sin?* (1973) to the subject of rape: "Rape, for example, is characteristically less a sexual act than a form of assault and mayhem—a form of hurting, debasing, and destroying another person for power-drive satisfaction. That's sin!"[17] He is attempting to clarify the confusion between sex and sexual violence.

Like many traditional legal definitions, *Baker's Dictionary of Christian Ethics* (1973) defines rape as "a man's unlawful carnal knowledge of a woman, without her consent, by resort to force or fraud."[18] This definition emphasizes the important issues of consent and force, but adds that "corroboration by evidence other than the woman's testimony"[19] is required. A doubt remains as to a woman's trustworthiness. It also is interesting to note that this definition limits rape to male-female assault and does not recognize same-gender rape, or female-male assault.

The *Dictionary of Moral Theology* (1962), a Roman Catholic resource, emphasizes the violent nature of rape: "In the terminology of modern theologians, *rape is* a violent sexual relation . . . violence is understood not only as a physical but moral force (serious threats, deception)."[20] Added to this definition is the injustice of the "violation of the right of a woman to use her generative faculty according to her own choice."[21] But then it goes on to say that the rape of a virgin is a greater injustice because "virginity is a good of greatest value, distinct from the right that she has to the use of her own body according to her free choice."[22] Here the concern for sexual chastity overrides the principle of women's right to bodily integrity and autonomy. This concern is further emphasized: "In a case of violence, the woman is obliged to use all the means at her command to avoid *the sexual act* [emphasis added], short of exposing herself to the danger of death, or to other grave harm . . ."[23] This is one step short of the example St. Maria Goretti gave the world. She was made a saint because she resisted her rapist; although he did murder her, she remained a virgin. Finally, the ethical concern expressed here focuses on the maintenance of a woman's sexual chastity, which, at its core, is a concern for male property rights just as Hebrew scripture suggests.[24]

> The unjust aggressor is obliged to make reparation of all damages due to his crime. In particular, he must enable the woman to contract marriage in the same manner as if she had never been violated, *even by marrying her himself,* [emphasis added] provided that all other conditions are favorable. . . . *Often the best form of reparation is marriage,* [emphasis added] if it can be properly arranged and offers a reasonable prospect of success.[25]

The *Dictionary of Moral Theology* echoes Deuteronomy with its suggestion that a rape victim *marry* her rapist and that such a marriage would make reparation *to her* for the crime![26]

In the *Biblical View of Sex and Marriage* (1960), Otto Piper goes to the extreme of traditional interpretation and describes rape (along with masturbation) as that which results "when a normal satisfaction of the sexual desire is impossible."[27] He regards insatiable sexual need as the source of sexual violence and "never a conscious volition."[28] If never a conscious volition, then, we can conclude, rape is nothing that a rapist can be held accountable for.

In late 20th-century Christian ethical discussion, even less attention was given to incest than to rape. The primary concerns expressed were the potential for hereditary defects in children of an incestuous union[29] (although the scientific basis for this genetic concern is questionable), the impact of incest on the parents' relationship, and the need to maintain the "natural order of procreation."[30] These sources of ethical discussion made no reference to incestuous abuse being destructive to child victims or to it being a violation of the parent/child relationship.

Unlike *Baker's Dictionary* and the *Dictionary of Moral Theology*, Noonan does raise the ethical issues posed by comparing rape and incest. In his discussion, however, there is a mixture of accuracy and inaccuracy which limits its usefulness.

> Except where it merges with actual rape, incest is not necessarily attended by fear or bodily injury. In the paradigm case of father and pubescent daughter, it is typically attended by trauma for the child. It creates the possibility of a conception without responsible parents. *It does not invade the child's privacy without her consent.* [emphasis added] It does not express hatred. It does distort the relation of a father to a daughter. It does involve a betrayal of the child's trust. The infliction of the trauma, the risking of a pregnancy, the distortion of the parental role, and the betrayal of trust are injuries to the individual and to society.[31]

There is often fear and bodily injury even without penetration. In fact, the typical case involves a father and a three- to six-year-old daughter when the abuse begins. There is definitely trauma for the child. For the pubescent female child, the possibility of enforced conception is very real and must be addressed by the Church. Noonan describes the damage and yet suggests that there is no invasion of privacy which is the basis for that damage done. While the incestuous abuse may not express hatred, it expresses a total disregard for the well-being of the child. Noonan accurately sums up the nature of the injury and its consequences. But he erroneously believes that the incest taboo is functioning to prevent incest.[32] Again there is minimal understanding of the ethical questions of consent, power, and powerlessness, harm, and the protection of children.

In *Dirt, Greed and Sex* (1988), William Countryman makes perhaps the strongest theological and ethical assertion:

> Theft of sustenance or space is the most obvious kind of violation of property; yet, violations of that trust which is the foundation of human community or of the freedom of choice are at least as grave. . . . When committed by a stranger, it violates the victim's freedom of choice; when committed by a family member or presumed friend, it violates the bonds of human community as well. The metaphorical space which surrounds each of us and which we characterize as "mine" is of the essence of our being human. It offers some protection for the freedom to develop and become what God is calling us to be, which is the principal goal of being human. When it is opened voluntarily to another, it is also a means of community. But when

it is broken into by violence, the very possibility of being human is at least momentarily being denied to us. As there is nothing more precious to us than our humanness, there is no sexual sin more serious than rape.[33]

He rightly places the discussion in the context of theft, not of property, but of self.

In *Embodiment* (1978) by James Nelson, one of the most useful books written in the late 20th century on Christian sexual ethics, the author cites rape as a social justice issue and as a crime of "violence used to keep women 'in their place.'" This is a valuable insight but beyond this, his treatment of rape is minimal.[34]

In Nelson's later anthology (with Sandra P. Longfellow) *Sexuality and the Sacred* (1994), they do include three articles on sexual violence and pornography.[35] In the 1990s, we began to see some attention to sexual violence in the discussion of sexuality and ethics. In 1995, Toinette Eugene summarized the sin of sexual violence:

> A womanist-informed definition of sexual abuse is constructed in terms of the experiences of African-American women within a historical context, and in terms of the ethical, religious, and psychological issues regarding sexual violence. Therefore the elements of sexual abuse are the violation of one's bodily integrity by force and/or threat of physical violence. It is the violation of the ethic of mutuality and care in relationships of domination. It is a violation of one's psycho-spiritual-sexual integrity by using sexual abuse to control and express violence. Sexual abuse is the violation of the Spirit of God incarnate in each of us.[36]

Despite lip service to the contrary, it appears that 20th-century Christian teaching, like traditional teaching, viewed sexual violence generally as either a sexual impropriety or a violation of male property rights. The occasional exceptions to this view are too few to challenge the dominant position of both Scripture and tradition significantly.

The Christian tradition itself offers even less than Scripture in providing clarity and direction for an ethical perspective on sexual violence. Too often the teachings of the tradition confuse sexual activity with sexual violence. In doing so, they focus on the sexual rather than on the violent aspect of sexual violence; they blame the victim; and they fail to hold the offender accountable. They ascribe agency to the victim and not to the perpetrator. There is virtually no mention of the victim of sexual assault as the one who is offended directly. The context of justice is almost never put forth. Restitution *for the victim* is rarely mentioned. While there is some concern in Scripture for the impact of sexual violence on the whole community, the implications of this are never drawn. The tradition treats sexual assault as an embarrassing individual experience rather than as a cause for community outrage. Moreover, the traditional teachings contribute to the negative, ill-informed, and contradictory attitudes about female sexuality and homosexuality.

This critical review of scriptural and traditionally oriented contemporary sources leads to the conclusion that Scripture and Christian tradition alone are inadequate for helping to address sexual violence as an ethical issue. Thus, it is clear that to engage constructively in ethical discourse, we must be willing to set aside that material which is ill-informed and perpetuates confusion, and draw more deeply on our faith and experience.

Using these resources, we must then reframe the ethical questions presented by sexual violence, clarifying the confusion between sexual activity and sexual violence, and asking what is the real violation which takes place when a person is raped or sexually abused. We must name the unmentionable sin.[37] Then we must struggle with the demands that justice makes in response to the sin of sexual violence. Finally, we must consider the implications for contemporary Christian sexual ethics.

## What's Wrong with Rape?—A New Ethical Framework

### Harm

The early work of Ann Wolbert Burgess and Lynda Lytle Holmstrom who presented "rape trauma syndrome" to begin to describe and measure the harm of rape on victims represented an effort to develop a clinical and hence objective measure but was in fact also a moral argument. The question of harm is the strongest criterion which specifies negative consequences for the victim as central to an ethical argument. Judith Hermann's work on linking rape to posttraumatic stress disorder emphasized the particularity of sexual violence by calling it "complex post-traumatic stress disorder" and continued to make the case for "harm" as a violation of a moral good.[38] In Ann Cahill's extensive discussion of ethics in *Rethinking Rape*, she examines the question of harm and summarizes her view of the wrong of rape:

> In the act of rape, the assailant reduces the victim to a nonperson. He (for the overwhelming majority of rapists are male, another aspect of the sexually differentiated nature of the act) denies the victim the specificity of her (for the overwhelming majority of rape victims are female) own being and constructs her sexuality as a mere means by which his own purposes, be they primarily sexual or primarily motivated by the need for power, are achieved. . . . [T]he victim's difference from the assailant—her ontological, ethical, and personal distinctness—is stamped out, erased, annihilated.[39]

The focus on the *harm* done to the victim is the primary measure of moral wrong. Although in some ways this highly subjective norm may be a problem for legal norms which prefer objective, behavioral measures, it is nonetheless appropriate in shaping an ethical, pastoral or therapeutic response. Perhaps it may also be significant in shaping the response to the perpetrator in an appeal to his/her empathy for the consequences of his/her actions on another person.[40]

A focus on harm done to the victim also is not entirely dependent on the victim's perception. The community has an overriding interest at points in positing harm done even in contradiction to the victim. For example in statutory rape, the law specifies that sexual contact is illegal between an adult and teenager even if the teenager sees her/himself as consenting. This social and legal norm based on the inability to consent due to imbalance of power asserts harm done to a teen by sexual involvement with an adult.

In any case, beginning with the question of harm done to the victim does not rely on resolving the issue of the intent or psychological motivation of the assailant (sex or violence?) to determine the wrong of rape. In fact it allows us to posit the question: why does it matter what the motivation of the assailant is? If he (or she) is acting out of a desire for power and control or a desire for sexual contact (or both), and denies the autonomy and choice of another person, he (or she) has violated an ethical norm and should be held accountable. This insight from the secular consideration of ethical norms and sexual violence strengthens our consideration of the theological and scriptural foundations for positing specific ethical norms related to sexual violence.

## THEFT

Another common lay interpretation of the wrong of rape or sexual abuse is often articulated by survivors of childhood sexual abuse or abuse by clergy or other trusted helpers. Frequently, survivors use phrases such as "what I lost" to describe the consequences of the betrayal of trust they experience. In this they are reaching for a moral norm by which to establish the wrongness of their experience. Of course the flaw here is that this language of "loss" completely avoids agency or responsibility on the part of the perpetrator. The passive voice of loss ultimately reflects on the survivor and her/his carelessness in "losing" something valuable. This is a reasonable effort again within a patriarchal context in which support for placing responsibility for an offense (betrayal of trust and violation of boundaries) on the person with power (parent, teacher, clergy, etc.) is unlikely. But it seriously distracts from a viable ethical norm which should focus on theft. This is not to revert to the property discussion above, but rather to acknowledge that in fact something is taken from the victim (not a third party) by the perpetrator that does not belong to him or her. It is not the property of a victim's sexual goods but rather the trust that one carries in one's world, in relationships, and also one's future. The sexual abuse of a child means that that child's future is dramatically impacted and for better or worse probably will require some expenditure of energy and resources as an adult to address the childhood experience. A child's future is stolen by sexual abuse. This does not mean that it cannot be recovered. But if the actions of an adult who took something that did not belong to him/her did not occur, this child would have a very different future.

A sexual attack makes it clear that something has been taken away *by someone*. *Someone* has taken another's power away. *Someone* has stolen another's bodily integrity. The power to decide, to choose, to determine, to consent or withhold consent in the most concrete bodily dimension, all vanish in the face of a rapist or child molester. In the poem "Stolen, Not Lost," written in 1993 by Marian Lovelace, a survivor of childhood abuse by multiple Catholic priests illustrates the distinction between theft and loss. The author describes learning about responsibility, realizing that in abandoning the shame and blame, certain gifts were stolen, although not lost.[41]

Finally, the sin of sexual violence brings us back to the 10 Commandments. But it is not the 7th Commandment which is usually invoked that should concern us: "you shall not commit adultery." The problem with sexual violence is not that it represents "sex outside of marriage." Rather is it the 8th Commandment: "you shall not steal" (Deuteronomy 5:19 and Exodus 20:15). It is not theft in the sense of rape or sexual abuse of a woman or child being the theft of property belonging to the male head-of-household. It is rather the theft by the assailant of the security and well-being of the victim, the betrayal of trust, and the theft of her/his future.

## The Sin of Sexual Violence

Fundamentally, rape or sexual abuse are not sins because they are "sexual," in other words, because there is some form of genital contact, and specifically outside of marriage. So adultery is not the ethical category within which to consider sexual violence.[42] Neither is homosexuality although confusion on this point is rampant. Using Genesis 19 (Sodom and Gomorrah) and Judges 19 (the unnamed concubine), historical and contemporary interpretations of both of these stories focus on the sexual sin of homosexuality. This appears to be based on the fact that the gang of men in each case threatens to assault other men, the male guests, which would involve genital contact between males. In fact, the stories vividly describe sexual assault, first threatened against men, suggested against the daughters, and carried out against the concubine in the Judges version. All of this mayhem occurred in the context of a profound violation of the hospitality code and of the concubine herself which are the real ethical issues at stake here.

In neither the scriptural interpretation of the stories, nor in more current hermeneutics do we hear any reference except among feminist biblical scholars[43] to the sin which is inflicted upon the woman, that is, the violation of her bodily integrity and sacrifice of her life. Certainly no one asked the concubine whether she would choose to offer herself to a gang of rapists in order to protect her master from this fate. Once she found herself facing the gang, it was apparent that the gang's purpose was to violate and destroy her, not even because she was a person in her own right, but because she was the property of the guest. Since he was the real target of the gang of assailants, assaulting the concubine, his property, was the next best thing to being able to assault him directly.

The sin of sexual violence is a violation of the victim her/himself which causes physical and emotional harm. Why is it unethical to violate the sexual boundaries of another person?

Sexual violence is a personal sin:

- a violation of bodily integrity which denies a person the choice to determine her/his own boundaries and activities.
- a violation of personhood because it objectifies the other making them a nonperson.
- an action which creates a victim, that is, renders a person powerless by stealing her/his resources and sense of self.
- a violation which distorts and misuses sexuality.
- an action which causes pain and suffering, that is, harm.

Sexual violence is a relational sin:

- a betrayal of trust in a relationship which destroys the possibility of relationship between people.

Sexual violence is a social sin:

- which thrives in an environment of sexism, racism, and heterosexism to sustain subordinate/dominant relationships which encourage or silently condone individual acts of sexual violence, creating a hostile environment particularly for women and children.
- which destroys community because it creates an atmosphere of fear and distrust among family, friends, coworkers, and acquaintances.

In a non-peer relationship in which there is an inequality of power (e.g., a relationship between parent and child; teacher and student; pastor and congregant, etc.), there are additional dimensions to the sin of sexual violence:

- With a child, a violation of the adult role vis-à-vis the child. The adult should be protecting and providing for the child's welfare.
- A misuse of the power and authority of the adult or leadership role, which takes advantage of vulnerability.
- A denial of authentic consent.

In sum, sexual violence is a sin because it causes harm to another person and brings suffering. For Christians, this contradicts God's purpose attributed to Jesus in John's Gospel: "The thief comes only to steal and kill and destroy. I came that they may have life, and have it abundantly" (John 10:10).

In addition, the responsibility articulated by the prophet Ezekiel in Chapter 34 draws on the Hebrew hospitality code which mandated the entire community to protect those who are vulnerable: orphans, widows and sojourners (Psalms 146:9). This important mandate was given to the Hebrews with a reminder: because *you* were once slaves in the land of Egypt (Deuteronomy 10:19). The reminder is that all humans experience vulnerability at different times in our lives and so we are to protect one another in those circumstances.

Sexual violence is a sin against the community. Hebrew Scripture references an offense which disrupts community life. They describe the upset of male property arrangements which resulted from sexual violence. But reinterpreted from the perspective of the victims, we can better understand the disruption of the community to mean the fear, mistrust, and limitations which sexual violence imposes on all members of the community. In Hebrew Scripture, the words describe the havoc, folly,[44] and emptiness which result from sexual assault. A picture emerges of a hostile, alien environment which diminishes the possibility of meaningful relationships within the community, particularly between women and men. From a Christian perspective, the sin of sexual violence is also a sin against the community of faith as a whole. Because through baptism, all Christians are joined together as one body, whenever any one of its members is violated or injured, the whole body suffers from the sin.

Some criteria are needed to help judge the seriousness and the sinfulness of human behavior. But the criteria should be based on the degree to which a particular behavior causes harm or suffering to a person. Once the ethical question is reframed in this way, principles and criteria can be formulated to guide behavior and society's response to particular behaviors. Establishing the criterion of harm done to the victim and theft of the person does not rely on resolving the issue of the psychological motivation of the assailant (sex or violence?) to determine the wrong of rape. In fact it allows us to posit the question: why does it matter what the motivation of the assailant is? If he (or she) is acting out of a desire for power and control or a desire for sexual contact (or both), and denies the autonomy and choice of another person, he (or she) has violated an ethical norm and should be held accountable. It is the offender's sin—a sin against God, the victim, and the community with serious ramifications for all.

In asserting a new ethical framework, we face the real challenge presented by Catherine MacKinnon's position that rape is the "normal" consequence of the established social and political domination of women by men. As such it is hard to find an ethical norm to challenge it. If it is "the way things are," it is therefore "normal," therefore moral. The ethical norm is defined by those with power. Carol Adams quotes MacKinnon and Judith Hermann:

> "The fact is, anything that anybody with power experiences as sex is considered *ipso facto* not violence, [i.e. not wrong] because *someone who matters enjoyed it* [emphasis added]." (1987) . . . Judith Hermann offers a confirmation of this: if "the normative social definition of sexuality involves the eroticization of male dominance and female submission, then the use of coercive means to achieve sexual conquest might represent a crude exaggeration of prevailing norms, but not a departure from them." (1988)[45]

This is the tacit subtext to the history of western thought on the subject of the ethical wrong of rape. It has rested on the experience and interpretation of the one with power and virtually ignored the consequences for the one without. Therein lies the difficulty of establishing and implementing social and judicial remedies for this unjust behavior. The question of "who decides?" whether it was sex (i.e., normal/moral) or violence (i.e., aberrant/immoral) is finally a political as well as an ethical and legal question yet to be determined and acted on in the 21st century.

## Notes

1. Albert Bandura, *Aggression: A Social Learning Analysis* (Englewood Cliffs, NJ: Prentice Hall, 1973), 5.

2. "Justices, 6–3, Legalize Gay Sexual Conduct in Sweeping Reversal of Court's '86 Ruling," *New York Times*, June 27, 2003.

3. See Lori B. Girshick, *Woman-to-Woman Sexual Violence* (Boston, MA: Northeastern University Press, 2002).

4. See Barrie Levy, ed., *Dating Violence: Young Women in Danger* (Seattle, WA: Seal Press, 1998).

5. See also Tikva Frymer-Kensky, "Deuteronomy," in *The Women's Bible Commentary*, ed. Carol A. Newsom and Sharon H. Ringe (Louisville, KY: Westminster/John Knox Press, 1992), 56–59.

6. "The laws focus mainly upon external threats to the man's authority, honor and property, though they may occasionally serve to define and protect his rights in relation to members of his own household." Phyllis Byrd, "Image of Women in the Old Testament" in *Religion and Sexism*, ed. Rosemary Ruether. (New York: Simon & Schuster, 1974), 51.

7. Ann Cahill, *Rethinking Rape* (Ithaca, NY: Cornell University Press, 2001), 168: "The wrong committed here is not one of violence against the female victim, but of trespass on another man's property, which constitutes a threat to the rights, and therefore the political and social identity, of the owning male. This trespass (especially insofar as it represented a financial loss on the part of a father whose daughter was now damaged goods relative to the market of marriage) was perceived with social outrage and therefore punished severely. . . . in certain cases, most notably if the victim was a virgin, rape could be understood as a theft of an irreplaceable piece of property for which the real victim (usually the father in this case) deserved financial compensation."

8. See also Ron Clark, "The Silence in Dinah's Cry: Narrative in Genesis 34 in a Context of Sexual Violence," *Journal of Religion and Abuse*, Vol. 2, No. 4, 2001.

9. See Anita Diamant, *The Red Tent* (New York: Picador USA, 1997), for a very different interpretation of Dinah's experience and the aftermath.

10. See Ron O'Grady, *The Hidden Shame of the Church: Sexual Abuse of Children and the Church* (Geneva, Switzerland: World Council of Churches, 2001).

11. "Underage" refers to boys and girls under 16 or 18 years old depending on state statutes. The more effective statutes indicate that underage persons are by definition unable to consent to sexual contact with an adult.

12. U.S. Dept. of Health and Human Services, *Child Sexual Abuse: Incest, Assault, and Sexual Exploitation* (Washington, D.C.: U.S. Dept. of Health and Human Services, 1981), 1.

13. David Finklehor, "What's Wrong with Sex Between Adults and Children?" *American Journal of Orthopsychiatry*, Vol. 49 (October 1979), 694–96.

14. U.S. Dept. of Health and Human Services, 1.

15. U.S. Federal Equal Employment Opportunity Commission.

16. John T. Noonan, "Genital Good," *Communio*, Vol. 8 (Fall 1981), 200–201.

17. Karl Menninger, *Whatever Became of Sin* (New York: Hawthorn Books, 1973), 140.

18. Carl F. H. Henry, ed., *Baker's Dictionary of Christian Ethics* (Grand Rapids, MI: Baker Book House, 1973), 565.

19. Ibid.

20. *Dictionary of Moral Theology* (Westminister, MD: Newman Press, 1962), 1017.

21. Ibid.

22. Ibid., 1017–18.

23. Ibid., 1018.

24. In this we see the reflection of Thomas Aquinas who was most concerned about injury done to husband or father rather than to the rape victim herself. Oscar E. Feucht et al., *Sex and the Church* (St. Louis, MO: Concordia Publishing House, 1961), 70.

25. *Dictionary of Moral Theology*, 1018.

26. This text is the only one cited here which addresses the question of what happens if a woman does conceive from rape: "It is a disputed question whether, immediately following intercourse, the woman may use positive means to prevent conception or must let nature take its course." *Dictionary of Moral Theology*, 1018. While moral theologians discuss the intricacies of this question, women are left to decide whether to abort a fetus which results from rape with little moral guidance or pastoral help from the Church.

27. Otto A. Piper, *The Biblical View of Sex and Marriage* (New York: Charles Scribner's Sons, 1960), 62.

28. Ibid.

29. *Baker's Dictionary* 319; *Dictionary of Moral Theology*, 614.

30. *Dictionary of Moral Theology*, 614.

31. Noonan, 203.

32. Ibid., 205.

33. William Countryman, *Dirt, Greed, and Sex* (Philadelphia, PA: Fortress Press, 1988), 248.

34. James Nelson, *Embodiment* (Minneapolis, MN: Augsburg Publishing House, 1978), 262.

35. James Nelson and Sandra Longfellow, *Sexuality and the Sacred* (Louisville, KY: Westminster/John Knox Press, 1994).

36. Toinette Eugene, " 'Swing Low, Sweet Chariot!': A Womanist Ethical Response to Sexual Violence and Abuse," in *Violence Against Women and Children: A Christian Theological Sourcebook*, ed. Carol Adams and Marie Fortune (New York: Continuum Press, 1995), 186–87.

37. See Marie M. Fortune, *Sexual Violence: the Unmentionable Sin* (Cleveland, OH: Pilgrim Press, 1984).

38. Cahill, 194–95.

39. Ibid., 192–93.

40. This idealistic notion assumes that the assailant's sociopathy or narcissism does not obliterate the assailant's potential for empathy.

41. See Marie M. Fortune, *Response To Clergy Misconduct: A Handbook* (Seattle, WA: FaithTrust Institute, 2009).

42. The 2002 revisions to the U.S. Roman Catholic Bishops' Dallas Policy on the sexual abuse of children held some interesting revelations. The Bishops directly tied the definition of sexual abuse to a moral standard based on the Sixth Commandment in Hebrew scripture. "You shall not commit adultery." If this is the basis of their ethical understanding of sexual abuse, then no wonder the perception persisted that the bishops simply didn't "get it." The average layperson would rightly ask, "I thought adultery was about adults having sex with

someone they are not married to. What does sexual abuse of kids have to do with adultery?"

43. The exception is found among feminist biblical scholars and preachers, e.g., Phyllis Tribble in *Texts Of Terror*.

44. "Folly" defined as "wickedness or wantonness."

45. Carol Adams and Marie Fortune, eds., *Violence Against Women and Children: A Christian Theological Sourcebook* (New York: Continuum Press, 1995), 26.

# CHAPTER 11

# An Articulation of a Theology of the Body for Queer Theory

*Marie Cartier*

This chapter makes connections between butch-femme lesbian reality, queer theory, and spirituality, via Christianity. Connecting theology and lived religious reality with butch-femme realities is at the core of this work. The chapter explores how pre-Stonewall lesbians viewed the body to define themselves and the sense of community they developed in the lesbian bars of the period. Such community building functioned through a sense of common faith in each other, and was the grounding for what I call a theology of community that made sacred seeing and befriending each other, in a world where there was no other space that allowed for that. The argument that Joan Nestle begins with in her seminal article, "Butch-Femme Relationships: Sexual Courage in the 1950's," and that Henking and Comstock continue by including it in the critical anthology of writings on "being queer" and "being religious" *Qu(e)rying Religion,* is crucial to this undertaking. They wrote, "The unspecified connection between religion and homosexuality is provided by Joan Nestle's personal account of butch-femme lesbian relationships in New York City in the 1950s . . . she makes no overt claims; but she does articulate a strong belief statement about communal lesbian survival and uses such terms as "erotic independence," "essential pleasure," "celebration," and "erotic heritage," that suggests religious language and lend themselves to religious categorization."[1] Methodologically, each section begins with a question to establish clarification around definitions, identities, norms for particular behaviors, matters of history and heritage to help unpack the complexities of butch-femme realities.

The butch-femme community of the 1950s created its own spirituality in the context of a corporeal theology between couples and individually. These couples/individuals were also part of this larger "bar community" that created a space for the community to refine this theology in terms of self-defining a community. This self-defined community functioned for its members in many of the same ways any religious community functions that is held together by a common faith and/or theology.

The lesbian bar culture of the butch-femme community in the 1950s and 1960s created its own faith community, theology, and "places of worship"—the bars in which they "congregated," weekly. By reframing the gaze on theology/spirituality, it is possible to re-envision the reason why this community was and remains so important to contemporary lesbians and feminists, straight and gay, and allows us a reinterpretation of the experience of the butch-femme community.

For the basic functions of a faith community—weekly meetings, commitment to a theology—in this case a praxis of sacred corporeality, commitment to the members of the community, shared ideology, refusal to deny identity, and willingness to endure extreme danger to one's physical being/psyche to continue to practice one's "faith," and ensure "communal survival," were all present in the bar culture of the 1950s. There is a verifiable model of theology present in its functioning that is useful to queer culture and the culture at large.

## WHAT DEFINES A RELIGIOUS COMMUNITY?

A "community," is defined as "a social group or class having common interests," and "religious" is defined as "extremely faithful, scrupulous, conscientious," and finally, "religion" itself means "the expression of [a person's] belief in and reverence for a superhuman power recognized as the creator and governor of the universe" or "any particular integrated system of this expression," or "any objective attended or pursed with zeal or conscientious devotion."[2]

A religious community then could be a social group or class whose common interests include faithful and conscientious expressions of belief in and reverence for a superhuman power recognized as creator of the universe, or simply a group that pursues an objective with zeal.

## WHAT IS THEOLOGY?

Theology is "the study of the nature of God and religious truth," "rational inquiry into religious questions," or a "formalized body of opinions concerning man's relationship to God."

An expanded definition[3] is that "theology" is "the science of God," classically defined as "faith seeking understanding." Amid divine mystery, theology continuously seeks but ultimately never finds answers. While theology occurs in academic settings, it needs to occur in and on behalf of a believing community. Religious studies, for example philosophy of religion, conversely occur only in the academy.[4]

When we leap from this sacred definition to a sacred, yet secular definition of "gay theology," we begin to see the possibility for locating a theology within the bar culture. Ronald Long suggests that a contemporary use of the term theology is not a church matter exclusively. Rather, theology should be a public endeavor where individual persons or communities critically think about its purpose and life's course. Thus, gay theology explores what one can and ought to say religiously based on lived gay experiences, contributing directly to public discourse, rather than seeking to clarify what religious bodies teach or have taught about homosexuality.[5]

So, while theology *may* be practiced within an academic setting, it *should be* practiced within a believing community. This praxis of "faith seeking understanding" then in terms of gay theology should not be defined in the "academic" setting of the church hierarchy, but within the believing community *itself*—as a public enterprise of that culture's reflection on its direction.

Finally, since theology is not about seeking final answers, it is appropriate that its primary praxis is exploration, rather than formal teaching. Theology then is "practice," something which is *done* within the believing community.

Corporeal theology would then be theology or practice done within a believing community that is "characteristic of the body," or "tangible." Recently, feminist religious and secular theorists and religious ethicists have suggested that we rethink our understandings and attitudes about spirituality and sexuality, frequently using the concept of embodiment. Human beings are physical, spiritual, physical beings; thus, Western Christian thought that makes the body subordinate or inferior to the soul denies the existence of our flesh and blood.[6]

The idea of an embodied spirituality, resting in a corporeal praxis, is highlighted in the work of several contemporary gay and lesbian theologians/religious writers, as well as heterosexual writers. Among them are the Reverend Nancy Wilson (*Our Tribe: Queer Folks, God, Jesus and the Bible*), James Nelson (*Body Theology*), Riane Eisler (*Sacred Pleasure*), Alison Webster (*Found Wanting: Women, Christianity and Sexuality*), and Andrew Harvey (*The Gay Mystics*).

This Christian view is reinforced, particularly for women by the contemporary writings on religions commonly known to embody corporeal practice, such as tantric Buddhism.[7] Several theologians have spoken of an embodied theology for lesbians and gay men that employs corporeal praxis, and said that this theology should be drawn from the lived experience of the community itself.

## WHAT IS A "SHARED IDENTITY?"

Identity is defined as "the collective aspect of the set of characteristics by which a thing is definitively recognizable," or "the set of behavioral characteristics by which an individual is recognizable as a member of the group" or "the personality of an individual regarded as a persistent entity."

To "share" an identity is "to participate, use, or experience something in common," with that identity. To be a community with a "shared identity" means then that community participates in a "collective aspect," sharing and or *using* behavioral characteristics to become recognizable members of that group. If we understand religion as personal relations with a venerated reality, then an individual or group's religious life has multiple things they revere and hierarchical realities which may involve a relation with a morally ideal, wonderful, sacred reality.[8]

So, religion, theology, community, and sacrality are necessarily exclusive, but by reframing the gaze on what constitutes "revered reality," we can suggest that the praxis of a sacred life, may or may not include interaction with a "morally perfect" reality. Long himself is not claiming "being gay is religious in character," and he says that "while the valuation of male beauty and homosex that anchors gay life is itself religious, it is a reverential tie that will probably take its place among other sacred ties," not claiming gay life as being a cult or pertaining to gay men's religious practice.[9]

There are some contradictions here with lesbian life, especially as evidenced in butch-femme culture, but when articulating a theology for this period, it by no means connotes that by adopting this "theology," the community dissolved all other "sacred ties."

## WHAT WAS THE DEFINITION OF "BUTCH-FEMME" AND DID THAT DEFINITION INCLUDE A POSSIBLE THEOLOGY?

All commentators on twentieth-century lesbian life have noted the prominence of butch-fem roles. Before the 1970s their presence was unmistakable in all working-class lesbian communities . . . butch-fem roles not only shaped the lesbian image but also lesbian desire, constituting the base for a deeply satisfying erotic system.

. . . These (roles) were at the core of the community's culture, consciousness and identity.[10]

As Kennedy and Davis explain it in this same passage, when they began the research for their history *Boots of Leather, Slippers of Gold*, they thought that butch-fem roles would be incidental and marginal, as had been suggested by, among others, Lillian Faderman in the book that is called "the definitive study of modern lesbian life," *Odd Girls and Twilight Lovers*.[11]

Faderman suggests that "butch women *would not* be covert and the femmes who *let* themselves be seen with them often led dangerous lives." Her writing involves an implicit charge against overt expression of the butch-femme model. Instead of seeing these roles at the core of a developing community, she sees them as marginal, and detrimental to that development. Faderman says of butch-femme couples that they, "courted violence." She agrees that many of them were "certainly courageous in their insistence on presenting themselves in ways that felt authentic," but she feels that "their bravery made them victims." She also acknowledges the class differences these communities felt when she writes, that "middle and upper class lesbians could be comforted by the presence of policemen . . . but butch-fem couples did not have the luxury of that illusion."[12]

However, the 12-year study by Kennedy and Davis creates the community histories that support the claim that butch-femme roles were not marginal, that they were the majority; that they were not "optional"; therefore, it was not that butches "would not" conform to societal expectations; it is that they "could not."

A 70-plus-year-old narrator said that she was "stone butch until about fifteen or twenty years ago . . ." and said the following, "butch-femme . . . it's what goes beyond sex . . . it goes into your whole being . . . it's part of your whole make up . . . even though I'm butch sexually . . . my sex is only part of this . . . but being butch is how I am, how I feel . . ."[13]

By "stone butch" the narrator means that she would not let her lover penetrate her, or possibly make love back to her. She has changed this because of her lover's desire, not her own: "I always made love to them, and I always got a thrill out of it . . . I enjoy being on top. You know what I mean? Being the one who's overtly sexual."[14] In recent years, she conceded she has stopped this practice, and let lovers be more overtly sexual with her.

The issue of the "stone butch" is a very interesting conception, especially if we consider it in the light of a new theological model of corporeality originating within the people it serves. A contemporary butch articulated this same idea, that butch is something she "could not" not be rather than "would not be."

When I came out "butch" was not in my vocabulary (she came out in the 1975),

I was just a lesbian. But when I did (learn) that word it gave me a context to be Ok in . . . I'm proud that I can claim it. That I understand my history now . . . it defines who I am . . . I'm a lesbian . . . and I always was butch . . . I didn't have an understanding of what it was . . . just "athletic," . . . then an "Amazon."[15]

Butch women themselves do not feel mutable, or marginal, but feel permanently marked on the landscape of gay and lesbian history. That they were the strongest agents of a movement for gay and civil rights is supported by the research of Kennedy and Davis. For while the small, educated homophile movement was gathering strength while working for "assimilation," the butch and femme were aggressively claiming and holding space in large and visible numbers.

For their partners, "femme" women, it is much harder to find and therefore interview femme women of the period. Femme women have been ridiculed as "tools of the patriarchy," and not allowed ownership of their story as one of historic consequence. Because we lock ourselves into a binary position of gendering whether it is masculine, feminine, butch, or femme (see the work of Judith Butler and others), it is difficult to place the femme woman who owns femininity within the female lesbian body as different as the female who owns femininity within the heterosexual body. And therefore it becomes problematic to encode her historical significance to the butch-femme movement in terms of "courage"—because after all, the "only" thing she was doing differently than a heterosexual woman was . . . dating a masculine looking woman, "letting herself be seen with . . ." butches. However, the femme women were courageous in their choices and were deeply marked as homosexual when they walked arm in arm with a butch lover. This type of courage is reminiscent of what Christians have gone through throughout the ages in terms of fighting for their right to a faith practice. Most of these women were kicked out of their churches of birth and the bar culture was the only place that accepted them.[16] This was however a radically transgressive act. And it is in this act, and that of the gendering of the stone butch that much of the "theology" will originate.

Butch and femme, while they are owned individually, are relational terms, primarily indicating a sexual position or being desirous of one. So, it stands to reason that without "femme," "butch" loses much of its potency. "Butch femme has become a form of self-representation for lesbians; it gives lesbian desire a partial sometimes reluctant entry into the symbolic realm of language and culture. In the hegemonic sense, we are women, but we are something else, too."[17]

The following quotes are from self-identified femme authors who lived during the urban period 1945–1975, prior to Stonewall and its liberating effects, and serve as an illustration of their self-placement on this landscape, and not with the conscription that they were "letting" themselves, as Faderman suggests, be coupled with butches, but, for the most part, that they saw themselves as courageous partners, not victims, in the dance. The spirituality that I see in these authors work is in their defiance of a system that would erase them, the dominant heterosexual culture of their time, and on the face of that, their belief and struggle toward owning their humanity. Since they were kicked out of all major and minor religions, the only religion left to them was one of their own choosing. Again, I call their lives religious in that they chose, despite the odds, to see and validate humanity in each other. As the following quotes articulate:

I fly to you/To be soothed in the wings/of your Butch tenderness hidden under fierceness necessary as mine/to ride your feathers, fingers & tongue . . ."[18]

. . . I do like tough women, butch women, big, confident, strong women, It is then that every part of me opens . . . Satisfaction. Determined grown-up satisfaction that denies silence, all silences, most particularly the long silence of my girlhood, the denial of a lesbian girlchild who was never meant to survive.[19]

. . . I wanted her to see my competent femme self, self-supporting and sturdy, happened. We kissed for a few minutes and soon her hands knew I was not afraid . . . I strained to take and give to her, had never felt so beautiful . . . She reached deep into me, past the place of coming, into the center of my womanness.[20]

. . . perhaps some would say I have betrayed womanhood with you, that we are traitors to our sex. Traitors to our sex, or spies and explorers across the boundaries of what is man, what is woman? My body yawns open greedily for what you are not afraid to give me.[21]

These stories from women "in the life" are supplemented herewith by quotes from more contemporary "femmes" and /or lovers of butch women. From a poem "Ode to the American Butch," Michelle Clinton an African American bisexual/ femme poet writes:

. . . inside wild gay territory/. . . will take you to places of foreign knowledge/ w/out the heart to recognize/anything you used to think/was home.[22]

What is "the place of foreign knowledge" which the above author states that the butch and femme go to? In the context of historical or contemporary butch-femme participation it was a community based on theology, as defined through corporeal praxis: "the experience including the sexual experience, of every human being in every time and place is distinct from that of every other human being, and that the social matrix in which she or he lives will determine that experience."[23]

Above I have drawn similarities between theology, butch-femme bar culture of the 1950s and contemporary culture, without doing a disservice to either the traditional definition of theology, or to the historic or contemporary cultures. I continue this discussion by answering the following questions.

## WHAT WAS THIS COMMUNITY'S SHARED IDENTITY?

Since gender recognition requires performance, being viewed by someone else, gender characteristics become labeled and classed as feminine or masculine.[24] Performing gender is a requisite and shared praxis. From the statements from femmes and butches, this praxis had to do with sexual loving that took the participants to another "place," the "center"—sexuality that was transcendent. One informant said that she has more "respect for women and for femmes now . . . I have a better understanding . . . Butch femme relationships give me the freedom to be me. Femmes appreciate me being me, my body, my size and strength . . . it's appreciated by femmes."[25]

In other sources, butches also talk about sharing technique (i.e., information on praxis) with each other. And femmes talk about sharing information with each other, and specifically about teaching butches' praxis—or how to make love. If there is tangible corporeal embodied theology present in this community, then it is being developed within the community itself, and passed to its members by its members. These life experiences connect to faith praxis as we open theology to include body theology, queer theology, feminist theology, all of which contain elements of embodied thought, or discourse on the sacred.

In *Stone Butch Blues,* the Jess narrator remembers being told by a femme she was with that she, the butch, had two choices when making love: All I remembered was Jacqueline's warning: *You could make a woman feel real good . . .or you could make her remember all the ways she's ever been hurt.*[26]

I call this a theology of praxis, a theology of the body as these women, with no help from the culture surrounding them, decided to make each other "feel good," to humanize each other, rather than to heed the call of the culture surrounding them that labeled them sinners. This theology of the body that was practiced between these women was passed perhaps mainly from femmes to butches, and is perhaps the same *type* of information in the tantric tradition of Buddhism on transcendental praxis that was passed from women to men, from femininely gendered beings to masculinely gendered beings. And that these women, in both cultures, *could be* considered sacred bearers of knowledge. In tantra, the praxis of indigenous Hindus, the secret oral instruction that a Female tantrika (or embodiment of the Goddess) gave included the inner yogas that form the basis of the sexual practices. The yogi in question was accepted as a consort by a female Tantric and proceeded to practice with her, in some cases for several months and in others for many years.[27] This Tantric tradition relates to Christian practice. In the Bible Jesus allows Veronica to wash his face as he walks to Calgary and leaves an impression on the cloth; he is only witnessed by Mary, who then must tell the disciples of His rise from the dead. These stories show how often it is the women who must initiate the embodied contact—the touching, the seeing, and how that phenomena of human physical contact becomes often more sacred than text.

What appears to be the authentic passing of sexual expertise in terms of lovemaking to a woman's body appears to come from this research from women, rather than from men. This type of knowledge—how to actually and really make love to a woman—is usually not sought by men, but apparently is sought by *masculinely gendered* women, that is, butches. Perhaps, this, as has been suggested by Esther Newton, is part of "Mary's story." Mary is the lover of Radclyffe Hall's protagonist, Stephen Gordon, in *The Well of Loneliness*, who must return to men, leaving Stephen bereft at the end of the novel. "Hall was unable to publicly articulate—perhaps to believe in—the persona of a real lesbian who did not feel somehow male. If sexual desire is masculine, and if the feminine woman only wants to attract men, then the womanly lesbian cannot logically exist. Mary's real story has yet to be told."[28]

What does it mean to create a community where the sexuality of women is honored? Outside of the butch-femme contemporary and historical community, the intense "worship" of female desire cannot easily be found in *community*, except for the aforementioned example of tantric Buddhism. If there is an embodiment theology, then the following quote regarding lesbianism and the scientific community in the second half of the 19th century shows how it was lesbians perhaps that saved embodiment for women at all. For "the mannish lesbian" dominated the discourse about female homosexuality. This community believed that sexual desire "was not considered inherent in women," and that "the lesbian was endowed with a trapped male soul giving her active lust." Richard Kraft Ebing articulated "the fusion of masculinity, feminist aspiration and lesbianism" that remains an *article of faith* in Anglo-American culture" (italics added).[29]

If it is an "article of faith" that sexual desire cannot be held in a woman actively, but only in a masculinely gendered woman, what does it mean to live in an opposing culture like butch-femme where sexual desire in femininely gendered women is expected, and then honored? This type of alternate "faith" begins to constitute a radical theology of difference—a corporeal theology rooted in sexual praxis designed to bring the genders, in this case both embodied in the biological female, into union with one another.

One could draw a comparison here to tantra, and possibly an analogy to the union of human with the divine—especially when "human" is seen as "man" (generic) and "God" (Divine) as "Holy Spirit, or female," through the

Eucharist. The Eucharist and its sacrament are an embodied experience—you "eat the body, drink the blood," therefore entering into union with Divinity, Christ (male), but also then filled with "the Holy Spirit" (female). Is "Mary's story" then this priest-like role? And is Stephen's story that of supplicant? Certainly a contemporary reading indicates this worship/worshiper speculation as more probable that not. One femme writes of this newly acquired ability for the femme woman to articulate desire and claim embodiment: "I contemplate myself as femme, deliberately cross-dressing myself in femininity as drag, constructing myself as a spectacle for woman's eyes: Queen of Desire. The woman to be desired who declares herself a desirer of women: Queen femme."[30]

## What Were the "Rules" for Enduring Danger, and Exposing/Denying Identity? How Did These Rules Function or Not Function as Spiritual Praxis?

When we talk about butch-femme, we are talking about a people under siege—nightly bar raids by police, gang rape, and beatings by heterosexual men were all part and parcel of the experience of being part of this community (see Kennedy and Davis, Feinberg, Nestle, and others for documentation)— but we are also talking about sexual freedom and the ability to belong to a "new Church"—that of butch-femme. "The time period of the fifties . . . sets the stage for the freedom we have now . . . (it's important to) put it in people's faces so that they have to see it.[31] Heroic action was necessary for the survival of something this community believed in—something that they could not have found elsewhere—such as in the "discreet" life style of the homophile middle-class movement. What they were standing their ground for, in the face of severe life-threatening harassment, was the ability to love with "persistent desire."[32] This is the title of Nestle's most famous work on the subject, and it remains a moniker for this society's driving theology—"persistent desire." When 1970s lesbian feminists complained in the early 80s of "lesbian bed death" (the syndrome where long-term lesbian couples would stop having sex), this was a recent lesbian phenomenon. Butch-femme couples were seen, and are seen, as having "persistent desire." Lesbian feminist couplings came to be associated with "bed death." Why?

Throughout the 1940s and 1950s fems were central to the building of all working-class lesbian communities and most relationships were based on butch and fem; social life was unimaginable without both. Fems patronized bars despite the risk and they avoided their families' attempts to control them. "In the context of severe oppression, fems desired butches . . . embraced an erotic dyad that was predicated on fem sexual pleasure." They built relationships that lasted; however, their contributions to history/herstory have not been recognized. "Esther Newton's 1984 comment that the history of femmes is yet to be written still holds true today."[33]

So, perhaps the "faith seeking understanding" here is that of "Mary's" story, especially as she impacts "Stephen's." One informant said, "It's such a stigma . . . even now . . . all the classifieds in the *Lesbian News* . . . people who advertise for no butches; we're in a negative classification of things people don't want . . . but it feels like I feel powerful in the world being butch . . ."[34]

However, with *lesbians who identify as femmes*, the butch, even the "stone butch" is desired, and wanted, as is the femme—the masculine woman whose desire is to "please" and the feminine woman whose function in the dyad is to be "pleased." "Pleasure" is an ambiguous termif what you desire to do *is please*, and then you are *being pleased* in that action.

The primary rule of belonging to this group was hard-core courage to endure the historical oppression. What compelled them to risk losing job, family, life—if not something "greater than themselves"—something that felt like "reverence for a superhuman power," to use the definition of Divinity-worthy of worship?

To be in the company of others who had an understanding of, acceptance of, and a sense of celebration of alternative gendering coded into sexual and spiritual praxis approximated that Divinity that faith communities do feel they will "die for," if necessary.

Within this complicated reality, by virtue of being viewed through a nec-essarily dominant heterosexual lens, the identity—"stone butch"—becomes pragmatic and useful when viewed through the butch-femme lens.

> It's hard to talk about something like giving up power without it sounding passive. I am willing to give myself over to a woman equal to her amount of wanting. I expose myself for her to see what's possible for her to love in me that's female. I want her to be open to it. I may not be doing something active with my body, but more eroticizing her need that I feel in her hands as she touches me.[35]

Femmes created and create the space for the butch to hold and perform mas-culine gender. Because of this, the butch can feel "normal" in a society wishing her to classify herself as "abnormal." The femme says I create space for you. Conversely, the butch creates the space for the femme to hold sexual desire in an otherwise female body traditionally gendered. Because of this, the femme can also feel normal, in a society which wishes her to feel abnormal.

Elizabeth Kennedy writes that femme's emphasis on pleasure, and that emphasis in the relationship between butches and femmes, assured a type of balance to the relationship, "making the pursuit of satisfaction legitimate for each partner. . . . Butch fem relationships were gendered relationships without being fully integrated into a heterosexual system of male supremacy."[36]

In response to the stone butch, Halberstam suggests that the creation of the stone butch, if viewed outside of heterosexist culture, is a creative and workable "solution" to masculine gendering within a female body. Reviewing a definition of "pleasure," as Halberstam suggests, a stone butch only cautions against "unmediated genital contact. Although some stones chose (and choose) to not orgasm with a partner, others have and do receive pleasure from their partners through a variety of sexual practices such as tribadism (*or rubbing*)" (italics mine).[37]

What is interesting is that one's own pleasure can "provoke unwarranted rage not only from a gender conformist society that cannot comprehend stone butch gender or stone butch desire but also from within the dyke subculture, where the stone butch tends to be read as frigid, dysphoric, misogynist, repressed or simply pre-trans-sexual."[38]

Halberstam writes that "the burden of butchness is resolved by the assumption of the stone butch identity." The outrage against the butch may not be *merely* because she is coded by the dominant cultures as "frigid," "mannish," etc. but also because her praxis directly facilitates the space for the unfolding of, nurturing of, and celebration of femme desire. Historically femme or female desire has been seen as dangerous and curtailed through historical actions such as witch burnings, rape, and so on.

To create a systematic way to nurture female desire and to create a "worship" of that desire has not been seen as possible within history. In the sexually repressed 1950s, butch-femme created a theology of *love* with desire that was possible for not only femininely gendered women, but also masculinely gendering "beings," in this case, women. In so doing, it presented a model for change and, therefore, became a major threat to the dominant paradigm of masculine gendered repression of love and feminine gendered repression of desire.

## SUMMARY OF THE THEOLOGICAL IDENTITY OF THIS COMMUNITY:

Butch-femme honored female masculinity, but also and perhaps more radically, honored *non-traditionally gendered* feminine women. Butch-femme is one of the few spaces in all of history that honored as important, the feminine, the femme, "the "Mary," especially in her sexual self. Historically, we find evidence for the femme gendered erotic pleasure being the focal point for the butch-femme community. The ability to generate and teach this body of erotic knowledge, and the passing of it from the feminine to the masculine gender, and the praxis of it, may constitute the foundation of the "theology" of this community.

## WHAT IS THE FEAR OF THE EROTIC NATURE OF BUTCH-FEMME?

It is not that working lesbians just appeared "stupid" and embraced "masculinity" because, as has been suggested, the 70s rejected traditional femininity as well as masculinity. This culture was rejected because it was overtly sexual, and to *assimilate*, the 50's "discreet" lesbian could not be overtly sexual—never mind mannish.

A popular women's magazine, *True Story*, in 1954, called the "femme" who seduces another woman, an "athletic" woman.[39] What is seen as dangerous in this traditional "ladies magazine," is not the mannish woman—but the feminine woman. She is the one who is not originally detected, bears no visible signs of deviance, and therefore, is especially dangerous to "normal" society. In her first encounter with this woman, the protagonist says: "Something was happening that I didn't understand, or even want to happen; yet I was powerless to stop it. I felt as though some gigantic force had taken possession of my will and spirit and brain driving me relentlessly to what?"[40]

The "to what?" is apparently to orgasm, that comes from *merely holding* the "femme"—the dangerous femme who does nothing except hold "desire." Our protagonist in fact is the aggressor, and can't "help herself . . . hardly conscious of what I did, I pulled her to me, my arms holding her closer and closer . . . like one of those sky rockets they shoot off on the Fourth of July, zooming into limitless space. Suddenly the rocket burst, and millions of stars flooded the room."[41] Perhaps there is theological significance in the phenomenological experience of "zooming off into limitless space." I also believe that the ability to hold someone closer and closer however and let go into and with that person is at the heart of embodied theology—our discourse of God begins with seeing God in the other.

The protagonist in angst goes to a psychiatrist, and he advises that she was "completely vulnerable when Marcy (the "femme") came along. She was experienced and practiced, and knew thoroughly the art of seduction. *You didn't stand a chance.*" He encourages this "athletic" woman to resist and date men and that "little by little mental readjustments will come, but it won't be over night . . . you must have patience and courage." At the end of the article, our narrator still thinks of Marcy, her "femme," but says now that she thinks of her with "pity and compassion . . . I hope someone will help her . . . and give her back the destiny that can only be achieved through the right kind of love."[42]

It is the femme then that can "bring out the butch" in a woman. Halberstam writes that the multiple modes of complementarity between stone butches and various forms of femme pleasure that stake out a central place for the stone butch within both historical butch-femme bar life and present-day queer sexual subcultures.[43] This staking out of a *central place* that is a space of complementarity for butches and femmes *specifically created for pleasure* is so dangerous. Sexuality that is not reigned in by the heterosexual dominant paradigm is seen as one of the most dangerous forces there is.[44] To couple lesbian sex *with intense desire*, as is apparent in butch-femme, and its actual *care and love*, as opposed to "just sex," is an extremely potent mixture, and certainly not a position an assimilationist would take in the '50s.

Women should not enjoy sex. This is driven home to the point that the only *dangerous* thing our protagonist in *True Love* has happen to her is her orgasm! The fact that this woman/femme "brings this out" in her is what is dangerous. The medical advice given her is not just given "fictionally." In the postscript to this article, the publishers notes that "The medical facts of this story have been checked for accuracy by Dr. Albert Ellis, New York psychologist and marriage counselor and author of the recently published book, *The American Sexual Tragedy*.[45] Thus, the advice is to "Go out with every man who asks you. It won't be easy, at first, but in time, it will become a habit. If a man kisses you, force yourself to respond, no matter how distasteful it may be."[46]

Anything is better than to be "under the spell" of femme *out of control* sexuality, in which one "would not have a chance." Flo, in her seventies, said that even though in the 30s through 50s when they put a bounty on the heads of homosexuals—she still went to the bar—despite the danger. She said, "They were offering $25 if you turned in a homosexual to Bellevue (in New York).

They had 72 hours then to try him out, and then they could keep you. Anyone could turn someone in . . ."[47]

Even though this is the atmosphere that surrounded her sexual expression, she still went to the bar. Why? "It was really cheesy. But it was the only place you could go, and feel like you were part of a family."[48]

It is little wonder that lesbians endured hardship to be part of a family. For the lack of understanding and compassion for their physical beings and the expression those beings sought is brutally marked in many accounts, among them a book, not so amazingly by, an upper-class lesbian. She begins quoting one of her interviewees: "A dyke looks just like man, but is a hundred times better as a lover. She just wants to please the woman. A man is a brute. He just wants a woman for his own pleasure."[49] She then goes on to analyze this woman's statement as follows: "The femme who is attracted to the transvestite often is simply a carbon copy of the kind of woman she would be if she were a heterosexual. . . if they were normal, they would look for the same kind of man they now have in a transvestite. . . . He might be a wonderful, gentle lover, . . . but like the "little boy" a lot of transvestites are, he probably won't be able to hold a job long."[50]

Of course, this analysis leaves very little room for the economic reality of a butch woman trying to get a job when very few jobs allowed a woman to wear pants, or when few employers would hire someone obviously butch (see Feinberg and others).

If a lesbian were to emulate the femme role, to assimilate, she might make choices primarily based on the quality of her lover's lovemaking. That she makes this a priority stigmatizes her. This is the centuries old virgin-whore complex that women get trapped in. If she decides to do something based on the needs of her body she is a whore; if she denies her body by definition she is then a virgin. Christianity has left very little room for most women to negotiate this dilemma and lesbians of mid-century even less so, for they were left out of the discussion altogether, since they were sinners, not sinning, but sinners. However, their decisions to choose their bodies as sites of independence sand self-definition have religious significance and the lesson for contemporary women of all faiths, particularly Christian women, might be that self-identification might mean ostracism, and it also might mean independence, joy, and community building with others of like mind. What does it mean to make the needs of your body a priority? As women we have only begun with the second wave of feminism to look at this question. These women, as Nestle suggests, were ahead of their time.

## What Lessons Are There in "Erotic Independence, Essential Pleasure, and Celebration"?

Joan Nestle wrote that when she was asked to speak in prison, she wanted to honor lesbian sex in prison, to honor the women who wanted each other, not because there were no men available but because they were lesbians. "My life has taught me that touch is never to be taken for granted. How in such a world as this, where guns and governments crush tenderness every day, can you find your way to that small, hidden woman's place? . . . Never will I take for granted in this world your generosity of exploration, how you have listened to my body . . . a woman reaching for my breast or parting my legs is never a common thing."[51]

As Nestle so eloquently puts it elsewhere in the article, in terms of lessons, the "only shame I ever feel now, after so many years of women's touch, is never saying thank you enough."[52] The "lesson" here is that it is possible, even in a world that labels a femininely gendered being's holding of desire as parody or worse impossible—to find that desire and live *without shame*—except for this grateful "shame" that Nestle corrects through her prose. *The only shame* she ever feels is in not saying thank you enough for good lovemaking, and what it has brought her.

## WHAT LESSONS ARE THERE IN AN "EROTIC HERITAGE"?

One informant told me, "Nowadays a lot of lesbian history is ignored. It's important that people know it was not easy in the fifties; they put their lives on the line to fight for the right to be who they are, to have their corner of the world: The bill of rights. They wanted it, too, and they were denied it because of their sexuality. It's my history, that's all.[53]

When we do not know, or misread our history, someone can make a statement like this directed to Joan Nestle: "You say you don't want to romanticize butch/femme relationships but that's exactly what you do . . . you white-wash your experiences and your sexuality like that, you trivialize yourself."[54] However other lesbians counter that, "there is a material power differential between men and women. Lesbians may be playing with power, but we don't have it."[55] Without knowledge of our erotic heritage, it is easy for history to repeat itself, and for history to be misinterpreted. Butch-femme needs to be seen, if possible, in the light in which it was lived.

According to poet Judy Grahn butch-femme had roots in the gay subculture and manifested not so much as an imitation of heterosexual roles as an exploration of different ways of being female.[56] One of the greatest lessons that the exploration investigates as sexual and theological praxis is that butch-femme offers the knowledge that women/lesbians/and femininely gendered people *have* an *erotic* heritage—an embodied ownership of sexuality. This is at the basis of all body theology and any work that deals with the issues of our embodiment and our embodiment as our connection to any transcendence. For these women to claim embodiment was the first step to their possible embodied transcendence.

## DOES AN "EROTIC HERITAGE" TRULY MAKE A SPACE FOR THEOLOGY? DOES IT ALLOW FOR A REVISIONING OF SEXUALITY AS WE "REFRAME THE GAZE" AROUND BUTCH-FEMME?

Revisiting lesbian sexuality in the 1950s allows us to revision our own sexuality. Especially as we consider the contemporary feminist theorist dilemma that "Mary's story" has not been told. Perhaps in revisiting the 1950s, where "Mary's story" was being lived in such an audacious way, is a path to begin to tell that story. In the telling of, and exploration of, that story, we may begin to fashion a corporeal theology, based on the sexual praxis of butch-femme, as it was lived in the 50s. However, the 50s were what they were. As one narrator remarked, when questioned of who she socialized with, "We hung out with prostitutes, pimps, drug dealers because you've got to hang out with somebody and we were felons then. Don't forget that. We were criminals . . . so we hung out with criminals."[57]

Although this was not an "ideal community" it was also not at all a "marginal community." And there is serviceable material here for the contemporary lesbian or straight woman to learn from, and an ability to reframe the histories that have been written, in a new light, based on new interpretations, particularly of gender.

When a majority of one's history has been captured and trivialized, the reasons for its trivialization provide great lessons for contemporary societies, as well as a new window to the past. There is evidence here—in the butch-femme culture—from which to create a "new" theology, based on interpretations of theology from comparison groups, and from revisioning this period itself, without damaging the authenticity of either.

## WHAT CAN WE CLAIM AS SPIRITUAL HISTORY, IF ANYTHING, FROM REVISITING THE HERITAGE OF THE 50S BUTCH-FEMME CULTURE?

There are many different things that an individual can lay "claim" to. One must be careful as was suggested earlier by Boswell, that one allows people the dignity of interpretation belonging to their time and place. Reclaiming the "persistent desire" of butch-femme allows us a link to a true erotic heritage.

Elizabeth Say and Mark Kowalski in their ethnography learned from their informants that "the erotic is far more than sexuality, though it is also this."

> They ask us to revalue the erotic and see that it offers us two lessons in citizenship. The first is to embrace passion . . . those things which stir us most deeply give us energy to sustain us in our work and to find joy in life. . . . The second lesson we can draw from erotic power is a reminder that we are all embodied beings . . . If we want a society where people do not live in fear, we must teach future citizen that physical bodies, real human people, are sacred and that avoidable human suffering of any sort is sin.[58]

Butch-femme allows the "space" to acknowledge an erotic heritage that we as women did not know we had, one that legitimates the need for desire in our lives. This essay begins to make connections between butch-femme reality, queer theory, and spirituality. I believe this historic butch-femme culture offers lessons for women and their contested embodiment. Religion has often taken away the control of women's bodies—via control of reproduction, marriage, and sexual-preference choice. These have not even been possible choices for women of most faiths, and since America has been and remains primarily Christian, then most particularly in the United States, for women of Christian faiths. The lessons of courage and independence that the mid-century butch-femme culture and the choices its members made, choices of passion and kinship directly related to ownership of their bodies, offer much to our knowledge of embodiment and how one connects an unspoken but lived theology of praxis, in this case that of one's own body, with one's lived religious reality.

## NOTES

1. David Gary Comstock and Susan E Henking, ed., "Part III: Culture and Society," *Qu(e)erying Religion: A Critical Anthology*, p. 284, in ref. to Joan Nestle's, "Butch-Femme Relationships: Sexual Relationships in the 1950's," (New York: Continuum, 1993), pp. 323–29.

2. William Morris, ed., *The American Heritage Dictionary of the English Language*, (Boston: Houghton Mifflin, 1981). All dictionary definitions, unless otherwise noted, are from this source.

3. Richard P. McBrien, general ed., *The HarperCollins Encyclopedia of Catholicism* (New York: Harper Collins, 1995), "theology," p. 1250.

4. Ibid.

5. Ronald E. Long, "The Sacrality of Male Beauty and Homosex: A Neglected Factor in the Understanding of Contemporary Gay Reality," in *Qu(e)erying Religion: A Critical Anthology*, ed. David Gary Comstock and Susan E. Henking (New York: Continuum, 1993), p. 280.

6. Elizabeth A. Say and Mark R. Kowalewski, *Gays, Lesbians and Family Values* (Cleveland, OH: Pilgrim Press, 1998), pp. 75–76.

7. Miranda Shaw, *Passionate Enlightenment: Women in Tantric Buddhism* (Princeton, NJ: Princeton University Press, 1994).

8. Long, p. 275.

9. Ibid., p. 275.

10. Kennedy and Davis, p. 5.

11. Lillian Faderman, "Butches, Femmes and Kikis: Creating Lesbian Subcultures in the 1950's and '60's" (Chapter 7), in *Odd Girls and Twilight Lovers* (New York: Columbia University Press, 1991), pp. 158–87.

12. Ibid., pp. 184–85.

13. Flo Fleischman, Personal Interview with Author, Los Angeles, CA, September 1998.

14. Ibid.

15. "Nan Am azon."(pseudonym), Personal Interview with Author, December 28, 1998, Los Angeles, CA.

16. Almost all of the 80 informants that I interviewed while I was studying this culture said that the lesbian bar of the period was "the only place" that they could find an accepting community.

17. Sally Munt, ed., *butch/femme: Inside Lesbian Gender*, (London: Cassell, 1998), p. 4.

18. Chrystos, "I Fly to You," *Fire Power* (Vancouver, Canada: Press Gang Publishers, 1995), p. 52.

19. Dorothy Allison, "Femme," in *Skin: Talking About Sex, Class and Literature* (Ithaca, NY: Firebrand Books, 1994), p. 152.

20. Joan Nestle, "Esther's Story," *A Restricted Country* (Ithaca, NY: Firebrand Books, 1987), pp. 43–44.

21. Minnie Bruce Pratt, "Mimosa," in *S/He* (Ithaca, NY: Firebrand Books, 1995), pp. 117–18.

22. Michelle Clinton, "We're All Gringos on this Bus/Ode to the American Butch," in *Good Sense and the Faithless* (Albuquerque, NM: West End Press, 1994), p. 80.

23. John Boswell, "Concepts, Experience and Sexuality," in *Qu(e)erying Religion: A Critical Anthology*, ed. David Gary Comstock and Susan E. Henking (New York: Continuum, 1993), p. 117.

24. Michelle Atherton, "Feminine and Masculine Personas in Performance: Sade Huron: A Drag Queen with a Dick," in *Acts of Passion: Sexuality, Gender and Performance*, ed. Nina Rapi and Maya Chowdhry (London: Haworth Press, 1998), p. 230.

25. "Amazon Nan"(pseudonym), Personal Interview with Author, December 28, 1998, Los Angeles, CA.

26. Leslie Feinberg, *Stone Butch Blues* (Ithaca, NY: Firebrand Books, 1993), pp. 71–72.

27. Miranda Shaw, *Passionate Enlightenment: Women in Tantric Buddhism* (Princeton, NJ: Princeton University Press, 1994), p. 180.

28. Esther Newton, "The Mythic Mannish Lesbian: Radclyffe Hall and the New Woman," in *Hidden from History: Reclaiming the Gay and Lesbian Past*, ed. Martin Bauml Duberrman, Martha Vicinus, and George Chauncey Jr. (New York: New American Library, 1989), p. 293.

29. Ibid., p. 287.

30. Wendy Frost, "Queen Femme," in *The Femme Mystique*, ed. Leslea Newman (Los Angeles, CA: Alyson Publications, 1995), p. 303.

31. Nan Amazon, Interview.

32. Joan Nestle, ed., *The Persistent Desire: A Butch-Femme Reader* (Boston, MA: Alyson Publications, 1992).

33. Elizabeth Lapovsky Kennedy, "The Hidden Voice, Fems in the 1940's and 50's," *Femme: Feminists, Lesbians and Bad Girls,* ed. Laura Harris and Elizabeth Crocker (London, England: Routledge, 1997), pp. 15–16.

34. Nan Amazon, Interview.

35. Amber Hollinbaugh and Cherrie Moraga, "What We're Rollin' Around in Bed With: Sexual Silences in Feminism," in *Powers of Desire: The Politics of Sexuality,* ed. Ann Snitow, Christine Stansell, and Sharon Thompson (New York: Monthly Review Press, 1983), p. 398.

36. Elizabeth Lapovsky Kennedy, "The Hidden Voice: Fems in the 1940's and 50's," p. 25.

37. Judith Halberstam, "Lesbian Masculinity: Even Stone Butches Get the Blues," in *Female Masculinity,* Chapter 4 (Durham and London: Duke University Press, 1998), pp. 124–25.

38. Ibid, p. 129.

39. Anonymous, "She Was Different: A Story of Warning for Young Girls," *True Story,* September 1954, pp. 64–95, all quotes in this example, found within this story.

40. Ibid.

41. Ibid.

42. Ibid.

43. Halberstam, p. 128.

44. Many feminists have spoken of this, particularly Adrienne Rich in her essay, "Compulsory Heterosexuality."

45. *True Love,* 1954, p. 95.

46. Ibid.

47. Flo Fleischman, Personal Interview with Author, Los Angeles, CA, September 1998.

48. Ibid.

49. Ann Aldrich, *We, Too Must Love* (New York: Fawcett, 1958), p. 94.

50. Ibid., pp. 94–95.

51. Joan Nestle, "Our Gift of Touch," in *A Fragile Union: New and Selected Writings* (San Francisco: Cleis Press, 1998), pp. 143–45.

52. Ibid., p. 144.

53. "Amazon Nan" (pseudonym), Personal Interview with Author, December 28, 1998, Los Angeles, CA.

54. Sarah Schulman, "What We're Fighting About When We Fight About Sex," *Womanews,* July/August, Undated (probably 1981, according to interior dates within article itself), archival document from "Butch Femme" folder at June L. Mazer Lesbian Collection, Los Angeles, CA.

55. Ibid.

56. Andrea Weiss and Greta Schiller, *Before Stonewall: The Making of a Gay and Lesbian Community* (Tallahassee, FL: Naiad Press, 1988), p. 51.

57. Flo Flieschman, Personal Interview with Author, Los Angeles, CA, September 1998.

58. Say and Kowalewski, p. 112.

## REFERENCES

Aldrich, Ann. *We, Too Must Love.* New York: Fawcett, 1958.

Allison, Dorothy. "Femme." In *Skin: Talking About Sex, Class and Literature.* Ithaca, NY: Firebrand Books, 1994.

Anonymous. "She Was Different: A Story of Warning for Young Girls." *True Story,* September 1954, pp. 64–95, all quotes in this example, found within this story.

Atherton, Michelle. "Feminine and Masculine Personas in Performance: Sade Huron: A Drag Queen with a Dick." In *Acts of Passion: Sexuality, Gender and Performance*, ed. Nina Rapi and Maya Chowdhry. London, England: Haworth Press, 1998.

Boswell, John. "Concepts, Experience and Sexuality." In *Qu(e)erying Religion: A Critical Anthology*, ed. David Gary Comstock and Susan E. Henking. New York: Continuum, 1993.

Chrystos. "I Fly to You." In *Fire Power*. Vancouver, Canada: Press Gang Publishers, 1995.

Clinton, Michelle. "We're All Gringos on this Bus/ Ode to the American Butch." In *Good Sense and the Faithless*. Albuquerque, NM: West End Press, 1994.

Comstock, David Gary and Susan E. Henking, ed. "Part III: Culture and Society." In *Qu(e)erying Religion: A Critical Anthology*. New York: Continuum, 1993.

Faderman, Lillian. "Butches, Femmes and Kikis: Creating Lesbian Subcultures in the 1950's and '60's" (Chapter 7). In *Odd Girls and Twilight Lovers*. New York: Columbia University Press, 1991.

Feinberg, Leslie. *Stone Butch Blues.* Ithaca, NY: Firebrand Books, 1993.

Fleischman, Flo. Personal Interview with Author. Los Angeles, CA, September 1998.

Frost, Wendy. "Queen Femme." In *The Femme Mystique*, ed. Leslea Newman. Los Angeles, CA: Alyson Publications, 1995.

Halberstam, Judith. *Female Masculinity.* Durham and London: Duke University Press, 1998.

Hollinbaugh, Amber and Cherrie Moraga. "What We're Rollin' Around in Bed With: Sexual Silences in Feminism." In *Powers of Desire: The Politics of Sexuality*, ed. Ann Snitow, Christine Stansell, and Sharon Thompson. New York: Monthly Review Press , 1983.

Kennedy, Elizabeth Lapovsky. "The Hidden Voice, Fems in the 1940's and 50's." In *Femme: Feminists, Lesbians and Bad Girls*, ed. Laura Harris and Elizabeth Crocker. London, England: Routledge, 1997.

Long, Ronald E. "The Sacrality of Male Beauty and Homosex: A Neglected Factor in the Understanding of Contemporary Gay Reality." In *Qu(e)erying Religion :A Critical Anthology*, ed. David Gary Comstock and Susan E. Henking. New York: Continuum, 1993.

McBrien, Richard P., general ed., *The HarperCollins Encyclopedia of Catholicism*. New York: Harper Collins, 1995, "theology," p. 1250.

Morris, William, ed. *The American Heritage Dictionary of the English Language*. Boston, MA: Houghton Mifflin, 1981. All dictionary definitions, unless otherwise noted, are from this source.

Munt, Sally, ed. *Butch/femme: Inside Lesbian Gender*. London, England: Cassell, 1998.

"Nan, Amazon" (pseudonym). Personal Interview with Author, December 28, 1998: Los Angeles, CA.

Nestle, Joan. "Esther's Story." In *A Restricted Country.* Ithaca, NY: Firebrand Books, 1987.

Nestle, Joan. "Our Gift of Touch." In *A Fragile Union: New and Selected Writings*. San Francisco: Cleis Press, 1998.

Nestle, Joan, ed. *The Persistent Desire: A Butch-Femme Reader*. Boston, MA: Alyson Publications, 1992.

Newton, Esther. "The Mythic Mannish Lesbian: Radclyffe Hall and the New Woman." In *Hidden from History: Reclaiming the Gay and Lesbian Past*, ed. Martin Bauml Duberman, Martha Vicinus, and George Chauncey Jr. New York: New American Library, 1989.

Pratt, Minnie Bruce. "Mimosa." In *S/He*. Ithaca, NY: Firebrand Books, 1995.

Say, Elizabeth A. and Mark R. Kowalewski. *Gays, Lesbians and Family Values*. Cleveland, Ohio: Pilgrim Press, 1998.

Schulman, Sarah. "What We're Fighting About When We Fight About Sex," *Womanews*, July/August. Undated (probably 1981, according to interior dates within article itself), archival document from "Butch Femme" folder at June L. Mazer Lesbian Collection, Los Angeles, CA.

Shaw, Miranda. *Passionate Enlightenment: Women in Tantric Buddhism*. Princeton, NJ: Princeton University Press, 1994.

Weiss, Andrea and Greta Schiller. *Before Stonewall: The Making of a Gay and Lesbian Community*. Tallahassee, FL: Naiad Press, 1988.

# CHAPTER 12

# Sexuality, Politics, and Faith

*Shari Julian*

O ne cruel night in the recent past, in the extinguishing of a brilliant flash of light, I was transported to the dark side of the moon. My ability to generate and reflect light was forever changed. In that instant, I was no longer a moon to a sun, reflecting a status and identity as part of an established identifiable system of suns and satellites. I was that most invisible of bodies, the widow. As a woman, no matter how many achievements I had accomplished on my own, my light was always as a married woman, in the eyes of others, a reflected light from some other sun: my father, my husband, my children, society, and my church. With the death of a husband or the loss through divorce, the role of a woman in the social order immediately changes. Society reclassifies her and expects her abruptly to change her friends, life activities, social roles, and often financial status. A woman alone, unlike a man alone, becomes the extra woman, an unbalanced number. In that devastating instant, I went from being the desired, attractive, lovingly validated partner of a funny intelligent husband, to the extra woman at a couple's event or the single number on a cruise or in a hotel. I was now a threat to other's security or someone who needed to be taken care of, rather than a woman loved beyond all reason by a partner all my own.

In many societies, the widow or a divorced woman is a woman left behind. Many societies expect the widow to become invisible. She wears visible signs of mourning and grief for her lost partner, ceases to be a sexual being, and people expect her to conform to some social idea of proper widow decorum. Not long ago, in many Indian cultures, they immolated the widow on the pyre with her dead husband, as she was no longer useful in any other

247

function than as a wife and a financial burden on others, with no one left to take care of her. In scripture and in stories , including Elijah and Jesus, we read notions of the widow's mite. In the Old Testament, we read of Ruth and Naomi and the duties and role of a widow. The role of a widow is one of the aspects of a woman's power and role in society. Women, power, faith, social roles, and cultural norms are intertwined elements. Religions celebrate the contribution of women, while still strictly defining their roles in the church hierarchies, functions, and interactions.

This chapter explores the dichotomies of messages surrounding women's power, faith, social roles, and cultural norms, particularly that of the widow, while analyzing women's lived experiences. We examine how faith and social norms conscribe women in ways that distort their experience of power and identity and render them vulnerable within a sexist, male-biased culture. We will explore the myth and the reality of female power and the role of church teachings and hierarchy, faith, law, ethics, norms, gender sexuality, and a dualist social ethic. This treatise analyzes how women are responsible for the values and behaviors of women and men; and yet, the men primarily determine the criterion for measuring the success of those values, unexamined social precepts and the church. This criterion is neither woman built nor in many cases woman appropriate. The role of women is to maintain the delusions and the conflicting myths by which they are emotionally entrapped.

The stage is set by analyzing the interactions and emotions of Johan and Marianne, the fictional protagonists in Ingmar Bergmann's film *Scenes From a Marriage*. The film is a clinical look at the beliefs of a powerful woman in a marriage of presumed equals. In the film, which is set in Sweden, a historically egalitarian society, Marianne is convinced that her life is not influenced by the elements of female oppression and gender role definition inherent in other more socially constricted societies. She learns the reality of her situation as her marriage disintegrates and she is forced to confront the truth that her power and presumed equality are a myth. Using this example as a jumping off point, the essay then: explores women's vulnerability, victimization, and invisibility; examines cultural blindness and religious and social controls; analyzes scriptures whose interpretation demonizes women; and reviews two case studies. It concludes by focusing on how women and men can regain the light and achieve true growth in the church and society.

## From Radiance to Invisibility: Women Left Behind

Ingmar Bergmann in his brilliant movie *Scenes From a Marriage*[1] illustrated the role of society and family in constructing perceptions of a woman about herself. Marianne, a successful matrimonial attorney in egalitarian Sweden, opens the story as the powerful professional partner of her husband Johan, a physician. The film begins with them being interviewed on their secrets of a perfect marriage. Johan immediately responds and speaks, disregarding Marianne at every opportunity about their partnership being the key. It is apparent during that interaction, that their marriage is a dance of self-delusion and an exercise in parallel play rather than collaboration. Soon after, Johan tells Marianne that he is leaving her and immediately moving in with a much younger woman. As Marianne rushes around to help him pack everything he will need for that trip, he cruelly refuses to discuss his reasons except that it is best for him. He abruptly leaves, heedless of the devastation he has done to Marianne. She discovers that their friends have known all along of his affair and have colluded to help him deceive her. Cut off from any support system and unsure of who she is without Johan, Marianne tries to reconstruct how she arrived at her present state. Intellectually, she attempts to gather the data that would give her current circumstances meaning. She devalues her real achievements and lived reality: a brilliant law career, a compassionate spirit, an exquisite mature beauty, a successful role model for her daughter, and a loving nature. Her perception of her self-worth all boils down to her lack of desirability in Johan's eyes. She obsesses over a younger woman co-opting her life, without ever seeing that Johan's values and maturity were all an illusion that she helped to craft.

From being a powerful woman, she immediately becomes vulnerable and disposable to Johan and her friends. They justify their betrayal by assuring her that a woman as powerful as she seemed will pick herself up and move on past her characterized self-pity. She is expected to think of Johan's needs and his unhappiness at growing older and losing his appeal. They are all astonished about her fury at that response.

In the most insightful scene in the movie, Johan returns to her during a brief trip back home seeking sex and solace. His young lover is growing distant and his ego needs the unconditional love and support that he once found with Marianne. She tries to tell him that she has gone through fire during his absence and has in the process learned a great deal about her own self. Seeing a chance to win her confidence and to insinuate himself into a sexual encounter, he begs Marianne to tell him what she has learned. She begins by going over the family album to talk about the effect her childhood and family acculturation had on forming her understanding of herself as a woman. She pours out the deepest secrets of her heart, only to look up and see that Johan is fast asleep.

The scene where Marianne analyzes the unspoken rules of her childhood resonates. She was raised to be good and meet others' standards for behavior. She was expected to be ladylike, compliant, self-abnegating, submissive, and second in all matters of partnership. She was expected to always be watchful of others' feelings and to tailor her behavior, appearance, and morality to their expectations, not her own. If she was successful in these endeavors, she could then, in the remaining space, meet her own needs. Johan determined her desirability as a sexual being, and when he declared her unfit to keep his wandering eye under control, it was her failure, not his character that was to blame. However, Johan, their friends, and society all punished her for that failure.

## VULNERABILITY, VICTIMIZATION, AND INVISIBILITY: WOMEN UNDER THREAT

Vulnerability and victimization are, in Western society, terms that few men are able to connect to their life experience and perceptions. Victimhood is almost entirely reserved for women. As a forensic behavioralist specializing in sexual crimes and behaviors, I learned this early on while interviewing male prisoners. When I asked if they had ever been sexually or physically victimized in their past, the answer was no. I changed the interview language and asked about their history of early sexual behaviors and heard the most terrible cases of sexual exploitation reframed as sexual conquest and power. When I would attempt to reframe their horrific histories as victimization, the response was almost always the same, "I see why you might think that, but I was actually in control." Once, so frustrated by this gender blind spot, I cried in frustration, "You were six and she was forty, does that seem like a power position to you?" The response, "I asked her how men and women fall in love so I was responsible." I have had many cases where men have taken responsibility for crimes where they were the victim not the perpetrator, to avoid being seen as the depowered party.

Society expects men to deny victimization or lose their power place in society. This expectation yields poor coping mechanisms and little under-standing of the need to express and rectify powerlessness to relate to women and to right social wrongs. Victimization of others is an opportunity to steal power and grow in strength to win some ill-defined game. As a result, some male victims act out against others while others seek to keep the pain bur-ied through addiction and self-loathing behaviors. While the minds of male victims are often blocked by an inability to recognize and label their own histories, their bodies, and personas often seek to reframe and regain what has been lost. Since we train women from birth to yield this power, women are frequently the target. This insight was borne out by the lack of research in the mid-80s when I first began this work. I could find almost no references in the literature to exploitation and victimization of males, particularly if the victimizer was a female.

Female invisibility is another form of victimization that is often not artic-ulated. Women, who received accolades and success in their youth when beauty and desirability was a factor, often find that when sexual appeal to men is out of the picture, so is she. I have a friend, a world famous anthropologist, who in her youth worked with Margaret Mead and met and charmed many prominent and fascinating men. Never married and now in her eighties, still charming and fascinating and working, she reports that she can travel safely anywhere in the world and work in the most dangerous of places. "No-one sees me. When I was young, my sexuality made me vulnerable. Now that I am old, I am invisible and a threat to no-one."

I saw some of the invisibility of women when I was young and living in a small northeastern U.S. town, where my parents owned several Victorian homes that they cut up into boarding houses. Women, alone, occupied all the tiny one-room apartments. One was an elderly farmwoman who had been a mail order bride from Hungary. Her husband worked her merci-lessly on the farm and beat her when she slowed down. He died and she was totally on her own, with no pension or resources. She had only one possession of worth, a pair of earrings from her childhood. Her small farm had been sold which gave her enough money to live below the poverty level. Many months she paid her rent with pound cakes that she baked for extra change. She told me that her husband was her only option for a girl born into poverty and that she was simply waiting for death, but not to be with him. My parents, to save her from a pauper's grave, paid for a burial and a headstone in a plot all her own.

Another boarder who had absolutely nothing material had once been a famous female fencer. She fell in love with a movie star of the twenties and had an affair with him. He left her after awhile and she drifted to the fringes of show business. Alone with only her pictures and her fencing foils, she often spoke of her life as a woman used and left. Their stories and others served as a life-long impetus for me to prepare to be a woman of indepen-dent means. I still remember their sad lives, one light bulb for light, toast and one egg for dinner, and clothes from the charity drives. My parents paid to bury the fencer also. From an early age, I observed and opined that an older woman alone with no skills other than as a wife lived in a half world. I resolved at a really young age to prepare myself never to have that experi-ence. I got an education, raised wonderful children, surrounded myself with terrific friends, saved some money, and worked hard at building a career that I controlled. Over time, I have learned something that no one can know at a young age: for women there is no guaranteed way to build relevancy as long as men are the gatekeepers for the criterion of relevancy.

Sometimes, these signals are subtle. For example, President Obama's new rules on continuing COBRA now extend to 36 months for the involuntarily terminated, but leave the terms at 18 months for the widow. My late spouse certainly did not voluntarily terminate his employ and would be distressed to know that his widow had so short a time for health coverage. In an instant, I went from being half of a couple to being a woman alone. My home, which seemed too small for our needs the day before my husband's death, became a big white elephant that I was encouraged to sell. Other relatives immediately fought over our goods and furnishings because, obviously, I would have no use for them without a husband. While I was trying to mourn, others encouraged me to put aside my own feelings to meet the needs of the children, who are now adults with their own families. As if a giant eraser came down from the sky, the defining edges of my personhood began to be blurred. No matter that I have multiple degrees and a notable career of my own, the main question asked was "what will you do now without your husband?" The day before his death, I was a prominent professional and a warm, sexually desired being, adored by a husband who saw me as ageless, beautiful, and wonderful. The day after his death, I became a middle-aged unclaimed woman of past desires: I became a widow, one of those persons who become invisible due to cultural blindness.

## CULTURAL BLINDNESS, RELIGION, AND SOCIAL CONTROL

This cultural blindness extends not only to sexual behaviors, but also to gender expectations. Victimization is a niche more comfortably occupied by women. The returning male soldier traumatized by the horrors of war and unable to fight again is a slacker, not a victim. As a result, the messages of the dangers presented by the powerful female to the stability of society and the social order control virtually every aspect of the acculturation of women. Even though words in the English language do not have, as they do in the romance languages, male and female designations, there are definitely words that assign only to females. Applying these words to males either has no social context or designates the male as being unworthy of society's notice. For example, designating a woman's genitalia to another woman as a pussy connotes an entirely different meaning than calling a man a pussy. A man characterized as a pussy is a half man. A woman who has balls has so forgotten her social and gender role that she is reframed as female dog wearing a prosthesis to borrow power from a man.

Since the earliest history, woman's sexuality has been a weapon to be feared and controlled. Woman's gender roles as mother and wife and anchor of the home and the family unit have always been a cage to contain and control female power. Presently, in the most progressive of times, female slavery, rape, and abuse are on the rise. Women still do not have a real and equal voice in public policy or governance and are still expected to yield to male control regarding the scope of their behavior and the expression of their sexuality. Any attempt by women to define their own self-expression and identity for themselves calls up the forces of social stasis and control to punish the effort. For some reason, many believe that men are capable of making wiser decisions than women by virtue of having a penis. Even though the penis has no brain tissue, it connotes power and wisdom and control over women, the weaker sex. Even if a man is not as educated as a woman is, or is as wise about a certain area of knowledge, society usually expects that she will defer to him and his decisions. Oft quoted is the justification, supposedly based on religious doctrine, that someone has to make the final decision. If my years as a marriage counselor have taught me anything, it is that someone making a decision over the head of the partner only results in resentment and a bad outcome. Any issue that the couple cannot resolve together either indicates that the couple lacks the right communication skills or needs to table the issue for further examination, unless one partner is physically or emotionally unable to participate. Many societies raise males with a sense of power entitlement that unfortunately often includes depowering the female to maintain the illusion. Part of that power becomes visible by controlling women, particularly controlling their bodies.

From early history, societies have linked the dark internal workings of a woman's body with the idea of temptation and the fear of castration. Women bleed, an unclean act, associated with injury and death. A man enters a woman hard and powerful and leaves her body weak and flaccid. What dark and evil machinery inside of her controls his power so completely? When a woman bewitches a man, he is not in control. To regain control, he must add the element of involuntary submission and violence. For the male, there is within the female, the ability to lose his own way. She is both sacred and profane. Men must always be vigilant that the interior Lilith does not escape and destroy him. Therefore, much of human history involving male/female interaction references the struggle for who is ultimately in charge. As a social phenomenon, we must fear, reject, or denigrate the idea of female dominance over male, at all times. A man depowered by a female is not only low on the social totem pole. He is effectively under the totem pole.

The process of protecting a woman from her weaker side is the defining pattern for male-female interaction. Woman is emotional and guided by her menses, which makes her irrational and childlike. Woman is venial and always looking for a way to castrate men. A man raised only by a woman or viewed as controlled by women is only a half man. Woman and her behavior under the control of males is a reflection on him and his honor. Men are accustomed to the implied power position and therefore expect that advantage as their due. Women are needy and always must conform to achieve male validation. Women who are no longer fertile are no longer visible. Power and women are a dangerous mix and must be depowered when their glory or opinion does not mix with the male's agenda or needs. A woman's power can only be ratified if it is displayed in a manner agreeable to men. For example, in many African nations, an uncircumcised female is considered an irresponsible child who is not allowed to run for office.

Thousands of years after the early references to female power being allied with unnatural and dark forces, women still struggle daily with legitimacy of their contribution and worldview. This has resulted in a systemic framework inherent in the world's largest faiths within which women cannot achieve political power or process equality. No female pope, or Eastern or Western priests, or Imams, or Orthodox rabbis are legitimately ordained within the most literal of church constructs. Women occupy a lesser place in the faith hierarchy, no matter how strong her devotion. Men are priests and women are handmaidens or helpers to the priest or workers on the most elemental level. In some faiths, women have no voice unless it is uttered through a man's mouth and no will, unless it is his will. To permit a woman to achieve the fullness of her potential, she must first meet the checkpoints of a mythic life. Before she has permission to fulfill herself, she should be able to cook, clean, take care of a family, bear children, raise the children, and perform all tasks needed as a helpmate to her spouse. Many women choose not to follow this path; but ultimately, they are rated less than a complete woman.

This results in bizarre double life and consciously assumed personas. A woman in public life must also be feminine, deferential, twice as bright as most men, but adept at concealing it, and able to pass a multiplicity of criterion imposed on her by public judges. Men do not have to pass nearly as many tests to prove their validity. People accept that a busy public or professional male will not have time to parent. People do not expect him to be a hands-on parent; his wife is. A male's wardrobe is not scrutinized by society as evidence of public acceptability. A woman's is. If a political woman is out in public, commentators and pundits use her clothes choices as barometers of her personality. Hillary Clinton and Michelle Obama, both brilliant Ivy League attorneys, face evaluation of their clothes and hairdo choices rather than the quality of their minds. People scrutinize and evaluate their child-rearing practices, even though both have raised children who are exceptional. Men in public life do not have to concern themselves with their hair, clothes, manicures, and affects before they are able to utter a word about weighty matters. Society measures the quality of a woman's utterances by her tact and voice quality. Is she an aggressive harpy, a Greek monster that was half woman and half bird of prey, who will stop at nothing to serve herself, or is she a spineless ninny who serves at the whim of her mate? The bar is always higher for women to achieve the smallest gain than for a male to climb the heights. This bar and the need to control occur in society at large, and religion in particular.

One of the most significant ways that religion and power still influence women today is the debate over who controls a woman's body and reproduction. The logical disconnect is that society expects a women to do anything she can to alter her appearance for seduction. A heavy woman must lose weight. A small-breasted woman more than likely feels more desirable with implants. Many designers of women's clothing often have no attraction to women and therefore have a theoretical conception of female desirability. However, when it comes to the end game of seduction, the rules change. A pregnant woman who does not desire to carry a child and terminates her pregnancy is a murderer. A woman who uses birth control is denying God's laws. A woman who decides to sterilize herself is denying the intended function of her body. In many cultural and religious contexts, the woman who seduces her husband is a wanton and shameless hussy. If the husband wants sex, she must provide it, or he gets to take it. Until the last 20 or so years, laws did not recognize marital rape as a crime; and, it is still hard to get prosecution for rape especially when the perpetrator is known to the victim. The rare doctor who is brave enough to offer abortion services to women is often characterized as a killer or is killed by someone who thinks his death is justifiable. Men who receive vasectomies are not greeted by crowds screaming murderer at him.

Women will never be free until they control their own reproduction and bodies. Although it didn't apply to my developmental situation at the time, I am old enough to remember before *Roe v. Wade* when abortions were not available and birth control was illegal. People still had unprotected and extramarital and premarital sex and unintended consequences still resulted. I personally remember two women older than I, who died from backstreet abortions and several more who were maimed. The idea that society should force a woman to carry a baby and then give it up for adoption or be forced to keep it is barbaric. I have had the opportunity to work with women who were raped during wars on various continents. Rape of the women of a culture is the fastest way to depower the men and to defeat the culture. I have seen scores of women (some of them just mere girls) forced to keep the babies of their rapists. Whole cultures still exist that celebrate her stoning or murder as a mandate response for "getting herself raped." In a closed community, these babies are her shame and her responsibility, no matter what the circumstances of conception. To minimize or deny the death and crippling of women in filthy backstreet rooms is to deny her value as anything other than a means for baby making. The argument of original sin as a justification for the decision to keep the fetus and sacrifice the woman goes back to the idea of making her pay for the conception and the sin; the dad is usually not held accountable. The baby is without sin and therefore deserves to be saved; she, on the other hand, is expendable and responsible for an act that she did not do on her own. Almost every abortion is conflated by opponents as the result of a loosely moraled woman who finds the thought of a baby to be inconvenient and disposable. The same groups who point their fingers and condemn her for not wishing to carry a baby also, in general, have a policy against preventive birth control.

This concept goes back to the notion of a woman as a birth vessel who happens to have a head and other appendages. The whole process of growing a child, experiencing the body changes, and feeling that child's growth and life within should be one of volition, of personal will. To go through the whole process of baby development and then have to give up the child is the denial of all emotional connection within the woman that occurs during gestation and birth. To suggest this as a viable alternative because the woman has no other legal choice is to deny her worth and humanity. Of course, if a woman chooses to go through this process, it is her decision and under her control. She is still making her own decisions about her body.

Women experience challenges of having opportunities to make decisions not only when it affects her body, but also when it affects the bodies of those in her social and governmental communities. In the most developed nations on earth, the intellectual input of women is devalued. Iceland, rated the most developed nation on earth, for example, had no women involved in making the economic decisions that led to the nation's recent bankruptcy. Women were excluded from the councils of economic decisions in a nation that has long heralded its male-female equality. However, the women now have to live with the consequences of the men's decisions and figure out how to feed their families in a ruined economy. Even in the United States, systemic sexism or gender bias against women often deny the intellectual leadership of women. Primarily male decisions triggered the most recent global economic crisis. The one woman, Brooksley Borne, who tried to sound the alarm years before the crisis hit, was marginalized and ridiculed for her predictions. A nation that does not value the input of its women is a nation that will continue to take the wrong path over and over again. However, worldwide, few women occupy real positions of power. When women such as Indira Gandhi, Golda Meir, and Margaret Thatcher did get the opportunity to lead their nations, they proved to be savvy and strong leaders.

Why listen to the input of women on world matters or policy decisions? The perspective and priorities of women are very different than those of men. Microeconomists working in underdeveloped countries will not lend money to men. When the woman receives the loan, she uses it to build equity and assets for her family. She may buy a cow and sell butter to others while also using it to feed her family. Her profit from the butter may lead to buying a second cow. The microeconomists report almost no loan repayment failures and the use of the money to shore up small communities and make them economically viable. In great nations with many assets and options, women still are not policy makers. While more women are active in the public, some women continue to be more concerned about the home and children along with the infrastructure of a society. They rarely resort first to a bellicose response. Women are trained from birth to be watchers of faces and the readers of moods. Therefore they are often more aware of the nuances in situations and other options for response. Whether nature or nurture, religious scriptures have had a strong say about women's place in public and private spaces.

## TESTAMENT OF PUNISHMENT: WOMEN DEMONIZED IN SCRIPTURE AND PRACTICE

What might be one ongoing cause of women's oppression? Could this have to do with images of the divine, of God in society and faith? There are no famous images of God as a female in the Western Judeo-Christian literature. There are no scriptures addressing the god of Judeo-Christianity tradition as "She" although some scholars define the third person of the Trinity (Father/Creator, Son, Holy Spirit), as feminine, as Sophia. In addition, some scholars have been able to rally from more inclusive language for the divine and humanity, where the divine's name remains gender-free. Nevertheless, most images, directives, and sacred text come from an implied understanding that God is a "He."

Females, no matter how elevated by the function of birth and nurturance, are not the equal of a man in scripture. One of the earliest references to a powerful female deity in Hebrew and Christian literature and sacred text is Lilith. She appears as Adam's first wife. Lilith is born as a piece of Adam that is later separated from his body. Her great mistake, which damns her for evermore as a creature of evil, was to assert to Adam that she is an equal to him in the eyes of God.

In the *Alphabet of Ben Sira*, Lilith is described as Adam's first wife. The actual date of the origination of the *Alphabet* is debated by scholars, but probably is somewhere around the eighth century, BCE.[2]

After God created Adam, who was alone, He said, *"It is not good for man to be alone"* (Gen. 2:18). He then created a woman for Adam, from the earth, as He had created Adam himself, and called her Lilith. According to Jewish tradition, Adam and Lilith were born joined back to back with each other. They were unhappy in this position so G-d took mercy on them and separated them. Adam and Lilith began to fight. She said, "I will not lie below," and he said, "I will not lie beneath you, but only on top. For you are fit only to be in the bottom position, while am to be in the superior one." Lilith responded, "We are equal to each other inasmuch as we were both created from the earth." However, they would not listen to one another. When Lilith saw this, she pronounced the Ineffable Name and flew away from the garden into the air. G-d had forbidden her to leave the garden so Adam stood in prayer before his Creator: "Sovereign of the universe!" he said, "the woman you gave me has run away." At once, the Holy One, blessed be He, sent these three angels to bring her back.

Said the Holy One to Adam, "If she agrees to come back, fine. If not she must permit one hundred of her children to die every day." The angels left G-d and pursued Lilith, whom they overtook in the midst of the sea, in the mighty waters wherein the Egyptians were destined to drown. They told her G-d's word, but she did not wish to return. The angels said, "We shall drown you in the sea."

"Leave me!" she said. "I was created only to cause sickness to infants. If the infant is male, I have dominion over him for eight days after his birth, and if female, for twenty days."

When someone or something cannot overtly control a woman, the female character often becomes demonized. The reward for her independence and assertions of her equality in the eyes of God sets the stage for the framing of the independent and powerful woman in religious process and practice as a succubus, or a woman demon who has sex with men, a stealer of men's power. Women are connivers and seducers.

Society and early Western philosophy have programmed men to believe that they must always be watchful of the power that women wields because she is able to use guile and sex to depower men, lead them astray, and ultimately ruin them. Any attempt to seek equality must be punished before it fuels a woman's power to defeat man. The creation story in Genesis is a case in point.

In Genesis 1, God creates humanity all at once and pronounces them good. Yet, in Genesis 2, God creates Adam and Eve, creating the man first; thus, contrary to all laws of mammalian reproductive behavior, a man, with the assistance of God, is the biological source of woman. God has taken the dust from the ground, formed the body of Adam (in Hebrew the *adamah*, earth creature) and breathed life into him. God then populates the Garden of Eden with all manner of wonderful beings and plants along with the Tree of Knowledge. Genesis 2:18–24 discusses the creation of woman. God puts

Adam to sleep and from his rib creates woman (of man). Throughout the centuries, interpreters have taken this story as a literal explanation of the inferior status of woman and have said that her role was to be man's help-mate rather than an equal being. Genesis tells us that even though Eve knew she was forbidden to eat the fruit of the Tree of Knowledge, her yielding to the seductions of the snake caused her not only to disobey God, but to ulti-mately condemn Adam and all the rest of their descendants to shame, hard work, painful childbirth, and suffering. Many theologians later interpreted her actions and shaped their understanding into the concept of original sin. The subtext of this story is that woman is born of lesser status than man and that man around woman becomes a flawed sinful being. To those groups and individuals who believe in the fundamental or literal interpretation and iner-rancy of the Bible, they insist that this story guides all their perceptions of woman and the power of her ability to sin and lead the man along with her.

In the Hebrew *Book of Judges 16*, Delilah entraps Samson by playing on his self-absorption and using his love for her to betray him to the Philistines for silver. She repeatedly asks Samson to tell her the secret of his strength. Finally, when he reveals to her that he has not cut his hair as a part of a vow to God and that the uncut hair is the source of his great power, she lulls him to sleep and has a man come in and cut Samson's hair. He has made himself vulnerable to her by sharing his secrets and relaxing his vigil, and she rewards this trust by deception.

Throughout biblical and mythic literature, the theme of a man's need to control woman's behavior and power or to risk betrayal occurs. Even the most saintly of women are not allowed a powerful voice in the church. In the New Testament Gospels, Mary, for all her elevation and worship in the Catholic Church, speaks only a few scriptural words in the Magnificat (Luke 1:46–55). Her femaleness and worldview are not shared. Nor is there an explanation of the internal processing of her perspective as a central player in one of the most unique and phenomenal events in world history. Her role is male defined and explained. Her impregnation is not sexual but immaculate. The birth of her child is a virgin birth and not the result of a biological coupling. Unschooled and poor, she accepted God's will. Under the most extraordinary circumstances, she birthed a child who would change the world as few other men ever had, yet how she reasoned about these events unfolding around her, remains a cipher. Her historical role is not that of a breathing thinking female trying to internalize this wondrous and never-to-be-repeated event, but rather that of a birth vessel obeying the will of a male god.

Religious practice has long associated the inclusion of women in the process of prayer as a distraction from God and a temptation to man. As long as a male in the context of religious tradition, either in the role of priest or as the spiritual leader of the family, is the primary channel to God, women remain in a secondary role in prayer life. The justifications for this secondary role are the events around original sin and Eve's transgressions. To be fair, this perspective is often so wrapped in sexist justification and religious mysticism that it is never questioned. For example, a sophisticated and scholarly friend of mine who is able to enjoy the intellectual equality between men and women still believes that the separation of men from women during prayer services is important so that a man can concentrate on prayer without sinful distraction and thoughts. The idea that prayer as a couple together builds on the erotic and emotional context of coupling is seen as sinful rather than healthy. Praying together and opening up the spirit as a couple is erotic and vulnerable and wonderful. The love between a couple is God-generated and therefore eroticism should be an extension of that process and growth. A man who prays alone is denying his mate the pleasure of growing together with him in the spiritual realm. This is a sharing of power and frightening in its implications for the power structure of the church.

The power structure of almost all faiths lies in the primacy of men. The same bodies that are celebrated for the birthing of a child are denigrated as unclean during the months when no child resides in the womb. Depending on the faith, the punishment of women for menstruating varies from no contact between the sexes, to the cause for emotional immaturity, to a proof that woman is so unclean that she cannot ever be elevated to a priestly role within true orthodox faith. The teachings of most faiths on sexuality are so conflicting that they require women to maintain a schizoid perspective.[3]

Traditionally, the truly religious woman retains her virginity until marriage so that she is not tainted goods. In the most rigid social contexts, this has led to horrible abuses against women. Society often views a raped woman as a consenting woman. A woman fooled by an elaborate sham marriage or lies is spoiled goods for any other relationship. A woman is a war vessel that militia can use to dilute or impregnate the cultural identity out of a bloodline. When the armies leave, they leave her with the child who is her problem and payment for her inability to die during the assault. An incest survivor is a murderer if she does not wish to carry the baby of her family. A virtuous woman is not a sexually aggressive woman who enjoys and asks for sex. Society expects a sexually unschooled woman to wait to learn from the man how to make love. No matter that he is brutal, or unschooled, or just plain lousy at lovemaking, she is expected to subordinate her own needs to follow his lead. Many faiths find the sexually active woman tainted and therefore not allowed to serve God. The sexually prolific man is following the leads of the prophets and elders and is therefore doing God's work. Scripture and the church tell the husband to love his wife as Christ loved the church and she is told to obey him, although there are things that a husband does for a wife that Christ cannot and does not need to do for the church. The Catholic priest cannot serve two masters, again the other master presumably being the wife who will lure him into sinful thoughts. Many view the fundamentalist husband as the leader of the home and final arbiter of decisions, even if he is not as educated or knowledgeable in that decision arena as his wife. The wife's role is to protect the ego of her husband and elevate his status while subordinating her own wants and thoughts to his and the children's desires and needs. It is no surprise that society forces many women, in their pursuit of self-understanding and realization, to chose between coupling and going life alone. Some, who did not go it alone, may end up dying wishing that they had.

## WOMEN TRAUMATIZED: SOCIETY TRESPASSES

Individually and socially, women have experienced domestic violence since the beginning of time. Sadly, in the 21st century, honor killings of women, dowry murders, and control killings of women and their children are becoming more and more commonplace in developed societies. No longer confined to cultures where the male is entitled by birth, and cultural and religious norms, to kill the female for real or imagined infractions against his honor, these types of killings are happening more and more in developed countries. One of the most famous recent cases occurred in Dallas: one Christmas ago a Moslem Egyptian father shot his daughters in his taxicab for becoming too Westernized. For a long time, many agencies and the media avoided the term honor killing for fear of upsetting the religious community. When the consensus came regarding this deadly deed as an honor killing, the father, who had escaped with the help of sympathizers, was long gone back to his native country.

So often, women are vulnerable victims, without recourse to family, church, or the law. Protective orders are still hard to obtain in the cases of threatened domestic violence. The perpetrator first has to act in some way that finally convinces a district attorney or the police that a danger exists. Many times that is after something terrible and final has occurred.

Yet, there are examples in which women have chosen to standup for justice, against all orders, on behalf of themselves, their children, and their communities. Two cases are Mothers and Grandmothers in Argentina, and the LDS (Latter-day Saints) Mothers in Texas.

An excellent example of the female approach is the Grandmothers (Abuelas) of the Plaza De Mayo and the Mothers of the Plaza de Mayo in Argentina. During the time in Argentina known as the Dirty War (1976–1983) when the military junta ruled Argentina, they carried out horrible civil rights abuses.[4] For the junta to consolidate their power, they created a milieu of terror, which they blamed on internal traitors. In truth, anyone who spoke out against junta's tactics of false imprisonment and torture and kidnapping was considered a traitor. The people the junta abducted in the night and made disappear were often the students and the human rights workers who worked with the poor. There were never trials, charges filed, or public airings of complaints. People were just accused of being traitors and taken. Some who escaped later reported that they were kept in large warehouses of torture where they were subjected to horrific mental and physical abuse by hooded torturers. Eventually, they took the abducted individuals out and killed them. People became afraid to say anything to anyone for fear of being misinterpreted and of becoming another victim. The women were raped and sexually assaulted before they were killed. If they were pregnant, the junta kept them in filthy warehouses before being killed and having their children turned over to be adopted by the very individuals who tortured them. The mothers of the disappeared began to meet one-on-one with each other to see if they could find out what happened to their children.

The mothers began to see that government and religion were in collusion regarding their destruction. Faced with the same consequences as their children and crippled by the absence of any rights to protect them, the mothers tried to go through appropriate government channels to ask for help. The authorities dismissed the mothers with no help and in some cases imprisoned and punished them. The Catholic Church colluded with the government in many cases by betraying the activities of the mothers as they met in churches. In one famous instance called the Night of the Pencils, some schoolchildren protested for bus passes to go to school. Their priest turned them in, and the junta killed them. In another case, they kidnapped the mother who had been the guiding force in organizing the other mothers; and she disappeared as she worked on posters inside a church.

Mothers of the disappeared were for the most part homemakers. Some had little education and no skills outside keeping a home. In a society where they were forbidden to speak out or even meet, they devised a *female* form of protest. They walked to the Plaza de Mayo, the large square in front of the government building in Buenos Aires, in pairs of two. To identify themselves, they wore a white baby blanket on the head as a scarf. Forbidden to speak and told to keep moving or they would be arrested for holding an illegal meeting, they kept walking in a slow circle around the plaza . All they asked for was that they be told the fate of their children. Later, when it came out that their children were probably dead and that their grandchildren had been kept and adopted by the persecutors and murderers of their children, the group for the grandmothers of the disappeared was formalized. To counter the brutality of the junta, they formulated a defense and protest plan that would eventually confound the junta, who based their repression in cruelty and brutality. When the authorities would ask one woman for papers, all would rush forward and demand that they take their papers. When the police would try to arrest one of the grandmothers, the rest would rush forward and demand to be arrested. Every Thursday, they marched, silent and inevitable. Eventually, they attracted the interest of foreign journalists. When Jimmy Carter became president, he imposed sanctions on Argentina, which helped create some legal movement for the mothers. Ronald Reagan, who wanted to do business with Argentina, quickly discontinued this help. As a result, the junta continued their oppression. For years, the mothers and grandmothers marched, asking only for word of their children. In some cases, families lost two and three children to the policies of the junta.

When the junta declared war on the Falklands or Maldives Islands, as they are known in Argentina, to divert attention from the problems at home, they suffered a humiliating defeat at the hands of the British forces. The deaths of the soldiers and the incompetence of the military during this conflict weakened the hold of the junta and transition in government took place. However, there still was little help for the mothers because the new governments wanted to move beyond the actions of the past and did not want to uncover the abuses of the junta. About that time, mass graves began to be discovered in pits around Argentina and barrels filled with bodies were fished out of the River Plata. Convinced that their children were now dead and they would never get any real help, the mothers began to publish their own exposés of government doings and the names of the dead. They continued to silently walk and parade their grief and despair until they captured the eyes and the anger of the world.

Eventually, these actions resulted in the changing of laws and some government cooperation in finding their abducted grandchildren. The mothers demanded that the government do DNA testing for free on all individuals who suspected they were taken from their biological families during the junta's reign of terror, so that they might be repatriated. They also demanded that the government establish a DNA data bank for the families of the disappeared to assist in the repatriation of their families. To this date there are over 70 children who have been repatriated.

The mothers and grandmothers continue to march wearing the white head scarf embroidered with the name Mothers and Grandmothers of the Disappeared. An internationally acclaimed organization and a former nominee for the Nobel Peace Prize, they are now recognized throughout the world as an example of female ingenuity and power against oppression and as a champion for the rights of parents, children, and the oppressed.

One beautiful Thursday in October 2008, carrying their flag, I marched with the mothers around the Plaza de Mayo, and wept as they walked with me and told me their terrible personal stories of terror and loss and their history of quiet resistance. Aa very large contingent of riot police in full gear stood and watched a short distance away.

The second case took place in San Angelo, Texas in the United States, a nation that has constutional guarantees against unlawful search and seizure, and for the rights of privacy and the primacy of the family. In 2008, I worked as an expert in the highly publicized case of *Texas v. the LDS church and the Yearning for Zion Ranch*. The LDS church hired me as their only expert. My charge was to advise the church authorities as to the least disruptive way to keep the families together while protecting the children from greater trauma. I spent a great deal of time researching the literature and consulting with authorities before finally concluding that the best plan would be to keep the children and the mothers at the ranch so that the children had the familiar things such as their room and spring gardens around them. I suggested that guards, from the center of the compound, wall off the men so that the children could remain safe and the compound cattle and fields could be tended without any danger of the men getting close.

I went to San Angelo, met with countless mothers, and heard tales that horrified me of warrantless searches and new babies torn from their mothers' breasts. Because the mothers were women of faith that differed from the mainstream beliefs, people perceived them as weak and controlled. Some of these women shared a husband and worked on the religious compound. Their clothing and hair were distinctive and differed from modern standards of beauty and fashion.

However, in the course of speaking with these distraught mothers, I discovered that many of the women held college degrees. The greater bulk of women I spoke with were not one of a series of multiple wives but rather a partner in a monogamous relationship with one husband. The standards of the community called for group work and worship, natural and nourishing meals, no premarital or extramarital sex, no television or outside movies, prayer, hard work, and devotion to God. At a previous time, Warren Jeffs, who was at the time in prison for his inappropriate and illegal acts involving underage girls, had led this faith group. The group had attempted to expunge Jeffs and his actions from their community. However, they refused to turn their back on the girls who were underage and pregnant.

The authorities moved in and removed the children and women with weapons and the fear of force. They carried women and children by bus to a central location where the mothers were called into an auditorium for a meeting on the requirements of the state. Once in there, they locked the doors and then told the mothers to leave. They put the children, who had never before been alone with strange men, into rooms with communal beds where men with guns patrolled at night. Terrified, the young girls slept under the beds while the older girls sat up all night to protect them. These children came from a culture where even the adults don't see each other naked. All the children wear long johns and long sleeves. The prairie dresses are long and concealing.

Authorities shipped off young boys, characterized as predators in the making, to facilities and foster homes far away from the ranch and their families. Once away from their parents, the children's appearances were altered by short haircuts and revealing outfits. The mothers who attempted to fight for the return of their children were marginalized and reframed as automatons and mindless victims of the men. The dislocation and trauma to these religious families was incredible. With no charges, a bogus outcry from a known prank caller, and no evidence of abuse, the authorities stepped in and violated the constitutional rights and all protections of the individuals under the law to dismantle this community and punish the mothers for their sexual and lifestyle choices.

One of the first things the authorities did was destroy and violate their tabernacle, a magnificent limestone edifice carved and built by the community. To this day, it stands empty and defiled. Church is held in the eating hall. As the lone expert allied with the women against the power of the state, I saw firsthand the absolute inability of the mothers to get justice or reasonable action. The authorities forced many of the mothers to move hundreds of miles away from their home even to visit their children. The state characterized these modest religious women as trainers for the sexualization of their children with absolutely no evidence to support those charges. Articles appeared in the paper describing the new looks given the children and their delight at being exposed to candy for the first time. I sat with these women and wept at their and my inability to do anything to help them.

Contrary to the state's charges, I saw neatly dressed happy, loving children who worked hard and loved their community life. I saw loving mothers and fathers, not automatons, and I saw citizens who tried over and over to work with the system to regain their families. Instead of looking for the least traumatic way to investigate the charges, the state and the authorities chose the most traumatic and disruptive options possible. The women were punished for their life and sexual choices by the loss of their children, and the public rejection and branding of them as unworthy mothers and robotic tools of the men. The men were punished for not adhering to the local concept of an appropriate Christian father and husband. Even though a large percentage of the couples were monogamous, the plural marriage position of the greater group resulted in all the males (including infants) being characterized as pedophiles and sexual predators. The women, presumed to be an extension of the men without a will of their own, were punished for the alleged sins of the men. The assumption that plural marriage results in pedophilia is not borne out in the scientific literature. As a group, in the eyes of the surrounding community, they were irredeemable sinners and had to be punished by secular law for moral, not legal, lapses.

Two years later, there have been only a few charges filed. Many of the children, forever altered have finally been returned. The cost in dollars and emotional disruption was enormous for both the citizens of Texas and the families. To regain their children, the families had to undergo counseling and the children had to take courses in sexual protection even though there was no evidence that the alleged perpetration had taken place. Many of the families, afraid of future actions and severely traumatized, left the compound vowing to never return.

## From the Absurd to Hope: Rekindling the Light

As a forensic behavioralist, I have made a long career out of the inequity between the sexes and the differences in opportunity for the sexes. In a country where the bulk of college graduates are women, and women head the majority of single parent households, the idea that women are childlike and have to be protected from their choices is toxic and absurd. Women have to have a major voice in the formation of public policy because the internal social infrastructure is in crisis. Schools are failing; children are not receiving the medical and nutritional help they need. Mentally ill and learning-different children have no real programs for assistance. The cost of living is rising and the ability of the single mother to provide is falling. Collecting child support from the appropriate father is a difficult and slow process. Most states will not help with DNA testing or tracking of the missing father. Again, it is the woman who juggles jobs, home responsibilities, and children to keep home and hearth together. How tragic that for as much as things have changed, much has remained the same.

At the time that I received my doctorate, my discipline's honor society did not allow women members. My few female classmates and I had to stand by and watch as men who graduated lower in the class with less rigorous dissertations were sworn into a society that by rights we should have had entrée into. I can still remember challenging the faculty advisor about our exclusion. With a straight face, he told me over and over that I needed to understand that women lowered the academic level of such an honor. I still remember how stunned I was at that explanation. I can remember telling him that if we scored higher in class but were expected to lower the intellectual level of the honor society, something was wrong with the criterion for either the degree or the honor. Years later when they finally invited me to join, I declined on principle. Then and now, an ugly male can still be a genius, an ugly female is just ugly and that opinion extends to her ideas and input. A female actor over

40 is getting over the hill. A male actor is still considered sexy enough that he can play a romantic interest for a female half his age. Female sexiness is not a standard set by women for women; it is strictly evaluated against male approval.

The ultimate place that a woman can attain some power is in her job setting. Yet, despite sexual harassment training, sexual harassment cases are rising. A woman with few resources is forced to do anything she can to keep her job. I have been involved in cases where that means servicing the boss sexually or experiencing degradation in front of everyone. In even the most heinous cases, the perpetrator usually forces the victim to defend her honor and behavior; the threat of being without any means to live if favors are not granted does not constitute consensual. Yet, consensual is usually the defense. In a case I had recently, I discovered that the boss opening the doors in the middle of the night to gain favors from his female employees who lived on the premises was hard to prove as assault in court. Women executives who are forced to conduct business in men's clubs are told that they should have known that it is part of the job. Bosses who grope and touch usually characterize the female employee as hysterical and a poor sport. All of these behaviors are a way to keep women depowered and not a threat in the workplace. I know of no woman, no matter how old, unattractive, or educated, who has not been assaulted and harassed multiple times in her career. Behaviors that would never be tolerated by male co-workers are normative in the lives of working women. These behaviors are not so much about attraction as they are about disempowerment.

As a clinician and a specialist in sexuality, I have had the opportunity to visit with women from all over the world and from all of the major faiths. Men, by and large, define female appearance, behavior, status, and choices. It is no accident that the big-bellied male is still an object of desire and the fat-bellied female needs a lap band and some will power. The current trend of reality television increasingly celebrates and rewards the worst possible images of females as empty-headed, vapid, materialistic, vain, and promiscuous. People often paint the scholarly female as aggressive, plain, and antimale. The over 40 female is irrelevant, predatory, or past her prime and angry. Women are the highest proportion of citizens in the most progressive nation on earth, and the least represented in the halls of power. As long as this is the case, political power and ideology, after 2,000 years, will still be male in structure, perspective, and application. Many persons, female and male, with more literal biblical views and conservative practices engage in subjugation, give women lesser status, and celebrate the lack of female input in policy, practice, and compassion. Such thought assumes that women are to understand and validate the inequality of opportunity and choices. They would celebrate with prayer and song their own lesser status.

What is the answer? As women of faith, we must form our own female-led communities to lobby for programs and laws that grant women true equality as citizens. As the Beatles said, "So you think you want a revolution?" We must answer yes; we need a revolution of women centered policies, power, and ideas. We need a place at the table in the halls of religious and political power. Our priorities are critical for a healthy society. Women must serve as scholars, thinkers, and designers of government priorities rather than as handmaidens. Social programs that rebuild our cultural infrastructure must have the same priority as military and financial concerns. Women must get involved with economic policy decisions. Our nation needs a microeconomic as well as a macroeconomic plan and programs. We must offer the mentally ill, disenfranchised, and sick services other than jail. We must become leaders in religion rather than followers of policies and rules that benefit males in power. We are still vulnerable, depowered, and invisible. The male hegemony has to end and an era of partnership and mutuality must begin. Women have to have a voice in foreign policy. We see the world and options for change very differently than men. Women the world over must support the education and empowerment of other women. As long as the rate of crimes against women continues to rise around the world, we will never as a gender have an equal place at the table and an equal voice in the dialogue. We must work with parents to help them learn liberating ways of socialization for their children. We must work with liberated men who can join us in our struggle for true equality for all. This cooperative alliance must create a faith foundation which preaches love, compassion, and a structured equality of partnership.

## NOTES

1. *Scenes from a Marriage* (Swedish: *Scener ur ett äktenskap*) is a 1973 Swedish film and mini-series written and directed by Ingmar Bergman. (USA release, 1974), Criterion Collection.

2. In addition, the Haggadah, which is a rabbinic text used to describe the passages of the Bible, references Lilith. The Haggadah is extracted from the teachings of the Talmud. It is in this text that the story of Lilith is fleshed out.

3. See the following texts:

Leviticus 15:19—30:

19 When a woman has her regular flow of blood, the impurity of her monthly period will last seven days, and anyone who touches her will be unclean till evening.

20 Anything she lies on during her period will be unclean, and anything she sits on will be unclean. 21 Whoever touches her bed must wash his clothes and bathe with water, and he will be unclean till evening. 22 Whoever touches anything she sits on must wash his clothes and bathe

with water, and he will be unclean till evening. 23 Whether it is the bed or anything she was sitting on, when anyone touches it, he will be unclean till evening.

24 If a man lies with her and her monthly flow touches him, he will be unclean for seven days; any bed he lies on will be unclean.

25 When a woman has a discharge of blood for many days at a time other than her monthly period or has a discharge that continues beyond her period, she will be unclean as long as she has the discharge, just as in the days of her period. 26 Any bed she lies on while her discharge continues will be unclean, as is her bed during her monthly period, and anything she sits on will be unclean, as during her period. 27 Whoever touches them will be unclean; he must wash his clothes and bathe with water, and he will be unclean till evening.

28 When she is cleansed from her discharge, she must count off seven days, and after that she will be ceremonially clean. 29 On the eighth day she must take two doves or two young pigeons and bring them to the priest at the entrance to the Tent of Meeting. 30 The priest is to sacrifice one for a sin offering and the other for a burnt offering. In this way he will make atonement for her before the LORD for the uncleanness of her discharge.

Genesis 31:35

35 Rachel said to her father, "Don't be angry, my lord, that I cannot stand up in your presence; I'm having my period." So he searched but could not find the household gods.

Isaiah 30:22

22 Then you will defile your idols overlaid with silver and your images covered with gold; you will throw them away like a menstrual cloth and say to them, "Away with you!"

Ezekiel 36:17

17 "Mortal, when the house of Israel lived on their own soil, they defiled it with their ways and their deeds; their conduct in my sight was like the uncleanness of a woman in her menstrual period.

4. A military junta removed Isabela Peron, the legally elected president and the widow of Juan Peron, from office in 1974 and controlled Argentina for the next decade. The junta began what is now known as the "Dirty War" against those who opposed them. As many as 30,000 Argentineans "disappeared" and were never heard from again.

## REFERENCES

Atwater, Tony. "The Illusion of Power and Control: The Deception in Violence Against Women," *The Penn*, April 7, 2006.

Chodorow, Nancy. *Femininities, Masculinities, Sexualities: Freud and Beyond.* Blazer Lecture Series. Louisville: University of Kentucky Press, 1990.

Gilman, Sander L. *Freud, Race and Gender.* Princeton, NJ: Princeton University Press, 1995.

Hirsch, Irwin. "From Helplessness to Betrayal to the Illusion of Strength." *Gender and Psychoanalysis* 4 (1999): 291–306.

Ho, Stephanie. "Number of Female Leaders Around World Growing." *Amazons When Women Lead,* biography.com, 2009.

Nordau, Max. *De la Castration de la Femme.* Paris: Adrien Delahaye et Emile LeCroisnier, 1892.

Yan, Sophia. "A New Dynamic: Women Leaders Around the World." *International Intelligencer,* May 2007. http://www.internationalintelligencer.blogspot.com/.

# PART V

# Women, Worldview, Religious Practice

# CHAPTER 13

# Women and Christianity in the Caribbean: Living Past the Colonial Legacy

## *Althea Spencer Miller*

There are two ways to tell the story of Christianity and the Caribbean's women.[1] One is to examine the formal Church and recount the history, spotlighting issues of women's roles, the founding of all girls' schools, women's programs, and the application of particular doctrinal issues that affect women. Though that approach is important and informative we better capture the relational tension between the Church and women by mapping stories of women as colonial and postcolonial peoples onto the Church's presence as a Eurocentric, and latterly, a geopolitically influenced institution with an evolving relationship to the Caribbean. Thus, we see an institution that became rooted, not quite influential nor thoroughly perduring, but somewhat disconnected from the pulse of the people.

This chapter maps portions of Caribbean women's history through the lens of gender and sexuality to understand the processes that constructed this irony. I discuss the ways colonial sexual behavior was addressed by ideological discourse. The essay maps slave sexual behavior as resisting or ignoring the churches' declared morality, and traces ways Christianity perpetuated the regnant gender ideology, a form of misogyny, revealing unwillingness on the Churches' part to find the divine impulse in Caribbean history that departs from Eurocentric Christian doctrine and its racialized misogyny. The term misogyny here does not reference individual psychological aberrations resulting in intensively negativity against and hatred toward women. Rather misogyny reflects the systematization and institutionalization of colonial misanthropies expressed acutely in the use and abuse of female sexuality. That expression today finds articulation and practice in doctrinal issues concerning female ordination and leadership within the churches and in the micromanagement of personal morality—especially women's.

The inhabited Caribbean has a history at least as old as Christianity itself, though its Christian history is not as old. The narrative of the Caribbean's earliest inhabitants, the Arawaks,[2] and the Caribs date from the first century CE up to the disruption of their existence with the 1492 arrival and collusion of Christopher Columbus, Spaniards, and Roman Catholics, yoking complicity of the Church in Rome, Spain, and Portugal with the royal will for imperial expansion.[3] Western Europe developed into separate nation-states with a unifying sensibility of shared history and a common civilization—Western. The Spaniards' efforts to convert indigenous Arawaks[4] resulted in the extinction of the Arawaks and their religion[5] and the entrenchment of Christianity as the proper religion of the newly expanded boundaries of Western (European) civilization. Further, it presaged a colonial history where women's bodies were commodities in the slave economy. The gender[6] ramifications of that encounter continue in formal institutions of Caribbean society despite decades of political independence and development of regional and national cultural identities.[7]

Caribbean colonial history includes uneasy and too easy sexual relationships between colonizers and the colonized. In the postcolonial period, it survives with class lines replacing the colonial lines of demarcation. The Roman Catholic and Protestant missions were and remain impotent in corrective, retributive, and restorative action on behalf of slave women and other women deemed to be inconsequential, exposing the complexity of gender relations amidst imperial power and ecclesiastical abdication of faithful duty. The ideology that emerged is readily accessed through analysis of women's sexuality. As Barbara Bush notes, "The stereotyping which was particularly damaging to black women characteristically fell into the realm of sexual morality."[8]

The interweaving of Christian teaching with colonial gendered ideological discourse informs Christian presuppositions in today's Caribbean.[9] The hidden narrative of gender in Caribbean Christianity permits Church and society to legislate, articulate, perpetuate, and validate a misogynistic Christian masculinist frame that derives from the colonial mentality that adopts Eurocentric mores about women in economic history, producing a meta-narrative that continues the ideological discourse begun in slavery times, replicating an idealized European woman, perpetuating, and producing an ironic tension between women and the Church. Newer narratives celebrating the admission of women into ordained ministry or in Caribbean ecumenical leadership have not changed that meta-narrative.

To chart the terrain of women's sexuality regarding the contemporary Caribbean Church, I render a selective account of the relationship developed between the Church and colonial powers beginning with the arrival of the Spanish. Thereby we will see the dependence of the Church on the plantocracy's favor and financial support. The story of Codrington College in Trinidad illustrates how this dependence evolved into commodifying female slave sexuality, which compromised the Church's ability to restore enslaved African humanity. The commodification justified European male's rapacious sexuality and aided development of European superiority. This ideological discourse also obscured interracial parity of sexual proclivities and active participation of European women in the informal slave economy, sanitized European women such that they embodied purity and superiority of European ethnicity, and propagated the black woman's body as African depravity and inferiority: the heritage of the Church's approach to women in the Caribbean. Women's ordination and leadership in Church and Para-Church organizations occur amidst this ideological narrative. Despite a strong tradition of women's heterodox behavior that manifested profound dissatisfaction with the conditions of slavery, the colonial and contemporary Church sympathetically and avidly perpetuated the dominant ideological heritage.[10] This chapter examines that heritage through the lens of the colonial woman's sexuality.

## CHRISTIANITY'S CARIBBEAN HISTORY: AN ABBREVIATED VERSION

Beginning in Mexico in 1520 and spreading to all Spanish colonies, the *Encomienda Doctrina*[11] system was the official tool that combined Christianity via Roman Catholicism with Western civilization in the New World. Thus, the Spanish crown intentionally colluded with the Church in acculturating the indigenous population into Western civilization, a relationship of symbiotic expectations that continues today. The British later followed suit.

The British presence continued the union between Church and State in England, as mandated when King Charles II commissioned Governor Edmund D'Oyley in 1661 to encourage good behavior of protestant ministers so that would have due reverence,[12] though the commission lacked actualization in the colonies as in the Church in England.[13] A lack of standards and the resultant encouragement of negative opportunism meant the colonies attracted many who bore vices rather than the virtues of Anglicanism. The English systematized the ministry to settlers and the governance of the islands by subdividing the islands into parishes with the state financing the parish priests.[14] In the Caribbean colonies, the Church of England was dull, blasé, and ethnocentric because it regarded itself as an extension of England

and directed its attention to the European settlers anxious to rid themselves of the shackles of English propriety and decorum.[15]

Perhaps for these reasons, the Anglican Church was generally incompetent at managing the moral life of its colonies. The unbounded, profligate sexual life of settlers, the existence and brutal treatment of slaves, and the lack of integrity in church governance—each bespoke a fundamental turpitude in British characters who colonized the West Indies. Ironically, the Church, as servant of the Crown, became the guardian of one of the most execrable and sustained examples of intrahuman, interethnic violence of an unprecedented and unrepeated scale and duration in the Caribbean: the horror of plantation slavery, where gendered experience had different meanings for female and male slaves. Female slave sexuality had a unique place in the economy of slavery.[16] Developments in the early years of Codrington College in Barbados provide an account of that development and its institutionalized justification.

## CODRINGTON COLLEGE[17]

When Christopher Codrington III died in 1710, he bequeathed three sugar estates to the Society for the Propagation of the Gospel. The conditions of the bequest included continuation of the three estates and the means to educate students.[18] The society, charged with developing the constitution of the college, also committed to ensuring conversion and education of all the estates' slaves. Codrington died just before the peak of sugar production in Barbados. By 1770 there were disastrous financial outcomes for the estates. The bequest inextricably linked the plantations' economic well-being and Codrington College in Barbados. Fluctuations in the estates' finances negatively impacted the Society's ability to fulfill its mandate and realize its ideals.

In 1783, an absentee named Braithwaite rented and returned the estates to success.[19] Braithwaite enabled Codrington College eventually to actualize in Barbados a bold vision for educating inhabitants of different social classes and equipping them with skills needed for developing and maintaining the colony. The bolder vision, the evangelization through catechism of the slave population,[20] suffered many pitfalls. Therefore, slave education disappeared but the college continued educating privileged children and preparing young men for ministry. A fundamental factor in solving the economic woes of the estates was the employment of enslaved female sexuality and reproductivity as early as the 1760s.

Their employment became the means to reduce costs of replacing slaves. With humane intent, planters agreed to take care especially of young children and childbearing women. Despite intended humaneness, ultimately institutionalization and entrenchment of slave women's reproductive capacities emerged within slave economics. In the 1770s, women received money for delivering healthy babies; enslaved midwives received more money than mothers, reflecting slave owners' concern regarding midwives and high infant mortality rates.[21] These practices signal the dependence of Christian desire for evangelization of slaves upon estate economics, which contextualizes colonial denouncements of slave morality in general, and slave women's morality in particular. Codrington developed a tradition of persons who sought to humanize the treatment of enslaved persons, a tradition compromised by slavery economics. The institution deemed to ennoble slaves became guardian of an egregious degradation: motherhood for sale, because of the Church's dependence on estate economics and attendant politics.

## THE CODRINGTON LEGACY AS TYPE

Although Codrington College was not alone in its alliance with using slave sexuality for reproductive purposes,[22] it serves as a high-profiled pointer to the emergent importance of female sexuality and reproductive capacities in the colonial estate economy. Ironically, Codrington College was one of the few institutions that took seriously the welfare of slaves. The use of slave sexuality linked Christianity and slave women's sexuality and reproductive capacities and left little room for its representatives to critique that development. Further, concern for slave well-being did not necessarily preclude sexual exploitation of slave bodies. The Codrington situation illuminates the prioritization of ruling class concerns over morality for the slaves and Christian practice.

Codrington College succumbed to the exploitation of the female slave body and her nurturing capacity for the interests of the Gospel and contemporary economics, exemplifying presumptive arrogation of anatomical proprietorship toward a "higher purpose." Here, the "higher purpose" occluded materialistic considerations that fostered the need for arrogation. The naturalization of proprietorship seeped into Caribbean Christianity's legacy. Eurocentric definitions of civilization with evangelism as mediator and gateway to that civilization, focusing only on female reproduction, masculinist monopoly on decision-making, and selective bestowal of humane treatment, place the colonial Church in collusion with colonial interests and prejudicial relations with women. The emergent theology/ideology was that Eurocentrism as sole example of civilization's pinnacle was the appropriate cultural matrix for transmission and living of the Christian gospel. Doctrinally, European ethnicity had controlling rights over other ethnicities that permitted invasion of their innermost being through deculturation and sexual commodification, done under the name of Jesus Christ.


## FEMALE SEXUALITY: COMMODIFICATION AND IDEOLOGY

Concerns about colonial European population growth led to a gender ideology that cast the European female as model moral female. This ideology used character depictions that contrasted behaviors of European and African women. Contrastively, English ideologues located African/slave women as morally negative. The derogation of African/slave women served as rational proof of a foundational ideology about European moral superiority, which continues to inform the Caribbean Church today and undergirds demarcations of acceptable sexual behavior aligned with Caribbean class stratifications.

Hilary McD. Beckles finds class stratifications among colonial European women important for understanding the evolution of the foundational ideology. Beckles begins in the 18th century when, poor, single white women worked alongside slaves and endured a similar social status on the estates, and were regarded as "sluts" and "white slaves." In the 19th century, white women's situation was very different in some territories.

> In 1815, white women owned about 24 percent of the slaves in St. Lucia; 12 percent of the slaves on properties of more than 50 slaves, and 48 percent of the properties with less than ten slaves. In Barbados in 1817, less than five of the holdings of 50 slaves or more were owned by white women, but they owned 40 percent of the properties with less than ten slaves. White women were 50 percent of the owners of slaves in Bridgetown, the capital, on properties stocked with less than 10 slaves. In general, 58 percent of slave owners in the capital were female, mostly white, though some were also "coloured" and black. Overall, women owned 54 percent of the slaves in the town. The typology of slave owning in the West Indies as a whole shows a male predominance in the rural areas, and a female predominance in the urban areas where property sizes were relatively smaller.[23]

Moreover, Beckles states that in Barbados's capital, Bridgetown, white females outnumbered white males. Thus, many white females were unmarried and forced to be self-sustaining. Urban slavery was not plantation based. So many white women

> operated on the periphery of the urban economy, dominating the ownership and management of enterprises in the service sector such as taverns,

sex-houses, slave rental services, petty shopkeeping and huckstering. . . . Many white and free-coloured families, and quite often single white women, made their living from the wage earnings of hired female slaves who worked not only as prostitutes but as nannies, nurses, cooks, washerwomen, hucksters, seamstresses, and general labourers. The hiring out of women for sex ran parallel to these markets.[24]

Apparently, white women, free coloreds, and manumitted women participated in the commodification of slave women's sexual bodies. This reality occurred within a masculinist enterprise of social construction, male dominance, and an economic structure intended to benefit European plantocracy.[25] Unmarried white women were unaccounted for and unattended in societal formal and legal structures; they were relegated to the economic margins. By the 18th century, black slave women outnumbered poor white women. Beckles theorizes that they were "cocooned within another system of representation that denied [their] social identity and right to autonomous self-expression."[26] He accuses 18th-century historians of Caribbean life of introducing "considerable fiction into the storehouse of historical writing."[27] While the implications are many, the focal ramifications point to poor, single, white women's exclusion from all discourse of representation. This meant that Europeans could freely maintain pretensions of purity and moral superiority of Western over, above, and against African civilization.

Depictions of white women tended to exclude them from the crud of society. Debasement and immorality were assigned to the black woman despite the fact that white women shared in it. There is evidence of the sexual profligacy of European women, notably Elizabeth Moore-Manning, wife of Edward Manning, a member of the House of Assembly. Her husband sought to divorce her based on allegations that she enjoyed sexual liaisons with numerous black men on the estate:[28] one example of the contradiction between practice and representation of the elite European woman.[29]

Simultaneously and despite preferential representation, elite white women were losing ground against the mystique and allure of black women; that is, they could not compete against white male desire to explore "the female brute." The norm of, and increase in, black slave women warranted grave concern about the ability of Europeans to self-replicate. This was a crisis requiring ways of enhancing the attractiveness of European women for their men. Their image was needed to sustain white superiority ideology.

The rhetoric that stigmatized enslaved and manumitted black women and ennobled white women intensified. One, it ensured the education of European women to improve her marriageability. Second, it was no longer possible to equate white women and slaves. By legislation, birth to a white woman guaranteed a child's freedom, no matter the father. The slave woman's child automatically was born into slavery, assured by conjoining legislation and representation. As Beckles states, white women were "constitutionally placed to participate in the slave-based world as privileged persons." Further, "the linking of white womanhood to the reproduction of freedom meant that the entire ideological fabric of the slave-based civilization was conceived in terms of sex, gender, and race."[30]

The next step was to control the white woman's sexual freedom. The premium value of the black slave woman's body was the reproduction of labor. The European female's premium value was the reproduction of freedom or, "the reproduction of patriarchy," the sustenance of male rights to all women.[31] If slave women were sexually profligate then there was parity of behavior between slave and European women, but not parity of freedom or status. White woman's sexual profligacy was absorbed into rhetoric of white upper-class female purity. European historians' egotistical ethnocentrism could exclude sexual escapades of lower-class white women from their accessible records. The Church could pontificate and evangelize slaves into pretensions of Western civilization with the purity of white femaleness as arbiter. Sadly, the Church's doctrinal transmission adhered to ideology rather than reality.

The Elizabeth Moore-Manning divorce case highlights white female sexual profligacy with male slaves and white male hypocrisy, suggesting that the white upper-class female was sexually indistinguishable from epithets that adorned her lower-class counterpart. Moore-Manning's indignant husband exercised his male prerogative of divorce despite his dalliances with black slave women. Perhaps the Mannings reflect the Church's inability to relegate colonizers' sexual proclivities into its preferred norms, which continues today. The Church inherited a notion of the sexually pure, ethnically white woman. Plainly put, the Church today still believes that better behavior models European culture. Exacerbating this racialized morality are the denominations in the Caribbean that address social issues, Christian character, women's roles, and sexuality by modeling white Evangelical Christianity in the United States of America.

Whereas Caribbean Christianity has a long history of female lay leadership and although the ordination of women is approximately 75 years old, younger denominations influenced by white evangelical Christianity in America continue to resist ordaining women. Yet, even among those denominations, there are opportunities for women to give teaching and artistic leadership within affiliated para-church organizations. Some Pentecostal denominations have had ordained females and female bishops although generally they locate women as the subordinate gender. In these denominations, the pneumatological impulse outweighs gender considerations for ordination, as women often participate in worship as readers, speakers, and interpreters of glossalalia (a technical term for speaking in tongues), singers, aisle stewards, dancers, and leaders of women's study groups though not as preachers when adult males are present.[32]

## WORSHIP, WOMEN, AND SEXUALITY

Historically, worship service has been the main event for transmitting European superiority. European Christian worship was an experience in staidness and rigid propriety. Dancing as a response to life was especially negated. Edward Kamau Braithwaite has described dance as "African architecture."[33] Of worship, he says it is

> an essentially Euro-Christian word/concept that does not really describe the folk/African situation in which the congregation is not (cannot be) a passive one entering into a monolithic relationship with a superior god; but an active community which celebrates in song: sound: *dance*,[34] the carnation of spirit/powers (*orisha/loa*).

The songs and the sounds, minus dance, were present but not African. Church edifices were testaments to European creativity. There was no testament to African slave creativity within Christianity. The disallowance of dance, which Africans did with all parts of their body, emphatically concentrated in the waist region, expressed the negation and derogation of Africanisms. As Braithwaite further states:[35]

> . . . because this music and dance was so misunderstood, and since the music was based on tonal scales and the dancing on choreographic traditions entirely outside the white observers' experience—not forgetting the necessary assumption that slaves, since they were "brutes" could produce no philosophy that "reach[ed] above the navel"[36]—their music was dismissed as "noise,"[37] their dancing as a way of (or to) sexual misconduct and debauchery.[38]

Africanisms signaled negative morality. Purity was inextricable property of Western civilization and thus precluded anything African. Roman Catholic, Protestant, and Evangelical Churches inherited the representation of European woman as icons of purity, allied that purity with doctrines of sexual behavior, and continued to replicate it by restricting use of the body in worship.[39] Males had rights to profligacy and control of female sexuality for masculine dominance. In addition to inheriting conflicts between representation and reality, the Church also inherited an alienation from the Africanizing impulse that exists on many levels within the Caribbean today. That impulse survives due to an "immanent nature . . . which made its amazing and successful ('miraculous') transfer from Africa to the New World/Caribbean, even under the extraordinary conditions of slave trade/slavery . . ."[40] Dance outside churches, Carnival in the Southern Caribbean, and ongoing traditions of calypso and dancehall attest to that continuity, albeit detached from legitimizing and defining African traditions. Europeans arrogated the right to derogate African dance. The Church sanctified its exclusion.

## FEMALE SLAVE SEXUALITY AND THE CHURCH

Sexuality remained an area of much concern for the Church. There were two fronts for the management of female slave sexuality: already mentioned is the legislative front, centered in economic estate management concerns for maintaining slave numbers and managing freedom. Access to and management of enslaved female reproduction directly impacted marriage and family, primary concerns of Christianity, was the second front. It was impossible for slaves to maintain stable unions and families. Missionaries required marriage of slave and free colored converts to the faith if they were in stable relationships. Stable relationships were encouraged by churches and this constituted a conflict with concerns of the plantocracy for biological reproduction of slaves. The concern for slave familial stability was a conflictual front for management of slave sexuality.

Prior to Emancipation, internal slave trade, trade between plantations, compounded problems of stable unions and created havoc for the Church's desire to develop stable family life among enslaved peoples, a requisite qualification for church membership. (To this day, many churches do not permit women and men who are in long-term, monogamous, common-law relationships to be full members while they cohabit with their partner.)[41] The churches had a variety of responses to this situation that included contralegislative matrimonies, guidelines for multiple family situations, and a willingness to tolerate slave versions of polygamous relationships. In the late 18th century, the Moravians permitted baptized men to retain any wives they had prior to their baptism. If a spouse's sale ruptured a marriage, each partner was permitted to form new unions in the permanent absence of the other—an early form of serial monogamy, particularly where young children were present. Throughout the Anglophone Caribbean the Presbyterian, Methodist, Moravian, and Baptist denominations recorded many covenant-styled marriages where legal sanctions were prohibited.

Generally, churches circumnavigated and alleviated neglect and abuse of this aspect of slave humanity. Indeed, churches were subversive of the plantocracy's need for multiple and profligate slave reproduction. Despite this, clearly, the churches seamlessly imported Europe's masculine domination of marriage rules into their understanding of gendered stakes in matrimony. The Baptist missionary H. M. Waddell explained the Church's expectations regarding marriage. There were regulations for a man having many women who could reasonably expect to be married to him. They laid out a hierarchy of rights that prioritized "the first more than the last, the older 'sister' more than her younger rival, the mother of [the man's] children more than her that has never borne."[42] The presumption of masculine priority and the contemporary naïve view of female sexual desires did not recognize any necessity for giving concomitant regulations for women who may have had more than one suitor or father to consider. During slavery, it is implausible that no women were in such a position. There seems also to have been no regulations for men who, in conforming to the Church's hierarchy of rights, may have perforce married women with multiple fathers for their children.[43] Possibly, men who considered and regulated these circumstances with uncontested assumptions about women intended to be sympathetic to women and perhaps curtail excessive masculine sexual proclivity. Nonetheless, regulations restricted those seeking membership in the churches. Marriage was requisite for cohabitants, presumed to be sexually monogamous. There were no accommodations for unmarried cohabiting women. Perhaps unmarried women could be members as long as they were not cohabiting with men. Presumably, because the Church was concerned to acculturate the enslaved within Western civilization, it did not recognize a need to address white women's marital status. Perhaps the marital status of white women was taken as a given. These conditions, where women face the larger portion of difficulties and insufficient consideration, continue to be effective.

We must credit churches for their efforts to achieve some enslaved familial stability. However, assumption of masculine priority rather than naïve assumptions about female sexuality aligned the churches' presumptions of gender relationships amidst colonial ideological underpinnings. Further, the churches' concern for slave marriage must remain contextualized by their dependence on estate economics, planter favor, and their convictions regarding the brutishness and moral incapacity of slaves and superiority of Western civilization's institutions for managing sexuality. The churches' accommodations for slave marriage did not subvert interstate slave trade. Missionaries, largely, did not confront slavery itself, nor should one idealize their efforts toward slave marriage as being libratory or prioritizing of slave interests. This was a consequence of Crown/Church/Estate collusion and of Christianity as the arbiter of Western civilization. Further, usage of female sexuality, in its complexity, should not obscure misogynistic underpinning of the presumed masculine right to regulate women's sexuality toward an agenda where women have not contributed. Here, the Church enacted assumptions of male priority. We cannot overlook Eurocentric racializing of morality that framed the churches' insistence on one female to one male as the norm for marriage.


## WOMEN'S RESISTANCE

Yet, throughout the centuries slave women and their ancestors continued to act in ways that flouted the stereotypes and frustrated discursive constructs of white superiority and female delicacy as well as management of female sexuality. Colonialism bequeathed a legacy of color gradations and class alliances where lighter complexioned families characterized the top of the social scale while darker skins characterized the lower socioeconomic classes. Previously, slave women and their midwives found ways to lower the birth rate of enslaved children and so frustrated the production of a cheap labor force.[44] They were suspected of exercising some kind of African abortion method as an antislavery protest. In addition to flouting the Church's standards, abortion would be the most effective method of countering the planter's system for cheaply increasing the labor force and having an economically competitive product.[45]

Today, dancers of calypso and the dancehall movement defy strictures against Africanisms in riotous rebellion and joyous, defiant, affirmation of African dance. This is true of the dancehall movement, rooted in Jamaican society's lower classes. In the dancehall movement, dominated by sexual expressions, the churches meet a challenge to its Eurocentric dominance. Donna P. Hope, a dancehall scholar, understands the dancehall movement's mores as "reflecting and reinforcing the lived realities of its adherents and, further, legitimiz[ing] their personhood and social identities."[46] When Hope defines the dancehall movement as representing a "shift in the terrain of culture 'towards popular, everyday practices and local narratives; and towards the decentering of old hierarchies and grand narratives,'"[47] she identifies the hallmark of an era where churches lost the moral right to be arbiters of culture in Jamaica and throughout the Anglophone Caribbean. Caribbean Plebeians no longer need the churches to legitimize their lifestyles and determinedly ignore the churches' morality pronouncements. The moribundity of Eurocentric practices of historical churches and the importation of Euro-Americanisms by younger evangelical and neo-Pentecostal denominations lack resonance with the Africanization of the culture through music, dance, art, and the emergence of the underclass as legitimate vehicles and articulators of authentic Jamaican culture.[48] While Pentecostal churches traditionally appealed to the underclass, they too upheld Eurocentric mores on sexuality and iterated doctrines that perpetuated gender hierarchies and classist heritage of Western civilization.

Further, Hope identified a transfer of power between the sexes within the dancehall context, which, while not numerically important, is notable. Through increasing financial independence, there was a transformation in the role and status of many women where they could discard the "other woman status" that attended the lives of many lower-class women.[49] With financial independence, these women were less inclined to be wives and were content to be "maties."[50] Flourishing dancehall women became "owners of men." They owned a man "because they could provide him with resources such as a car, expensive clothing, jewelry, and gifts. This relationship was, therefore, based on the principle of exchange and these women called the shots."[51] The notion of ownership carries discomfiting overtones of commodification of sexuality. Discomfiting though it may be, it signals an emergence of female control over her sexuality. Instead of competing masculinities, the dancehall movement highlights competing femininities,[52] a radical departure from the heritage of colonial representations and the comfort zone of churches. Like many of her female slave ancestors, the dancehall woman subverts Christian masculinist discourse on proper society and the role and status of women within it. Marginalized women are defining their own center and placing themselves at its core. The Church continues to define female sexuality and delineate its proper spheres for activity. The female continues to function under and outside the radar of that definition. For its membership, the Church insists on upholding tenets of Western civilization. Women in Caribbean society will eventually find their way back to truer expressions of their mangled African heritage concerning their bodies and its desires with or, more likely, without the Church despite its history of determining women's social heterodoxy.

## THE EMERGENCE OF FEMALE LEADERSHIP IN CARIBBEAN CHRISTIANITY

Osborne and Johnston in *Coastlands and Islands* provide the earliest, indigenous, anecdotal snippets of colonial women's Christian activities.[53] Some of their accounts reveal fracture lines in relationships between various denominations and women who did "para-church" work. Some of these stories are incidental to Osborne and Johnston's main point. However, for a female-oriented history, women's stories are the main point. Osborne and Johnston narrate stories of three outstanding women that highlight women's exercise of heterodox authority in ways that surpassed imposed limits and expectations. Ellen's story is one of a slave woman's unwavering faith during a storm at sea that contrasted with the panic of European Christian women. In an interview where her understanding of the faith was assessed, her responses read like a catechist's primary manual, which cast a shadow on her authenticity. Her steadfast faith in severe circumstances, established her capacity to understand fully the meaning of her conversion. Ellen's examiners eventually conceded her authenticity.[54]

The examiners' acceptance of Ellen's authenticity contrasts to Thomas Knibb's response to another African woman, Mammy Faith. A Baptist missionary, Knibb denounced Mammy Faith, describing her as an example of those who are "ignorant of the gospel," but "preach to, and live upon the people, and tell them tales that are as ridiculous as they are irreligious."[55] Further, Mammy Faith, according to Knibb, "pretends to forgive sins to all she pleases, and many of the negroes are so weak as to fall down before her to obtain pardon. These people cry aloud for help."[56] Clearly, Mammy Faith exercised a ministry that was sufficiently successful and outstanding to attract attention of and perturb the Baptist Missionary Society. We can infer that the sector of society for which she had appeal did not readily make a gender distinction concerning the human channel of God's miraculous working and ensured her survival.

Mammy Faith may or may not have been a charlatan; probably she was a maverick, a rival to the Baptist mission, unaccredited, and feared. She exercised an idiosyncratic mission that the Church could not accommodate as readily as it did the missionary strivings of George Lisle (alternatively spelled Liele), Moses Baker, and James Mursell Phillippo.[57] Yet, the three pillars of Mammy Faith's ministry are similar to those of missionaries in general—proclaiming a gospel of forgiveness, acquiring a following, and receiving financial support for work done. The difference between Mammy Faith and endorsed missionaries may not be only her message; for her heterodoxy[58] lay in her independence of both the plantocrats and the denominations seeking establishment; and, she was a woman doing a man's job.

There are other examples of heterodox behavior by women. Mrs. Mary Able Smith[59] was moved by necessity to defend the Methodist missionary Reverend Dr. Thomas Coke. Mrs. Smith protected Dr. Coke by standing between him and a band of drunken men who were intent on physical attack. Her intervention further incensed them to violence. Mrs. Smith responded, "You may do as you please, but the first man who lays a violent hand upon him shall have these scissors thrust into his heart."[60] Certainly, this is an example of indecorous, unseemly behavior on the part of a colonial European woman. Ecclesiastically, the oversimplified, unidimensional, stereotypical picture of the genteel, colonial, European woman conceals the varied and complex humanity of colonial European womankind.

Another remarkable woman is Mary Wilkinson. Her ethnicity is unascertainable though she did notable work among the slaves.[61] Mary Wilkinson is remembered for two subversive and resistant activities in 19th-century

Jamaica. Wilkinson was an informal religious teacher, leader, and subversive. In exercising her will to teach, she acted in multiple unorthodox ways. She taught Christian doctrine to slaves. She became a self-appointed marriage officer by "devising and [using] a wedding service"[62] for sanctifying unions of slaves for whom the laws forbade marriage. When the irate response of white estate owners reached critical mass, Wilkinson left her hometown, Manchioneal, for Kingston. She joined Coke Methodist Church,[63] also known as the Parade Society. During the period 1807 to 1815, the government enacted legislation prohibiting the chapel's use for any Christian activity. Wilkinson, an outstanding lay leader, continued her teaching ministry in the Kingston Parish Church.[64] Undeterred, Wilkinson continued her activities which included meeting at different locations in Kingston with her Methodist Class group during the "Seven Years' Night."[65] Occasionally she met with them in the Parade Society's chapel yard after dark. Her most daring activity may have occurred within the environs of the very denomination at odds with missionary denominations, the Anglican Church. On Sundays, Wilkinson worshipped at the Parish Church. She grasped opportunities after worship to pew visit with congregants. She held conversations about God with any who "stayed behind to listen to her message."[66] At the end of the "Seven Years' Night," the membership of the Parade Society had increased, under dangerous and threatening circumstances, from 560 to 1723. The miracle of Wilkinson derives from the results of her ministry and that of others like her. The fact of her socially resistant behavior is even more remarkable.

Importantly, Osborne and Johnston memorialize three remarkable women. One reason for this might lie in the oft-stated feminist truism that a woman has to be thrice as good as a man to be acceptable. Church records are replete with activities, opinions, and judgments of un-extraordinary ordained men. Women's stories remain incidental and occasional to those moments when our actions affect the masculine sphere. There is a dearth of historical material focusing on and analyzing lives and contributions of the laity and its subcategory, the laywoman. Therefore, we may never be able to determine whether these women were exceptions or part of a female heterodoxy. Here we may utilize their memorialization as representative of a subjugated memory. They profile a collective historical ambivalence that existed regarding colonial missionary churches to colonial governments, the estates on one side, the home churches on another side, and ultimately to the slaves they also came to serve. Today, the Anglophone Caribbean Church collectively continues to subjugate these memories and therefore transacts and transmits an unreflective and inadequately analytical understanding of its heritage in relation to gender and class within the Caribbean. It tends to fossilize and glorify, in its ecclesiastical life, the missionary's version of the history.

## MORE WOMEN

Yet, as Hilary Beckles points out, the social positionalities of colonial women regarding dominant discourses "were not fixed, neither were they ideological polarities, but fluid interactions that yielded varied results overtime but no distinct pattern."[67] Beckles's observation on secular society is also true of women's collective and individual participation in colonial Christianity. Therefore, it would be a disservice to portray Christian women as standing only on the outside of religious and social orthodoxy. There were, for example, two slaves whose leadership preceded the Hart sisters in Antiguan Methodist history. Writing in 1859, Dr. Abel Stevens[68] notes that on January 17, 1758, 28 years before the Methodist missionary Reverend Dr. Thomas Coke arrived in the Caribbean, an Antiguan planter, Nathaniel Gilbert, and two of his slaves heard John Wesley preaching in London, England. The name of one slave was Bessie; the other remains anonymous. Quite possibly, the two slaves were women though there is some uncertainty about this.[69] Gilbert went to London for medical treatment. This unhappy happenstance positioned Gilbert and his two accompanying slaves to hear John Wesley preach. All three had their hearts touched by Wesley's preaching and they returned to Antigua intent on propagating his message. Mr. Gilbert began preaching and Stevens comments thus on the Antiguan response to him, "That a man of his position, with the dignity of Speaker of the Legislative Assembly, should take the character of lay preacher, excited surprise; but that he should become a preacher to the negroes excited contempt."[70] By 1760, Mr. Gilbert and his two female slaves had founded Caribbean Methodism with a following of about 200 slaves.

Upon the death of Mr. Gilbert some years later, his two female slaves assumed leadership of the Methodist movement and led it until the arrival of Reverend Dr. Thomas Coke in 1786. Bessie is an example of a Christian slave who functioned within the orthodoxy of incipient Methodism. In Bessie's case, gender was not a handicap partly because of Nathaniel Gilbert's sponsorship. Her moral behavior and her social demeanor, which remained within the paradigm of Eurocentric ideological purity, strengthened her position. As a Europeanized woman, albeit a black woman, she is memorialized as one of early Methodism's heroes.

After Dr. Coke's departure, Anne and Elizabeth Hart, sisters who were free coloreds, became the Methodist leaders in Antigua. The Hart Sisters of Antigua and Sarah Ann Gill of Barbados were daughters of the plantocracy who inveighed against the ills of slavery. The Hart sisters pioneered free women's invective against slavery. Slave owners publicly abused them. Elizabeth especially campaigned for "public education for slaves, and the protection of slave women from the sexual tyranny of white males." In Antigua, the sisters did fundraising for the Ladies Negro Education Society.[71] In the 1820s, Gill received the wrath of an outraged slave-owning white society. She campaigned that a "good Christian could not be a slaveholder." She and other women "developed sophisticated philosophical critiques of the slave system as representing a moral contradiction of humanist and Christian values." Such was the turbulence surrounding her that the Methodist Church that she represented reassigned her to South Africa. There she continued her antislavery campaign.[72] Again, the image of Christian women is diverse. One cannot predetermine all responses to slavery based on color or class, nor infer from the nature of an activity the color or class of the woman involved. These realizations destabilize fixed representations of women that are color or class based. They destabilize the ideology of European superior capacities and black passive acquiescence. Further, they destabilize the polarizing capacity of the received racialized moral representations that exalt an angelic Eurocentrism and demonize Africanisms.

## THE MEANING OF WOMEN

When Knibb critiqued Mammy Faith and sought to distance the Baptist Church from her activities, he possibly had concerns to protect his denomination from social censure and its consequent vulnerabilities. If he did, he would have been in the same position as earlier Moravian and later Methodist and Presbyterian missionaries throughout the Caribbean. Women such as Mammy Faith and Mary Wilkinson placed the Missionaries in positions where they would have to explain that their denominational activities did not subvert, by interest or effect, the dominant social order. This was a real problem and threat to their missions' survival. The missionaries' success in proclaiming the Gospel of spiritual freedom also planted in the enslaved hearts and minds the desire for, and an expectation of, cognate social benefits. Yet, missionaries themselves had to curtail and contain expressions of slave frustration and resistance to the social order, in the name and for the sake of the same religion that implanted freedom's desire within them. The ironic duality of the missionary colonial existence was rooted in the presumption that colonial governments were Christian in religious orientation and practice. Yet, to serve the Christ to whom both governments and missionaries gave allegiance, Christians had to engage in activities that resisted the sociopolitical order. This paradoxical existence was sociopolitical heterodoxy in the service of a subversive religious orthodoxy. This was the work of those marginalized by gender and race.

The stories of Mammy Faith, Mary Wilkinson, and Mary Able Smith, Bessie, and the Hart sisters, are indicators that the will to resistance and subvert did not reside in the missionaries. There are no strong stories of similar efforts by missionaries. In actuality, the missionaries, though showing many signs of great discomfiture with the slave system and rather loose colonial morality, were more inclined to placate the plantocracy.[73] Indeed, in many cases, this was a strategic necessity for the survival of the nonestablishment denominations. In sum, then, masculinist missionary fidelity to the Christian faith lay in required acquiescence to the social order, no matter how corrupt and unjust it might have been. Lay people exercised the fidelity that led to extreme steps for the cause of spiritual orthodoxy and authenticity. The ethos of historic Caribbean Christianity today foregrounds, in precept and practice, the masculinist missionary acquiescence, even though the strategy is neither necessary nor relevant but antiquated, ideological, and vestigial. And so, churches today coexist with Caribbean society in an untenable, conflictual tension. Led by descendants of slaves, they ironically perpetuate this ideological heritage.

Within churches, the primary access to these women comes through oral recounting of their stories. Their memories are kept alive through regular sermons, anniversary sermons, and moments within Christian Education when retelling the history of Caribbean Methodism. Mary Wilkinson is a heroine within that tradition. These women—Ellen, Mary, Bessie, and the Hart sisters—are maintained within a tradition of religious and social orthodoxy. With an autobiographical diversion here, I disclose that I grew up hearing these women's stories. These accounts were devoid of theoretical analysis, being panegyric and paranetic, that is, exhortatory, in intent. In my youth, I imagined the comportment of these women as befitting the stereotypical image of the sedate and cultured European grand dame sitting in her parlor for afternoon tea. I found it impossible to entertain images of them in sermonic ecstasy or acting with the throes of bodily gyrations. I certainly appropriated these women in a European mode. In addition to attesting my Eurocentric orientation through Christian discipline and the success of the missionary subtextual legacy, the comportment that I imposed on these women also resembled that of the women in leadership who surrounded me.[74] Perhaps this heritage transmission was inevitable as Bessie and the Hart sisters were, arguably, the model predecessors of later women who attained leadership within Caribbean Christianity. Subtly, these women, whatever their ethnicity, were domesticated as the ecclesiastical bearers of a racialized morality.

## ORGANIZATIONAL WOMEN'S LEADERSHIP

On July 30, 1941, several denominations in Jamaica, represented by denominational heads, formally constituted and institutionalized the ecumenical movement as the Jamaica Christian Council.[75] The book *Men of Vision*,[76] published in 1981, briefly narrates the first 40 years of its history. The title may be taken literally, as the first 20 pages are devoted to the men who shaped, led, and forged both the foundations and future of the movement from its nascence to its more mature form in 1981. Fortunately, the publication also contains a photo history that includes Sister Marie Theresa (Roman Catholic), Lieutenant Colonel Dorothy Pursar (Salvation Army), and Sister Bernadette Little (Roman Catholic), who served as vice presidents of the Council in 1973–75, 1977–79, and 1981, respectively, and Miss Dorritt Bent who was the Assistant General Secretary from 1979–81. Miss Bent was a laywoman.[77] After 1981, Reverend Dr. Marjorie Lewis Cooper served a term of office as General Secretary to the Jamaica Council of Churches.

The account of women's leadership in Caribbean Christianity would be incomplete without acknowledging their leadership in the Caribbean Conference of Churches and some indication of the development of women's ordination. Most memorable is the contribution of Dr. Oluwakemi Banks who served multiple terms as a vibrant, spirited, Afrocentric member of the council of Presidents, the Presidium. In addition, the Presbyterian Church in Jamaica[78] was the first in the Caribbean to enjoy the ordained ministry of a woman. Reverend Dr. Marjorie (Madge) Prentice Saunders[79] was ordained in England in the 1960s. As a founder and organizing secretary of the Girls' Club, she oversaw its expansion to the Bahamas, Haiti, Guyana, and Trinidad. In 1966, she led a contingent of women to Ireland, England, and Scotland where the movement was called the Girls' Brigade. She was ordained by the Presbyterian Church in England, the first black woman to be so honored in the denomination there. She later returned to Jamaica and exercised fully ordained ministry of the Jamaican Church. She began a tradition of female ordination with Reverend Dr. Hyacinth Boothe, a former Deaconess in the Wesley Deaconess Order of the Methodist Church becoming the first female presbyter in that denomination.[80] Much later, in the early 1980s the Moravians in the Eastern Caribbean sent women to be trained for their ordained ministry beginning with Reverend Cicely Athill. So did the Presbyterians in Guyana. By the late 1990s, the Jamaica Baptist Union ordained their first woman, Reverend Angela Morgan. The Reverend Remia Gordon was ordained by the Free Baptists in 1991.[81] There is a proud tradition of women's ordination in the Caribbean. Modeled by Reverend Dr. Marjorie Saunders, our influence continues to irradiate beyond the region. In the *Jamaica Gleaner* of March 16, 2008, there was a report that Reverend Rose Hudson-Wilkins became the first black woman in England to be appointed to the Queen's Chaplains. Reverend Hudson-Wilkins is a Jamaican who began her ministry in the Jamaican Anglican Church Army.[82]

## CONCLUSION

Had this essay covered the record of women's ordination, church, and para-church leadership throughout the Caribbean it would have addressed a rich but simpler heritage. However, the relationship of Christianity and women in the Caribbean needs further and deeper analysis. This essay is an initial effort to begin that analysis while providing a truncated history of that relationship. To view that history from the perspective of sexuality and gender is to provide an analytical entry point. We can infer that the Church had a complex relationship with colonial powers that compromised its ability to critique the planters, colonial governance, and the construction of a racial and misogynistic ideology. At times, despite an idealistic intent to civilize the slaves into Christianity, the compromised missionary movement found itself compelled to maintain the interests of the planters. It cannot be gain-said that the fact of slavery itself, the issuance of the missionaries from the colonizing force, the connection between the Church and the vested interests of Western civilization together constitute compelling evidence of the contemporary churches troubling relationship to colonization. The gendered approach is another, and inadequately explored, element in that troubled relationship.

Did European men in the 18th through 20th centuries think of them-selves as engaging in social construction and in creating an ideologically based discourse of race and gender? They may not have used this postmodern language. There is, however, overwhelming documentary evidence that they were actively engaged in creating legal, psychological, moral, emotional, and social distance from those they enslaved. Collectively, their journals, histories, letters, and commentaries attest to that effort and expose the clichés of language and thought that attended their distancing. Much effort went into deprecating the capacities of enslaved women regarding their sexuality, suggesting irresponsible motherhood and profligacy. It is difficult to distinguish whether the missionaries' lament of the European males' depravity was caused by their sexual irresponsibility or by their involvement with the "brutish" African women. Whichever it was, the Church allied itself with the propagation of European ethnicity's grand narrative and the degradation of Africanisms. The African woman's body, like the European woman's, became the icon of both value discourses. The Church in its preaching and practices perpetuated and actualized this iconography. This was both moral superficiality and ideological collusion.

The moral impotence of the Church in the pre-emancipation Caribbean was due to its collusion with imperial powers. Through marriage and social fraternization, many missionaries came to a sympathetic understanding of the planter's viewpoint. Thus, they were unable to destabilize the balance of power within the system. It was clearly to the advantage of the missionaries to be seen by the plantocracy as supportive of the slave system and to avoid commenting on the immorality of the system itself. This was compounded by the missionaries' focus on slave morality to the exclusion of the lax moral behavior of the owners. "As Herbert Gutman has pointed out, modern theories of the slave family grew out of the racialist notions of slave owners. The twin evils of familial instability and sexual immorality arising from this are still used to describe black family life both in slavery and freedom."[83] Gutman's comment is still relevant in 2008.

Its relevance is most active in the social class structure in the Anglophone Caribbean. The tiers tend to have the poorest strata manifesting the most dynamic African retentions and reminiscences. Within those strata are found the women whose social and economic location make them most vulnerable. In the postcolonial Caribbean, they too have found the elite male ready and willing to cavort but not to roost. Large statistics on extramarital childbearing cluster at this social level. The elite male sexual partners of the lower-class women have no problems retaining their church membership. The women must overcome social and religious stigmas. The template for this relationship lies in the colonial past.

Barbara Bush recognized that religious abolitionists and pro-slavery advocates held similar attitudes toward the black woman. Neither denied her infantilism, promiscuity, and moral inferiority. Pro-slavery advocates exploited her for their own entertainment, lasciviousness, promiscuity, and satisfaction. Religious abolitionists wanted to save her from herself and the promiscuous male plantocrats.[84] Thus, while their ends diverged, they shared the same ideological position. Black and white women's bodies were the symbols, and their activities the lived articulation of ideology. Given the template, the class ramifications, Christian collusion, and doctrinal stances—women's sexuality, as the most accessible marker of morality, clarifies the ideological heritage of the Church as partial to Eurocentrism. Clearly, liturgical dances control body movements, and lower-class women (urban especially) can be treated more severely based on sexual reproduction. The Church can continue to function from a position of moral superiority while it identifies with Eurocentrism. An Afrocentric Church, by honed instinct, seems oxymoronic and a bad risk.

Today Caribbean Christianity remains synonymous with acculturation into European ethnic elitist mentalities. The Church has received ideology and representation as substance and attempted to canonize them as ideals. Despite a progressive history in some denominations of ordination and female lay leadership, the Church continues to require female members to control their sexuality with mores that reflect the European elite female as *represented* rather than as she *lived*. Caribbean Christianity clung to an ideal that may never have been fully realized anywhere. Women, especially black women, have borne the clutter of disproof. Elite Caribbean woman must actualize something that never really existed. The lower-class woman must divest herself of the culture of her survival and adapt her behavior to a European template that did not quite work—not even for indigenous Europeans in the colonies. Christianity in its doctrine, liturgy, ethics, and social activism provided the coherence and hinge for activation and relational symbiosis of religion, ethnicity, class, gender, and ethics, with a will toward homoeostasis at the ideological level. Caribbean Christianity guides women of any class or ethnicity toward this ideological homoeostasis. This is the legacy's narrative: the transmission of denunciatory rhetoric, supposedly reflecting a moral high road though accompanied by active cruelty. The perpetuation subscribes to the ideology of the inferiority of anyone and any cultural mores that do not reflect the behavior of whites. For women "the alleged physical and moral inferiority of black women, in contrast to European women, . . . establish[ed] them firmly in the role of the 'other woman'; one set of moral standards was applicable to white women, another less honorable set to black; the superiority of white women was stressed."[85] This was an impossible situation for black and white women, even where they invested their lives in the ideology. White women bore the purity their men did not in general achieve. Black women bore the burden of the underachievement of European men, European women, and the African male. Today, the perpetuation of both misogyny and ethnocentrism generates the ridiculous phenomenon of black people being subtly racist against ourselves with Christianity persisting in propagating and legitimizing that phenomenon.

The next stage in theological history for Caribbean Christianity is to undertake serious probing and sustained discussions about the ideological heritage of colonialism vis-à-vis gender. This requires an ideologically astute identification, analysis, and critique of its grand narrative beyond the effort of this paper. Reverend Dr. Lesley Anderson offered some clues to helpful elements in approaching the task. In his sermon at the Caribbean Conference of Churches' (CCC) Seventh General Assembly, held in Panama in 2005, he averred that the vision of the CCC ". . . implies breaking down the walls of oppression, conflict, sexism, racism, and anything else that separates and threatens to destroy a healthy relationship between people."[86] The challenges he identifies are part of the human fabric but their expressions in the Caribbean were peculiarly molded by the Colonial experience. If the challenges are to be more than flaccid terms, and to include Caribbean homophobia, gender needs to be engaged as a deconstructing category of analysis. The Caribbean is very aware of the heritage of the colonial experience. However, the Church can extend its approach by engaging its ideological heritage and its perduring denial of Africanisms.

The prism of female sexuality and the colonial heritage leads to hopeful anticipation of a more legitimate fecundity. Advancement of women in church and para-church leadership in the Caribbean is to be celebrated and lauded. However, that advancement does not conclude by its structural forms the triumph of gender in the Caribbean. The impact of our Europeanized heritage upon the models we employ for our moral life and the ongoing construction of morality in de-Africanized systems and structures need to be examined. Church leaders, male and female, may question the assertions of the paper by querying the feasibility of utilizing alternative structures for sexual morality to marriage. One step is to elevate the heritage of heterodoxy bequeathed by women and examine it for answers. That heterodoxy includes resistance to all manifestations of injustice within the status quo emerging from our foremothers, including embracing the entire range of woman types as formative for our understanding of women and women's capacities. Another is to relinquish our adherence to the Eurocentric status quo and embrace the legitimacy that arises within the very valid quest for Caribbean identity by breaking the Eurocentric stranglehold on moral definitions, worship, and behavior. Perhaps this last is the most difficult to articulate and access. One way is to learn from the colonial heritage of social construction, and see how we gender immorality in female terms both practically and symbolically, interpret women in scripture, construct images of goodness in ways devoid of Africanisms, and how we uncritically import cultural behavior based on geopolitical influences.

Gender analysis is not the only route to understanding nonindigneous influences on Caribbean Christianity. However, if we do not include gender we will be blinded to ways we replicate the ideological heritage of Eurocentric, misogynistic gender stereotypes and idealizations to the disadvantage of our women. Today's Caribbean women, like their foremothers, live the struggle to survive religious and social systems that hamstring them in multiple ways. Their means, devious or forthright, ought to be celebrated, acknowledged, and lifted up just as male examples are. What gender analysis does is to highlight the complex lives of women and their stories. Their histories, especially enslaved women's reveal platforms for gendered construction of morality as well as its racialization. They challenge Caribbean churches to relinquish the shackling meta-narrative of our colonial heritage. To relinquish those shackles is to be freed to participate in the construction of the Caribbean's hybridized identity and an appropriate concomitant meta-narrative. Then, there may be many ways to tell the story of the Christianity and Caribbean women.

# NOTES

1. The collective term, "women" references a diversity of female experiences whether slave, mulatto, or European women are under discussion. The limitations of space prohibit comprehensive representation and analysis. In his discussion of the status of gendered history in the Caribbean, Hilary Beckles in 1999 thought that "the post-structuralist assertion that the term 'woman' is but a social construct . . . has struck no central nerve" in Caribbean feminist historiography, a situation that Beckles began to address in Hilary McD. Beckles, *Centering Woman: Gender Discourses in Caribbean Slave Society* (Kingston: Ian Randle Publishers, Princeton: Markus Wiener Publishers, Oxford: James Currey Publishers, 1999), xiv. This essay continues in that direction by deconstructing the Church, gender, power axes in Caribbean Christianity's colonial heritage albeit from an Afrocentric perspective. It will not address the relational problems of Caribbean women of Carib, Dutch, French, Hispanic, or Indian ancestries.

2. The Arawaks were called Tainos in Cuba, Jamaica, and Haiti and have been linked to the Amerindians who migrated either from the Amazon Basin to the Orinoco Valley, through Venezuela to Trinidad and then through the Lesser Antilles to the Greater Antilles. An alternative theory of origins, Julian H. Steward's circum-Caribbean theory posits the origins as a dual movement of the Tainos. One group radiated from the Columbian Andes to the West Indies. The other radiated from the Andes into Central America, the Guianas, Venezuela, and the Amazon Basin. See Irving Rouse, *The Tainos: Rise and Decline of the People Who Greeted Columbus* (New Haven, CT: Yale University Press, 1993), 30–48 and Dale Bisnauth, *History of Religions in the Caribbean* (Kingston, Jamaica: Kingston Publishers, 1989), 1.

3. The collusion occurred when Pope Alexander VI issued the Papal Bulls that "granted half the world to the Spanish crown and proposed the dividing line between the Spanish and Portuguese dominions." Bisnauth, *History of Religions,* 11.

4. The Caribs were a fiercer group and aggressively violent. Therefore, the efforts toward association and evangelization focused on the various Arawak groups beginning in Hispaniola in 1493.

5. Arawak religion was ancestor based. Deceased ancestors became zemiis and were the objects of propitiation, adoration, and worship. In addition, an invisible, benign, and merciful Supreme Being did not need propitiation.

6. I use the term "gender" to connote the social construction of roles and relationships that impose upon rather than define biosexual characteristics. It is an analytical tool that readily relates to the rhetoric of definitions and discursive universes. It abstracts the discussion away from nature and points to the use of language as a tool of nurture.

7. See Barbara Bush, *Slave Women in Caribbean Society, 1650–1838* (London: James Currey, Ltd., Jamaica: Heinemann Publishers (Caribbean), 1990), xi, xii.

8. Bush, *Slave Women,* 13.

9. Barbara Bush is repeatedly insistent on the persistence of colonial racist and classist attitudes to today. See ibid., 1–10 esp.

10. Current Caribbean evangelicalism does not share in this history. However, at the level of gender ideology they are influenced by U.S. evangelicalism, which follows the lines of male dominance/female subordination.

11. The *repartimiento-encomienda* system established in Hispaniola in 1499 preceded the *Encomienda Doctrina.* First used by the Spaniards in the Canary Islands in 1489 the *repartimiento-encomienda* system commended the Indians to the Spanish *conquistadores* and gave the *conquistadores* the right to exact labor or tribute from the Arawak/Tainos. In return, the *conquistadores* were to instruct the Arawak/Tainos in the Christian faith. See Bisnauth, *History of Religions,* 16. The *Encomienda Doctrina* was a development from this.

12. J. B. Ellis, *The Diocese of Jamaica,* 30 with quote excerpted from Osborne and Johnston, *Coastlands and Islands,* 25 with incomplete citation in Endnote 4.

13. In the late 17th century the Church of England was still recovering from the Reformation and its own secession from the Roman Catholic Church. The unsettledness and its emergent liberal form were reflected in the export of English State Religion to the Caribbean.

14. This occurred in Barbados as early as 1630 and in Jamaica by 1681.

15. Francis J. Osborne and Geoffrey Johnston, *Coastlands and Islands: First Thoughts on Caribbean Church History* (Kingston, Jamaica: UTCWI, 1972), 27.

16. See Beckles. *Centering Woman,* esp. 22–37. Adrienne Davis describes a similar situation for slave women in the Americas, Adrienne Davis, "'Don't Let Nobody Bother Yo' Principle': The Sexual Economy of American Slavery," in Sharon Harley and The Black Women and Work Collective, *Sister Circle: Black Women and Work* (New Brunswick, NJ: Rutgers University Press, 2002), 103–127.

17. Today, Codrington College is a highly respected seminary that trains men and women for the Anglican priesthood.

18. The terms of the bequest were that "the plantations continued intire [entire] and three hundred negroes at least kept always thereon, and a convenient number of Professors and Scholars maintained there, all of them to be under the vows of poverty, chastity and obedience, who shall be obliged to study and practise physick and chyrugery as well as divinity . . ." Quote obtained from Osborne and Johnston, *Coastlands and Islands,* 34 and cited from Frank J. Klingberg, ed. *Codrington Chronicle,* 16.

19. Osborne and Johnston, *Coastlands and Islands,* 36.

20. This was the earliest effort in a British colony to Christianize slaves. Bisnauth, *History of Religions,* 103.

21. See Beckles, *Centering Woman,* 159.

22. The Moravians and the Lutherans went further by actually owning slaves. For the Lutherans see Bisnauth, *History of Religions,* 46.

23. Beckles, *Centering Woman,* 63.

24. Ibid., 65.

25. The entrepreneurship of women was not an expression of liberation and independence. It is part of the colonial legacy for Caribbean women but continues today with mixed reasons for its existence.

26. Ibid., xviii.

27. Ibid., xix.

28. Ibid., xx.

29. Another very popular example is that of the Jamaican White Witch of Rose Hall who is thought to have killed seven husbands and to have suffered from sexually transmitted diseases.

30. Ibid., 62.

31. Ibid., 62.

32. Judith Soares describes female leadership in the neo-Pentecostal movement represented by a few selected congregations in Barbados. See Judith Soares, "Eden after Eve: Christian Fundamentalism and Women in Barbados" in *Nation Dance: Religion, Identity, and Cultural Difference in the Caribbean* (Bloomington: Indiana University Press, 2001), 104–117. Some para-church organizations that have used female leadership in these ways include Youth for Christ, Campus Life, and the Student Christian Movement.

33. Edward Kamau Braithwaite, *Folk Culture of the Slaves in Jamaica* (London, Port of Spain, New Beacon Books, 1971, Revised Edition 1981), 13.

34. Emphasis, mine.

35. Braithwaite, *Folk Culture,* 17.

36. The phrase is from Derek Walcott's *In a Green Night* (London 1962), 26.

37. See, for instance, Bryan Edwards, *The History, Civil and Commercial, of the British Colonies in the West Indies,* 2 vols. (London 1793) 3 vols. (London 1774), Vol. II, 106; R. Renny, *A History of Jamaica* (London 1807), 168.

38. See, among others, *The Diary of William Jones, 1777–1821* (London 1929), 12; W. J. Gardner. *A History of Jamaica* (London 1873), 99–100.

39. Liturgical dancing is very popular across the spectrum and there is a certain freedom of movement in Pentecostal and Neo-Pentecostal denominations that is absent from the others. Liturgical dancing is controlled and choreographed. The African penchant for dancing with a gyrating waist is disapproved in both cases.

40. Braithwaite, *Folk Culture,* 13.

41. This restriction particularly affects women who are more often than not the partner who faithfully attends worship services and nurses the desire for full membership.

42. Osborne and Johnston, *Coastlands and Islands,* 65 quoting from H. M. Waddell, *Twenty Nine Years in the West Indies and Central Africa,* 40. The order of the listing is not necessarily an indication of the order of each group's priority.

43. There are limitations in access to sources that require the acknowledgment that such "irregular" situations may have been considered. The limitations in Osborne and Johnston's quotes may reflect their priorities more so than the actual ecclesiastical regulations of the colonial period.

44. See Beckles, *Centering Woman,* 159.

45. See ibid., 159, 164.

46. Donna P. Hope, *Inna di Dancehall: Popular Culture and the Politics of Identity in Jamaica* (Jamaica, Barbados, Trinidad, and Tobago: University of the West Indies Press, 2006), 20.

47. Hope, *Inna di Dancehall,* 21. Here she quotes Stuart Hall, "What is 'Black' in Black Popular Culture?" in *Stuart Hall: Critical Dialogues in Cultural Studies,* eds. David Morley and Kuan-Hsing Chen (New York and London: Routledge, 1996), 446.

48. In Jamaica, a very strong movement toward using local rhythms grew into an annual national gospel competition and festival that rivals the annual reggae festival for attendance and stellar performances. There remain restrictions in dancing, the flexibility of the waist and fluidity of the body, as well as the constraint on general participation. These are some indicators of the suppression of Africanisms.

49. In a replication of colonial practices, these women had extramarital relationships with middle class men. Often, these men were members in good standing of churches but experienced no marginalization within the churches. Their affairs were either very secret or part of the entrenched behavior of many Caribbean men and so defied judgment.

50. "Matie" is the sweetheart or the "other woman."

51. Hope, *Inna di Dancehall,* 58–59.

52. For variations on the theme of competing femininities, see Beckles, *Centering Woman,* 174 and Hope, *Inna di Dancehall,* 59 and 36–85 for a fuller discussion of the role of sexuality in dancehall culture.

53. They also exclude some significant stories of women's activities that others include. For example, in recounting the beginnings of Methodism in Antigua they omit the women who were integral to its development. For example, see John W. Poxon, *Coke, The Man and His Mission: The Church in Early Years* (Kingston, Jamaica: The Jamaica Methodist Church, A Bicentenary Publication: January 1989) and Dr. Abel Stevens, *The History of the Religious Movement of the Eighteenth Century Called Methodism, considered in its different denominational forms and its relations to British and American Protestantism: Vol. II: From the Death of Whitfield to the Death of Wesley* (New York: Carlton and Porter, 1859).

54. Osborn and Johnston, *Coastlands and Islands,* 62–63.

55. I suspect that Mammy Faith incorporated tales from African spirituality and cosmology into her messages. If she did then she was a prototype of postcolonial scholarship.

56. Ibid., 63. The source of the quotation is unacknowledged there.

57. These were other foundational and memorialized Baptist missionaries of the colonial period. They and Knibb were freed slaves from the United States. The Baptists were renowned for their work among slaves. It is virtually impossible to explain their antagonisms without resorting to class sensitivities and the vulnerability of their mission in the light of planter and Anglo-ecclesiastical resistance.

58. I intend the word "heterodoxy" to insinuate an alternative orthodoxy and inscribe legitimacy to these women. This lifts their actions to the level of paradigmatic exemplariness.

59. Mary Able Ann Smith is sometimes identified as Mary Akle Ann Smith. She was born in America to Scottish parents. She may have migrated to Jamaica during the American War of Independence.

60. Poxon, *Coke,* 14.

61. For this reason, the absence of any attestation to her ethnicity is a significant loss, as it would have added to our knowledge and sense of unorthodox and orthodox alliances in colonial times. I am using the terms orthodox and unorthodox in their relationship to socially, legally, and religiously accepted codes of behavior and without any intention of ascribing a negative or positive assessment on the morality of the designated action.

62. Ibid., *Coke,* 47.

63. Then called the Parade Society.

64. The Parish Church was the chief Anglican congregation in Jamaica. The Parish Church was located on the south side of Parade Square and Coke Church on the east side.

65. "Seven Years' Night" references the period from 1807–15 when the Parade Chapel was closed.

66. For this information on Mary Wilkinson see Ibid., 46–47.

67. Beckles, *Centering Woman,* x and 174.

68. Stevens, *The History of the Religious Movement of the Eighteenth Century Called Methodism,* 355.

69. Some records say that the slaves were a male and a female.

70. Ibid., 355.

71. See Beckles, *Centering Woman,* 183–84 and Moira Robinson, "The Hart Sisters: Early African Caribbean Writers, Evangelicals, and Radicals." The available bibliographic information for this article is incomplete.

72. See Beckles, *Centering Woman,* 182–83.

73. See Osborne and Johnston, *Coastlands and Islands,* 79, endnote 22 for a discussion with Elsa Goveia who argued, "By preaching submission to the slaves the missionaries were making a highly significant contribution to the maintenance of the slave system and slave society."

74. Here I speak of my perception of these women in the oral situation of worship and Christian education. The history of their role in Caribbean church history is documented as indicated in previous footnotes.

75. The Jamaica Christian Council was renamed the Jamaica Council of Churches in 1962.

76. The Jamaica Council of Churches, *Men of Vision* (Jamaica: Montrose Printery, 1981).

77. *Men of Vision,* 27. Other photographs, scattered throughout the booklet, attest to the presence of women in the elected offices of the Council.

78. The Presbyterian Church in Jamaica along with the Congregational Church became the United Church of Jamaica. Many years later, the Disciples of Christ joined the union. The denomination was renamed the United Church in Jamaica and the Cayman Islands.

79. Sources for the following stories of ordained women are not readily available. Despite thorough searches of denominational web sites, I did not find any specific information on the history of women's ordination in the Caribbean. At this time, the acquisition of information is dependent on personal awareness of these women and the transfer of information within the circle of women who know each other. An initial history of women's ordination and service in the Caribbean is urgently needed before a generation of eyewitnesses passes.

80. In 1982 and 1984 Revds. Winnie Bolle and Venice Guntley were ordained to the Episcopalian Church in the United States of America and in Canada. They are both Jamaicans. Rev. T. Anne Daniel (née Williams), Mrs. Eslyn Sonaram-Bryan, and Rev. Dr. Althea Spencer Miller were the first women accepted to train as presbyters in the ministry of the Methodist Church in the Caribbean and the Americas who had not been deaconesses.

81. Deaconess Dr. Rachel Evelyn Vernon provided information about the Baptists in footnote 76 from her unpublished dissertation on the history of the ordination of women in the Church in the Province of the West Indies (the Anglican Church).

82. Reported in the *Jamaica Gleaner,* March 16, 2008, http://www.jamaica-gleaner.com/gleaner/20080316/out/out5.html. Ironically, Rev. Hudson-Wilkins and Rev. Dr. Marjorie Saunders' ascendancies have roots in the colonial relationship with England.

83. Herbert G. Gutman, *The Black Family in Slavery and Freedom, 1750–1925* (Oxford, 1976) 329. Cited in Bush, *Slave Women,* 5.

84. Bush, *Slave Women,* 18.

85. Ibid., 17.

86. Rev. Dr. Lesley Anderson, President of the Caribbean Conference of Churches, "Healing and Transformation Given in Christ, Fulfilled Through the Spirit," Sermon preached at the Caribbean Conference of Churches Seventh General Assembly, Panama, June 2005, http://www.ccc-caribe.org/eng.genassem05/homily_Anderson.pdf.

## REFERENCES

Beckles, Hilary McD. *Centering Woman: Gender Discourses in Caribbean Slave Society.* Kingston: Ian Randle Publishers, Princeton: Markus Wiener Publishers, Oxford: James Currey Publishers, 1999.

Bisnauth, Dale. *History of Religions in the Caribbean.* Kingston, Jamaica: Kingston Publishers, 1989.

Braithwaite, Edward "Kamau." *Folk Culture of the Slaves in Jamaica*. Revised Edition. London, Port of Spain, Trinidad: New Beacon Books, 1971.

Bush, Barbara. *Slave Women in Caribbean Society, 1650–1838*. London: James Currey, Ltd., Kingston, Jamaica: Heinemann Publishers (Caribbean), 1990.

Dookham, Isaac. *A Post Emancipation History of the West Indies*. Great Britain: Collins, 1968.

Gregory, Howard. *Caribbean Theology: Preparing for the Challenges Ahead*. Bridgetown, Barbados, Jamaica, Trinidad and Tobago: Canoe Press, University of the West Indies, 1995.

Harley, Sharon and The Black Women and Work Collective. *Sister Circle: Black Women and Work*. New Brunswick, NJ: Rutgers University Press, 2002.

Hope, Donna P. *Inna di Dancehall: Popular Culture and the Politics of Identity in Jamaica*. Jamaica, Barbados, Trinidad and Tobago: University of the West Indies Press, 2006.

Jamaica Council of Churches, (The). *Men of Vision*. Jamaica: Montrose Printery, 1981.

López Springfield, Consuelo, Ed. *Daughters of Caliban: Caribbean Women in the Twentieth Century*. Bloomington: Indiana University Press; London: Latin America Bureau, 1997.

Osborne, Francis, S. J. and Geoffrey Johnston. *Coastlands and Islands: First Thoughts on Caribbean Church History*. Jamaica: UTCWI, 1972.

Poxon, John W. *Coke, The Man and His Mission: The Church in Early Years*. Jamaica: The Jamaica Methodist Church, A Bicentenary Publication, January, 1989.

Rouse, Irving. *The Tainos: Rise and Decline of the People Who Greeted Columbus*. New Haven, CT: Yale University Press, 1993.

Sankeralli, Burton, Ed. *At the Crossroads: African Caribbean Religion & Christianity*. With an Introduction by Rev. Dr. George Mulrain. Trinidad and Tobago: Cariflex Limited, 1995.

Shepherd, Verene, Bridget Breteton, and Barbara Bailey. *Engendering History: Caribbean Woman in Historical Perspective*. New York: St. Martin's Press, 1995.

Stevens, Abel, Dr., *The History of the Religious Movement of the Eighteenth Century Called Methodism, considered in its different denominational forms and its relations to British and American Protestantism: Vol. II: From the Death of Whitfield to the Death of Wesley*. New York: Carlton and Porter, 1859.

Taylor, Patrick. *Nation Dance: Religion, Identity, and Cultural Difference in the Caribbean*. Bloomington, Indianapolis: Indiana University Press, 2001.

Williams, Eric. *From Columbus to Castro: The History of the Caribbean 1492–1969*. Great Britain: Andrè Deutsch, 1970.

## INTERNET SOURCES

Anderson, Lesley. "Healing and Transformation Given in Christ, Fulfilled Through the Spirit." Sermon preached at the Caribbean Conference of Churches Seventh General Assembly, Panama, June2005, http://www.ccc-caribe.org/eng.genassem05/homily_Anderson.pdf.

Simpson, Trudy. *Jamaica Gleaner*, March 16, 2008, http://www.jamaica-gleaner.com/gleaner/20080316/out/out5.html.

# CHAPTER 14

# Maternal Practices as Religious Piety: The Pedagogical Practices of American Latter-day Saint Women

*Amy Hoyt*

Women within the Church of Jesus Christ of Latter-day Saints (LDS) offer an instructive lens through which to view how maternal practices, specifically childbirth and raising children, shape traditional religious women and contribute to their religious devotion.[1] Drawing upon an ethnographic study, this chapter explores how maternal practices are religious practices that act to alter the interior of women, particularly women from an American LDS community. As such, they are pedagogical tools that contribute to subjectivity, or personhood, and have the potential to transform women into more pious subjects. After introducing the LDS church, and the ethnographic and methodological specifics of the study, this chapter will examine pedagogies of maternity as religious praxis and explore the ensuing theoretical implications; analyze notions of agency and subjectivity; and reflect on the pedagogies and transformative gifts of parenthood.

## THE CHURCH OF JESUS CHRIST OF LATTER-DAY SAINTS

There are currently over 13 million Latter-day Saints throughout the world.[2] One sociologist, Rodney Stark, has made the controversial prediction that if the Church of Jesus Christ of Latter-day Saints continues to grow at its current rate that it will be on track to become the next major world religion.[3] Headquartered in Salt Lake City, the Church of Jesus Christ of Latter-day Saints now employs hundreds of men and women to help administer the affairs of the church. With over 52,000 full-time missionaries serving in hundreds of locations, the church has continued to grow at an astonishing pace. There are members of the LDS church residing in 160 countries around the world, and in 2005 more than 240,000 people joined the LDS church.[4] The LDS church is currently led by Thomas S. Monson, who was named the 16th president of the LDS church on February 4, 2008, at the age of 80.[5]

## ETHNOGRAPHIC PARTICULARITIES

The ethnography focuses on a community of Latter-day Saints who are located within four wards (congregations), each adjacent to one another in a suburban environment in northern California. Although the field notes are comprised of Sunday services in one ward, interviewees came from the members of several of the wards bordering the congregation that was observed, which altogether only comprises about 10 square miles. For confidentiality reasons and ease of reading, the community is referred to as Bay Town, a pseudonym.

Within the LDS church, wards are constructed by geographical boundaries, upon the approval of church leaders in Salt Lake City, Utah. Thus, members are discouraged from attending congregations if they do not live within the geographical boundaries. Ward members are brought together by geography and expected to build a cohesive congregation, despite differences.[6] Of course, geography can produce many similarities, mainly relating to socioeconomic variances, which might be reflected in racial and ethnic diversity, or lack thereof.

The LDS community that was studied in Bay Town, California, consists of an array of families, including those who are single, single parents, widows, traditional families, and couples without children. While a typical congregation consists of approximately 240 to 350 members, only about 45 to 50 percent attend weekly services. The ward I attended has about 95 families, of which roughly 45 attend weekly church services; and it is approximately 85 percent Caucasian, mostly middle-aged and middle-class. There are some variations in age, racial and ethnic background, and class, but the average congregant is a white, middle-class family member in the throws of raising children. The racial and ethnic diversity of the particular LDS community that I worked with, albeit slight, consists of families who are Chinese, African, African American, Tongan, South American, Mexican, Malaysian, and Vietnamese. While my interviews consisted of both women and men inside and outside of the Bay Town ward, my observations of Sunday meetings came solely from this particular ward.

Like any social group, each ward has its own culture, a subtle form of implicitly agreed upon mores. These communal mores are also informed by the larger LDS society within the United States, and are an important source for glimpsing the culture produced by those that constitute the community.[7] The ward and community that I worked with portrayed a high level of integration with the local community, including through work, volunteerism, school, and extracurricular activities.

## METHODOLOGY

In-depth interviews were conducted with 31 women and 15 men, ranging in ages from 27 to 79. The women and men had varying family situations, from those who are single and never married, to those in blended families, divorced, widowed, or both. Most interviewees had children. The socioeconomic status of these subjects was mostly middle-class but a few were working-class or upper-middle-class. Overall, there was a continuum of different life experiences. Because of the complementary gender norms embedded within the LDS cosmology, I worked with both men and women for clarity toward gaining a wider picture of the community, while primarily focusing upon women. Insights and conversations with the men helped delineate differences, similarities, and nuances probably not apparent when exclusively interviewing women.

## LATTER-DAY SAINT GENDERED THEOLOGY

To understand why maternal practices are considered acts of piety for LDS women, it is necessary to recognize the primacy of the belief in a pre- and postmortal existence, and the belief in the "mutuality of spiritual and material worlds."[8]

Latter-day Saints believe that in a pre-mortal existence, or an afterlife, "spirits" were created from matter that had existed forever. In this way, "human spirit, or "intelligence," is eternal, without "a beginning or an end."[9] For Latter-day Saints the belief in a pre- and postmortal existence includes gods who create spirits, which become embodied and, in turn, create additional beings. In this way, subjectivity, or personhood, does not change; it merely becomes embodied. According to LDS belief, spirits need bodies to progress toward eventual deification, which is dependent upon a male/female partnership, or what the LDS call "eternal marriage."[10]

Within the pre-mortal construct, or the life before birth, Latter-day Saints believe that gendered spirits gathered to hear and vote on a plan that included corporeality, moral agency, redemption through Jesus, and an eventual return to live with God.[11] According to LDS belief, God unveiled His plan for humans to become embodied and live on the earth so that they could prove themselves by using moral agency to obey God. For the LDS, the fall was part of God's plan, and since humans would exist within a fallen world (subject to temptations and sin), it was important to provide a way for them to become pious enough to return to live with God.[12] The role of Jesus as a savior was proposed as a way to redeem the sinful nature of humankind.

Latter-day Saints believe that agency, which is typically defined by feminist theorists as the ability to act "freely" (a concept I will critique below), is a principle that existed before mortality, is essential to existence, and that mortal or human agency was enabled by Jesus's atonement.[13] Most Latter-day Saints define agency differently than many feminist theorists have traditionally defined it. For the LDS, agency is the ability to choose between obedience and disobedience to God. During this same pre-mortal meeting, where God revealed God's plan, Lucifer offered an alternate plan, according to the LDS, which was to compel humans to obey God, thereby limiting their moral agency. The two plans were voted on. The LDS believe a war in heaven ensued, where Lucifer and the spirits who voted with him, about one-third of the spirits who existed within the pre-mortal world, were cast out and denied the opportunity for embodiment.[14]

For the LDS, this set in motion the ongoing battle between good and evil where Lucifer began his never ending attempt to sway humans away from God.[15] In short, Latter-day Saints believe in pre- and postexistences where subjectivity, or personhood, does not change, but becomes embodied: gendered spirits fought in a pre-mortal existence to come to earth and become embodied to someday progress to become gods and goddesses in a post-mortal existence. As gods and goddesses, with their kin connected to them forever, men and women continue the process of creating spirit children. This perpetual cycle of partnering and reproduction makes post-mortal existence, or an afterlife, necessary.

The eschatological beliefs of the LDS center upon a post-mortal existence that includes three kingdoms or "degrees of glory," which are hierarchically organized.[16] The belief in three kingdoms of glory within the post-mortal realm is a central aspect of LDS cosmology. They are referred to as the celestial, terrestrial, and telestial kingdoms. The celestial kingdom is considered to be the "highest" kingdom where the most pious will go after their death to live with Heavenly parents.[17] The terrestrial is for those who "were good people on earth, but they did not have faith in Jesus and did not obey all of the commandments."[18] The telestial kingdom, considered the "lowest" kingdom, is for those who did not obey God's commandments while living in the mortal world and who have no desire to do so.

Within the highest kingdom, the celestial kingdom, the LDS also believe that there are three degrees of glory, and exaltation is considered the highest degree of glory within the highest kingdom. Exaltation, according to Latter-day Saint belief, is the ability to eventually become gods and goddesses, which is made possible by the creation and perpetuity of spiritual offspring, which can include literal offspring and adoptive children. Future progeny follow the same process as mortals, by vast kinship networks, that are bound together forever by a covenant with God, which is made within an LDS temple. Thus, in part, one becomes a god or goddess by the adoption or creation and production of offspring. Reproduction, within a covenant marriage, is central to exaltation for Latter-day Saints.

Due to the primacy of marriage and reproduction, exaltation requires reciprocity between men and women; neither may be exalted without the other. While individuals may be saved, or attain salvation alone, to become exalted men and women, they are reliant on one another.[19] Contrary to previous observations, men may not reach exaltation without women, and vice versa.[20] Past LDS church President Gordon B. Hinckley explains, "in attaining the highest degree of glory in the celestial kingdom, the man cannot enter without the woman, neither can the woman enter without the man. The two are inseparable as husband and wife in eligibility for that highest degree of glory."[21] Thus, exaltation is dependent upon interdependence between men and women. Interdependence must be formally recognized by participating in a marriage ceremony within an LDS temple. During this ceremony, men and women are married "for time and all eternity" or "sealed" together. The marriage covenant continues past death into the post-mortal world. Within the LDS religion, marriage in an LDS temple is necessary in order to attain godhood.

The marriage ceremony within the LDS temple solidifies the cosmological belief in an afterlife because a temple marriage remains in effect past the mortal existence, if both partners live piously. Belief in the continual bonds of kinship is one of the most important theological principles within the Church of Jesus Christ of Latter-day Saints. Because the LDS believe that families can be bound together beyond the mortal world, the concept of a Mother and Father in Heaven as divine parents exemplifies the ultimate model of an "eternal family," and provides a framework, based upon individual parental duties, that undergirds the earthly family.[22]

Within contemporary LDS culture, the Heavenly Mother is not necessarily a symbol of women's autonomous value.[23] Her value is derived within the realm of kinship and marriage; she is the essential female component within a system that believes that marital and parental interdependence of men and women is the only way to obtain exaltation. As Heeren, Lindsey, and Mason have observed, because of the highly distinct gender notions that

Latter-day Saints claim as divinely instituted within patriarchy, Heavenly Mother appears "as a superior god for women's *specific* functions," and as such "patriarchy and belief in a goddess go hand-in-hand in the Mormon case."[24] In this way, most contemporary Latter-day Saints do not look to Mother in Heaven as a model for women's liberatory possibilities, but as a model of interdependence within a highly gendered patriarchal order that takes the possibility of family deification as its central mortal goal.[25]

As should be clear, the concept of family, including gender notions, is critical to LDS theology.[26] At the heart of LDS belief is the idea that men and women are radically different from one another and that they can become perfected only through their ongoing interdependence. The significance of an existence before birth and after life is important because of the *gendered* cosmology, or worldview, within the LDS faith. Gender remains consistent for persons before birth, during their life on earth, and in the afterlife.

Parental roles, framed by world views and faith, are highly distinctive and categorized along gender lines; humans are considered able to reach their greatest spiritual potential by engaging in maternal practices. The LDS I worked with consider embodied practices of maternity one way of achieving spiritual growth and maintaining religious devotion. They understand childbirth and parenting, within a nuclear family, as pedagogical processes that have the potential to train their interior into pious shapes.

Maternity, or childbirth, is fundamental to understanding the LDS female. Bearing children within the nuclear family is one of the highest priorities for most LDS women.[27] The primacy of the heterosexual family and a commitment to bearing multiple children have always been central for LDS church members.[28] For the women I studied, marriage presupposes children, and the ideal family consists of a husband, wife, and children, although this is far from some women's lived reality. Regardless of marital status, racial or ethnic background, political affiliation, educational level, age, or economic circumstances, virtually *every* woman I worked with expressed the importance of bearing and raising children, even the self-identified feminists. Tellingly, even those women who were not married or did not have children reiterated the importance of family and children. Similarly, the men I studied, with one exception, named family and children as their highest priority. These LDS members find their greatest potential through maternal, paternal, and parental practices within an explicit patriarchal family.

Both fatherhood and motherhood are considered pedagogical processes which can train one's mind and/or spirit, although motherhood is emphasized far more often for women than fatherhood is for men within the LDS church. For LDS women, bearing children is not what women do because it is what they are made for; bearing children is how women are *transformed* into devoted subjects. The goal is to transform oneself into a more pious form, through training that comes from practices of parenting. By using the body as a means of transforming the spirit and mind, these women do not consider themselves to be reduced to their anatomical *essence* but understand themselves as participating in a physical manifestation of their spiritual potential.[29]

## PEDAGOGIES OF MATERNITY

As I have stated, bearing children is a process that leads to spiritual progress, as it assists the women I worked with in meeting their spiritual potential. The actual physical act of giving birth is a principal way that LDS women embody their tradition. In part, this is how they practice their religion, by bearing and raising children devoted to Godly pursuits.

Having children fulfills a deeply held religious belief that the family is an everlasting unit, instituted prior to birth. Although a heterosexual marriage in an LDS temple, coupled with a lifetime of devoted piety, is the requirement for attaining celestial glory, the implication is that celestial glory is synonymous with progeny that will continue forever. Thus, technically, bearing children is not necessary for attaining Godhood in the next life, although it is widely understood that children are part of the process of becoming divine.[30]

As should be clear, fecundity or fertility is highly influential in self-formation. These LDS women met their potential, in part, by practicing piety vis-à-vis the body. One of the ways to receive a righteous disposition is to bear children. Anna, an Arab woman in her late twenties explained this to me:

> I would say having children is the most spiritual decision out all of the decisions, or at the top of religious decisions that we make. And we would pray about it if it's right and I've actually had a lot of spiritual feelings about having children and the need to have children. I think religion plays a big part in it too because the whole focus of our religion is bringing children, I feel like it's important. Bringing children to life and how rewarding it is.

For Anna and nearly every woman I encountered, having children is a religious act; the primary concern, even for those that had never been married and did not have children.

These women believe that women who have not had the opportunity to be mothers "in this life," will have the "blessings" of children in the next life. This belief is comforting to those who have not been able to bear children for various reasons, whether due to the inability to find a suitable marriage partner or because of infertility. Thus, most LDS women believe that every woman has the potential for motherhood in the next life, if she is able to live piously in this one.

Arden, a 38-year-old, graduate-level educated Caucasian woman who has never married, did not list children or getting married as a top priority when I asked about her goals or priorities. When I pressed her about the difficulty of being part of a church that focuses so much on family and parenthood, she insisted:

> I mother in other ways. I have my nieces and nephews and I don't feel that I'm missing out at all because I mother in other ways. I know that I'll have the opportunity to be a mother in the next life, so I'm not worried about it.

Her top priorities were her career and working on the relationships with her extended family, her parents, and siblings. However, her own future maternal possibilities also fundamentally inform how she understands herself. Arden went on to explain:

> A few weeks ago you and I were talking about a sense of hope, in regards to marriage and family, and I really can't overemphasize enough for me that that is what grounds me. I don't have to worry about it, I don't have to fret about it in this life, I don't have to be driven by a desire to have a biological child or a desire to somehow feel my life is valuable because I'm attached to someone through marriage. I do not have to feel that way and that is a direct result of my understanding of the afterlife. I don't know how I would be without that understanding, but it allows me to be happy with who I am and the way I am. In a way that I don't think I could be as a member of this church if I didn't have that hope.

Clearly Arden still holds motherhood as a valuable part of her subjectivity, but she envisions that this is a future event for her, a role that she will embody in another life. Arden is not focused on trying to find a spouse and create a family because she feels confident that she will have that opportunity in the future. Arden's attitude seems rare in this religious culture though. Other members of her social circle seemed overly concerned with whether she dates and if she has any prospects for marriage, although Arden indicated that these inquiries have lessened as time goes by. Most of the single women I interviewed seemed quite concerned about finding a spouse and creating a family; Arden was the exception.

Sarah, a graduate-level educated Caucasian woman in her fifties, who has never married, placed her number one priority as finding a mate. Her desire for marriage and her lamentation of being single were known within the community. Although she had a stellar career, her greatest desire was to find someone to share her life with. Clearly beyond the years of being able to reproduce her own children, Sarah still felt the import of family and was actively engaged in trying to actualize this desire. Is Sarah weak and needy? Despite a great career, she only wants to "find a man." This is certainly one reading of her life. However, this reading forecloses interesting questions and insights about the importance of marriage and family for these LDS women. Marriage, family, and children are all ways these women (and men) meet their greatest potential, embarking upon a pedagogical process, which can potentially reconfigure one into a more pious subject. In this light, Sarah's desire is one of religious piety, to progress personally.

The diverging commitments and explicit priorities between Arden and Sarah demonstrate the range of responses elicited within a religious system that places a high premium on heterosexual marriage and maternity. For both women, marriage and family are important, but the way they practice their commitment to family and marriage differs radically. Importantly, even for single LDS women, who do not have children, motherhood is a major representation of their subjectivity. They firmly believe that they will have children in the life to come, and thus, maternity is still a primary way they understand themselves, for it embodies a version of their spiritually fulfilled self.

For women who have had children, embodying the ancient command to "multiply and replenish" is one way of becoming pious followers within the LDS church.


## THEORETICAL IMPLICATIONS

Although maternal practices are important for traditional religious women, within the field of religious studies, traditional religious women are often studied and assessed by criteria that do not take the importance of childbirth and child rearing into consideration. This has often resulted in painting women who participate in unapologetically patriarchal religions as either oppressed or working from within the tradition to change it.[31] Scholars within religion have noted this simple dichotomy. Ann Braude has observed that within U.S. religious history, women need to be approached less as victims or empowered actors but as *"meaning-seeking actors* who simultaneously shape and are shaped by both the religious systems and the material realities they inhabit."[32] Similarly, Saba Mahmood, a scholar of anthropology and religion, has called for feminist theoreticians working in the field of religion to find out *how* women have become pious or devoted and to resist simply looking for acts of resistance within these traditions.[33] Both scholars indicate the need for traditional religious women who sustain patriarchy to be examined without quickly fitting them into a victim/empowerment scheme and to study and take seriously the practices that sustain traditional religions.

Maternity and parenthood are important to women in many religious traditions. Although the focus of my ethnography is on LDS women in the United States, the critique of Braude and Mahmood is important in order to validate women in all traditional religious cultures. Traditional religious women, whether Muslim, fundamentalist Christian, or Roman Catholic, would all benefit from the effort of religious scholars to study them by criteria that are germane to their worldview, including maternal practices.

Brenda Brasher, in *Godly Women*, found that women in two U.S. Christian fundamentalist congregations, Bay Chapel and Mount Olive, considered child rearing within a nuclear family a partial manifestation of their religious devotion.[34] Brasher conducted a six-month ethnographic study of both congregations, including the women's ministry groups, or enclaves, that function outside of institutional channels. By interviewing women who convert to fundamentalism, but had previously affiliated loosely with Christianity, Brasher is able to attend to motives for women's participation in traditional religious organizations. Brasher notes that a "sacred canopy" covers congregational life at both locations and that it includes theological ideas that are largely predicated upon gender, which "functions as a sacred partition that literally bifurcates the congregation in two, establishing parallel religious worlds," that include a symbolic congregational world for men and a symbolic world for women.[35]

Brasher also found that within the family, gender is structured around complementarities, not unlike other traditional religious cultures, and male headship is touted as the ideal. Submission is encouraged, but is usually interpreted to mean mutual submission between husbands and wives.[36] Brasher points out that despite the patriarchal rhetoric within the family structure, actual behaviors are much messier and do not lend themselves to easy theorizing.[37] Family is extremely important within Christian fundamentalism and while individual salvation is sought after, it is conceived within the framework of a nuclear family.[38]

Contemporary Roman Catholicism, although it is in an interesting phase, still maintains a strong commitment to maternal practices.[39] Despite the vast differences among members, Catholic belief highly encourages maternal practices, especially procreation. In *Sexing the Church* Aline Kalbian explains that within Roman Catholic cosmology, or worldview, God requires order and order prescribes and describes "what believers perceive as the proper state of relationship in the created universe."[40] Within this cosmic vision, gender is at the heart of Roman Catholic order.[41] This happens at the individual and communal level, and is made normative through theological teachings on marriage and sexuality. In this way, sexual acts and gender derive proper meaning through the teachings on marriage. This sense of order is based upon a complementarity model between men and women, and humans fulfill their purpose, in part, by living out their normative gender notions.[42] Proper gender roles are designed to play out within the sacrament of marriage, and procreation is the primary purpose of marriage. In this way, Roman Catholic worldview prescribes highly distinct gendered relationships, solidified through the sacrament of marriage, and propelled through *procreation*, which offer the ultimate model for all of creation to God.

Clearly, there is potential for religious scholars to shed light on an array of traditional religious women by studying and validating maternal practices as part of women's religious devotion. Although I primarily focus on LDS women within the United States in this essay, these findings can be extrapolated out, in a general way, to encourage scholars to take seriously the practices that influence how traditional religious women form their self-reference, or subjectivity.

## AGENCY AND SUBJECTIVITY

To work through the theoretical dilemmas that have been constructed and to better understand women's piety, feminist theoreticians within religion have been refining the debate of analytical categories of agency and subjectivity. Agency manifests itself through embodiment, an activity potentially with interior components, such as thought processes that may (or may not) occur prior to enactment. Agency consists of actions that lead to the formation of a subject. Thus, subjectivity is a result of embodied knowledges and behaviors, which can contribute to self-reference. Simply put, agency *informs* subjectivity. Agency has become particularly important and the discussion has taken many forms. Until recently, feminist scholars have rarely questioned an underlying premise: mainly that agency consists of acts that resist norms.[43] Since resistance has been equated with agency, women's acts that sustain traditional religions have not been viewed as constituting agentive behavior. Under this construct, women in traditional religions can only exhibit agency when they are *rebelling* against their traditions. This has resulted in a host of research that examines various ways that women resist, rebel, and subvert their traditions and has left those religious behaviors that sustain, support, and propel patriarchal religions largely unexamined.

Saba Mahmood's work *Politics of Piety* explicitly deals with the feminist theoretical category of agency. Mahmood aims to shift the analysis of agency within religious practices from a singular focus on resistance toward culturally and religiously specific frameworks that consider *both* resisting and supporting religious norms as valid examples of agency. Mahmood argues that liberal and progressive politics have become naturalized within the study of gender and that due to the twin commitments of feminist theory and analysis and politics, freedom has become normative to feminism.[44] This has occurred because liberalism has married notions of freedom with the idea that self-fulfillment comes from individual autonomy.[45] Within this framework, as long as one can demonstrate that they are acting autonomously "even illiberal actions can arguably be tolerated" as one is thought to be living out one's "true" desires.[46]

It is difficult to locate autonomy or freedom when one is compliant of norms, even if this is her "true" desire. As a result, within feminist theory, resistance has become valorized as a demonstration of one's capacity to act freely and enact one's true desires.[47] Independence, autonomy, and freedom are not necessarily appropriate goals for women who seek out patriarchal religions and actively work to further their agenda.[48] These goals may run contrary to the way in which they form their subjectivity, or self-reference. Traditional religious women tend to engage in interdependent relationships, either within kinship systems, community, or religious culture. Put simply, these women often understand themselves through connection, not separation.[49] In short, feminist theorists run the risk of projecting a desire for freedom and autonomy upon women who do not necessarily share these goals. For women participating in traditional religious cultures, this is especially problematic because most of their behaviors target supporting and upholding religious norms, not subverting them.

A similar challenge of defining agency as resistance is that feminist theory has also inadvertently obscured knowledge about the subjectivity of traditional women by determining what behaviors and practices contribute to configuring the subject. This is closely related to agency but differs in important ways. As stated above, agency implies action, action uses the body, and the body helps form a self-reference—part of a person's interior (mind or spirit, depending upon the context).

The body has been traditionally devalued within scholarship, and feminist theorists have been highly concerned with the denigration of the body. Because women have been typically associated with corporeality and men have been associated with mental capacities, the valorization of embodied action has become an important focal point. Much of Western metaphysics is built upon the dichotomy between mind and body. As many feminist theorists have pointed out, privileging the mind over the body, à la Descartes, has left numerous unexplored areas within a range of disciplines.[50] Some feminist theorists claim that because of Western culture's high premium upon the interior, women have been disadvantaged to some degree because of their historic association with embodiment.[51] To address the disparity between research privileging the mind and that of the body, in recent years, the body has become a fruitful area of scholarship.[52]

Saba Mahmood's work on embodiment is particularly useful as she shifts the analytical framework within feminist theory and religion by examining embodied actions as influential to the formation of subjectivity. Mahmood turns to the body to examine how a range of embodied religious practices form a more pious subject. Mahmood asks how the work of the body helps subjects to be formed by inhabiting *and* diverging from particular norms. Thus, subjectivity is formed, in part, by bodily comportments that act to train the interior in ways that *sustain* religious norms.[53] Mahmood is interested in how ethical subjects transform themselves through exterior behaviors that alter their interior. By focusing on how bodily actions train the interior of the Egyptian Muslim women she worked with, she reverses the dichotomy of mind/body.

Drawing on the work of Aristotle, Mahmood asserts that while the interior of the self dictates the exterior behavior, it is the actual behavior of the body (exterior) that transforms the spirit and/or mind (interior).[54] Mahmood draws upon Aristotle's concept of *habitus*, which is the idea that excellence is achieved in morals through learned acts that are repeated until they leave an indelible print upon the character of the person. "Thus, moral virtues are acquired through a coordination of outward behaviors with inward dispositions through the repeated performance of acts that entail those particular virtues."[55] Habitus differs from habits in that habits are repeated acts, whereas habitus leaves a permanent mark upon the individual and becomes part of her subjectivity.[56]

Looking specifically at Islamic women who choose to veil, Mahmood contends that the embodied act of veiling transforms the interiority of the Egyptian women she worked with into more pious forms of their selves. The act is transformative, not the desire to act, according to Mahmood. In this analytic move, she places the body as a primary site of analysis and allows for subjectivity to be constituted by *practices* that *sustain* religious norms.

I find Mahmood's rendering of subjectivity helpful because it suggests that a range of embodied behaviors instructs the way that subjects come to be formed, or how their interior is shaped. However, I depart from Mahmood on an important point. While Mahmood implies that the interior (mind and/or spirit) and exterior (body) are in a mutual relationship, her principal focus is on how the women she worked with utilize the body to transform their interiors into more pious subjects. Like the women Mahmood studied, the women I worked with are engaged in a belief system that strongly emphasizes bodily experiences as necessary for attaining piety, but that also strongly emphasizes spiritual experiences as having the potential to alter behavior (bodily acts). While it may seem like a small difference, it would be a monumental point of departure for the LDS women I worked with. For them, *both* the body and the spirit have the potential to be engaged in a *reciprocal* pedagogical process that informs their subjectivity.

For example, the women I studied demonstrate how the interior desire to be a mother influences the choice that is made (in most cases) to bear a child. However, the physical act of birthing and raising children can leave an indelible mark upon the self. The interior and exterior are mutually dependent upon one another, in a reciprocal, nonhierarchical fashion. *Both* the interior and exterior simultaneously influence each other and encourage the formation of the subject. These women believe that the spirit and the body are engaged in a mutually dependent relationship.

As stated above, the reciprocal relationship between the body and spirit within the LDS religion has its doctrinal roots within the belief in a pre-mortal life where spirits fought a "war in heaven" to be able to enjoy material human experience.[57] As such, the spirit could not progress without a material form. The mutuality between spirit and body is also apparent in the LDS belief that after death, humans will have an opportunity to have their "spirits" reunited with their bodies, if they live piously.[58] Corporeality is paramount; spirits struggled for it pre-mortally; they cannot progress to deification without it, and their spirits will be re-embodied in the post-mortal existence.

With the dual emphasis on the spirit and body within LDS traditional culture, the daily acts of subjects, their exteriority, influence the status of mind and/or spirit, their interiority. When one reads their scriptures daily, they are able to develop their spirit into a stronger form that will thus enable them to direct the body. In this way, body and spirit act reciprocally, reinforcing one another. To act unfaithfully, vis-à-vis the body—for example, to engage in sexually impure behavior—damages the spirit and thus the "weakened" spirit is unable to facilitate the body to act piously. But the spirit can be strengthened, by praying, reading scriptures, and attending church, to train the body to obey other commands, such as sexual purity. Thus, maintaining sexual purity assists the body in maintaining its integrity, which in turn shapes interiority. The body is invested in integrity so that the spirit can be maximized, and the spirit is concerned with converting the body into its "best" self. They are dependent upon one another for Latter-day Saints. The following ethnographic vignettes demonstrate how maternal practices contribute to subject formation for the LDS women I worked with and have the potential to contribute to their piety.

## AGENCY AND FERTILITY

While maternity is the embodied act that trains the interior, the mind and/or spirit also influences the body. The women I interviewed have a range of beliefs, which their actions support and diverge from. To attribute this gap to hypocrisy or subversion would be a simplification. Rather, these women are dedicated to a lifetime of bettering themselves and are highly concerned with working toward developing a consistent commitment to their religious beliefs. More than anything, these women desire to be pious. Although they believe that bearing and nurturing children is their highest calling, there does not seem to be a doctrinal or cultural "magic number" of children that one has to bear to be considered pious, although bearing only one child did not seem like a viable option for any of them.

On average, the women had 3.4 children. Birth control was used by virtually every woman I interviewed, both to space children and to prevent them, either at the beginning of their marriage or after they had borne their desired number of children.[59] Permanent forms of birth control such as tubal ligation and vasectomies were also fairly common among these particular LDS women and men. One of the most surprising findings was that only 13 percent of the men wanted more children than their wives did. Conversely, 87 percent of the women either wanted the same number or more children than their husbands wanted. Although giving birth is important for the women, many have put considerable thought into their ability to provide emotional, physical, and material resources for the children they bear. Here, agency mediates between one's interior (desires) and exterior (physical) actions and beliefs, and accounts for various behaviors the women employed, and thus, the various subjectivities. Let me illustrate with one vignette.

Karen, a Caucasian college graduate and stay-at-home mother of four in her early thirties, explains how she and her husband have dealt with her desire for additional children:

> Once I started having kids, I was like okay, four is probably the most I can do, being pregnant, etc. Once we got to three I think Kent was ready to be done. But I [thought] "I'm having the kids." So, I'm like you know what, either I've got to have the baby now or years down the road I'm going to want to have another baby . . . so I said, "we have to do it now." I finally talked him into it, I got pregnant, and up until recently, I feel like he has been punishing me ever since, you know. So, that was a tough one, but I think he will eventually see the light and get over it.

Conferring with his wife, Kent, a Caucasian graduate-level educated professional in his early thirties explained:

> I haven't been able to be there for her as much as, because even though I said "okay," well let's do it . . . I just was not . . . anytime something would happen, I'd just be thinking yeah . . . "I wouldn't be dealing with all this stress if" . . . I just can't . . . I can't give you anything else. I'm at my limit.

Kent goes on to explain that his principal concern with having additional children was the ability to care for them financially and emotionally. While Karen felt strongly about bearing another child, Kent deferred to her because ultimately, "Karen's feeling was 'this is my body . . .' that was the only argument that I was actually able to listen to." Both Kent and Karen negotiated about the size of their family, and eventually Karen employed agency to uphold a cultural norm of having slightly larger than average families. She desired children and sought to materialize that desire. Conversely, her embodied fecundity brought both her and her husband an additional child, and an opportunity to continue the pedagogical process through the act of birth and parenting. Kent was also changed by this act. Although he feels pushed to his emotional limits, his transformation may not be toward his potential self; that remains to be determined by how they each negotiate parenting and the other complexities of their lives. Although Kent exemplifies the majority of men that I worked with, who generally want fewer children than their wives, some men want more children than their spouses want.

Lynn, a Chinese convert in her late twenties with graduate-level education explained:

> We—I wanted four before we got married, I thought it would be so fun . . . and he wanted two before we got married. But now it is completely reversed and he wants four but I want two, so then we compromised on three. I still want to see if I can do two before I could do a third one, so three will be the maximum children to have, two will be the minimum.

In an interview with her husband, Barry, he shared this view with Lynn and explained that Lynn would have the final say on the number of children they would have. When I asked him how they decided on the number of children to have, he responded, "she decided." He elaborates, "Now, I kind of want three; I wanted four before. She's all, 'well two,' and so we tried to compromise at three. She says after the second one she doesn't know if she can have a third." This vignette demonstrates a few important ethnographic insights. Lynn uses agency to mediate between different levels of fecundity. Second, Lynn and Barry's ideal family size has shifted throughout their marriage, and may continue to do so. Agency continues to moderate between these different fecund behaviors, and strands of subjectivity derived from these behaviors will continue to shift, as they are formed and reformed throughout this process of creating and parenting within their family.

Allen, a Caucasian 36-year old with a college degree, stated that deciding on the number of children to have entailed "some negotiation with my wife" because she wanted two children and he wanted three or four. Allen explained that his wife was concerned with her age and career and that these factored into her decision to have fewer children. Most of the LDS interviewed justified their desire for smaller families by speaking about the need for emotional, physical, spiritual, and financial "health." I never actually encountered a woman who said that she wanted fewer children due to her career aspirations. Allen was the only man that explicitly stated that his wife took her career into consideration when they decided on the number of children to have. For almost every other person, putting off or curtailing the number of children for a woman's career would be unacceptable within the church's culture, despite the number of women who were employed outside of the home. Instead, women talk about not being able to "handle" a lot of children and the emotional and financial pressures of raising "good" children.

These vignettes demonstrate how agency negotiates the number of children, or the level of fecundity, that these LDS women and men engage in. Pious fecundity, while crucial to spiritual progression of these women and men, is ultimately mediated by their agency, a simultaneous engagement between self, kin, and community, whether the community is religious, social, or cultural.

Once a child is born into an LDS family, the pedagogical process becomes ongoing, as agentive parental practices transform the interior of mothers and fathers. Parenting, the ongoing daily responsibilities of both motherhood and fatherhood, also influences subjectivity, with the potential to transform them into varying shapes of piety. Raising children is an intensive, all-consuming pedagogical opportunity that took considerably different forms.

## PEDAGOGIES OF PARENTHOOD

Parenting, and specifically mothering, is an important aspect of subjectivity for these LDS women. Many of them talked about how much they had changed as a result of bearing and raising children. Some expressed that they had learned more from raising children than they could have ever learned without the experience. Thus, bearing children followed by the daily acts of parenting is a pedagogical learning tool that promotes transformation. Some women, although they loved their children, were transformed by the daily acts of mothering, but did not feel that this was an improvement; they were isolated, lonely, and overwhelmed. Other women seemed to relish their role. The women's lives and experiences are quite complex.

Most of the women had children, and the majority of them genuinely seemed to enjoy many aspects of this job. However, every one of them either expressed or demonstrated frustration or exasperation as they struggled through the daily tasks of raising children. For many of them, these feelings were disrupted by moments of joy and satisfaction, bringing feelings associated with practicing parenting into balance. For others, the frustration outweighed these moments, and they struggled to make it through the day-to-day tasks of parenting. But none of the women discounted the import of bearing and raising children. Rather, they highly valued their children and accepted the struggles as part of the mortal natal experience. Notably, several of these women worked full-time and their level of satisfaction or frustration was not radically different from the women who stayed at home and raised children full-time. Instead, the added pressure of having an outside career brought a complication to their lives that did not alleviate the pressures of parenting. Regardless of the employment status of these mothers, each embarked upon daily embodied acts of parenting that left an impression upon their interior—they were changed by the *repeated* tasks of parenting.

If "the space of ritual is one among a number of sites where the self comes to acquire and give expression to its proper form," then everyday acts of parenting are an avenue that these women and men I studied use to transform themselves, with the goal of becoming more pious.[60] What are their daily rituals within the realm of parenting? They include feeding, dressing, transporting, listening, disciplining, teaching, praying, and loving. Everyday rituals also include teaching their children to pray and read the scriptures, and training them to be "good people," "followers of Christ," to "know God," and to be "good citizens."

Some of the women were divorced and were raising their children without a partner to bear some of the daily responsibilities. For them, motherhood was exhausting and scary. The burden of raising children without someone to offer help was intense, as was the financial responsibility. One woman seemed very overwhelmed by her newly single status. As a mother of two young children, she had always had a full-time career. After her divorce she had a very difficult time finding time and energy to be the sole provider and sole parent. She almost never socialized outside of her family, except on the rare occasion that her ex-husband took the children overnight. Since her divorce was ongoing throughout my research, I saw her go through an array of emotions and responses to her changing status. She loved her children, but she seriously doubted her ability to provide everything for them adequately. She indicated that she felt a large sense of support from her fellow congregants. This particular sentiment was not shared by all of the single women I interviewed; it varied depending upon the ward and their bishop. In this sense, single mothering was indeed transformative but not necessarily positive.

Parenting takes on many forms, but overall, it is a process that is pedagogical and transformative. Regardless of how parents employ their agency to mediate between different parental practices, raising children is a religious command that has the potential to transform the self into a more pious form.

## CONCLUSION

Maternal practices within the LDS religious culture offer an interesting framework for examining how agency informs subjectivity and how corporeal acts are considered transformative to one's interior. Daily maternal acts, particularly parenting, are considered significant within the LDS culture, as they are embodied religious practices that have the potential to transform one's interiority into a more devout form.

Feminist theory has drawn upon the body as a valid site of research and theorization, in part to elevate the status of the body, thereby displacing the harmful binary Western metaphysics has constructed. While this has proven analytically stimulating, feminist theorists must be attuned to the tendency to discount communities whose privileging of the body may not look exactly "feminist." If the body is valorized within a community, is a woman's use of her body for reproduction detrimental to her subjectivity, or is it a reiteration of the import of the body? If the body is valorized, isn't women's own chosen use of their differing bodies a concrete way of reinforcing this valorization? Can Western feminist theorists claim that the body should be a privileged site of inquiry and then disavow the use of the body if it is for reproductive purposes within an unapologetic patriarchal religion? Does valorizing the maternal body necessarily mean limiting women's activities *only* to bearing children? How can scholars study these women without imposing upon them an ideology that runs contrary to their entire religious culture?

One challenge between Western feminist theory and the LDS women in this study is that their valorization of maternal practices seems to maintain gender essentialism or set in concrete women's unchanging role as mothers at the expense of other options. Many feminist theorists are reluctant to encourage any practice that remotely supports placing limitations upon women. In this way, some Western feminist theorists shy away from issues of motherhood, as it is perceived to reduce women to their most essential or significant characteristic, their wombs.

The category of essentialism depends upon the fixity or stability of essences. Gender essentialism, the theory that women have a fundamental nature, including a primary role of reproduction, is highly contested within current Western feminist theory, which has resulted in a knee-jerk opposite reaction. The reigning theory within Western feminist theory proposes that subjects are constructed and fluid. Thus, *the essence of gender essentialism is stability.*

The claim that these LDS women engage in strict gender essentialism is called into question when the stability that is central to essentialism is disrupted by the deployment of agency, which results in a *multitude* of subject positions. Using agency to engage in various parental practices, which can potentially alter one into a more pious form of the self, is another way that the practices of these women are not captured by an essentialist framework. Additionally, the claim that a focus on reproduction forecloses women's other options discounts how some women engage in *chronological* role prolifera-tion, or take on different roles at different times in their lives. Agency, dif-fering parental practices, and a proliferation of roles each rely on the ability to shift and change, to be fluid and flexible. In this way, these LDS women inhabit multiple subject positions throughout a lifetime that are anything but stable, even though they collectively valorize maternity.

These LDS women point toward a need for Western feminist theory to reexamine what is blurred when scholars use essentialism to discount other lifestyle forms and to explore ways of rethinking how the philosophical cat-egory of essentialism is conceptualized when factoring in agency. Hopefully, Western feminist theory will engage itself in a serious critique of the phobias surrounding gender essentialism to remain radically open to women whose practices do not fit neatly within the analytical categories and political com-mitments of Western feminist theory.

## NOTES

1. The Church of Jesus Christ of Latter-day Saints is often called the LDS church or the Mormon church and its members are referred to as LDS or Latter-day Saints.

2. The Church of Jesus Christ of Latter-day Saints, http://newsroom.lds. org/ldsnewsroom/eng/statistical-information. Accessed 2/20/2009.

3. Rodney Stark, "The Rise of a New World Faith," *Review of Religious Research*, 26, no. 1 (September 1984):18 and "Extracting Social Scientific Mod-els from Mormon History," *Journal of Mormon History*, 25, no.1 (Spring 1999): 176.

4. The Church of Jesus Christ of Latter-day Saints, http://www.lds.org/library/display/0,4945,40–1-3474–2,00.html.

5. The Church of Jesus Christ of Latter-day Saints, http://newsroom.lds. org/ldsnewsroom/eng/news-releases-stories/thomas-s-monson-named-16th-church-president.

6. Terry L. Givens, *The Latter-day Saint Experience in America* (Westport, CT: Greenwood Press, 2004), 167.

7. Ethan Yorgason, *Transformation of the Mormon Culture Region* (Chicago, IL: University of Illinois Press, 2003).

8. Brooks, *The Refiners Fire: The Making of Mormon Cosmology 1644–1844* (New York: Cambridge University Press, 1994), 12; Erich Robert Paul, *Science, Religion and Mormon Cosmology* (Chicago: University of Illinois Press, 1992), 146; also D. Michael Quinn, *Early Mormonism and the Magic Worldview* (Salt Lake City, UT: Signature, 1987).

9. Brooks, 241, 254.

10. The LDS do not use "eternal" in the classic sense of timelessness but use the term to denote a sense of infinity. See Sterling M. McMurrin, *The Theological Foundations of the Mormon Religion* (Salt Lake City: University of Utah Press, 1965).

11. McMurrin, 13. Sterling McMurrin has noted that few ideas are as important to Latter-day Saints as that of "eternal progression."

12. Ibid., 64. Although early members of the LDS church seemed to believe that Eve was to blame for the fall and that God cursed her and all women because of her actions, current LDS beliefs about Eve often portray her in a positive light, as a hero who ushered in mortality. See James E. Faust, "What It Means to Be a Daughter of God," *Ensign* (November 1999), 100. Also, Jolene Edmunds Rockwood, "The Redemption of Eve" in *Sisters in Spirit: Mormon Women in Historical and Cultural Perspective*, eds. Maureen Ursenbach Beecher and Lavina Fielding Anderson (Chicago, IL: University of Illinois Press, 1987).

13. David A. Bednar, "And Nothing Shall Offend Them," *Liahona* (November 2006): 89–92. Bednar explains moral agency as "the capacity for independent action and choice."

14. James E. Faust, "The Forces That Will Save Us," *Liahona* (January 2007): 2–7.

15. L. Tom Perry, "'Give Heed unto the Word of the Lord'," *Ensign* (June 2000): 22.

16. Ibid.

17. "The Family: A Proclamation to the World," *Ensign* (June 2006): 104.

18. "The Three Kingdoms of Heaven," *Friend* (February 1986): 20.

19. Mormons make a distinction between salvation and exaltation. Salvation is possible through living a pious life, but exaltation is granted by living a type of "higher law." Only exaltation offers the potential to become divine. Jan Shipps has noted that within the LDS theology, individuals may be saved but families are exalted as units. See Jan Shipps, *Mormonism* (Chicago: University of Illinois Press, 1985).

20. See Jennifer Busquait, "Reproducing Patriarchy and Erasing Feminism," *Journal of Feminist Studies in Religion*, 17, no. 2, (Fall 2001): 5–37. Busquait makes the claim that men may be exalted without women, which I have found no evidence for.

21. Gordon B. Hinckley, "Daughters of God," *Ensign* (November 1991): 97. Hinckley was not the president of the church at this time but was in the First Presidency, the highest authoritative body within the LDS church.

22. Although the LDS identify as monotheistic because they *worship* one God, they do believe that pre-mortal spirits are created by a Heavenly Father who has a female partner, Heavenly Mother. John Heeren, Donald B. Lindsey, and Marylee Mason, "The Mormon Concept of Mother in Heaven: A Sociological Account of Its Origins and Development," *Journal for the Scientific Study of Religion*, 23, no. 4 (December 1984): 396–411; 399.

23. This is particularly troubling for LDS and Mormon feminists because Heavenly Father is worshipped autonomously, despite the model of parent and family member that the term "father" implies. In other words, although He is the Father (in a partnership with a Mother) He is worshiped separately and thus His independent worth is implied at the same time His partnership with a Mother is emphasized.

24. Heeren et al., "The Mormon Concept of Mother in Heaven," 409. Italics added for emphasis.

25. There are exceptions to this, of course, and some LDS women, including LDS feminists, do look to Heavenly Mother as a symbol of women's potential for empowerment. See Carol Lynn Pearson, "Healing the Motherless House," in *Women and Authority*, ed. Hanks, Maxine (Salt Lake City, UT: Signature Books, 1992); Linda Wilcox, "The Mormon Concept of a Mother in Heaven" in *Sisters in Spirit: Mormon Women in Historical and Cultural Perspective*, eds. Maureen Ursenbach Beecher and Lavina Fielding Anderson (Chicago: University of Illinois Press, 1987); See also Margaret and Paul Toscano, *Strangers in Paradox: Explorations in Mormon Theology* (Salt Lake City, UT: Signature Books, 1990).

26. Kathleen Flake, "'Not to be Riten': The Mormon Temple Rite as Oral Canon," *Journal of Ritual Studies*, 9, no. 2 (Summer 1995): 13.

27. Lawrence Foster, *Religion and Sexuality* (Urbana: University of Illinois Press, 1984), 239.

28. Melissa Proctor, "Babies, Bodies and Birth Control," *Dialogue*, 36, no. 3 (Fall 2003): 159–75.

29. Mahmood, *Politics of Piety*, (Princeton, NJ: Princeton University Press, 2005), 147. See Giorgio Agamben, *Potentialities: Collected Essays in Philosophy*, ed. and trans. D. Heller-Roazen (Stanford, CA: Stanford University Press, 1999), 179. I am using potential in the Aristotelian sense, where potential stands for something that is possible because of specific knowledge or training.

30. Physically bearing children is not the only way that the women I worked with conceived of fulfilling their eternal potential as mothers. Adoption was a viable option for some women and theologically, the LDS church believes that if children are adopted they can still be "sealed" with their adoptive families in the temple, thus creating the eternal bond that is necessary for a timeless family.

31. The tendency for feminist scholars of religion to measure traditional religious women in America against liberative norms, such as independence, autonomy and equality, comes out of the inheritance of liberal feminism within the United States and Europe. Liberal feminism has enjoyed particular influence over most types of feminisms because most other feminisms have replicated its commitment to the liberal human subject. See Rosemary Tong, *Feminist Thought: A Comprehensive Introduction* (Boulder, CO: Westview Press, 1989); Sheila Ruth, ed., *Issues in Feminism* (Mountain View, CA: Mayfield Publishing, 1995), 445–51; Wendy Brown, *Politics out of History* (Princeton, NJ: Princeton University Press, 2001); Saba Mahmood, *Politics of Piety*.

32. Anne Braude, "Forum: Female Experience in American Religion," with Rosemary Skinner Keller, Maureen Ursenbach Beecher, and Elizabeth Fox-Genovese, *Religion and American Culture*, 5, no. 1 (Winter 1995): 10. Italics added for emphasis.

33. As quoted in Pamela Klassen, "Agency, Embodiment, and Scrupulous Women," *Journal of Religion*, 84, no. 4 (October 2004): 592–603. Klassen was quoting from page 281 of Mahmood's unpublished manuscript.

34. Brenda Brasher, *Godly Women* (New Brunswick, NJ: Rutgers, 1998), 129–30.

35. Ibid., 4–5.

36. Ibid., 130–31.

37. Ibid., 133.

38. Brasher, 129.

39. Mary Jo Weaver, "Who Are the Conservative Catholics?" in *Being Right: Conservative Catholics in America*, eds. Mary Jo Weaver and R. Scott Appleby (Bloomington: Indiana University Press, 1995), 1–14. Within North America, congregations are comprised of both members who long for a return to the pre-Vatican II days, and members who anxiously wait for women to receive the priesthood, as well as a host of congregants who do not fit neatly into either camp.

40. Aline H. Kalbian, *Sexing the Church* (Bloomington: Indiana University Press, 2005), 7. Kalbian's main focus is on metaphor and imagery and she explicitly attempts to read contemporary Roman Catholic texts with an eye for ruptures that allow for women's empowerment. Kalbian believes that the metaphor used to explain the Catholic Church's relationship to Christ lends itself to a disruption in the complementary gender scheme that is prescribed between men and women, because the church is sexed female and is considered united with Christ in marriage.

41. Ibid., 141.

42. Ibid., 20.

43. Several theorists have critiqued this feminist assumption within the last few years. See Mahmood, *Politics of Piety*; also Pamela E. Klassen, *Blessed Events: Religion and Home Birth in America* (Princeton, NJ: Princeton University Press, 2001); Mary Keller, *The Hammer and the Flute: Women, Power and Spirit Possession* (Baltimore, MD: The Johns Hopkins University Press, 2002).

44. Other scholars have made the argument that feminism includes both analysis and politics but Mahmood is unique in linking the twin commitment to the tendency to define agency strictly in terms of resistance. For other scholars who have written on the dual role of feminist theory see Diane Fuss, Judith Butler, Marilyn Strathern, and Wendy Brown.

45. Saba Mahmood, "Agency, Performativity, and the Feminist Subject" in *Bodily Citations: Religion and Judith Butler*, eds. Ellen T. Armour and Susan M. St. Ville (New York: Columbia University Press, 2006), 184. Italics added for emphasis.

46. Saba Mahmood, "Agency, Performativity, and the Feminist Subject," 184.

47. Mahmood, *Politics of Piety*, 8.

48. Elizabeth Fox-Genovese, *Feminism Without Illusions: A Critique of Individualism* (Charlotte, NC: University of North Carolina Press, 1992); Crystal Manning, *God Gave Us the Right* (New Brunswick, NJ: Rutgers, 1999), 124–27.

49. This does not mean that they devalue having free time and making choices within their lives, but overall, the choices they make engage others.

50. Diana Fuss, *Essentially Speaking: Feminism, Nature and Difference* (New York: Routledge, 1989).

51. See Naomi Schor, "This Essentialism Which Is Not One: Coming to Grips with Irigaray," *The Essential Difference*, eds. Naomi Schor and Elizabeth Weed (Bloomington: Indiana University Press, 1994).

52. Within religious studies, see R. Marie Griffith, *Born Again Bodies* (Berkeley: University of California, 2004).

53. Mahmood, *Politics of Piety*.

54. Mahmood, *Politics of Piety*, 119–22.

55. Ibid., 136.

56. Mahmood distinguishes between Aristotle's concept of habitus and Pierre Bourdieu's reinterpretation of Aristotle's work and finds value in the pedagogical emphasis that Aristotle places upon bodily forms. Additionally, she finds Aristotle's notion of habitus leaves room for different ways in which the habitus can be employed and is not contingent upon a collective function, as Bourdieu's concept of habitus seems to be. Ibid., 138–39.

57. Kent C. Condie, "Premortal Spirits: Implications for Cloning, Abortion, Evolution, and Extinction" in *Dialogue*, 39, no. 1 (Spring 2006): 35–56, 40.

58. Erich Robert Paul, *Science, Religion and Mormon Cosmology* (Chicago: University of Illinois Press, 1992).

59. This differs from earlier work that found that LDS use birth control to space children but not to prevent them. Heaton, Tim B., Kristen L. Goodman, and Thomas B. Holman, "In Search of a Peculiar People: Are Mormon Families Really Different?" in *Contemporary Mormonism: Social Science Perspectives* eds. Marie Cornwall, Tim B. Heaton and Lawrence A. Young (Chicago: University of Illinois Press, 1994).

60. Mahmood, *Politics of Piety*, 131 and regarding ritual, 128–30.

# Suggested Reading

Althaus-Reid, Marcella. *From Feminist Theology to Indecent Theology: Readings on Poverty, Sexual Identity and God.* London: SCM Press, 2004.

Aquino, Maria Pilar, Daisy Machado, and Jeanette Rodriguez, eds. *A Reader in Latina Feminist Theology.* Austin: University of Texas Press, 2002.

Armour, Ellen T. *Deconstruction, Feminist Theology, and the Problem of Difference: Subverting the Race/Gender Divide.* Chicago, IL: University of Chicago Press, 1999.

Baker, Dori Grinenko. *Doing Girlfriend Theology: God-talk with Young Women.* Cleveland, OH: Pilgrim Press, 2005.

Baker-Fletcher, Karen. *Sisters of Dust, Sisters of Spirit: Womanist Wordings on God and Creation.* Minneapolis, MN: Augsburg/Fortress, 1998.

Baker-Fletcher, Karen and Garth Kasimu Baker-Fletcher. *My Sister, My Brother: Womanist and Xodus God-talk.* Maryknoll, NY: Orbis Books, 1997.

Balmer, Randall Herbert. *Protestantism in America.* Columbia Contemporary American Religion Series. New York: Columbia University Press, 2005.

Beattie, Maija Lisa. *The Difference That Difference Makes: Womanist Challenges to White Feminist Theology.* Thesis. Berkeley, CA: GTU, 1990.

Beattie, Tina. *Eve's Pilgrimage: A Woman's Quest for the City of God.* London: Burns & Oates, 2002.

Bednarowski, Mary Farrell. *The Religious Imagination of American Women.* Bloomington: Indiana University Press, 1999.

Biezeveld, Kune, and Anne-Claire Mulder, eds. *Towards a Different Transcendence: Feminist Findings on Subjectivity, Religion, and Values.* Oxford: P. Lang, 2001.

Brock, Rita Nakashima. *Journeys by Heart: A Christology of Erotic Power.* New York: Crossroad, 1988.

Brock, Rita Nakashima and Rebecca Ann Parker. *Proverbs of Ashes: Violence, Redemptive Suffering, and the Search for What Saves Us.* Boston, MA: Beacon Press, 2001.

Brock, Rita Nakashima and Susan Brooks Thistlethwaite. *Casting Stones: Prostitution and Liberation in Asia and the United States.* Minneapolis, MN: Fortress Press, 1996.

Carmody, Denise Lardner. *Christian Feminist Theology: A Constructive Interpretation.* Cambridge, MA: Blackwell Publishers, 1995.

Carter, Stephen L. *The Culture of Disbelief: How American Law and Politics Trivialize Religious Devotion.* Reprint. Norwell, MA: Anchor Press, 1994.

Castelli, Elizabeth A. and Rosamond C. Rodman, eds. *Women, Gender, Religion: A Reader.* New York: Palgrave Macmillan, 2001.

Chopp, Rebecca S. *The Power to Speak: Feminism, Language, God.* New York: Crossroad, 1989.

Chung, Hyun Kyung. *Struggle to Be the Sun Again: Introducing Asian Women's Theology.* Maryknoll, NY: Orbis Books, 1991.

Clanton, Jann Aldredge. *In Search of the Christ-Sophia: An Inclusive Christology for Liberating Christians.* Mystic, CT: Twenty-Third Publications, 1995.

Collier-Thomas, Bettye. *Daughters of Thunder: Black Women Preachers and Their Sermons, 1850–1979.* New York: New York University Press, 2001.

Collier-Thomas , Bettye and V. P. Franklin, eds. *Sisters in the Struggle: African-American Women in the Civil Rights–Black Power Movement.* New York: New York University Press, 2001.

Cooey, Paula, M., William R. Eakin, and Jay B. McDaniel, eds. *After Patriarchy: Feminist Transformations of the World Religions.* Faith Meets Faith Series. Maryknoll, NY: Orbis Books, 1991.

Corrington, Gail Paterson. *Her Image of Salvation: Female Saviors and Formative Christianity.* Gender and the Biblical Tradition Series. Louisville, KY: Westminster/John Knox, 1992.

Crawford, A. Elaine Brown. *Hope in the Holler: A Womanist Theology.* Louisville, KY: Westminster/John Knox, 2002.

Dockery, Amie and Mary Alessi. *When Women Worship: Creating an Atmosphere of Intimacy with God.* Norwood, MA: Regal Books, 2007.

Donaldson, Laura and Kwok Pui Lan. *Postcolonialism, Feminism and Religious Discourse.* New York: Routledge, 2001.

Douglas, Kelly Brown. *Sexuality and the Black Church: A Womanist Perspective.* Maryknoll, NY: Orbis Books, 1999.

Eriksson, Anne-Louise. *The Meaning of Gender in Theology: Problems and Possibilities.* Uppsala, Sweden: Teologiska Institutionen, 1995.

Flinders, Carol. *Enduring Grace: Living Portraits of Seven Women Mystics.* San Francisco: Harper San Francisco, 1993.

Ford-Grabowsky, Mary. *Sacred Voices: Essential Women's Wisdom Through the Ages.* San Francisco: HarperSanFrancisco, 2002.

Fortune, Marie M. and Carol J. Adams. *Violence Against Women and Children: A Christian Theological Sourcebook.* New York: Continuum, 1995.

Fulkerson, Mary McClintock. *Changing the Subject: Women's Discourses and Feminist Theology.* Minneapolis, MN: Fortress Press, 1994.

Gebara, Ivone. *Out of the Depths: Women's Experience of Evil and Salvation*, translated by Ann Patrick Ware. Minneapolis, MN: Fortress Press, 2002.

Gilkes, Cheryl. *"If it Wasn't for the Women—": Black Women's Experience and Womanist Culture in Church and Community.* Maryknoll, NY: Orbis Books, 2001.

Gilson, Anne Bathurst. *The Battle for America's families: A Feminist Response to the Religious Right.* Cleveland, OH: Pilgrim Press, 1999.

Gilson, Anne Bathurst. *Eros Breaking Free: Interpreting Sexual Theo-ethics.* Cleveland, OH: Pilgrim Press, 1995.

Goldenberg, Naomi R. *Changing of the Gods: Feminism and the End of Traditional Religions.* Boston: Beacon Press, 1979.

Gonzalez, Michelle A. *Sor Juana: Beauty and Justice in the Americas.* Maryknoll, NY: Orbis Books, 2003.

Graff, Ann O'Hara, ed. *In the Embrace of God: Feminist Approaches to Theological Anthropology.* Maryknoll, NY: Orbis Books, 1995.

Graham, Elaine L. *Making the Difference: Gender, Personhood, and Theology.* Minneapolis, MN: Fortress Press, 1995.

Grant, Jacquelyn, ed. *Perspectives on Womanist Theology.* Atlanta, GA: ITC Press, 1995.

Grau, Marion. *Of Divine Economy: Refinancing Redemption.* New York: T & T Clark International, 2004.

Grey, Mary. *Feminism, Redemption, and the Christian Tradition.* Mystic, CT: Twenty-Third Publications, 1990.

Grey, Mary. *Introducing Feminist Images of God.* Cleveland, OH: Pilgrim Press, 2001.

Grovijahn, Jane M. *A Feminist Theology of Survival: Sexually Abused Women Reclaim Their Broken Bodies as Imago Dei.* Thesis. Berkeley, CA: GTU, 1997.

Harmon, Debra E. and Barbara J. Rhodes. *When the Minister is a Woman.* St. Louis, MO: Chalice Press, 2008.

Hayes, Diana L. *Hagar's Daughters: Womanist Ways of Being in the World.* Mahwah, NJ: Paulist Press, 1995.

Hogan, Linda. *From Women's Experience to Feminist Theology.* Sheffield, England: Sheffield Academic Press, 1995.

Hollies, Linda H. *Bodacious Womanist Wisdom.* Cleveland, OH: Pilgrim Press, 2003.

Hunt, Mary E. *Fierce Tenderness: A Feminist Theology of Friendship.* New York: Crossroad, 1991.

Isasi-Díaz, Ada María. *En la lucha = In the Struggle: A Hispanic Women's Liberation Theology.* Minneapolis, MN: Fortress Press, 1993.

Isasi-Díaz, Ada María. *Mujerista Theology: A Theology for the Twenty-First Century.* Maryknoll, NY: Orbis Books, 1996.

Isherwood, Lisa. *The Good News of the Body: Sexual Theology and Feminism.* Sheffield, England: Sheffield Academic Press, 2000.

Isherwood, Lisa and Elizabeth Stuart. *Introducing Body Theology.* Sheffield, England: Sheffield Academic Press, 1998.

Jacobs-Malina, D. *Beyond Patriarchy: The Images of Family in Jesus.* Mahwah, NJ: Paulist Press, 1997.

Johnson, Elizabeth A. *She Who Is: the Mystery of God in a Feminist Theological Discourse.* New York: Crossroad, 1992.

Jones, Serene. *Feminist Theory and Christian Theology: Cartographies of Grace.* Minneapolis, MN: Fortress Press, 2000.

Kanyoro, Rachel Angogo. *Introducing Feminist Cultural Hermeneutics: An African Perspective.* Cleveland, OH: Pilgrim Press, 2002.

Kathleen O'Grady, Ann L. Gilroy, and Janette Gray, eds. *Bodies, Lives, Voices: Gender in Theology.* Sheffield, England: Sheffield Academic Press, 1998.

King, Ursula, ed. *Feminist Theology from the Third World: A Reader.* Maryknoll, NY: Orbis Books, 1994.

Kirk-Duggan, Cheryl A. *Misbegotten Anguish: A Theology and Ethics of Violence.* St. Louis, MO: Chalice Press, 2001.

Kraemer, Ross Shepard and Mary Rose D'Angelo, eds. *Women & Christian Origins.* New York: Oxford University Press, 1999.

Kwok, Pui-Lan. *Introducing Asian Feminist Theology.* Cleveland, OH: Pilgrim Press, 2000.

LaCugna, Catherine Mowry, ed. *Freeing Theology: The Essentials of Theology in Feminist Perspective.* San Francisco: HarperSanFrancisco, 1993.

Lindley, Susan Hill. *You Have Stept Out of Your Place: A History of Women and Religion in America.* Louisville, KY: Westminster/John Knox, 1998.

MacHaffie, Barbara. *Her Story: Women in Christian Tradition.* 2nd edition. Minneapolis, MN: Augsburg/Fortress Press, 2006.

MacKinnon, Mary Heather and Moni McIntyre, ed. *Readings in Ecology and Feminist Theology.* Kansas City, MO: Sheed & Ward, 1995.

Maitland, Sara. *A Big-Enough God: Artful Theology.* New York: Mowbray, 1994.

May, Melanie A. *A Body Knows: A Theopoetics of Death and Resurrection.* New York: Continuum, 1995.

McAvoy, Jane. *The Satisfied Life: Medieval Women Mystics on Atonement.* Cleveland, OH: Pilgrim Press, 2000.

Miller-McLemore, Bonnie J. *Also a Mother: Work and Family as Theological Dilemma.* Nashville, TN: Abingdon Press, 1994.

Mitchem, Stephanie. *Introducing Womanist Theology.* Maryknoll, NY: Orbis Books, 2002.

Moltmann-Wendel, Elisabeth. *Liberty, Equality, Sisterhood: On the Emancipation of Women in Church and Society.* Translated from the German by Ruth Gritsch. Minneapolis, MN: Fortress Press, 1978.

Oduyoye, Mercy Amba. *Daughters of Anowa: African Women and Patriarchy.* Maryknoll, NY: Orbis Books, 1995.

Oduyoye, Mercy Amba. *Introducing African Women's Theology.* Cleveland, OH: Pilgrim Press, 2001.

Ortega, Ofelia. *Women's Visions: Theological Reflection, Celebration, Action.* Geneva, Switzerland: WCC, 1995.

Parsons, Susan Frank. *Cambridge Companion to Feminist Theology.* Cambridge, UK: Cambridge University Press, 2002.

Prichard, Rebecca Button. *Sensing the Spirit: the Holy Spirit in Feminist Perspective.* St. Louis, MO: Chalice Press, 1999.

Pui-lan, Kwok. *Postcolonial Imagination and Feminist Theology.* Louisville, KY: Westminster/ John Knox, 2005.

Raboteau, Albert J. *Canaan Land: A Religious History of African Americans.* New York: Oxford University Press, 2001.

Ramshaw, Gail. *God Beyond Gender: Feminist Christian God-language.* Minneapolis, MN: Fortress Press, 1995.

Ray, Inna Jane. *The Atonement Muddle: An Historical Analysis and Clarification of a Salvation Theory,* ed. Cheryl Kirk-Duggan. Berkeley, CA: Center for Women and Religion, Graduate Theological Union, 1997.

Richardson, Marilyn. *Black Women and Religion: A Bibliography.* Boston, MA: G. K. Hall, 1980.

Riggs, Marcia Y. *Plenty Good Room: Women versus Male Power in the Black Church.* Cleveland, OH: Pilgrim Press, 2003.

Ruether, Rosemary Radford, ed. *Feminist Theologies: Legacy and Prospect.* Minneapolis, MN: Augsburg/Fortress, 2007.

Ruether, Rosemary Radford, ed. *Religion and Sexism; Images of Woman in the Jewish and Christian Traditions.* Eugene, OR: Wipf & Stock Publishers, 1998.

Ruether, Rosemary Radford and Rosemary Skinner Keller, eds. *In Our Own Voices: Four Centuries of American Women's Religious Writing.* San Francisco: HarperSanFrancisco, 1995.

Sanders, Cheryl J., ed. *Living the Intersection: Womanism and Afrocentrism in Theology.* Minneapolis, MN: Fortress Press, 1995.

Saussy, Carroll. *God Images and Self Esteem: Empowering Women in a Patriarchal Society.* Louisville, KY: Westminster/John Knox, 1991.

Schneider, Laurel C. *Re-Imagining the Divine: Confronting the Backlash against Feminist Theology.* Cleveland, OH : Pilgrim Press, 1998.

Schrein, Shannon. *Quilting and Braiding: the Feminist Christologies of Sallie McFague and Elizabeth A. Johnson in Conversation.* Collegeville, MN: Liturgical Press, 1998.

Schüssler Fiorenza, Elisabeth, *Jesus: Miriam's Child, Sophia's Prophet: Critical Issues in Feminist Christology.* New York: Continuum, 1995, 1994.

Schüssler Fiorenza, Elisabeth and M. Shawn Copeland, eds. *Feminist Theologies in Different Contexts.* London, England: SCM Press; Maryknoll, NY: Orbis Books, 1996.

Sernett, Milton C. *African American Religious History: A Documentary Witness.* 2nd edition. The C. Eric Lincoln Series on the Black Experience. Durham, NC: Duke University Press, 2000.

Swan, Laura. *The Forgotten Desert Mothers: Sayings, Lives, and Stories of Early Christian Women.* Mahwah, NJ: Paulist Press, 2001.

Tatman, Lucy. *Knowledge That Matters: A Feminist Theological Paradigm and Epistemology.* Sheffield, England: Sheffield Academic Press, 2001.

Terrell, JoAnne Marie. *Power in the Blood?: The Cross in the African American Experience.* Maryknoll, NY: Orbis Books, 1998.

Thistlethwaite, Susan Brooks, ed. *Adam, Eve and the Genome: the Human Genome Project and Theology.* Minneapolis, MN: Fortress Press, 2003.

Thistlethwaite, Susan Brooks. *Sex, Race, and God: Christian Feminism in Black and White.* New York: Crossroad, 1989.

Torjesen, Karen Jo. *When Women Were Priests: Women's Leadership in the Early Church and the Scandal of their Subordination in the Rise of Christianity.* San Francisco: Harper Collins, 1993.

Townes, Emilie M. ed. *Embracing the Spirit: Womanist Perspectives on Hope, Salvation, and Transformation.* Maryknoll, NY: Orbis Books, 1997.

Townes, Emilie M. *In a Blaze of Glory: Womanist Spirituality as Social Witness.* Nashville, TN: Abingdon Press, 1995.

Tuttle, Myra F. *A Feminist Theological Perspective on the Practice of Preaching.* Thesis (D. Min). Berkeley, CA: Pacific School of Religion, 1991.

Weaver, J. Denny. *The Nonviolent Atonement.* Grand Rapids, MI: W. B. Eerdmans, 2001.

Weems, Renita J. *Just a Sister Away: A Womanist Vision of Women's Relationships in the Bible.* San Diego, CA: LuraMedia, 1988.

Weisenfeld, Judy. *This Far by Faith: Readings in African American Women's Biography.* New York: Routledge, 1995.

Whitson, Audrey Joan. *God as Female: Lover, Friend, Mother and Sister.* Thesis. Berkeley, CA: GTU, 1990.

Wiesner, Merry E. *Women & Gender in Early Modern Europe.* 2nd edition. Cambridge, UK: Cambridge University Press, 2000.

Williams, Delores. *Sisters of the Wilderness: The Challenge of Womanist God-Talk.* Maryknoll, NY: Orbis Books, 1993.

Williams, Maxine L. *An Examination of Exclusionary Practices Fostered against Women in Ministry in the Black Baptist Church Tradition, Using the Lens of Womanist and Liberationist Theologies.* Thesis (D. Min.). San Francisco: San Francisco Theological Seminary, 2002.

Wondra, Ellen K. *Humanity Has Been a Holy Thing: Toward a Community Feminist Christology.* Lanham, MD: University Press of America, 1994.

Young, Pamela Dickey. *Christ in a Post-Christian World: How Can We Believe in Jesus Christ When Those Around Us Believe Differently—or Not at All?* Minneapolis, MN: Fortress Press, 1995.

Young, Pamela Dickey. *Feminist Theology/Christian Theology: In Search of Method.* Minneapolis, MN: Fortress Press, 1990.

# Index

# About the Editors and Contributors

**Cheryl A. Kirk-Duggan,** PhD, is Professor of Theology and Women's Studies, at Shaw University Divinity School, Raleigh, North Carolina, and an Ordained Elder in the Christian Methodist Episcopal Church. Dr. Kirk-Duggan has written and edited over 20 books, including *The Sky is Crying: Racism, Classism, and Natural Disaster*, in response to Hurricane Katrina (2006). Dr. Kirk-Duggan has memberships in several professional guilds, is featured in Malka Drucker's *White Fire: A Portrait of Women Spiritual Leaders in America* (2003), and the 2009 recipient of the Excellence in Academic Research Award, Shaw University. With degrees in music and religious studies, Kirk-Duggan conducts research that is interdisciplinary, spanning religious and women's studies, culture, pedagogy, spirituality and health, justice, and sexuality. Known for her 6 P's as: professor, preacher, priest, prophet, poet, and performer, she is an avid athlete and musician, and embraces the quest for a healthy, holistic, spiritual life as the foundation for her worldview. She resides in Raleigh with her beloved husband, Mike.

**Karen Jo Torjesen** is Dean of the School of Religion of the Claremont Graduate University and Margo L. Goldsmith Professor of Women's Studies in Religion. She has taught Patristic Theology at the Georg August University in Germany, Christianity and Biblical Studies at Mary Washington College in Virginia, before coming to the School of Religion to teach Early Christianity. During her tenure at Claremont she founded the Women's Studies in Religion program that celebrates its 20th anniversary in 2010. Her book *Hermeneutical Procedure and Theological Structure in Origen's Allegorical Exegesis* reflects her interest in early Christian interpretation of the Bible and her recent book, *When Women Were Priests*, her interest in women's roles in early Christianity.

## Contributors

**Soyoung Baik-Chey** received her BA and MA degrees at Ewha Womans University in South Korea, majoring in Christian Studies and Christian Social Ethics, and acquired her ThD at Boston University School of Theology in 2003. Her dissertation title is "Transcending the World and Transforming the Church: Korean Non-Church Christian Movement, 1927–1989." She is now HK Research Professor at Ewha Institute for the Humanities, Ewha Womans University and an instructor in the Department of Christian Studies at Ewha Womans University. She has taught academic courses such as "Christianity and the World," "Religion and Human Being," "Feminist Ethics and Globalization," "Theology and Social Science," and "Christianity and Modern Culture," and has also led many lectures regarding religion and humanities for church congregations and youth. Her primary concern lies in the historical and ethical role of Korean Christian faith communities in the time of changing paradigms in the global world.

**Karen Baker-Fletcher** is Professor of Systematic Theology, Perkins School of Theology, Southern Methodist University in Dallas, Texas. She is the author of several books and numerous articles in the areas of women and theology, ecotheology, a womanist perspective on the Trinity, and womanist Christology. Her interests are in process-relational, ecowomanist and ecofeminist approaches to constructive theology with attention to divine love and the redemption of creation. She is the author of *Dancing With God: A Womanist Perspective on the Trinity* (2007), *Sisters of Dust, Sisters of Spirit: Womanist Wordings on God and Creation* (1998), and *A Singing Something: Womanist Reflections on Anna Julia Cooper* (1994). She coauthored *My Sister, My Brother: Womanist and Xodus God-Talk* (1997) with Garth Kasimu Baker-Fletcher.

**Tuere Bowles** is an Assistant Professor in the Department of Adult and Higher Education at North Carolina State University. Dr. Bowles, an expert narrativist, received her doctorate and qualitative research certificate from the University of Georgia. She specializes in oral history research and is currently developing a documentary highlighting black women experiences in the environmental justice movement. Complex analyses of social justice and equity education issues unify her research. Two specific themes persist in her scholarship. First, she explores socialization and educational experiences of people of color across the lifespan in formal (e.g., secondary and postsecondary) and nonformal (e.g., community, religious, and social movement) settings. Second, within gender and diversity in the environmental sciences and engineering, Bowles explores women's learning and knowledge construction in professional practice. Tuere Bowles holds a Bachelor of Arts degree from Spelman College and a Masters of Divinity degree from the Interdenominational Theological Center.

**Kathlyn A. Breazeale** is Associate Professor of Religion at Pacific Lutheran University in Contemporary Theology, focusing on feminist and womanist theologies. She is the author of *Mutual Empowerment: A Theology of Marriage, Intimacy, and Redemption* (2008) and several articles dealing with issues of sexuality and marriage from a feminist process theological perspective. Other areas of research and publication include the intersection of feminist theology, the arts, and social justice; religion and public life; and feminist pedagogy. Her current projects include developing a pedagogy for using film, art, service learning, and bioregional perspectives in teaching liberation theologies, and an ecofeminist theological analysis of how women and men who are considered "closer to nature" are denigrated, particularly the Sámi people of Scandinavia and the Spiritual and Shouter Baptists of Trinidad and Tobago. Kathi also expresses her theological and pedagogical interests in her work as a liturgical dancer.

**Pamela K. Brubaker** is Professor of Religion at California Lutheran University. Her publications include *Globalization at What Price? Economic Change and Daily Life* (2007, 2001), *Women Don't Count: The Challenge of Women's Poverty to Christian Ethics* (1994), and *Justice in a Global Economy: Strategies for Home, Community, and World*, co-edited with Rebecca Todd Peters and Laura Stivers (2006). She has published articles in the *Journal of Religion, Conflict and Peace, The Ecumenical Review*, the *Journal of Feminist Studies in Religion*, and *Union Seminary Quarterly Review*. She is a member of the World Council of Churches Advisory Group on Economic Matters and has served on the Board of Directors of the Society of Christian Ethics and co-chaired the Ethics Section of the American Academy of Religion. She earned her PhD in Christian Social Ethics from Union Theological Seminary in New York City.

**Marie Cartier** is a scholar, visual/performance artist, queer activist, poet, and theologian who has been active in many movements for social change. She teaches at University of California, Irvine, in their Film Department, and California State University Northridge in Women's Studies. She is finishing her PhD in Religion from Claremont Graduate University, with an emphasis on Women and Religion: feminist queer gender. She has published several articles regarding the possible sacrality of the butch-femme community at mid-century. Her book, *Baby You Are My Religion: 1950's Butch Femme Bar Culture in the U.S. as Possibly Sacred Community*, will be published in 2010.

She has three Master of Fine Arts degrees in film, theater, and visual art. She currently exhibits her installation performance project MORGASM, the Museum of Radical Gender and Sex Matrix, which explores female orgasm in a museum context.

**Jean T. Corey,** PhD, is Assistant Professor of English and Director of Writing at Messiah College, where she teaches literature and writing courses focused on ethnicity, race, religion, and gender. Jean earned her doctoral degree from Middle Tennessee State University in 2000 and Master's from Duke University in 1989. Her current research interests include literacy practices of basic writers, alternative discourse, and women's spiritual autobiography. Having spent most of 2005 in Kenya, she is currently engaged in research on the rhetoric of hope and the global AIDS pandemic. Having raised four biological children, Jean and her husband have started all over again. They reside in Harrisburg with their two Kenyan children, six-year-old Robert Baraka, and five-year-old Maya Achieng.

**Marie M. Fortune** grew up in North Carolina where she received her undergraduate degree from Duke University. She completed her seminary training at Yale Divinity School and is an ordained minister in the United Church of Christ. In 1977, after serving in a local parish, she founded the Center for the Prevention of Sexual and Domestic Violence, now FaithTrust Institute, where she served as Executive Director until 1999, and now serves as Founder and Senior Analyst. Today, FaithTrust is a multifaith, multicultural organization providing religious communities and advocates with training, consultation, and educational materials to address the faith aspects of abuse. She also was editor of *The Journal of Religion and Abuse* and served on the National Advisory Council on Violence Against Women for the U.S. Department of Justice and the Defense Task Force on Domestic Violence for the U.S. Department of Defense. For more information regarding FaithTrust Institute, please contact the Operations Associate at Operations@faithtrust institute.org.

**Amy Hoyt** received her PhD in Women's Studies in Religion from Claremont Graduate University in 2007. She teaches at Victor Valley College as an adjunct professor and is currently engaged in research on Latter-day Saint structures of masculinity in the 19th century. This article is based, in part, on her dissertation, *Agency, Subjectivity and Essentialism within Traditional Religious Cultures: An Ethnographic Study of an American Latter-day Saint Community*.

**Judith Johnson,** an independent researcher with Claremont (CA) Graduate University's School of Religion, teaches feminist theology studies for Global Ministries University. While the vice-president of the national (U.S.) Women's Ordination Conference, she was on the Executive Committee of Women's Ordination Worldwide. She set up the Women in Theology Center at the Catholic University of Louvain (Leuven) in Belgium; taught interdisciplinary courses for four American universities in Germany; and taught Catholic seminary students for the Archdiocese of Los Angeles. She has worked as a journalist, media instructor, advertising artist, Congressional press assistant, and editor of military and media publications. She coauthored *Holy Women, Holy Blood* (2002). Johnson received her doctorate in religion from Claremont (CA) Graduate University in 2002, with a concentration in Cultural and Women's Studies. She also has a Master of Arts in Religious Studies from the Catholic University of Louvain in Leuven, Belgium.

**Shari Julian,** MS, MEd, PhD, has been a licensed therapist in individual and marriage and family therapy for 24 years. In addition to her clinical degrees, she holds a doctorate in public policy and administration. Dr. Julian has worked all over the world in victimology, ethnic and gender studies, terrorism and disasters, sexual issues, and mass trauma. She has thousands of postdoctoral study hours and clinical work in sexuality and gender studies, organizational behavior, and criminology. She is a professor of criminal justice and victimology at Texas Wesleyan University. Dr. Julian also holds a postdoctoral certificate in forensic psychology and psychiatry. She currently serves as an expert for state and federal courts, and on several national committees dealing with terrorism, clinical approaches for victims of mass disasters, and treatment of military warriors with posttraumatic stress disorder and closed head injuries and their families. Dr. Julian is widowed and the mother of three sons.

**Joan M. Martin** is the William W. Rankin Associate Professor of Christian Social Ethics at The Episcopal Divinity School (EDS), Cambridge, Massachusetts. She has been a member of the faculty since the academic year 1993. Dr. Martin is author of *More Than Chains and Toil: A Christian Work Ethic of Enslaved Women* and Editing Collective Member, *Your Daughters Shall Prophesy: Feminist Alternatives in Theological Education.* She teaches a range of courses from the traditional introductory courses in Christian ethics to courses in contemporary issues such as "Womanist and Women of Color Ethics," "African American Christian Social Ethics," "Vocation and Work in Church and Society," and "The Church, Class, and the U.S./Global Economy." In addition to her teaching and committee responsibilities, she serves as the Doctor of Ministry Degree Coordinator. Dr. Martin is an ordained Presbyterian minister (PCUSA).

**Althea Spencer Miller**  is Assistant Professor of New Testament at Drew Theological School. As a student of the New Testament, Dr. Spencer Miller works within liberatory, postcolonial, and feminist hermeneutics and is experimenting with applying these perspectives to biblical translation using a dialect-based approach. Her publications include *Feminist New Testament Studies: Global and Future Perspectives*, co-edited with Drs. Kathleen Obrien Wicker and Musa Dube.

**Linda E. Thomas,**  PhD, is professor of theology and anthropology, Lutheran School of Theology at Chicago. She is a transdisciplinary scholar who works at the intersection and influence of religion and culture, rooted in a Womanist perspective. Her work focuses on African American women's experience. She is passionate about uncovering and exploring historical and contemporary experiences and ideologies governing actions, policies, and norms surrounding sex, race, and class. Her publications include *Under the Canopy: Ritual Process and Spiritual Resilience in South Africa,* which explores black South African's everyday lives trapped by structural poverty and ways religion and culture fueled their resilience during apartheid, and *Living Stones in the Household of God*, a collection of essays about black theology in the new millennium. She has published dozens of academic journal articles and contributed essays to several scholarly books. She has a forthcoming book, edited with Dwight N. Hopkins, titled *Walk Together Children: Black and Womanist Theologies, Church and Theological Education.*

Printed in the USA
CPSIA information can be obtained
at www.ICGtesting.com
LVHW011636110823
754951LV00005B/223